ZAGAT TRI-STATE RESTAURANT SURVEY

**Edited by Joan Lang,
Melanie Barnard,
Jacqueline White Kochak
and Joan Reminick**

Coordinated by Joan Lang

Published and Distributed by

ZAGAT SURVEY
4 Columbus Circle
New York, N.Y. 10019
212-977-6000

ISBN 0-943421-81-0

ACKNOWLEDGMENTS

The editors wish to express their appreciation to Carol Bennett, Marie Bianco, Lizann Bradshaw, Jan Bresnick, Sylvia Carter, Katharine Colton, Jerry Connelly, Terry DeMauro, Cara De Silva, Robert Doan, Jane Freiman, Joyce Gabriel, Peter Gianotti, Kathy and Peter Gogolak, Linda Giuca, Beth Hillson, Peggy Katalinich, Lea Lane, Bea Lewis, Elise Maclay, Madeline McEneny, Barbara and Ed Meyer, Linda O'Connell, Carol Pinard, Irene Sax, David Soskin, Beth Shluger and Herbie Wheeler.

TO ORDER

ZAGAT U.S. HOTEL, RESORT, SPA SURVEY

ZAGAT SURVEY:
AMERICA'S TOP 1000 RESTAURANTS

ZAGAT SURVEY:
AMERICA'S BEST VALUE RESTAURANTS

ZAGAT RESTAURANT SURVEYS
Atlanta; Atlantic City; Boston; Chicago;
Dallas/Fort Worth; Hawaii; Houston; Kansas City;
London; Los Angeles/Southern California;
Miami/Southern Florida; Montreal; New Orleans;
New York City; Ohio; Orlando/Central Florida;
Pacific Northwest; Philadelphia; Rocky Mountains;
San Francisco; Southwest; St. Louis;
Tri-State (CT/NY/NJ); Washington, D.C./Baltimore

ZAGAT NYC MARKETPLACE SURVEY
covering food, wine and entertaining sources

ZAGAT/AXXIS GUIDES
for desktop, notebook and handheld computers.
Comprehensive mapping software fully integrated
with Zagat restaurant and hotel ratings; available
by city on disk or nationwide on CD-ROM.

Call (212) 977-6000 • (800) 333-3421

or Write to:

Zagat Survey
4 Columbus Circle
New York, New York 10019

Regarding
Corporate Gifts and
Deluxe Editions, call
(212) 977-6000
or (800) 333-3421

CONTENTS

INTRODUCTION

Here are the results of our *Tri-State Restaurant Survey*, covering more than 1,000 restaurants on Long Island and in Connecticut, Southern New York State (including Westchester, Rockland, Putnam, Dutchess, Ulster and Orange Counties) and Northern New Jersey down to the Shore, all roughly within a 100 mile radius of New York City.

Over 3,400 people participated in our *Survey*. Since they dined out at average of 3 times per week, this *Survey* is based on roughly 530,000 meals eaten in area restaurants per year. By surveying large numbers of local restaurant-goers, we think we have achieved a uniquely reliable guide. Knowing that its quality is the direct result of their thoughtful voting and commentary, we thank each *Survey* participant.

We also thank our local editors: for Long Island, Joan Reminick, restaurant critic and columnist for *Newsday;* for Connecticut, Melanie Barnard, the restaurant critic for the *Stamford Advocate* and *Greenwich Times*; for Southern New York State, Jacqueline White Kochak, a freelance writer and restaurantophile; and Joan Lang, a freelance writer and restaurant columnist for *New Jersey Monthly*, who coordinated this entire project and edited the New Jersey section.

We invite you to be a reviewer in our next Tri-State Restaurant Survey. To do so, simply send a stamped, self-addressed, business-size envelope to ZAGAT SURVEY, 4 Columbus Circle, New York, NY 10019. This will permit us to contact you. Each participant will receive a free copy of our next *Tri-State Restaurant Survey* when it is published.

Your comments, suggestions and criticisms of this *Survey* are also solicited. There is always room for improvement – with your help!

New York, New York   Nina and Tim Zagat
May 1, 1993

FOREWORD

Now as never before, the dining scene in communities north, east and west of New York City has come into its own. The past decade has seen an explosion of new restaurants that rival their big-city counterparts in both quality and value.

Some of these spots, like Bertrand in Greenwich, CT, and Dennis Foy's Townsquare in Chatham, NJ, are the products of ex–NYC chefs. Others, like Sapore di Mare in Wainscott, LI, and the 1766 Tavern in Rhinebeck, NY, are the outposts of seasoned Manhattan hosts following an affluent clientele to their weekend and summer playgrounds. And many are simply the delicious provender of creative restaurateurs who have come to realize that any place that's home to sophisticated diners can be home to a sophisticated restaurant.

Then, too, there are the interesting ethnic pockets that have sprung up all around New York City – the Korean and Japanese enclaves in northern New Jersey, the Japanese communities of Long Island, the Indian neighborhoods in Westchester County, and the multicultural cities of central and southwestern Connecticut – enriching an already tasty stew. And, lest we forget, the Tri-State area has its share of lovely country inns.

All of this makes for satisfying and often very special dining. Not only are many of these restaurants the equal of Manhattan's; they are also significantly less costly and more accessible. It's no longer necessary to "go to the City" for a superior meal, and many hungry city-dwellers now find good reasons for traveling to the suburbs and beyond to dine in a rarified setting.

For instance, it's widely known that some of the best seafood around is available on Long Island; that you can get superb brick-oven pizza in Connecticut; and that you can literally taste the future at any of the four student-run restaurants at the Culinary Institute of America in Hyde Park, NY; and that some of the Northeast's best Spanish and

Portuguese restaurants can be found in the Ironbound section of Newark, NJ.

Moderately priced family-style Italians are all the rage across Long Island; one-of-a-kind American cafes are popping up in Connecticut; bistro French food is back in style all over New York State; old-fashioned steakhouses and Hong Kong–style Cantonese restaurants are opening at an aggressive clip in New Jersey. And everywhere there are new high-style, Californian-influenced cafes and Italian trattorias dispensing boutique pizzas and unpretentious comfort food for the '90s at everyday prices.

So there is plenty to sample throughout this diversified, multifaceted region, which has grown up and matured because of its ties – and proximity – to New York City, but now has a thriving, lively existence independent of it.

One other thing is worth noting: suburbanites and country-dwellers treat their local restaurants like second homes. Because they and their res-taurants are more spread out, proximity plays an important part in their choice of restaurants, and in turn they tend to be fiercely loyal to their favorites. We also note that the ratings in this *Tri-State Survey* are somewhat more lenient than in our *New York City Restaurant Survey*.

Jersey City, New Jersey   Joan Lang
May 1, 1993

EXPLANATION OF RATINGS AND SYMBOLS

FOOD, DECOR and **SERVICE** are each rated on a scale of 0 to 30 in columns marked **F, D** and **S**:

> 0–9 = poor to fair
> 10–19 = good to very good
> 20–25 = very good to excellent
> 26–30 = extraordinary to perfection

The **COST** column, headed by a **C**, reflects the estimated price of a dinner with one drink and tip. As a rule of thumb, lunch will cost 25 percent less.

An **Asterisk** (*) after a restaurant's name means the number of votes is too low to be reliable; **L** for late means the restaurant serves after 11 PM; **S** means it is open on Sunday; **X** means no credit cards are accepted. The paired number and letter in bold (e.g. **A6**) after the town indicates the restaurant's quadrant on the map for its area.

By way of **Commentary**, we attempt to summarize the comments of the *Survey* participants. The prefix **U** means comments were uniform; **M** means they were mixed.

The names of the restaurants with the highest overall ratings and greatest popularity are printed in solid capital letters, e.g., "**XAVIAR'S IN PIERMONT.**"

If we do not show ratings on a restaurant, it is either an important **newcomer** or a popular **write-in**; however, comments are included, and the estimated cost, including one drink and tip, is indicated by the following symbols:

> **I** = below $15
> **M** = $15 to $30
> **E** = $30 to $50
> **VE** = $50 or above

TOP RATINGS*

TOP 50 FOOD RATINGS
(In order of rating)

29 – Xavier's in Piermont — Piermont, NY
28 – Xavier's in Garrison — Garrison, NY
    La Panetiere — Rye, NY
27 – Jean-Louis — Greenwich, CT
    Mirabelle — St. James, LI
    Harrald's — Stormville, NY
    Robert Henry's — New Haven, CT
    Saddle River Inn — Saddle River, NJ
    Mill River Inn — Oyster Bay, LI
    Starr Boggs — Westhampton, LI
    Da Pietro's — Westport, CT
    Farmingdale House — Farmingdale, NJ
26 – Fine Bouche — Centerbrook, CT
    Freelance Cafe — Piermont, NY
    Restaurant du Village — Chester, CT
    Caterina de Medici — Hyde Park, NY
    Buffet de la Gare — Hastings-on-Hudson, NY
    Doc's — New Preston, CT
    Frank Pepe Pizzeria — New Haven, CT
    Bertrand — Greenwich, CT
    Union Place — Summit, NJ
    Chez Catherine — Westfield, NJ
    Chez Madeleine — Bergenfield, NJ
    Peter Luger — Great Neck, LI
    Cavey's — Manchester, CT
    L'Hostellerie Bressane — Hillsdale, NY
    Fromagerie — Rumson, NJ
    Culinary Renaissance — Metuchen, NJ
    Auberge Maxime — North Salem, NY
    Escoffier Room — Hyde Park, NY
    Cafe Panache — Ramsey, NJ
25 – Golden Lamb Buttery — Brooklyn, CT
    Sally's Apizza — New Haven, CT
    La Cremaillere — Banksville, NY
    Zeph's — Peekskill, NY
    L'Abbee — New Canaan, CT
    Yves — Montclair, NJ
    Meson Galicia — Norwalk, CT
    Box Tree — Purdy, NY
    River Palm Terrace — Edgewater, NJ
    Le Delice — Whippany, NJ
    Ruga — Oakland, NJ
    La Fontana — New Brunswick, NJ
    American Bounty — Hyde Park, NY
    Palm Restaurant — East Hampton, NY
    Navona — Great Neck, LI
    Marcello's — Suffern, NY
    Il Tulipano — Cedar Grove, NJ
    Max-a-Mia — Avon, CT
24 – Dennis Foy's Townsquare — Chatham, NJ

---

*Excluding restaurants with voting too low to be reliable.

TOP 50 OVERALL DECOR
(In order of rating)

28 – Dining Room   Short Hills, NJ
Golden Lamb Buttery   Brooklyn, CT
27 – Mayflower Inn   Washington, CT
Crescent   Bayville, LI
Robert Henry's   New Haven, CT
Bluffs Hotel   Bay Head, NJ
Highlawn Pavilion   West Orange, NJ
La Panetiere   Rye, NY
La Chateau   South Salem, NY
26 – Homestead Inn   Greenwich, CT
Box Tree   Purdy, NY
Abigail Kirsch   Tarrytown, NY
Harrald's   Stormville, NY
25 – Troutbeck Inn   Amenia, NY
Xaviar's in Garrison   Garrison, NY
Inn at Pound Ridge   Pound Ridge, NY
Grenville Restaurant   Bay Head, NJ
Bertrand   Greenwich, CT
Copper Beech Inn   Ivorytown, CT
L'Hostellerie Bressane   Hillsdale, NY
La Cremaillere   Banksville, NY
Bee and Thistle Inn   Old Lyme, CT
Randall's Ordinary   Stonington, CT
Stonehenge   Ridgefield, CT
Saddle River Inn   Saddle River, NJ
La Fontana   New Brunswick, NJ
Auberge Maxime   North Salem, NY
24 – Ram's Head Inn   Shelter Island, LI
Old Drover's Inn   Dover Plains, NY
Le Chambord   Hopewell Junction, NY
Escoffier Room   Hyde Park, NY
Bernard's Inn   Bernardsville, NJ
Riverview   Oakdale, LI
Plumbush Inn   Cold Spring, NY
Cavey's   Manchester, CT
Restaurant du Village   Chester, CT
American Bounty   Hyde Park, NY
St. Andrew's Cafe   Hyde Park, NY
Inn at Millrace Pond   Hope, NJ
Ryland Inn   Whitehouse, NJ
Black Orchid   Morristown, NJ
Pratos   Carlstadt, NJ
Cobb's Mill Inn   Weston, CT
Bird & Bottle Inn   Garrison, NY
Roger Sherman Inn   New Canaan, CT
Frenchtown Inn   Frenchtown, NJ
1770 House   East Hampton, LI
Xaviar's in Piermont   Piermont, NY
Three Village Inn   Stonybrook, LI
Apricot's   Farmington, CT

TOP 50 OVERALL SERVICE
(In order of rating)

27 – Harrald's — Stormville, NY
26 – Golden Lamb Buttery — Brooklyn, CT
Xavier's in Piermont — Piermont, NY
Xavier's in Garrison — Garrison, NY
La Panetiere — Rye, NY
Robert Henry's — New Haven, CT
25 – Mirabelle — St. James, LI
Fine Bouche — Centerbrook, CT
Jean-Louis — Greenwich, CT
Saddle River Inn — Saddle River, NJ
24 – Fromagerie — Rumson, NJ
Restaurant du Village — Chester, CT
Box Tree — Purdy, NY
Dining Room — Short Hills, NJ
St. Andrew's Cafe — Hyde Park, NY
Freelance Cafe — Nyack, NY
Le Delice — Whippany, NJ
American Bounty — Hyde Park, NY
Bertrand — Greenwich, CT
Union Place — Summit, NJ
Da Pietro's — Westport, CT
Caterina de Medici — Hyde Park, NY
La Fontana — New Brunswick, NJ
Mill River Inn — Oyster Bay, LI
Escoffier Room — Hyde Park, NY
Zeph's — Peekskill, NY
Troutbeck Inn — Amenia, NY
Copper Beech Inn — Ivorytown, CT
Arch — Brewster, NY
Auberge Maxime — North Salem, NY
Homestead Inn — Greenwich, CT
23 – L'Hostellerie Bressane — Hillsdale, NY
Cavey's — Manchester, CT
Yves — Montclair, NJ
Bistro Twenty-Two — Bedford, NY
Farmingdale House — Farmingdale, NJ
Le Chateau — Tenafly, NJ
Country Manor — Poughkeepsie, NY
Stonehenge — Ridgefield, CT
Il Tulipano — Cedar Grove, NJ
Bee and Thistle Inn — Old Lyme, CT
Grand Cafe — Morristown, NJ
La Pace — Glen Cove, LI
Jamie's — Englewood Cliffs, NJ
Le Petit Chateau — Bernardsville, NJ
La Mascotte — Commack, LI
Buffet de la Gare — Hastings-on-Hudson, NY
Depuy Canal House — High Falls, NY
Sestri — Gillette, NJ
Mayflower Inn — Washington, CT

BEST BUYS

TOP 50 BANGS FOR THE BUCK

This list reflects the best dining values in our *Survey*. It is produced by dividing the cost of a meal into the combined ratings for food, decor, and service.

1.	Frank Pepe Pizzeria	New Haven, CT
2.	Sally's Apizza	New Haven, CT
3.	Red Rooster	Brewster, NY
4.	Amarillo Grill	Hartford, CT
5.	Bloodroot	Bridgeport, CT
6.	Su Casa	Branford, CT
7.	Great American Cafe	Glastonbury, CT
8.	Bertucci's†	Westport, CT
9.	Congress Rotisserie	Hartford, CT
10.	China Pavilion†	Rocky Hill, CT
11.	Sunrise Pizza Cafe†	Norwalk, CT
12.	Hunan Village	Yonkers, NY
13.	Dublin Delights	St. James, LI
14.	Bricks	Norwalk, CT
15.	Panda Inn	West Hartford, CT
16.	India House	Montrose, NY
17.	Eddie's Pizza†	New Hyde Park, LI
18.	Abbott's Lobster	Noank, CT
19.	Eye of the Tiger	Hicksville, LI
20.	Bangkok	Danbury, CT
21.	Ahrash Cafe	Huntington, LI
22.	Tiger Bowl	Westport, CT
23.	J.J. Hwang	Merrick, LI
24.	St. Andrew's Cafe	Hyde Park, NY
25.	Mediterranean Snack Bar	Huntington, LI
26.	Thai Orchid	New Haven, CT
27.	Jani	Huntington Station, LI
28.	Uncle Dai†	Woodbury, LI
29.	Little Kitchen	Westport, CT
30.	Kabul	Huntington, LI
31.	Orchid	Garden City, LI
32.	Casa Comida	Long Branch, NJ
33.	Gail's Station House	Ridgefield, CT
34.	Chand Palace	Parsippany, NJ
35.	Max-a-Mia	Avon, CT
36.	Panda Pavilion†	Greenwich, CT
37.	King & I	Nyack, NY
38.	Jade Garden	Hauppauge, LI
39.	Hunan Gourmet East	Merrick, LI
40.	Baumgart's Cafe	Englewood, NJ
41.	To Fu	Farmingville, LI
42.	Pellicci's	Stamford, CT
43.	Imperial Wok	Yorktown, NY
44.	Paul Ma's/Shanghai	Yorktown, NY
45.	Hunam Restaurant	Levittown, LI
46.	Hunan Taste	Greenvale, LI
47.	Rigatoni	Rockville Centre, LI
48.	Arizona Flats	Bridgeport, CT
49.	Thai House	Huntington, LI
50.	Hot Tomato's	Hartford, CT

†Has multiple locations.

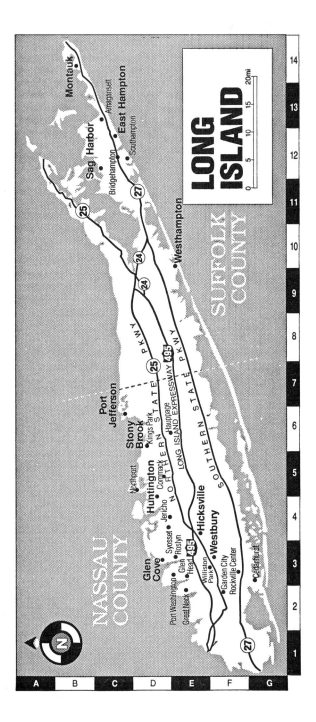

LONG ISLAND'S MOST POPULAR RESTAURANTS

Each of our reviewers has been asked to name his or her five favorite restaurants. The 40 spots most frequently named, in order of their popularity, are:

1. Peter Luger
2. Mirabelle
3. Mill River Inn
4. Coyote Grill
5. La Pace
6. Sapore di Mare
7. Millie's Place
8. La Parma
9. L'Endroit
10. Bryant & Cooper
11. Jolly Fisherman
12. Nick & Toni's
13. Dar Tiffany
14. American Hotel
15. Starr Boggs
16. La Marmite
17. North Street Grill
18. Riverbay
19. Casa Rustica
20. Palm Restaurant
21. Veranda
22. La Primavera
23. Fresno Place
24. Benny's Ristorante
25. Barney's
26. Navona
27. Milleridge Inn
28. La Mascotte
29. Three Village Inn
30. Trattoria Tulipano
31. Michael's – A Bistro
32. Karen Lee's
33. Sempre Vivolo
34. Maidstone Arms
35. John Peel Room
36. George Martin
37. Bruzell's
38. Due Torri
39. Caffe Spuntino
40. Laundry Restaurant

It's obvious that many of the restaurants on the above list are among the area's most expensive. However, all of New York City's surrounding areas have an abundance of bargain spots that are popular and worth noting. Long Island's Best Buys are listed on page 19.

TOP RATINGS*

TOP 40 FOOD RATINGS
(In order of rating)

27 – Mirabelle
    Mill River Inn
    Starr Boggs
26 – Peter Luger
25 – Palm Restaurant
    Navona
24 – La Pace
    Casa Rustica
    L'Endroit
    Nick & Toni's
    Fresno Place
    Gaetano's
    La Mascotte
    Sempre Vivolo
    Le Soir
    Piccolo
23 – Ross' North Fork
    Sapore di Mare
    Kokura II
    Veranda
    La Marmite

    Bryant & Cooper
    Chez Noelle
    La Primavera
    American Hotel
    Mirko's
    Coyote Grill
    P.G. Steakhouse
    Benny's Ristorante
    Riverbay
    Dave's Grill
22 – La Ginestra
    Villa Doria
    La Caravella
    Frederick's
    Maidstone Arms
    La Parma
    Karen Lee's
    Il Garofano
    Barney's

TOP SPOTS BY CUISINE

**Top American
(Contemporary)**
27 – Mill River Inn
    Starr Boggs
24 – Fresno Place
23 – Ross' North Fork
    American Hotel

**Top American
(Traditional)**
23 – Bryant & Cooper
20 – Jolly Fisherman
    Three Village Inn
    J. Dave's
19 – Post House

Top Chinese
22 – Lotus East
20 – Eye of the Tiger
19 – Hunan Taste
    Hunan Gourmet East
    Tung Ting

Top Continental
24 – La Pace
    L'Endroit
23 – La Primavera
    Mirko's
22 – Frederick's

*Excluding restaurants with voting too low to be reliable.

Top French
27 – Mirabelle
24 – L'Endroit
    La Mascotte
    Le Soir
23 – La Marmite

Top Hotel Dining
27 – Starr Boggs,
    Dune Deck Hotel
25 – Palm Restaurant,
    Hunting Inn
23 – American Hotel
22 – Maidstone Arms
    Ram's Head Inn

Top Italian (Northern)
24 – La Pace
    Nick & Toni's
    Gaetano's
    Piccolo
23 – Sapore di Mare

Top Italian (North & South)
25 – Navona
24 – Casa Rustica
    Sempre Vivola
    Veranda
22 – La Ginestra

Top Japanese
23 – Kokura II
21 – Sapporo
    Yamaguchi
20 – Kura Barn
    Ashai Tokyo

Top Newcomers/Rated
21 – Crescent
    Saffron
    North Street Grill
    Piccola Bussola
20 – Garden City Cafe

Top Newcomers/Unrated
—   Della Femina
—   I Santi
—   Siam Lotus
—   Stresa
—   California Grill

Top Seafood
23 – Ross' North Fork
    Mirko's
    Riverbay
    Dave's Grill
21 – Coast Grill

Top Steakhouses
26 – Peter Luger
25 – Palm Restaurant
23 – Bryant & Cooper
    P.G. Steakhouse
22 – Dar Tiffany

Top Thai
20 – Bangkok Palace
19 – Thai House
18 – White Sands
    Seeda Thai
17 – Siam Palace

Top Worth a Trip
27 – Starr Boggs,
    Westhampton
24 – Nick & Toni's,
    East Hampton
    Le Soir,
    Bayport
23 – Ross' North Fork,
    Southold
    Sapore di Mare,
    Wainscott

TOP 40 OVERALL DECOR
(In order of rating)

27 – Crescent/V
24 – Ram's Head Inn/V
   Riverview/V
   1770 House
   Three Village Inn/V
   L'Endroit
23 – Palm Garden
   Maidstone Arms
   American Hotel
   Starr Boggs/V
   North Street Grill
   La Pace
   Mirabelle
   Sapore di Mare
   Polo Grill
22 – Mill River Inn
   James Lane Cafe
   Coyote Grill/V
   Kokura II
   Veranda
   Sempre Vivolo

   56th Fighter Group/V
   La Caravella
21 – Benny's Ristorante
   La Marmite
   Dar Tiffany
   Due Torri
   Danford's/V
   Millie's Place
   Pappagallo
   Nick & Toni's
   Cafe Girasole
   Geo. Washington Manor/V
20 – La Coquille
   Villa Gattopardo
   La Mascotte
   Caracalla
   Barney's
   Capriccio
   Milleridge Inn

TOP 40 OVERALL SERVICE
(In order of rating)

25 – Mirabelle
24 – Mill River Inn
23 – La Pace
   La Mascotte
22 – Benny's Ristorante
   Mirko's
   Sempre Vivolo
   Casa Rustica
   Piccolo
   L'Endroit
   La Marmite
   Ross' North Fork
   Le Soir
   La Coquille
   Polo Grill
21 – Veranda
   Villa Doria
   Starr Boggs
   Mario
   Ram's Head Inn

   La Caravella
   Maidstone Arms
   Il Pozzo
   Pappagallo
   Gaetano's
   Three Village Inn
   Ristorante Orlando
   La Sila
   Il Garofano
   American Bistro
   Dar Tiffany
   Due Torri
   1770 House
   Capriccio
   Frederick's
20 – Iberian Restaurant
   La Ginestra
   Gordon's
   Palm Restaurant
   Giulia Ristorante

V = Also has an outstanding view.

BEST BUYS

TOP 40 BANGS FOR THE BUCK

This list reflects the best dining values in our *Survey*. It is produced by dividing the cost of a meal into the combined ratings for food, decor, and service.

1. Dublin Delights
2. Eddie's Pizza
3. Eye of the Tiger
4. Ahrash Cafe
5. J.J. Hwang
6. Mediterranean Snack
7. Jani
8. Uncle Dai
9. Kabul
10. Orchid
11. Jade Garden
12. Hunan Gourmet East
13. To Fu
14. Hunam Restaurant
15. Hunan Taste
16. Rigatoni
17. Thai House
18. Mother Kelly's
19. Pasta's Cafe
20. Lobster Roll
21. UB Loves Cafe
22. Honest Diner
23. Umberto's Pizza
24. Caffe Baci
25. Caffe Spasso
26. Lotus East/Lotus II
27. Hildebrandt's
28. Cafe Stefano
29. Country Pantry
30. Caffe Spuntino
31. Casa Margarita
32. Raay-Nor's Cabin
33. Tung Ting
34. Seeda Thai
35. Main Street Pasta
36. Mama Lombardi's
37. George Martin
38. Canterbury Ales
39. Spare Rib
40. Courtyard Cafe

Additional Good Values

Akbar
Alfredo's Pizza
Ashai Tokyo
Baja
Bangkok Palace
Bayou
Bonbori
Buckram Stables
Casa Luis
Chefs of New York
Cirella's
Colbeh
Dave's Downtown
DiMaggio's
El Tapatio
Estia/Amag. Fresh Pasta
Estoril Granada
56th Fighter Group
Fish Net
Fu Ho
G.D. Graffiti
Gumbo Alley
Hong Kong Seafood
Iberian Restaurant

Il Cappuccino
Jonathan's
Koenig's
La Famiglia
Lareira
Little Rock Rodeo
Mim's
Oriental Grill
Pasta-Eria
Peter's Inn
Rhumb Line
Robke's
Sasaki
Sea Shanty
Siam Palace
Silver's
Soho
Sri Lanka Gourmet
Stango's
Von Leesen's
West End Cafe
Wylie's Ribs
Yamato
Y.E. Coyote

Long Island
Area Code 516

	F	D	S	C

Abel Conklin's/S (Huntington) **D5** | 19 | 18 | 17 | $33 |
54 New St. (W. Carver St.), 385-1919
*M – A "new lower-priced menu" is bringing fresh faces
into the "clubby", "mildly stuffy" atmosphere at this North
Shore steakhouse; some diners find the food "solid and
dependable", and praise the "good wine list", while others
say the "nothing-special beef is hit or miss"; service,
though "good during the week", can be "slow on weekends."*

Adam's Grill/S (Roslyn Heights) **E3** | – | – | – | M |
388 Willis Ave. (bet. Cambridge & Harvard Sts.), 621-3636
*Californian cuisine, complete with rotisserie and
wood-burning oven, as well as a "smart" setting bring
pizzazz to this North Shore spot, owned by Cathy and
Carlo Lansa of Sotto Luna; judging by early reports, this
newcomer shows promise.*

Aegean East/S (Hicksville) **E4** | – | – | – | M |
392 Woodbury Rd. (S. Oyster Bay Rd.), 935-8685
*Not your typical gyro joint, this small but comfortable
East Nassau storefront puts a sophisticated spin on
Continental dining with a Greek twist; fans praise the
unusual "flowerpot dessert" and friendly service.*

Ahrash Cafe/S (Huntington) **D5** | 19 | 12 | 18 | $19 |
255 Main St. (New York Ave.), 423-1228
*U – Locals enjoy the "change of pace" provided by this
"bright and clean" Suffolk County Afghan – a Sleeper of
the Year – with bargain-priced, "lively, interesting food"
and "service that's special"; a few skeptics say the
restaurant's "enthusiasm exceeds its capacity" and it's
nothing to look at, as the low decor rating reflects.*

Akbar/S (Garden City) **F3** | 18 | 20 | 19 | $27 |
1 Ring Rd. W. (near Roosevelt Field Mall), 248-5700
*U – Our voters love this "elegant" Garden City ethnic for
its "fine Indian cuisine" ("the breads alone would tempt
many") and "gracious service"; a few say it's easy to
build up the bill, but note that a wallet-friendly option is
the "great lunch buffet" for $8.50.*

Alfredo's Pizza*/LS (Westbury) **F3** | 18 | 13 | 15 | $9 |
163 Post Ave. (Battler St.), 333-7877
*U – This longstanding Mid-Island favorite just might
have the "best pizza around"; while some call it a
"great family place", others maintain that, apart from
the pizza, there's "not much else"; but at these low,
low prices, who's complaining?*

Long Island

| F | D | S | C |

Alouette* (Melville) E4
| 15 | 11 | 15 | $26 |

526A Walt Whitman Rd. (Rte. 110, north of Amityville Rd.), 549-3033

M – Some say "oui" to the French food served in this "small" plain-Jane Melville "storefront", however, more gripe about "overpriced, tiny portions" of "too heavy", "pastry-wrapped entrees, appetizers and desserts" – ah, well, chacun a son goût.

Amagansett Fish Company/S (Amagansett) C13
| 19 | 11 | 16 | $29 |

Montauk Hwy. (next to IGA), 267-7592

M – "Simple yet au courant" seafood lends a "quality-of-life dimension" to this "noisy" East Ender; although a few surveyors cry "throw it back", citing prices out of sync with "paper tablecloths", most commend the "very fresh seafood" and don't even mind the "parking lot location."

American Bistro/S (Kings Park) D5
| 22 | 18 | 21 | $34 |

25 Main St. (Henry St. & Rte. 25A), 269-1199

M – Local foodies extol the "varied and imaginative" menu of chef-owner George Hirsch at this "sedate and pretty" North Shore Contemporary American, raving over "innovative" fare such as "fish in corn husks"; detractors say it "tries to be Manhattan" and doesn't quite make it, but the bottom line is "fine food, fairly priced."

American Hotel, The/S (Sag Harbor) C12
| 23 | 23 | 20 | $44 |

The American Hotel, 25 Main St., 725-3535

M – "A Sag Harbor must", this "step into history" is renowned for its "old-world charm" "and "excellent wine list"; reports on the Contemporary American food range from "wonderful" to "overrated"; however, defenders say it's "always a special treat"; to avoid the "high prices", opt for the Friday night $14.95 "dinner and movie combo."

Aragosta-Blue Lobster*/S (Bayville) D4
| 15 | 16 | 17 | $30 |

22 Bayville Ave. (Shore Rd. & Bayville Rd.), 628-3838

M – The view's the thing at this Italian-style seafooder overlooking the Sound; though the "seafood is always fresh", some folks say it's blanketed with "heavy tomato sauces" and is "just ok"; for best results, come "watch the sunset" and stick to the "pasta and salads."

Armando's Seafood Barge/S (Southold) B11
| 16 | 12 | 13 | $27 |

Main Rd. (Rte. 25), 765-3010

M – Tourists flock to this "no-nonsense" North Fork fish house for its "good view" and "noisy", "hectic", "camp atmosphere", and to chow down on seafood "so fresh it could almost swim to your table"; critics say "don't bother", citing "overpriced" and "uninspired cuisine."

Long Island

Ashai Tokyo/S (Glen Cove) **D3** | 20 | 12 | 15 |$24|
2 Village Sq. (Bridge St.), 671-8096
U – In a "plain but clean" setting, Japanese-food lovers can "satisfy the craving" with "very good" "fresh" sushi, "wonderful" sashimi and "tempura that's not greasy"; a few balk that "service is rushed" and the place "used to be more exciting", but how many Japanese restaurants do you know where "desserts are special?"

Baja*/S (Long Beach) **G3** | 17 | 17 | 18 |$21|
1032 W. Beech St. (Georgia & Kentucky Sts.), 889-5992
U – "Very crowded in season", this "beachy" South Shore Mexican cantina has plenty of fans for its reasonably priced, "consistently good" food and "innovative specials"; expect "friendly" service and "good value" at this "noisy", "trendy" spot.

Bangkok Palace/S (Woodmere) **G2** | 20 | 13 | 19 |$24|
1058 Broadway (Franklin Pl.), 569-1016
U – "You're treated like a houseguest" at this well-rated Woodmere Thai that our surveyors put "on a par with Manhattan"; it's "not a palace" by any means, but "very good food", "lovely service" and affordable prices are quite enough to satisfy.

Barney's (Locust Valley) **D4** | 22 | 20 | 20 |$42|
315 Buckram Rd. (Bayville Rd.), 671-6300
M – In a "unique old firehouse setting" that "feels like a New England country inn", devotees dine on "wonderfully fresh and flavorful" New American cuisine, including "good grill dishes" and "vegetables that one would never dream of"; phobes, a minority, decry "top prices" and "uncomfortable chairs."

Basilico/S (Southampton) **C12** | 20 | 19 | 17 |$41|
10 Windmill Lane (Jobs Lane), 283-7987
M – A certified Hamptons "place to be seen", this "stylish" "Nouvelle Italian" offspring of Sapore di Mare gets its share of criticism for more "attitude" than ability and "ear-splitting" noise; however, most diners praise this "chic", "trendy" trattoria's "surprisingly good" food.

Bayou/S (Bellmore) **F3** | 20 | 12 | 17 |$23|
2823 Jerusalem Ave. (bet. Wantagh Ave. & Newbridge Rd.), 785-9263
U – At this "crowded", "smoky" little "New Orleans funk" barroom, "the decor's a disaster" but "the best jukebox on Long Island" pumps out nonstop blues; folks gladly "wait hours" to feast on "superb" Cajun specials; a few report "the food's so hot, you can't taste what you're eating."

Long Island

Bayport House/S (Bayport) **F6** | 22 | 19 | 20 | $29 |
291 Bayport Ave. (Railroad St., 1 block south of Montauk Hwy.), 472-2444
M – This "quaint country" restaurant in a "charming" "old house" on the South Shore is "especially beautiful" to some, but our reviewers can't agree whether the Northern Italian fare is "delicious" or "mediocre"; solid ratings suggest that admirers constitute a clear majority.

Bellport, The/S (Bellport) **E7** | 20 | 17 | 17 | $30 |
159 S. Country Rd. (Woodruff Ave.), 286-7550
M – The "adventurous" Contemporary American food served at this "casual" but "elegant" "'in' spot" puts fans in mind of the high-priced "Hamptons transplanted" to the South Bay; a few critics call the food "weird", and more than a few complain of "uncaring" service.

Benny's Ristorante (Westbury) **F3** | 23 | 21 | 22 | $38 |
199 Post Ave. (Maple Ave.), 997-8111
U – If "the parking lot looks like a Mercedes Benz dealership", then the big-timers are there because "Benny really cares about his guests"; his loyal following feels "spoiled" by the "elegant atmosphere" and "solidly good" Italian food, though even they warn "don't go on a Saturday night" when "reservations are useless."

Best of Both Worlds, The/S | 17 | 16 | 19 | $30 |
(Williston Park) **E3**
280 Hillside Ave. (Willis Ave. & Herricks Rd.), 248-1891
M – A reincarnation of Your Place or Mine, this new Nassau Eclectic gets kudos for its "innovative" menu heavy on the "hot and spicy" Cajun numbers, as well as its "unusual decor"; some say the place is "not what it used to be" and "needs to concentrate on this world."

B.K. Sweeney's Steak House/S | – | – | – | E |
(Garden City) **F3**
636 Franklin Ave. (bet. 6th & 7th Sts.), 746-3075
In an ambiance of stained glass and warm wood, this comfortable Garden City steakhouse/pub serves dependable, if unremarkable, food that's popular with a convivial local steak-and-ale crowd willing to pay the price.

Blue Parrot Cafe/S (Roslyn) **E3** | 16 | 15 | 16 | $27 |
1363 Old Northern Blvd. (off Bryant Ave.), 621-2494
M – "Good eats and funky lights" attract "a young, yuppie crowd" to this West Coast–style Eclectic with pizza, pasta and "Mexican leanings"; fans are unfazed by "noise, noise, noise" and "too-close tables"; the disenchanted dismiss it as a "trendy Californian wannabe" where the "menu is more appealing than the food often tastes."

Long Island

| | F | D | S | C |

Boardwalk Restaurant/S | 9 | 15 | 11 | $21 |
(Wantagh) **F4**
Jones Beach (Field 4, off Boardwalk), 785-2840
U – A glorious "beach location" can't offset "cafeteria-style" seafood and "very slow" service at this "summertime restaurant"; "order the view only and maybe have a drink" or brunch – or "don't bother and just sit on the beach."

Bonbori/S (Huntington) **D5** | 19 | 15 | 18 | $25 |
14 Elm St. (New York Ave.), 673-0400
M – "Summer dining is heaven" in the "lovely outdoor garden" of this North Shore Japanese, but while most surveyors enjoy the "consistently" "fresh, flavorful sushi" and "light, crisp tempura", a minority complain of "just ok" food and a "long wait between courses."

Bruce's/S (Wainscott) **C12** | – | – | – | M |
Montauk Hwy. (Town Line Rd.), 537-3360
Though widespread confusion between this and another like-named LI restaurant makes evaluation difficult, be assured that "fantastic brunch" and a "great piano bar" draw crowds to this East End "country place"; its newish American cuisine is adequate but far from cutting edge.

Bruzell's/S (Great Neck) **E2** | 18 | 19 | 17 | $33 |
451 Middle Neck Rd. (Old Mill Rd.), 482-6600
M – While philes laud the "excellent chef" and "elegant" decor, phobes say this North Shore Eclectic is "not worth the price" and little more than "Great Neck glitz"; the popular $14.95 "sunset dinner" is "a good value."

Bryant & Cooper | 23 | 19 | 19 | $41 |
Steakhouse/S (Roslyn) **E3**
2 Middle Neck Rd. (Northern Blvd.), 627-7270
M – Red-meat aficionados happily hunker down at "too-close" "noisy tables" set up for "oversize portions" of "consistently good steaks"; some say this North Shore eatery is "overpriced", "snooty" and "nothing to rave about", but most find the restaurant "worth it."

Buckram Stables/S | 15 | 17 | 15 | $25 |
(Locust Valley) **D4**
31-33 Forest Ave. (Birch Hill Rd.), 671-3080
M – When the "horsey set" craves burgers, they head for this "North Shore collegiate" "yuppie bar" that's "good for a quick bite" of "basic bar fare"; more demanding types find the food "mediocre" at this "hangout for Locust Valley lockjaw types."

Cafe Girasole/S (East Norwich) **D4** | 20 | 21 | 19 | $36 |
1053 Oyster Bay Rd. (north of Northern Blvd.), 624-8330
M – As this newish North Shore Italian "improves with experience", the "charming", "airy" dining room with its "open kitchen" continues to serve "pleasant", authentic food; those less charmed cite "pricey" tabs, waiters with "attitude" and "pretensions above the quality of the food."

Cafe Max/S (East Hampton) **C12** | 18 | 16 | 17 | $37 |
85 Montauk Hwy. (Cove Hollow Rd.), 324-2004
M – Chef-owner Morris Weintraub (ex Maidstone Arms) presides at this popular Hamptons newcomer; some raters say his American fare is both "excellent" and "impressive"; others find the effort "mediocre", with "cramped tables" creating a "claustrophobic" atmosphere.

Cafe Stefano/S (Selden) **D6** | 19 | 18 | 17 | $24 |
The Shops of Selden, 280 Middle Country Rd. (Rte. 25), 696-9618
U – "People going to the East End get off the expressway" to eat at this "busy", "noisy" "gem of a storefront" that serves "delicious" "trattoria fare" at fair prices; "try the black linguine with calamari", urges one devotee, who exclaims "oh, their garlic!"; a smattering say "nothing exceptional", and wonder why "the food is so good and the service so poor?"

Cafe Testarossa/S (Syosset) **D4** | 17 | 16 | 16 | $28 |
499 Jericho Tpke. (bet. Jackson Ave. & Rte. 135), 364-8877
M – "Trendy customers pack" this sleek, "neon-lit" Italian known for "large portions" of pasta, pizza and assorted dishes that some find "very good", but others call "middle-of-the-road", "assembly-line" fare; moderate prices and a high-traffic location guarantee crowds.

Caffe Baci/S (Westbury) **F3** | 18 | 16 | 16 | $22 |
1636 Old Country Rd. (Merrick Ave.), 832-8888
U – Like its "brother restaurant", Cafe Spasso, this "noisy" "upscale" "modern Italian" is known for "cute pizza" and "pasta galore" at "great prices"; to some it's little more than a "TGI Friday's with an Italian accent."

Caffe Spasso/S (Carle Place) **F3** | 18 | 17 | 16 | $22 |
307 Old Country Rd. (1 block east of Meadowbrook Pkwy.), 333-1718
M – At this "grandaddy" of all the "blond wood and neon" pastarias dotting LI, folks "wait for hours" to stoke up on "great, fast pasta and pizza" at "moderate prices" in a "crowded, frenetic atmosphere"; a very few call the food "fake Italian" that puts "quantity above quality", but most give thumbs-up to this "slick", "fresh", "trendy" cafe.

Caffe Spuntino/S (Mineola) **F3** | 20 | 16 | 17 | $24 |

Birchwood Plaza, 348 E. Jericho Tpke. (Glen Cove Rd.), 747-8111

U – What makes this more than "just another Italian" is a "chef with imagination", who serves up "huge portions" of "consistently good" "sophisticated pasta" and "pizza with flair", not to mention "specials that are special"; its popularity produces a "noise level that's impossible", however, and owners constantly checking on tables strike some as "a nice touch", others as "arrogant."

Calabash/S (Baldwin) **G3** | – | – | – | M |

Fairview Shopping Ctr., 1187 Grand Ave. (south of Southern State Pkwy.), 538-7400

Chef Vincent Chin makes everyone feel at home at his cozy little Jamaican-Chinese newcomer where ethnic cookery soothes the soul and ignites the palate; the background reggae beat goes with the food, as does Jamaican ginger beer, and the prices don't hurt a bit.

Calamari Kitchen/S (Oyster Bay) **D4** | – | – | – | M |
(fka Village Landing)

North Cove Plaza, 62B South St. (E. Main St.), 922-2999

Garlic fills the air of this "very casual" BYO Southern Italian seafooder, where diners say it's "pleasant to watch" chef Robert Fitzharris do up amazing things (e.g. calamari meatballs); the prices are fair, the food is lusty, and, given the no-reserving policy, it's "best to go at off times."

California Grille/S (Glen Head) **E3** | – | – | – | E |

360 Glen Cove Ave. (Glen Head Rd.), 759-4100

Brand-new and an instant hit, this snazzy hot spot has shaken the North Shore dining scene like a California earthquake; early signs suggest the innovative food is satisfying and ungimmicky.

Canterbury Ales/S (Oyster Bay) **E3** | 16 | 15 | 16 | $21 |

46 Audrey Ave. (South St.), 922-3614

M – This refurbished North Shore pub, with its new chef and "recently upscaled menu", has a spiffy new "Boston fish-house" look and "the best oysters in Oyster Bay"; fans brave the noisy crowds for "properly prepared seafood" at this Conrad's sibling.

Capriccio Restaurant (Syosset) **D4** | 21 | 20 | 21 | $41 |

399 Jericho Tpke. (2 blocks east of Rte. 106/107), 931-2727

U – Under the new aegis of the owners of L'Endroit, this "posh" and "refined" sanctum of Classic French and Northern Italian "luxury-life eating" is "still excellent", according to most surveyors, who praise the "clubby ambiance" and "gracious service"; however, a few critics find "nothing interesting" and warn of "steep prices."

Caracalla (Syosset) **D4** | 21 | 20 | 20 | $42 |
102 W. Jericho Tpke. (west of Underhill Blvd.), 496-3838
M – "They make you feel at home", rave fans who praise the "sophisticated Italian" cuisine, especially the "excellent fish dishes", and the "beautiful decor" of this "pricey" Northeast Nassau place; those less captivated call the ambiance "stuffy", the service "haughty."

Casa Luis*/S (Smithtown) **D6** | 17 | 12 | 18 | $23 |
1033 Jericho Tpke. (1 mile east of Mayfair Shopping Ctr.), 543-4656
U – If North Suffolk folks are willing to overlook the "tight" weekend squeeze at this "casual", if "drab", roadside cantina, it's because they like the "good, hearty" and "authentic" Spanish and Mexican fare at moderate prices; "caring service" can't hurt, either.

Casa Margarita/S (Smithtown) **D6** | 16 | 15 | 19 | $22 |
67 W. Main St. (Maple Ave.), 360-0627
U – Some consider this "old standby" for Spanish and Mexican cuisine a faded "landmark" in need of "sprucing-up"; its "better-than-average" Spanish food gets stronger response than its "typical Mexican"; "avoid Tuesdays", when half-priced Mexican food means "crowds."

CASA RUSTICA (Smithtown) **D6** | 24 | 18 | 22 | $39 |
175 W. Main St. (bet. Edgewood & Landing Aves.), 265-9265
U – "Very Italian cuisine", including "wonderful" grilled fresh vegetables and "delicious tuna", explains why diners say a trip to this "homey", "rustic" Smithtown haunt "saves you a trip to Italy"; while a handful find it "pretentious" and "overpriced", many consider it "the best Italian on Long Island."

Chefs of New York*/SX | 16 | 12 | 17 | $15 |
(East Northport) **D5**
Tick Tock Ctr., 508 Larkfield Rd. (Clay Pitts Rd.), 368-3156
U – What keeps this small East Northport neighborhood spot "always jammed" is "pizza-pizza-pizza" plus other "decent", "typical" red-sauce favorites; low prices and "great servers" compensate for no ambiance.

Chez Antoine*/S (Baldwin) **G3** | 19 | 19 | 19 | $33 |
590 Sunrise Hwy. (Grand Ave. & Long Beach Rd.), 223-9426
M – On weekends, South Nassau residents crowd into this "colorful" and "very different" spot for "quality", though pricey, Caribbean and French cuisine; while some find it "strictly hit or miss" and the "Caribbean food better than the French", the less exacting like it all, especially the "interesting" desserts.

Chez Noelle/S | 23 | 18 | 20 | $43 |
(Port Washington) **E3**
34 Willowdale Ave. (near Port Washington Blvd.), 883-3191
U – North Shore residents may wonder "what's exquisite French food doing in a place like this?", but they're happy to have Noelle and Pierre Simonin's "elegant" "bit of France in Port Washington" – it may be "expensive" and "in a bad location", but it's a "gem of a restaurant."

Cirella's/S (Melville) **E4** | 18 | 16 | 18 | $25 |
14 Broadhollow Rd. (1 block south of Old Country Rd.), 385-7380
M – Seemingly just another "pastel-peach" pasta palace, this "trendy" but "casual" eatery wins accolades for a brand of "metropolitan flair" that includes "balsamic vinegar and virgin olive oil on every table", "large portions" of "nice" pasta and an "upbeat", "relaxing" atmosphere; critics, citing "spotty service", "smoke and noise", say it's "nothing great."

C.J. Thorne/S (Bridgehampton) **C12** | 18 | 14 | 18 | $34 |
Main St. (Ocean Ave.), 537-0667
M – This "comfortable" East Ender with its "cool atmosphere" is "hardly ever crowded" but nevertheless cherished by those who extol its Contemporary American "country salads", "grilled tuna done like sashimi" and LI's "best soup"; a few call the cooking "erratic."

Classico/S (Roslyn Estates) **E3** | 16 | 15 | 16 | $32 |
1042 Northern Blvd. (Searingtown Rd.), 621-1870
M – Our surveyors split on this neighborhood "storefront Northern Italian"; North Shore regulars go for the "good, solid", if "unremarkable", fare and say it's "fun on theme nights" and on "singles Thursdays"; detractors report "sloppy service" and "nothing-special food."

Claudio's/S (Greenport) **B11** | 13 | 14 | 15 | $27 |
111 Main St. (Front St.), 477-0627
M – Locals call this North Fork Seafood landmark a veritable "tourist heaven" that serves "too many fried items" and "the same sauce" on every dish, but the "great view" and relatively moderate prices explain why the outdoor patio is "a hangout" all summer.

Coast Grill, The/S | 21 | 14 | 17 | $36 |
(Southampton) **D12**
Noyack Rd. (next to the Peconic Marina), 283-2277
U – Combining "fine fresh seafood", "superior grill fare" and a "delightful water view" makes this "noisy", "crowded", "out-of-the-way" South Fork "fish house" a certified "don't-miss Hamptons spot"; though it's pricey for its "hole-in-the-wall" look, regulars say "don't judge a book by its cover."

Cody's/S (Uniondale) **F3** | 19 | 17 | 17 | $27 |
1166 Hempstead Tpke., 3rd fl. (Marvin Ave.), 538-0218
*M – Hungry diners huff their way up "two flights of steep
steps" for the "best food near the Nassau Coliseum"; the
Contemporary American menu is "eclectic" (some say
"erratic") and "innovative", but a few say it "tries too hard
to be chic and misses."*

Colbeh/S (Great Neck) **E2** | 18 | 15 | 16 | $26 |
785 North Station Plaza (near LIRR station), 466-8181
*M – For "delicious but simple grilled meats", this
affordable "Persian kosher" "hideaway" near Great
Neck's rail station has fans cheering "the exotic and
flavorful food and mood"; critics say "ok for what it is."*

Conrad's Bar & Grill/S | 19 | 20 | 18 | $29 |
(Huntington) **D5**
326 W. Jericho Tpke. (Jones Lane & Oakwood Rd.),
427-9728
*M – With its "knockout" architecture and "light and airy"
decor, this "crowded", "trendy" joint is a "best newcomer
according to a North Suffolk cheering section, who like
its "eclectic" Contemporary American menu; critics fault
the "high noise level" and "pretentious" service.*

Country Inn, The/S | 17 | 20 | 18 | $29 |
(Locust Valley) **D4**
29 Oyster Bay Rd. (Bayville Rd.), 671-1357
*M – "Charming" country coziness is the main draw at this
old Gold Coast manse; diners disagree about the Traditional
American food, however, some calling it "excellent" and
"fresh", while others fuss about "small portions" of
"mediocre" fare; "great burgers and drinks" assure a steady
pub clientele despite higher-than-diners prices.*

Country Pantry | 20 | 14 | 18 | $23 |
(Rockville Centre) **F3**
65 N. Village Ave. (Front St. & N. Village Ave.), 678-5286
*U – The new chef-owner of this "very small", "homey"
Contemporary American "storefront" continues to serve
a "beautifully prepared varied menu" at "down-to-earth
prices"; some say that service "needs work" and the place
is "much too crowded";"reservations are a must"; BYO.*

Courtyard Cafe (Bohemia) **F6** | 19 | 16 | 17 | $24 |
3318 Veteran's Hwy. (Washington & Sycamore Aves.),
467-4848
*M – To fans, e.g. the big "business lunch crowd", this
"adorable" place tucked away in a strip mall near
MacArthur Airport offers a sensibly priced, "creative"
Eclectic menu that includes "healthful dishes marked
with a heart"; to critics, the forest-green chintz decor is
"dark", and the cuisine "just above average."*

COYOTE GRILL/S (Island Park) **G3** | 23 | 22 | 18 | $34 |
104 Waterview Rd. (Waterfront Rd. & Pettit Pl.), 889-8009
*M – The beat goes on at this high-profile SW, now that
chef Keith Rennie has taken the reins; fans are wowed
by this "trendy" waterfront "'in' spot", where "watching
the cool set is half the fun" and the "jazzy" decor
competes with the "great view"; critics say "much too
noisy" and "too avant-garde for its own good."*

Crescent/S (Bayville) **D4** | 21 | 27 | 14 | $38 |
333 Bayville Ave. (on the Sound), 628-3000
*U – This "magnificent" new multi-level restaurant has
a "great view of the Sound" and an "innovative", daily-
changing Californian-style menu; even with "slow",
"amateur" service, it's the "best newcomer for
waterfront dining."*

Danford's Inn/S (Port Jefferson) **C6** | 15 | 21 | 18 | $32 |
25 E. Broadway (Rte. 112), 928-5200
*M – Locals call this "charming" old inn, in a "beautiful
dockside setting", "an overpriced tourist spot", but since
"there aren't too many choices" in Port Jeff, you may
want to try breakfast or the "nice Sunday brunch";
according to early reports, new chef Stephen Meade (ex
Garden City Hotel) has jump-started the kitchen.*

Dar Tiffany/S (Greenvale) **E3** | 22 | 21 | 21 | $40 |
44 Glen Cove Rd. (north of Northern Blvd.), 625-0444
*U – Although the "futuristic" "fortress" decor is called
everything from "Darth Vader Tiffany" to "Las Vegas
casino", North Shore high-rollers reserve in advance to
see and be seen over "terrific steaks" and other
American favorites here; budget diners favor the
"early-bird dinners" or the new grill room for "burgers,
salads and pizzas at moderate prices."*

Dave's Downtown/S | 16 | 14 | 16 | $24 |
(Montauk) **B14**
S. Elmwood Ave. (Main St.), 668-4200
*U – You'll find "funky family fun" in a "nice beachy
atmosphere" where the "decent" bistro food is "good for
Montauk" but "not as good as Dave's Grill"; patio dining
and a good-value daily breakfast buffet are pluses.*

Dave's Grill/S (Montauk) **B14** | 23 | 15 | 19 | $30 |
Flamingo Rd. (on Montauk Harbor), 668-9190
*U – "Casual" and "comfortable", this "favorite of baymen
in the know" takes "no reservations", but that doesn't
deter locals and summer folk who feel that the "good,
wholesome grilled fish" might be Montauk's "best fresh
seafood"; snag a table on the waterside patio and enjoy.*

Della Femina/S | – | – | – | E |
(East Hampton) **C12**
99 N. Main St. (Cedar St.), 329-6666
Who but advertising sparkplug Jerry Della Femina could light up the Hamptons dining scene with a late-season opening?; this is high-powered Nuova Cucina for a megawatt crowd, who don't mind paying high prices for handsome decor, heads-up service and a chance to mingle with everybody who's anybody.

Di Benardo's Bistro/S | 20 | 16 | 18 | $31 |
(Commack) **D5**
6300 Jericho Tpke. (Commack Rd.), 462-0800
M – After our Survey, this Commack Italian moved to its new location, changing the menu and becoming a bistro; our raters were divided about the old place – some calling the cuisine "memorable", "delicious" and "almost perfect", others saying "overrated" and "expensive"; however, the new venue promises lower prices.

DiMaggio's/S | 16 | 11 | 16 | $20 |
(Port Washington) **E3**
706 Port Washington Blvd. (Davis Ave.), 944-6363
U – For "food close to like Mama makes", this "little storefront" "neighborhood Italian" might be the best spot for pizza "before or after a movie"; bargain prices and friendly service nearly offset its lack of ambiance.

Diwan (Port Washington) **E3** | 19 | 20 | 17 | $28 |
37 Shore Rd. (Millpond Rd.), 767-7878
M – While loyal habitués say this North Shore Indian offers "wonderful food" and "attentive service" in "elegant", "gracious" surroundings, skeptics find the "pink and green" decor overly "ornate" and the cuisine "no match for the East Village"; the $8.99 weekday lunch buffet is an antidote to generally high prices.

Dublin Delights/SX | 19 | 11 | 18 | $18 |
(St. James) **D6**, 244 Lake Ave. (Woodlawn Ave.), 862-6900
(Miller Place) **C7**, 90 N. Country Rd. (Echo Lane), 331-4848
U – The friendly folks at this "best bang for the buck" duo serve "yummy Irish treats"; it's "the only place around for authentic shepherd's pie and Lancastershire hot pot", and the "alfresco" dining is "particularly nice at Sunday breakfast"; larger groups may find the new Miller Place venue a happier fit than the tiny St. James cafe.

Due Torri/S (Hauppauge) **E6** | 21 | 21 | 21 |$37|
330 Motor Pkwy. (Marcus Blvd.), 435-8664
M – "Rooftop dining" in "corporate elegance" atop a five- story office building with a "great view of the L.I.E. and Hauppauge Industrial Park"; fans laud the "consistently good", "sophisticated" Northern Italian fare and "old-world" service, but foes say it's a "good place to impress relatives", even if the food's "indistinguishable from other Italian places."

Eddie's Pizza/LSX | 21 | 6 | 15 |$15|
(New Hyde Park) **F2**, 2048 Hillside Ave. (Denton Ave. & New Hyde Park Rd.), 354-9780
(Mastic Beach) **E8**, 1355 Montauk Hwy. (William Floyd Pkwy.), 281-9516
(Cedarhurst) **G3**, 487 Chestnut St. (across from LIRR station), 295-9393
U – Eddie's makes the definitive thin-crusted pizza: "first-class", "paper-thin" and "no-guilt"; diners readily tolerate "long waits", "yucky decor" and "overrated" "Southern Italian cooking" for an "incredible" crust-biting experience – "so crispy it's almost matzoh."

Elbow Room, The/S | – | – | – | E |
(Jamesport) **D10**
Main St., Rte. 25 (S. Jamesport Ave.), 722-3292
World-famous marinated steaks are the draw at this '50s-era North Fork eatery where everything else seems beside the point; comfortable old-line ambiance and prices on the low side of high attract enthusiasts who wrote in to tell us about it.

El Tapatio/S (Great Neck) **E2** | 16 | 13 | 16 |$23|
4 Welwyn Rd. (east of LIRR station), 487-1070
M – Great Neck residents call this "off-the-beaten-path" Mexican a reliable "neighborhood standby" for "distinctive" south-of-the-border fare; no great shakes, perhaps, but "reasonable" prices and a comfortable ambiance that's both "corny" and "homey" have their partisans.

Emilia/S (Carle Place) **F3** | 21 | 17 | 20 |$35|
588 Westbury Ave. (near Glen Cove Rd.), 334-6858
M – Fans of chef-owner Vinnie Jurin's "cozy" Northern Italian say "if the owner tells you what to order, listen", praising "concerned service", "excellent seafood and pasta" and "cold appetizers"; skeptics find it "crowded" and "noisy", promising "more than it delivers."

Emilio's/S (Commack) **D5**　　| – | – | – | M |

Consumer's Ctr., 2201 Jericho Tpke. (east of Commack Rd.), 462-6267

More than just a pizzeria, this sleek little Commack eatery has an up-front pizza counter plus a multilevel wraparound dining area where locals chow down on huge portions of lush pastas and innovative off-the-menu specials.

Estia/Amagansett Fresh Pasta/SX | 15 | 9 | 13 |$20|
(Amagansett) **C13**

177 Main St. (center of town), 267-6320

U – By day, this "warm, friendly" luncheonette is a "basic greasy spoon" that's "great for breakfast"; at night, there's "always a wait" for "exotic" and affordable homemade pastas that some call "very good", but others find out of place in a coffee shop.

Estoril Granada/S (Mineola) **F3**　| 17 | 14 | 18 |$27|

149 Mineola Blvd. (Harrison Ave.), 747-7599

M – Though "tacky" and "worn", this is still "the best spot on LI for Spanish and Portuguese cuisine"; fans tout the "marvelous mariscada" and "great Spanish fried potato chips"; critics sigh "it's ok if you need a paella fix."

Eye of the Tiger/S (Hicksville) **E4**　| 20 | 19 | 19 |$22|

451 New South Rd. (B'way & Hazel St.), 931-1678

M – This "authentic", "cosmopolitan" Chinese is a bit more "expensive" than most ("tea costs extra"), but Sinophiles call it "a step above" the usual, with food that's "innovative", "fresh" and "beautifully presented"; dissenters say "pretentious", "overrated", "nothing special."

56th Fighter Group/S　　　| 12 | 22 | 14 |$26|
(Farmingdale) **F3**

Republic Airport, Gate 1 (Rte. 110), 694-8280

U – Whether you consider "eating in a WW II bunker" "wonderful nostalgia" or a "depressing concept", the Continental fare at this "gimmicky" stage set doesn't fly with those who'd "rather eat TV dinners"; families with kids and "airplane nostalgia buffs" should go for "the great Sunday brunch" – and "expect a wait."

Fish Net/S (Hampton Bays) **D10**　| 18 | 12 | 15 |$21|

122 E. Montauk Hwy. (bet. Ponquogue Ave. & the canal), 728-0115

U – Delivering "everything you'd expect from an honest seafood dive", this "ramshackle" little East End joint specializes in "fresh fish" at low prices, with an ambiance that "reminds you of a Greek diner" – no wonder it's always so "crowded"; wine and beer only.

Fountaine's Beacon/S | – | – | – | M |
(Hampton Bays) **D10**
322 W. Montauk Hwy. (Bess Lane & Jones Rd.), 728-2998
Chef Sean Fountaine, a veteran of New Orleans legend Arnaud's, delights locals with a reasonably priced Creole-Cajun–Continental repertoire that far outshines the lighthouselike exterior and bland interior; N.B. *"when they say a dish is spicy, believe them."*

Franina's/S (Syosset) **D4** | 21 | 15 | 18 | $38 |
58 W. Jericho Tpke. (bet. Robbins Lane & Underhill Blvd.), 496-9770
M – NE Nassau restaurant-goers can't get enough of this spot's "good, earthy", "well-prepared" Italian cooking, but many decry service with "auto-salesman" "attitude" and say the "decor needs a redo."

Frank's Steaks/S (Jericho) **D4** | – | – | – | E |
Jericho Office & Shopping Plaza, 4 Jericho Tpke. (Brush Hollow Rd.), 338-4595
Yes, they've got fish and chicken too, but high-quality, aged, premium beef is what this minimalist steakhouse is all about; that suits its beef-eater clientele just fine – so much so they wrote in to tell us about it.

Franzi & Nell's/S (Stony Brook) **D6** | – | – | – | E |
(fka Pasta Viola)
Stony Brook Village Ctr., 93 Main St. (off Rte. 25A), 689-7755
Smart and refined, this "imaginative" Californian-style bistro, which draws a professorial crowd from nearby SUNY, scores more hits than misses, though prices run a bit high for "casual fare"; seasonal outdoor dining and a $13 "bar special" dinner are pluses.

Frederick's (Melville) **E4** | 22 | 16 | 21 | $33 |
1117 Walt Whitman Rd. (south of Old Country Rd.), 673-8550
U – This "quaint" and "appealing" Suffolk County eatery serves "varied cuisines of Europe" in a "comfortable" (some say "cramped") "little house"; a "warm" ambiance and "accommodating staff" help make the place "a sentimental favorite."

FRESNO PLACE | 24 | 18 | 20 | $39 |
(East Hampton) **D5**
8 Fresno Place (Gingerbread Lane), 324-0727
U – A "good Hamptons choice" for "imaginative" American fare, this "cheery" spot is deservedly "popular", despite random grumblings of "quirky service", for being "a bit pretentious"; the "great drinks" and a beautiful "crowd" set the stage for an "interesting" social scene.

Fu Ho/S (Syosset) **D4** | 15 | 15 | 17 | $23 |

4 Berry Hill Rd. (Cold Springs Rd.), 364-2828
*M – Some sing the praises of the "creative menu" at this
Syosset Chinese as "almost as good as Chinatown",
others call it a case of "lots of linen and service for
ho-hum food"; though its scores have slipped, it's a
"good family choice."*

Fyodoroff/S (Carle Place) **F3** | 15 | 21 | 17 | $38 |

Country Glen Ctr., 144 Glen Cove Rd. (Old Country Rd.),
741-8311
*M – Our surveyors can't make up their minds about this
"expensive", "campy" Russian nightclub/restaurant that's
open only on weekends: the decor is "gorgeous" or
"depressing", the "heavy" food "authentic" or "mediocre",
the service "friendly" or "nasty"; all in all, it's a poor
second to Brighton Beach, but can be a "fun spot to
bring a group."*

GAETANO'S (Patchogue) **F7** | 24 | 15 | 21 | $36 |

337 E. Main St. (east of Rte. 112), 758-0477
*U – A South Suffolk "gem" for "excellent Italian", this
"tiny", "cozy" "storefront" wins accolades for its "fine
food" and "friendly service"; a few critics wish they'd
reduce the prices and fatten the portions, and the
"cramped and noisy" quarters will never win a prize.*

Garden City Grande Cafe | 20 | 20 | 19 | $33 |
(Garden City) **F3**

1100 Stewart Ave. (Endo Blvd. & Nassau Community
College), 222-2121
*M – "Hip", "ambitious" and "great for people-watching",
this mid-Nassau yearling sports a "creative"
Contemporary American menu ("try the alligator") that
appeals to a "young" crowd; more sedate types say
"forget the disco nights", when it's a "singles hangout."*

Garden Court Cafe/S | – | – | – | M |
(Rockville Centre) **F3**

Holiday Inn, 173 Sunrise Hwy. (bet. Village & Centre
Aves.), 678-1300
*Recently redecorated, this moderately priced American
serves a varied menu of burgers, pasta, seafood, veal
and the like in a pretty garden setting.*

Gasho of Japan/S (Hauppauge) **E6** | 17 | 19 | 18 | $27 |

356 Vanderbilt Motor Pkwy. (Washington Ave.), 231-3400
*M – Offering "slice 'em and dice 'em dining", this "typical
Japanese steakhouse" is "fun" for kids and out-of-
towners, but some are "unimpressed" by "small
portions" – "eat a snack before you go."*

G.D. Graffiti (Woodbury) **E4** | 14 | 15 | 13 | $21 |

Woodbury Common, 8285 Jericho Tpke. (Woodbury Rd.),
367-1340
*M – This bustling "food store/restaurant" newcomer
offers "innovative" American food, but ratings indicate a
bumpy start despite appealing prices; critics complain of
"slow service" and "noise"; though "it's good for lunch"
and "not bad for a quick supper."*

George Martin/S | 20 | 17 | 19 | $26 |
(Rockville Centre) **F3**
65 N. Park Ave. (bet. LIRR station & Maple Ave.), 678-7272
*U – "Wear comfortable shoes" and expect a "long wait" for
"big portions" of "creative" American "bistro cuisine" at
"moderate prices" served in a "congenial" setting of "shiny
brass and mellow wood"; a few detractors say it's "cramped"
and "noisy", but most surveyors call it a "local favorite."*

George Washington Manor/S | 16 | 21 | 18 | $31 |
(Roslyn) **E3**
1305 Old Northern Blvd. (Roslyn Rd.), 621-1200
*M – Ratings have risen at this "historically correct"
Colonial landmark; the "old-fashioned" (some say
"blah") American cuisine is still "nothing revolutionary",
but it's "good value" and great for "grandparents."*

Giulia Ristorante/S (Great Neck) **E2** | 21 | 18 | 20 | $36 |
570 Middle Neck Rd. (Brokauw Lane), 482-1510
*M – Devotees of this "warm", "plush" Great Neck Italian
laud the "sophisticated" food, "lively waiters" and
"hospitable" owner; nitpickers say it's "expensive",
"overcrowded on weekends" and "on a par with so
many that it's easily forgotten"; solid scores suggest you
see for yourself.*

Gordon's Restaurant/S | 20 | 15 | 20 | $41 |
(Amagansett) **C13**
Main St. (bet. Hedges & Miankoma Lanes), 267-3010
*M – History was made at this "old-fashioned" landmark
when the "jacket requirement was dropped", but the
"very-Hamptons" crowd is faithful to the "staid but
reliable" menu of "simply prepared fresh seafood" and
"great duck"; others decry stiff prices and say the place
is decidedly "past its prime."*

Gosman's Dock/S (Montauk) **B14** | 17 | 16 | 14 | $29 |
West Lake Dr., 668-2549
*M – There's "always a wait" at this "touristy but fun",
"not-too-expensive" waterside seafooder that's "a
Montauk must" for "lobster and the view"; seasoned
patrons caution "keep it simple and you'll survive."*

Gumbo Alley/S | 18 | 15 | 17 | $25 |
(Rockville Centre) **F3**
18 S. Park Ave. (Merrick Rd. & Lincoln Ave.), 766-9758
*U – "Spice lovers" find it "worth a trip" to South Nassau
for "hot, hot, hot Cajun food" in this "small", often
crowded eatery with its "busy bar" scene; most laud the
"best gumbo outside of New Orleans" and "great fried
sweet potatoes and blackened steak" at "moderate
prices", but a handful dismiss the food as "so-so."*

Gurney's Inn/S (Montauk) **B14** | 18 | 20 | 17 | $39 |
Gurney's Inn, Old Montauk Hwy. (east of Hither Hills
State Park), 668-2345
*M – A "gorgeous view" compensates for what some call
"pricey" "plastic" Continental cuisine at this spa and
resort whose decor evokes "the lobby of a '50s Reno
casino minus the slot machines"; loyalists insist it's
"dependable", with "nicely presented" spa cuisine.*

Hampton Square/S | 18 | 19 | 17 | $41 |
(Westhampton Beach) **E10**
10 Beach Rd. (Main St.), 288-1877
*U – This "cozy", "almost chic", Contemporary American
attracts "the green-pants crowd" (worn with navy blazers,
natch, since the rule is "jackets preferred"), but surveyors
are pleasantly "surprised by the good", "innovative" food;
a few critics cry "pretentious" and "overpriced", but fume
that they "can't get in during season."*

Hana*/S (Port Jefferson) **C6** | 20 | 15 | 19 | $26 |
21 Oakland Ave. (across from Mather Hospital), 473-9264
*M – For "fine basic Japanese" in a "reliable
neighborhood restaurant", this "good old" Port Jefferson
standard has a "pleasant modern setting" and a "very
light touch in the kitchen"; critics call the food
"inconsistent", and fault portions "the size of a pea."*

Harlequin Cafe/S (Sea Cliff) **E4** | 19 | 17 | 18 | $30 |
39 Roslyn Ave. (Sea Cliff Ave.), 676-1641
*M – This "cute spot" in "charming" Sea Cliff offers
"well-prepared, innovative" "modern American cuisine",
but beware of the "uncomfortable chairs"; "go early" if
"dancing, music" and a lively late-night "bar scene" are
not your scene.*

Harrington's Cafe Americain*/LS | 15 | 17 | 17 | $27 |
(Port Jefferson) **C6**
(fka The Original Elk)
201C Main St. (Arden Place), 928-4455
*M – Our critics were divided about this North Shore
jazz-with-dinner spot; some tout the "good food and
service", while others term the "trendy" American
cookery a little pricey and "highly irregular"; late hours
and live entertainment are pluses.*

Hildebrandt's (Williston Park) **E3** | 18 | 9 | 18 | $20 |
84 Hillside Ave. (bet. Willis Ave. & Roslyn Rd.), 741-0608
U – Wear your old saddle shoes and bring your appetite to this "no-atmosphere" "luncheonette from years ago" that, in addition to offering "excellent homemade ice cream" and "great hot fudge", boasts an "ambitious" International menu and a "caring staff."

Honest Diner/S (Amagansett) **C13** | 18 | 14 | 16 | $20 |
74 Montauk Hwy. (Abrahams Path), 267-3535
M – "Another hit" from husband-and-wife team Jeff Salaway and Toni Ross, this "trendy", "casual" "1950s diner", popular with "celebs", is good for "long lines any time of day" and "large portions" of "real good food"; critics bash it for "way-overpriced" "nothing-special diner food."

Hong Kong Seafood | 18 | 10 | 15 | $16 |
Restaurant*/LS (Amityville) **G4**
106 Merrick Rd. (west of Rte. 110), 691-8488
U – Delighted dim sum devotees "waddle out" of this "hole-in-the-wall" with its "unusual" Chinatown-style cuisine and "accommodating service"; prices are low, but there's a need for "more space" and "more help."

Hunam Restaurant/S (Levittown) **E4** | 20 | 12 | 18 | $20 |
3112 Hempstead Tpke. (near S. Berry Lane), 731-3552
M – "Close your eyes" ("the place could use a major overhaul") and "enjoy some of the best Chinese food on LI", say fans of this bastion of "suburban Szechuan" cuisine, who swear that with "one taste, you'll see why it's crowded"; the unimpressed assert that while the restaurant is "reliable", it's "nothing special."

Hunan Gourmet East/S | 19 | 14 | 17 | $20 |
(Merrick) **G3**
2035 Merrick Rd. (Merrick Ave.), 378-2323
M – Merrick regulars cherish this "better-than-average" "neighborhood" Chinese, a fixture since 1975 for "well-prepared" favorites served "as though you have a personal waiter"; a few vocal critics say there's "nothing new here" and lament "it used to be better."

Hunan Taste/S (Greenvale) **E3** | 19 | 15 | 17 | $21 |
3 Northern Blvd. (bet. Glen Cove & Willington Rds.), 621-6616
U – North Shore residents say there's "Chinatown variety in the suburbs" plus food that's "hot, hot, hot"; "excellent value" and "concerned service" win extra kudos, but dissenters say it's "starting to get shaky."

| F | D | S | C |

Iberian Restaurant/S ⎜20⎜14⎜20⎜$27⎜
(Huntington) **D5**
402 New York Ave. (bet. Rte. 25A & High St.), 549-8296
*U – Garlic-lovers say a night out at this Spaniard is "like
visiting a Spanish aunt's home" – one whose "dingy"
"interior needs a face-lift" – where everyone gets a
"warm welcome" plus sensibly priced "huge portions" of
"consistently good" food.*

Il Cappuccino/S (Sag Harbor) **C12** ⎜20⎜17⎜19⎜$26⎜
Madison St. (Main St.), 725-2747
*U – The secret's out about this Sag Harbor "Italian";
regulars say the "tasty", "moderately priced" "homestyle
Italian food", especially the "complimentary garlic rolls",
are reason enough to brave the crowds.*

Il Garofano/S (Bay Shore) **F6** ⎜22⎜18⎜21⎜$36⎜
118 Maple Ave. (near Maple Ave. dock), 665-8080
*M – This Bay Shore Italian hideaway may be "little
known", but devotees call its food and service
"consistently excellent", with particularly "good
pastas and veal dishes"; the less enchanted say
prices are highish and quality is "variable when the
owner isn't present."*

Il Pozzo Ristorante/S ⎜19⎜19⎜21⎜$36⎜
(Hauppauge) **E6**
760 Town Line Rd. (Hoffman Lane), 265-7475
*M – "You can imagine Grandma rolling out the ravioli" in
the kitchen of this "very romantic" little Italian that, for
most surveyors, succeeds at being "professional yet
homey"; critics, however, find the food "overrated" and
"unexpectedly expensive."*

Il Sapore/S (Roslyn Heights) **E3** ⎜19⎜16⎜17⎜$32⎜
177 Mineola Ave. (north of L.I.E. exit 37N), 621-0840
*U – There are "always people waiting" at this
"conveniently located" trattoria, so expect "noise" and
"bustle", but also "reliable" pizza and other Italian dishes,
"good service" and "fair prices"; a handful of naysayers
dub it "easy to forget" and just "another pasta place."*

Inn at Quogue, The/S (Quogue) **E10** ⎜19⎜19⎜17⎜$40⎜
The Inn at Quogue, 52 Quogue St. (Jessup Ave.), 653-6560
*M – There's a lot of potential at this "charming" country
inn that's more than just "another hotel restaurant";
though its American food is "not as great" as it could be
– new chef notwithstanding, the "relaxing atmosphere"
and "creative menu" have pulled ratings up since our
last Survey.*

I Santi/S (Water Mill) **D12** | – | – | – | E |
Shoe Town Shopping Ctr., 1020 Montauk Hwy. (east of
Deerfield Rd.), 726-7585
*Pietro Vardeu, former general manager of Sapore di
Mare and executive chef at Basilico, showcases the
cuisines of Tuscany and Sardinia with panache at his
spare and tastefully decorated new place; highish prices
leave the upscale Hamptons crowd unfazed.*

Jade Garden/S (Hauppauge) **E6** | 17 | 15 | 16 | $19 |
Shoe Town Shopping Ctr., 555 Rte. 111 (Town Line Rd.),
360-1646
*U – This "typical Chinese restaurant" serves "large portions"
of "fresh", "colorful" food from a small, mid-Suffolk shopping
center – modestly priced and "nice", say some, but
nothing to become excited about either.*

James Lane Cafe at the Hedges/S | 21 | 22 | 20 | $45 |
(East Hampton) **C12**
(fka Palm at the Hedges)
The Hedges Inn, 74 James Lane (Main St.), 324-7100
*U – Newly transformed but under the same ownership,
this "charming" but "very expensive" cafe where "flowers
abound" has established itself as an "in' spot"; Hamptonites
favor the new Contemporary American menu with its
Italianate slant, though a few miss the old Palm's
traditional steakhouse fare.*

Jani/S (Huntington Station) **D5** | 20 | 19 | 19 | $22 |
Walt Whitman Mall, 350 Rte. 110 (½ mile south of
Jericho Tpke.), 421-5264
*M – In "cool", somewhat "austere" surroundings, this
"hi-tech Chinese" "shopping-center shocker" serves spicy
"excellent" Szechuan and Hunan cuisine "priced right",
with the added kick of "delicious", "unusual" desserts
("chocolate cake in a Chinese restaurant"); some
complain of "small portions", "sullen" service and "noise."*

J-Dave's Old Inlet Inn (Bellport) **E7** | 20 | 21 | 18 | $35 |
108 S. Country Rd. (Station Rd.), 286-2650
*M – Under new management, this "charming" 1820s
landmark has a new menu of what some call "surprisingly
good" American food, including "great Cajun dishes";
critics fault "disappointing" changes and stiff prices.*

Jimmy Hay's Filet Mignon/S | 19 | 14 | 18 | $31 |
(Island Park) **G3**
4310 Austin Blvd. (Kingston Blvd.), 432-5155
*M – While some surveyors find this "clubby" "basic"
steakhouse a "friendly" "family place" for "good food",
others call it the "usual steak place" at above-moderate
prices and "nothing exceptional."*

Long Island | F | D | S | C |

J.J. Hwang/S (Merrick) **G3** | 20 | 20 | 19 | $23 |
217 W. Merrick St. (Chernucha Ave.), 867-3200
U – In a "very pretty" setting somewhere between "a ski lodge" and an upscale catering hall, diners delight in "unusual dishes" from China's Chengdu region; a "great host" adds to the "friendly atmosphere", where prices are reasonable for "fresh and different" fare.

John Peel Room/S (Westbury) **F3** | 17 | 17 | 17 | $32 |
Island Inn, Old Country Rd. (Zeckendorf Blvd.), 228-8430
M – A demographic cross-section of LI can be found at this cavernous Nassau "institution" that speaks American with an English accent; comments, too, are varied: "the optimum in English dining" that "never disappoints" vs. "overpriced" and "past its prime."

Jolly Fisherman/S (Roslyn) **E3** | 20 | 17 | 19 | $35 |
25 Main St. (Old Northern Blvd.), 621-0055
M – The darling of the senior set, this "sprawling" "standby" is "always packed" with North Shore people drawn to its Traditional American food and "lovely view overlooking Roslyn Pond"; regulars love the "standard, good seafood" and beef, but others lament that it's "not as good as it was" and is "too expensive."

Jonathan's/S (Huntington) **D5** | 19 | 16 | 15 | $25 |
15 Wall St. (bet. Gerard & Main Sts.), 549-0055
M – Tucked behind a gourmet shop is this European-style bistro that has expanded from lunch-only to a limited dinner format, serving "always imaginative", "good-value" "Californian-type" cuisine; as its ratings reflect, the service "needs polishing."

Kabul/S (Huntington) **D5** | 21 | 16 | 20 | $22 |
1153 E. Jericho Tpke. (Park Ave.), 549-5506
U – "Authentic Afghan" touches make you "feel like you're in another country" at this "charming" South Shore ethnic that serves "hearty", "interesting" fare with an emphasis on "grilled foods"; more good news: prices are modest and servers "anxious to please."

Karen Lee's/S | 22 | 17 | 19 | $39 |
(Bridgehampton) **C12**
Main St. (Corwith Ave.), 537-7878
M – Despite solid ratings, our reviewers divide over this Bridgehampton 'in' spot that's so popular "you can't get in"; fans praise the "concerned service" and "excellent food" made with "fresh ingredients", while detractors note "uneven" quality and "forgetful service", wondering "what's all the fuss?"

Koenig's/S (Floral Park) **F2** | 17 | 13 | 17 | $26 |
86 S. Tyson Ave. (Jericho Tpke.), 354-2300
M – The "hearty", "heavy", "homey" German food at this Floral Park institution offers "a lot for the dollar", but while locals, "senior citizens" and the "race-track set" accept the "dumpy" decor, those out for more highs and less heft might do better elsewhere.

Kokura II/S (Woodbury) **E4** | 23 | 22 | 20 | $34 |
8289 Jericho Tpke. (bet. Woodbury & Plainview Rds.), 367-4944
U – "Fresh", "flavorful" food in an "elegant" Woodbury setting have some calling this "class-act Japanese" the "closest thing to Japan on LI", making "reservations a must on weekends"; despite a solid score, some say the "service is not what it was in the past."

Kura Barn/S (Huntington) **D5** | 20 | 15 | 17 | $26 |
479 New York Ave. (south of Main St.), 673-0060
M – Controversy abounds at this "small" South Shore Japanese; fans praise the "fresh sushi", "airy, light tempura" and "typical, simple" decor that makes you "feel like you're in Kyoto", but dissenters decry tables that are "too close" and food that's only "ordinary."

Kurofune/S (Commack) **D5** | – | – | – | M |
77 Commack Rd. (Jericho Tpke.), 499-1075
Locals love this plain-Jane, typical Japanese restaurant where impeccably fresh sushi and a friendly staff keep customers – many of them Asian – coming back for more; lunch is a particularly good value.

La Bussola/S (Glen Cove) **D3** | 22 | 17 | 18 | $36 |
40 School St. (Glen St.), 671-2100
U – A North Shore favorite, this "solid" Italian standby satisfies regulars with "finger-lickin' big portions" of "traditional Italian cuisine"; a small minority calls it "overpriced and stuffy" – "ok, but nothing to write home about"; N.B. there's "a long wait on Saturdays."

La Caravella (Hicksville) **E4** | 22 | 22 | 21 | $40 |
294 N. Broadway (south of L.I.E., exit 41S), 938-0220
M – Rated "one of the finer Northern Italian restaurants in Nassau County", this "romantic spot" in Hicksville's business district is "always a treat" for its many fans; for others, it's just "another Italian" – "overpriced", "crowded" and "stuffy" – but ratings suggest they're easily outvoted by admirers.

Long Island

La Coquille/S (Manhasset) **E3** | 22 | 20 | 22 | $42 |
1669 Northern Blvd. (east of Shelter Rock Rd.), 365-8422
U – For years, North Shore Francophiles have treasured this "tiny", "quiet" "charmer" on Manhasset's Miracle Mile as their "special place" for "fabulous French" cuisine and "dignified, gracious service"; a few grumble about "small portions" and "high prices", but solid scores across the board suggest you give it a try.

La Dolce Sera*/S (Westbury) **F3** | 20 | 18 | 17 | $31 |
477 Old Country Rd. (across from Fortunoff's), 338-5932
U – Fortunoff shoppers who cross the street often "delight" in this airy, attractive Italian "sleeper", which offers family-style platters (and some single-portion options) of "surprisingly" good food and "great desserts"; some find it costly, and service gets mixed reviews.

La Famiglia/S (East Meadow) **F4** | 16 | 11 | 14 | $27 |
2366 Hempstead Tpke. (Newbridge St.), 579-3333
U – Hungry diners squeeze into "uncomfortable chairs" to mangia "huge" "family-style" portions of "not expensive", "stick-to-your-ribs" Italian cuisine, but some wonder "do we really need another family-style Italian restaurant?"

La Ginestra/S (Glen Cove) **D3** | 22 | 18 | 20 | $37 |
4 School St. (Glen St.), 671-3184
M – Fans praise this North Shore "relative of Trastevere in NYC" for its "lovely" (if "crowded") ambiance and "great pasta", insisting that "chef Enzo Alessandro's wood grill is the best" around; faulters find it all "noisy" and "very overpriced."

La Grange Inn/S (West Islip) **F5** | 18 | 19 | 19 | $31 |
Higbie Lane & Montauk Hwy., 669-0765
M – The "old-world charm" of this South Suffolk fixture appeals to a local clientele – "second- and third-generation" regulars who come for its "standard Continental" dishes and "old-style German cooking"; modernists find the food "boring" and the ambiance "tired" – "a big diner in an historic building."

La Marmite (Williston Park) **E3** | 23 | 21 | 22 | $41 |
234 Hillside Ave. (Mineola Blvd.), 746-1243
M – In the "refined atmosphere" ("country club spoken here") of an "elegant" old house, some Mid-Nassau restaurant-goers enjoy "divine French dining" that's "equal to a good NY restaurant"; less-enthusiastic raters think it's "not worth the expense."

LA MASCOTTE/S (Commack) **D5** | 24 | 20 | 23 |$41 |
3 Crooked Hill Rd. (Commack Rd.), 499-6446
*U – Ratings for this off-the-beaten-track "special-
occasion" French restaurant have risen since our last
Survey, with loyalists lauding the "caring" service and
"classy" presentations of "fine French food"; regulars
like to "go on weekday nights" for a "prix fixe dinner."*

LA PACE/S (Glen Cove) **D3** | 24 | 23 | 23 |$42 |
51 Cedar Swamp Rd. (Glen Cove Rd.), 671-2970
*U – In restaurant-rich Glen Clove, this "quintessential
Northern Italian" with its "lovely" "country-club decor"
and "attentive service" remains "a classic" to diners who
dote on the "top-drawer" traditional cuisine; to its few
critics, it's both "pretentious" and "overpriced."*

La Parma/S | 22 | 13 | 18 |$29 |
(Williston Park) **E3**, 707 Willis Ave. (Henry St.), 294-6610
(Huntington) **D5**, 452 W. Jericho Tpke. (east of Round
Swamp Rd.), 367-6360
(Oceanside) **G3**, 410 Merrick Rd. (¼ mile east of Long
Beach Rd.), 763-1815
*U – These temples of "lotsa food, lotsa garlic" attract the
faithful who find it "worth the very long wait" to engage in
"Italian family-style" "mass-gorging" and "feeding" fests;
despite "long lines" and a few complaints of "obnoxious
waiters", two new locations confirm the appeal of
"crowds", "noise" and "fun" at a moderate price.*

La Petite Maison Russe | 21 | 16 | 18 |$31 |
(Woodmere) **G2**
1066 Broadway (Franklin Pl.), 374-2591
*M – Some find this "small" and "very noisy" Five Towns
"French-Russian" "a welcome treat", with a "unique" menu
("delicious borscht and piroshki"); others call it "cramped",
"overpriced" and "deteriorating, like Mother Russia."*

La Piccolo Liguria | 22 | 16 | 21 |$36 |
(Port Washington) **E3**
47 Shore Rd. (Main St.), 767-6490
*M – This North Shore "neighborhood Italian" is labeled "a
real find" by some who say "the food is excellent", "the
decor is pretty" and "the staff bends over backward"; others
find its "high prices" more "memorable" than the food.*

La Primavera (East Hills) **E3** | 23 | 18 | 20 |$37 |
148 Glen Cove Rd. (north of L.I.E., exit 39N), 484-9453
*M – "On the North Shore's Restaurant Row", this
"crowded", "boisterous" "quality Northern Italian" attracts
regulars for its "excellent pastas" and "delicious chocolate
desserts"; however, highish prices and "tables that are too
close" keep others away.*

Lareira Restaurant*/S (Mineola) **F3** | 20 | 14 | 19 | $22 |
64-66 Jericho Tpke. (bet. Roslyn Rd. & Columbus Ave.),
248-2004
U – "Reminiscent of a great holiday in Portugal", this "casual" neighborhood spot offers lunch and dinner in either the conventional dining room or the lively bar; "grilled shrimp", "quail" and "paella" are "musts" at this "good", "inexpensive" ethnic.

La Sila (Inwood) **G3** | 22 | 19 | 21 | $35 |
233 Doughty Blvd. (Burnside Ave.), 239-2426
U – "The first time, you feel at home – the second time, you feel like family" at this "quaint", "romantic" South Shore French, offering "a nice quiet change from those noisy" places plus "very good", "imaginative" fare; a minority complain that "they charge extra for dressing their staff in tuxedos."

La Tavernetta/S (Woodmere) **G2** | 20 | 15 | 16 | $35 |
936 Broadway (bet. Lafayette Pl. & Neptune Ave.), 374-0993
M – At this pricey "Five-Towns 'in' place", the Italian fare is "consistently good" and "tastes homemade"; expect "cramped seating" and plenty of "noise"; a few complain of "quantity over quality" and warn "you must be a regular" to get good service.

Laundry Restaurant/LS | 20 | 19 | 18 | $37 |
(East Hampton) **C12**
31 Race Lane (Railroad Ave.), 324-3199
U – At the height of the season, it's "impossible to get a table" at this "trendy" Hamptons "meet-and-greet" "hangout" with "delicious" "innovative American cuisine"; some remain unimpressed by the "uppity-yuppity" scene that's "stuck on last year's spin cycle."

La Vigna/S (Greenvale) **E3** | 18 | 17 | 19 | $35 |
63 Glen Cove Rd. (north of Northern Blvd.), 621-8440
M – Recently reconcepted as a lower-priced "family-style" Italian (and with a new section for small, sensibly priced single-portion meals), this North Shore "favorite" wins raves for the pasta and veal, but some gripe about "rushed" service, "attitude" and quality that's heading "downward."

La Viola/S | 19 | 16 | 18 | $28 |
(Cedarhurst) **G3**, 499 Chestnut St. (north of LIRR station), 569-6020, 800-698-4652
(Syosset) **D4**, 41 Jackson Ave. (near LIRR station), 364-8383
U – This "Cedarhurst mainstay for good Italian food" has been "family-style" for over two years (for some this is "a step backwards", for others "great value"), offering "big portions" of garlic-intensive "homestyle" fare and "comfortable surroundings"; if you "stick with the specials and go with a large group", you should do fine.

L'ENDROIT (East Hills) **E3** | 24 | 24 | 22 |$43 |
290 Glen Cove Rd. (north of L.I.E., exit 39N), 621-6630
U – With its "excellent food" and "elegant decor", this is
"possibly the best on the North Shore's Restaurant
Row"; "lovely" surroundings, "consistently fine" "French
cuisine" and "first-class service" make this a top
performer in every category; the few complaints center
on "inflated prices" and a "stuffy" aura.

LE SOIR/S (Bayport) **F6** | 24 | 19 | 22 |$36 |
825 Montauk Hwy. (Bayport Ave.), 472-9090
U – "Très chic" and a "fine value" at the price, this
"unpretentious" "country" French on Suffolk's South
Shore is a "favorite of locals" and "a find" for
out-of-towners; its "excellent food" (including "devilish
desserts") is delightful, especially at "Sunday brunch"; a
dissenting few say it's "overrated" and "going downhill."

Little Rock Rodeo/S | 16 | 14 | 16 |$24 |
(East Hampton) **C12**
Montauk Hwy. (Cove Hollow Rd.), 324-7777
M – Surveyors split over this sprawling, "extremely
casual" "Tex-Mex for the Hamptons"; however, at press
time a sale was being negotiated that could turn this into
The East End Restaurant, dispensing American and
Northern Italiah dishes; check before you go.

Little Rock Yacht Club/S | 15 | 17 | 15 |$29 |
(East Hampton) **C12**
313 Three Mile Harbor Rd. (on the Harbor), 324-1111
M – The "view's" the thing at this "interesting"
indoor/outdoor eatery overlooking Three Mile Harbor;
friends cite the "thin pizzas (including "wonderful pizza
margherita"), "lovely setting" and "great fresh seafood",
but foes find it all "mediocre" except for the sunset.

Lobster Inn/S (Southampton) **D12** | 17 | 13 | 14 |$31 |
162 Inlet Rd. (end of Sunrise Hwy.), 283-1525
M – "Get a window seat and stick to lobster" at this
"touristy" barn that some call "a good fish restaurant"
but others say is "expensive" and "over the hill"; this is
the Hamptons, so expect "long waits" at peak season.

Lobster Roll/S (Amagansett) **C13** | 19 | 11 | 15 |$19 |
(aka Lunch)
Montauk Hwy. (look for flagpole), 267-3740
U – A summer-only "must-stop on the road to Montauk",
this "crowded", "no-atmosphere" "roadside" seafooder
serves "the definitive fresh lobster salad" sandwich as
well as "good" "no-frills seafood"; it's "not expensive",
and fans willingly "wait on line" – and even "claw their
way into the place."

Locust Valley Inn/S | 16 | 17 | 19 | $28 |
(Locust Valley) **D4**
225 Birch Hill Rd. (bet. Bella Vista St. & Alberta Pl.),
676-5427
*M – Locals say this "quaint" Gold Coast horse-country
Continental with its "nice fireplace in winter" is best for
hearty Italian fare, but others say the food's "nothing to
write home about" and hate the "loud bar trade."*

Lotus East/S (St. James) **D6** | 22 | 17 | 19 | $25 |
416 N. Country Rd. (Edgewood Ave.), 862-6030
Lotus II East/S (E. Setauket) **D6**
4020 Nesconset Hwy., 928-4343
*U – Suffolk residents find both addresses home to
"classy" (some say "superb") Chinese cuisine, with
"correct", if "cold" rolling-cart service; although the
consensus is "top-notch", with "above-average prices", a
few critics ask "what's so special?"*

Louie's Shore Restaurant/S | 13 | 13 | 14 | $29 |
(Port Washington) **E3**
395 Main St. (next to town dock), 883-4242
*U – "Location, location, location" ("it can be reached by
boat and the view is great") is the draw at this "folksy"
seafooder popular with "senior citizens"; most rate the
food somewhere between "fair" and "tired", and a few
report "canned-fruit-cocktail" sightings.*

Maidstone Arms/S | 22 | 23 | 21 | $43 |
(East Hampton) **C12**
Maidstone Arms, 207 Main St. (Village Green), 324-5006
*U – There's a "new look" (but still a "lovely old feeling")
to this "classy", "romantic", "very expensive" "East
Hampton mainstay", now under new ownership; raters
say it's "better than ever", praising the Contemporary
American cuisine, "great service" and "elegant" mien;
though a few call it "stuffy" for a beach town, most find
its appeal "timeless."*

Main Street Pasta/X (Smithtown) **D6** | 19 | 12 | 18 | $22 |
8 E. Main St. (next to Smithtown Movie Theater), 265-0540
*U – The line gets even longer after the early movie lets
out next door to this "small", "busy" "storefront"
specializing in "imaginative" "pastas that change with
the seasons"; despite "no atmosphere" and "very few
tables", the bargain prices, a "friendly chef" and "warm"
service make it worth the wait.*

Mama Lombardi's/S (Holbrook) **E6** | 22 | 16 | 19 | $26 |
400 Furrows Rd. (Main St.), 737-0774
*U – What began as a "pizza joint" evolved into a "family"
restaurant that's "very popular locally" as "an excellent
place to mangia" on "basic", "honest" "Sicilian" cuisine;
nobody seems to mind the "crowds", the din or the "long
wait" (no reservations) in light of "modest prices" and
"gargantuan portions."*

Mario/S (Hauppauge) **E6** | 22 | 17 | 21 | $34 |
644 Motor Pkwy. (Washington Ave.), 273-9407
*U – In the middle of a "busy" industrial park, this
"comfortable" "upscale" and "expensive" Northern Italian,
frequented by the business-lunch bunch, is praised for "very
good food", "comfortable" ambiance and "great service."*

McCluskey's Steakhouse/S | 17 | 11 | 15 | $28 |
(Bellmore) **F3**
157 W. Sunrise Hwy. (bet. Newbridge & Bellmore Aves.),
785-9711
*M – This "informal", "local cholesterol hangout" is known
for "moderate prices" and "good" – if "average" – steaks;
while critics say it's "greasy", "noisy" and "has had its day",
most agree it serves the "best bar burgers", "great" rings
and spuds, and "children are welcome."*

Mediterranean Snack Bar/SX | 20 | 8 | 17 | $17 |
(Huntington) **D5**
360 New York Ave. (Elm St. & Rte. 25A), 423-8982
*U – Ask people waiting in the "absurd lines outside" this
"no-atmosphere" Huntington magnet, and they'll call it a
"definitive Greek fast-food" joint, dishing out "cheap",
"huge portions" of superlative souvlaki, Greek salad,
shish kebab and gyro.*

Michael's - A Bistro/S | 21 | 19 | 20 | $35 |
(Roslyn Heights) **E3**
183 Roslyn Rd. (¼ mile north of L.I.E.), 484-4110
*U – Aficionados say dining at this "small, cozy" North
Shore "gem" ("good for a pre–LI Philharmonic dinner")
is "like eating in somebody's cushy living room"; they
cite the "innovative, appealing" Contemporary American
fare and "considerate" service; a minority find the staff
"cold" and "stilted", and the cooking "uneven."*

Milleridge Inn/S (Jericho) **D4** | 14 | 20 | 17 | $28 |
106-107 Hicksville Rd. (north of L.I.E., exit 41N), 931-2201
*M – A Colonial inn with eight dining rooms, "charming
gardens and grounds", a village of "shoppes" and the
staff dressed in "18th-century" costumes make this
Traditional American a mid-Nassau "landmark"; the
charmed say it's "great for the holidays", but others
prefer to pass on the "overpriced" "wedding-reception
food", "assembly-line service" and "forever" wait.*

Millie's Place/S | 20 | 21 | 18 | $31 |
(Great Neck) **E2**, 25 Middle Neck Rd. (bet. Grace Ave. &
Cutter Mill Rd.), 482-4223
(Manhasset) **E3**, 2014 Northern Blvd. (Searingtown Rd.),
365-4344
*M – These "chi chi" "nouvelle" American "bistros" are
"'in' spots" for the "jet-setters", "ladies who lunch" and
"so-called beautiful people" who "come to be seen" and
most definitely "heard"; despite complaints of
"overglitzed" LA-style ambiance, "snobby" attitude and
"overpriced food", most agree that Millie's "elevates
salad to an art form."*

MILL RIVER INN/S (Oyster Bay) **D4** | 27 | 22 | 24 | $45 |
160 Mill River Rd. (bet. Rte. 25A & Lexington Ave.),
922-7768
*U – Chef Michael Meehan is a "rising star" whose
"superb", "innovative" and "flawlessly presented"
Contemporary American fare has earned top marks for
this "snug", "classy" Gold Coast "romantic" spot; "superb
food", "great ambiance" and "fantastic" service "exemplify
the art" of "fine dining", despite a "high tariff."*

Mim's (Syosset) **D4** | 18 | 13 | 16 | $24 |
33 Berry Hill Rd. (Jackson Ave.), 364-2144
*U – The young-at-heart love this "crowded", "noisy"
place with "butcher-paper tablecloths", "crayons" on
every table and "huge portions" of "casual and creative"
"bar food" at moderate prices; while a few say it's just
an "overblown pub", most call it a "yuppie hangout" with
"family" appeal.*

Ming's HSF/S (Bridgehampton) **C12** | 18 | 16 | 16 | $29 |
Bridgehampton Shopping Ctr., Montauk Hwy., 537-0550
*M – A country cousin of the NYC HSFs, this "expensive"
and somewhat "cold" deco-style East Ender serves dim
sum and other Cantonese dishes; some say the food is
"great", others "not very good", but "if you need a
Chinese food fix in the Hamptons, it's the place."*

MIRABELLE/S (St. James) **D6** | 27 | 23 | 25 | $50 |
404 N. Country Rd. (north of Rte. 25), 584-5999
*U – Chef-owner Guy Reuge and his wife, Maria, have
created "the premiere Long Island French restaurant"
(No. 1 in overall ratings); "as close to France as you can
get in the suburbs", with "attentive" staff, "romantic"
"Country French decor" and food that surveyors call
"creative, artistic, delicious and expensive"; although a
small minority gripe about "chilly service" and "prices
that hurt", most consider it "simply phenomenal."*

Mirko's/S (Water Mill) **D12** | 23 | 19 | 22 | $38 |
Water Mill Sq. (Montauk Hwy.), 726-4444
U – "It's worth trying to find" this "overpriced" "hidden treasure" tucked behind a shopping plaza; "friendly owners" Mirko and Eileen Zagar and "great ethnic food" make for an entirely "delightful" experience.

Mother Kelly's/S (Cedarhurst) **G3** | 20 | 8 | 17 | $19 |
74 Columbia Ave. (Central Ave.), 295-5421
U – Crowded around tables that resemble a "dormitory" mess hall, serious eaters chow down on "gargantuan portions" of "great (and garlicky) homemade Italian dishes" – "wonderful pasta", "pizza to die for"; fastidious types may call it "just a sloppy neighborhood joint", but most enjoy the "down-home" spirit.

Nakisaki/S (Hempstead) **F3** | – | – | – | M |
276 Fulton Ave. (N. Franklin St. & Main St.), 292-9200
Worth seeking out, this sleek, stylish supper club serves unusual and distinctive Jamaican-Chinese fare to a smartly dressed crowd; later at night, there's live music (mainly reggae) and a disco; considering the prices, it's a reasonable night on the town.

NAVONA/S (Great Neck) **E2** | 25 | 18 | 20 | $39 |
218 Middle Neck Rd. (Hallanwood St.), 487-5603
M – For many surveyors, this North Shore favorite is "tops in Italian"; fans love the "excellent" food, including "incredible desserts made by the owners", and don't mind that it's "too crowded and noisy" on weekends; others feel alienated by the "Great Neck glitz" and warn "if you're not a regular, forget it."

Newport Grill/S (Garden City) **F3** | 19 | 18 | 18 | $27 |
176 Seventh St. (Franklin Ave.), 746-2592
U – On the site of the old Hunt Club, "friendly college kids" serve "surprisingly good", "innovative" and moderately priced American food in a "casual", "crowded" room; despite grumblings about "inconsistency", most report "everything tastes good."

NICK & TONI'S/S | 24 | 21 | 20 | $44 |
(East Hampton) **C12**
136 N. Main St. (Cedar St. & the Fork), 324-3550
U – "Wear your jeans, spurs and diamonds" to this "trendy", pricey, "see-and-be-seen" scene, where simple yet "fabulous" Tuscan cooking has helped create one of the Hamptons' hottest tickets; a few fault being "ignored if you're not a celebrity", but fans reply "sure, it's chic, but they pay attention to basics, like food and service."

Noodles/S (Port Jefferson) **C6** | – | – | – | M |

34 E. Broadway (across from ferry), 474-2233

This attractive newcomer boasts a modestly priced, varied Californian-style menu, plus a great harbor view from an outdoor deck; dancing, live entertainment and late weekend hours make for a lively scene.

North Street Grill/LS | 21 | 23 | 18 | $37 |

(Great Neck) **E2**

661 Northern Blvd. (Lakeville Rd. & Community Dr.), 466-0200

M – With Brendan Walsh as chef, this "hip" new, "expensive", "Frank Lloyd Wright–style" sibling of the Coyote Grill is mostly described as "fresh", "healthy", "interesting" "new-wave" Californian and as "exactly what suburban LI needs"; others call it a lot of "glitz" and "pretense."

Oakland's/S (Hampton Bays) **D10** | – | – | – | M |

Dune Rd. at Road H (end of Shinnecock Inlet), 728-6900

The beachy setting, water view and lively bar scene take center stage at this popular mid-priced East Ender, with simple seafood and pub-grub as a backdrop; there's a deck and marina, if you're looking to drop anchor.

Old Stove Pub/S (Sagaponack) **C12** | 18 | 10 | 14 | $38 |

3516 Montauk Hwy. (bet. Bridgehampton and East Hampton), 537-3300

U – "If you're a meat-eater, this is the place" for "charcoaled everything" – plus "good Greek food"; sure, it's "pricey" and some say the setting is "ugly", but for something thick, juicy and hot off the grill, it's hard to do better on the East End.

One Ocean Road | 18 | 17 | 15 | $38 |

(Bridgehampton) **C12**

One Ocean Rd. (Montauk Hwy. at monument), 537-1133

U – After "an uneven start", this "pretty, airy" Contemporary American "has settled into" the routine of "crowded Hamptons weekends", serving "fresh and imaginative" food in a "casual" atmosphere; prices are Hamptons-high, but we don't hear anyone complaining.

Orchid/S (Garden City) **F3** | 20 | 21 | 20 | $24 |

730 Franklin Ave. (bet. Stewart Ave. & 7th St.), 742-1116

U – "Polished" and "elegant", this "subterranean" Chinese "in the heart of Garden City" is a welcome oasis for shoppers; most find the "upscale" cuisine "beautifully prepared", a "notch above" the conventional neighborhood spot, but a small minority call the food "ordinary", the portions "small" and "overpriced."

Oriental Grill (Merrick) **G3** | 15 | 12 | 14 | $19 |
(fka L.I. Seafood Dumpling House)
Merrick Mall, 2126 Merrick Ave. (Smith Ave.), 868-8900
*M – A "vast" "barn" is the scene of an "all-you-can-eat"
"pig-out" in the "Mongolian BBQ mode" where you
select from a "smorgasbord" of raw ingredients, then
head for the stir-fry station; you'll find this either "a cute
idea" or "the kind of mass feeding the Army does better."*

Paddy McGee's/S (Island Park) **G3** | 16 | 17 | 15 | $27 |
6 Waterview Rd. (Waterfront Rd. & Pettit Pl.), 431-8700
*M – The "young" and "single" come to "frolic on the
deck" overlooking Reynolds Channel at this "lively,
congenial fish house" (sibling to Coyote Grill and North
Street Grill) where the "active bar scene" sizzles; if you
don't mind crowds and "waits", the affordable,
"interesting seafood" is reason enough to come.*

Palm Garden Restaurant/S | 19 | 23 | 19 | $39 |
(Roslyn) **E3**
Claremont Hotel, 1221 Old Northern Blvd. (1 block north
of Main St.), 625-2700
*M – Some find this "quiet", "elegant", "pretty little place"
in the new Roslyn Claremont Hotel "a miniaturized
Plaza Palm Court", hailing the Contemporary American
cuisine as "creative" and "lovely" – "one of the best-kept
secrets on LI"; others blast staff "attitude" and
"minuscule portions at astronomical prices."*

PALM RESTAURANT/S | 25 | 19 | 20 | $46 |
(East Hampton) **C12**
The Huntting Inn, 94 Main St. (Huntting Lane), 324-0410
*U – "Everything is à la carte" and "expensive" at this
"son of the NYC Palm", but that doesn't bother
insouciant Hampton carnivores who shrug off the
"zoolike atmosphere" and "snooty service" and gleefully
sink their teeth into "huge portions" of "superb-quality
man-food", which means "steaks to die for – and from."*

Panama Hattie's/S | – | – | – | M |
(Huntington Station) **D5**
872 E. Jericho Tpke. (2 miles east of Rte. 110), 351-1727
*Surveyors who patroned this spot in the past labeled it
"gimmicky" and "average", but recently the "inventive"
upscale New American cuisine at this "cozy"
brass-and-wood supper-club–style spot is winning
raves: "wonderful all around", "terrific", with friendly
service to boot.*

| F | D | S | C |

Pappagallo/S (Glen Head) **E3** | 21 | 21 | 21 | $37 |
716 Glen Cove Ave. (Chestnut Rd.), 676-3400
M – The grandaddy of Northern Italian cuisine on the
North Shore" has fans who love its "attentive service",
"beautiful skylit room" and "sumptuous" "classical" cooking;
a minority say "the place exists on its reputation alone."

Pasta-Eria/S (Hicksville) **E4** | 15 | 9 | 11 | $20 |
Woodbury Plaza, 440 S. Oyster Bay Rd. (Woodbury
Rd.), 938-1555
M – There's "good, cheap" pasta at this "new kid in
town" with a pizza counter up front and seating in back,
but critics say the scene is "too noisy" and food and
service are "uneven"; BYO.

Pasta Pasta/S (Port Jefferson) **C6** | – | – | – | M |
234 E. Main St. (opposite the post office), 331-5335
Candlelight, polished wood and attractive minimalist decor
are highlights of this North Shore oasis whose prosaic
name doesn't do justice to its mid-priced pastas and pizzas
that are more LA than Little Italy; wine and beer only.

Pasta's Cafe/S | 18 | 16 | 17 | $21 |
(Hicksville) **E4**, 96 N. Broadway (north of Old Country
Rd.), 937-0444
(Woodbury) **E4**, Woodbury Common, 8285 Jericho Tpke.
(Woodbury Rd.), 692-7000
(Manhasset) **E3**, A&S Center, 1106 Northern Blvd.
(Community Dr.), 365-5577
(Glen Cove) **D3**, 167 Glen St. (Town Path), 671-6500
U – All locations of this "trendy", "noisy" pastaria offer
"perfect al dente pasta" ("they actually cook it to order"),
with "a nice variety of sauces" plus "great salads" and
"yummy desserts", all at "good prices."

PETER LUGER STEAK | 26 | 17 | 20 | $43 |
HOUSE/SX (Great Neck) **E2**
255 Northern Blvd. (bet. Tain Dr. & Lakeville Rd.), 487-8800
U – Steak lovers maintain that "the best steaks in the
USA" are served in "he-man portions" at this "clubby"
"cholesterol castle" (the Great Neck cousin of the
Brooklyn original) where they also deliver "creamed
spinach", "tomatoes and onions", and "spicy" steak
sauce; though it's "high-priced" and service is "surly",
this remains LI's most popular restaurant.

Peter's Inn/S (East Northport) **D5** | 22 | 11 | 18 | $26 |
26 Laurel Rd. (Bellrose Ave. & 10th Ave.), 754-3516
U – "Serious food" seekers find this "plain-paneled"
"neighborhood bar" near the Northport LIRR station an
"unlikely setting" for "innovative" Contemporary
American "world-class dining"; curmudgeons claim it's
"expensive, considering the location", but prices are
"reasonable" on midweek "specials nights."

Petite Gourmet, The/S | 20 | 10 | 19 | $30 |
(Huntington) **D5**
328 Main St. (Green & Prospect Sts.), 271-3311
*M – Most like the "very good nouvelle Californian" food
and "unassuming" staff at this BYO "neighborhood
Mom's kitchen", and are unfazed by "minute tables" and
"no ambiance"; others call the experience "nothing to
write home about."*

P.G. Steakhouse/S (Huntington) **D5** | 23 | 14 | 20 | $40 |
1745 E. Jericho Tpke. (off E. Deer Park Rd.), 499-1005
*U – This "Peter Luger wannabe" serves "huge portions" of
"juicy steaks", "fantastic home fries" and "tasty salads" at
"hefty prices"; though a "close second to Luger", a "small
eating area" and "grouchy" service are drawbacks.*

Piccola Bussola/S (Westbury) **F3** | 21 | 14 | 18 | $28 |
649 Old Country Rd. (1 mile east of Fortunoff's), 333-1335
*U – Mid-Nassau Italian-food lovers flock to this "fun
family-style" eatery for "gargantuan portions" of
"down-home Italian" that's "heavy on the garlic" and
relatively light on the wallet; though "noisy" and
"crowded", most also find it "solid and reliable."*

PICCOLO/S (Huntington) **D5** | 24 | 16 | 22 | $32 |
Southdown Shopping Ctr., 215 Wall St. (bet. Southdown
Rd. & Prime St.), 424-5592
*U – Expect a "friendly, cheerful" greeting "when you walk
in" the door of this "small but enjoyable" strip-mall Northern
Italian; though you may "wait for a table", even with
reservations, you can expect "outstanding" – often "lavish"
– food along with a "high noise level" and crowding.*

Polo Grill/L (Garden City) **F3** | 22 | 23 | 22 | $40 |
Garden City Hotel, 45 Seventh St. (bet. Hilton & Cathedral
Aves.), 747-3000
*U – A popular site for "power lunch or a romantic
dinner", this "posh" Regional American has a new chef
in Richard Allen (ex Citrus and Checkers in LA), and
early signs are that his stylish hotel lobby dining room is
taking off; the "classy" "men's-club" ambiance and
"attentive service" help justify "high prices."*

Pomodoro | 20 | 15 | 17 | $30 |
(Huntington) **D5**, 62 Stewart Ave. (north of Rte. 25A),
549-7074
(Port Washington) **E3**, 294 Main St. (Shore Rd.), 767-7164
(Great Neck) **E2**, 132 Middle Neck Rd. (1 block north of
movie theater), 466-1159
*U – At all three locations, "deep dishes" of "robust" pasta
at "reasonable prices" are the rule – some "innovative", all
made with "fresh ingredients"; the "bright", "crowded"
setting has a "decibel level off the scale", so "bring your
earplugs, along with your appetite."*

Post House, The/S · | 19 | 19 | 19 | $35 |
(Southampton) **D12**
136 Main St. (Post Crossing), 283-9696
U – The "old Hamptons" live at this charmingly "warm and woodsily atmospheric" circa-1684 "country inn", where "good, basic" American cooking and "down-home friendly service" have withstood the winds of change; a few critics say it's "stuffy" and the food's "so-so."

Pumpernickel's/S (Northport) **D5** · | 17 | 14 | 17 | $27 |
640 Main St. (Rte. 25A & Waterside Ave.), 757-7959
M – North Suffolk habitués who come for the "hearty", "wholesome" German food praise the "good sausage and real mashed potatoes", "A-ok Wiener schnitzel" and tasty "rouladen" at this 20-year-old neighborhood standby; trendier folks find the "heavy" food "blah" and "dated", and call the "fake beer-hall" setting "too dark."

Raay-Nor's Cabin/SX (Baldwin) **G3** · | 18 | 11 | 16 | $20 |
550 Sunrise Hwy. (Rockwood Ave.), 223-4886
M – For "wonderful", "crispy" fried chicken, plus "great biscuits" and "the best pot pie", just "wait on line" at this '30s-era "log-cabin" institution serving "down-home" cookin' at "nostalgia" prices; to some, it's a "greasy spoon" well "past its prime", but most think it's "worth the cholesterol" for food "like Mom's."

Rachel's/S (Syosset) **D4** · | – | – | – | M |
Plaza 55, 57 Berry Hill Rd. (Muttontown Rd.), 921-0303
Seek out this out-of-the-way Northeast Nassau Italian for its great pizza, zesty pastas and pleasingly simple Californian-style grill fare; prices are reasonable and service is friendly, if not completely attentive; BYO.

RAM'S HEAD INN/S · | 22 | 24 | 21 | $41 |
(Shelter Island) **B11**
Ram's Head Inn, 108 Ram Island Dr., 749-0811
U – "Quiet and secluded", this "charming" inn is "worth the trip to Shelter Island" for "tasty" Contemporary American cooking and a "beautiful view of the water", "especially at sundown"; though pricey, it equals the best of "summer resort dining" – "reservations a must."

Rhumb Line/S (Greenport) **B11** · | 15 | 13 | 15 | $21 |
36 Front St. (bet. 2nd & Main Sts.), 477-8697
U – "Good basics" (chowder, burgers, "fresh" seafood) are the mainstays of this "dark", "warm" and "cozy" "nautical bar"; while nobody claims the food is memorable, this is a decent place "to stop after a ferry trip."

Rigatoni/S (Rockville Centre) **F3** | 20 | 13 | 17 | $21 |
27 N. Park Ave. (Sunrise St.), 678-2595
M – It's a tight squeeze on weekends, when the South Shore casual-dining crowd turns out for "great" pasta dishes and desserts in this "small, crowded" high-tech gourmet-grocery, but fans say "the talent in the kitchen" is up to the challenge; foes say the food "looks much better than it tastes."

Ristorante Orlando (Huntington) **D5** | 21 | 20 | 21 | $37 |
15 New St. (1 block south of Main St.), 421-0606
U – This landmark Gold Coast Italian wins praise for "attentive hosts", "courtly service" and "old-world charm"; while its modern decor may be passé, the "wonderful" "classic" food still satisfies; only a few diners call this place "another overrated, dated" Italian.

Riverbay/S (Williston Park) **E3** | 23 | 19 | 20 | $34 |
700 Willis Ave. (bet. Hillside Ave. & L.I.E.), 742-9191
M – Some seafood lovers maintain that this "trendy" and "attractive" fish house (a sibling of Bryant & Cooper) offers "the best seafood on LI" – "20 kinds of oysters", "great stone crabs" and "outstanding fresh fish"; others say "the waiters are fresh, too", and mind the high prices and the "noisy, pushy crowd" on weekends.

Riverview/S (Oakdale) **F6** | 18 | 24 | 18 | $34 |
3 Consuelo Pl. (Vanderbilt Blvd.), 589-2694
M – An incredible "view of the Great South Bay" is the setting for "good" seafood from "an always-changing menu" plus "exceptional service"; critics call the experience "average middle-American" and, despite the "pretty" surroundings, say it's "nothing special."

Robke's Country Inn/S | 19 | 9 | 16 | $24 |
(Northport) **D5**
427 Rte. 25A (Church St.), 754-9663
U – Despite reports that "it's just a bar and a poor one" at that, this "casual Northport institution" serves "humongous portions" of "homey", "reasonably priced" Italian-American food; though it's "not an inn and not really in the country", this "nothing-fancy" "roadhouse" stops traffic with the smell of its great charcoal pit.

Romantico/S (Glen Cove) **D3** | 20 | 18 | 18 | $36 |
50 Forest Ave. (Glen Cove Rd.), 759-0900
M – Some surveyors hail the "unique, authentic" food and "good service" of this Gold Coast Northern Italian newcomer, adding that the prix fixe dinner on weekdays "makes it a good value"; others, however, call it just "another Italian restaurant" – "good but not distinctive."

Long Island

	F	D	S	C

Rose Cottage/S (Amityville) **G4** — 20 | 16 | 19 | $31
(fka La Mansarde)
348 Merrick Rd. (Bryant Ave.), 691-6881
*M – Our surveyors are divided about this South Suffolk
Continental that recently changed hands; some say it's
"as good as ever" and "can't get enough of" the "quality
food at bargain prices" served by "extra-friendly"
waiters; others cite "unpredictable food" and a "staff
that's friendly only to those they know."*

Ross' North Fork Restaurant/S — 23 | 19 | 22 | $35
(Southold) **B11**
44780 North Rd., Rte. 48 (bet. Horton's Lane & Youngs
Ave.), 765-2111
*U – At this "classy" North Fork Contemporary American,
chef John Ross makes "good use of local products" in
an "ever-changing", "always wonderful" menu; the high
prices are matched by "attentive service" and an
atmosphere that's "clean, crisp" and "comfortable."*

Saffron/S (Westhampton Beach) **E10** — 21 | 17 | 17 | $44
23 Sunset Ave. (Main St.), 288-4610
*M – Chef Ali Fathalla brings a Mediterranean slant to his
new kitchen at Starr Boggs's former address; some
Hamptonites call it "a delightful newcomer" and "another
Starr in Westhampton"; critics say it's "too expensive"
and "no replacement for Boggs"; time will tell.*

Santosha/SX (Amityville) **G4** — – | – | – | M
40 Merrick Rd. (east of County Line Rd.), 598-1787
*The International fare at this offbeat Vegetarian, run by
a yoga-education group, is fresh and interesting; what
decor there is, comes straight out of the '60s.*

Sapore di Mare/S (Wainscott) **C12** — 23 | 23 | 18 | $48
Montauk Hwy. (Wainscott Stone Rd.), 537-2764
*M – "Superb" "Tuscan food" served in an "attractive setting"
delights the many East Enders who adore this "chic",
"upbeat", "'in' place" (the Wainscott offshoot of NYC's Coco
Pazzo); friends say "even without the starry clientele, it can
be heaven", while foes fault the "Gucci atmosphere", "snotty
attitude" and "Spago seating philosophy."*

Sapporo/S — 21 | 16 | 18 | $27
(New Hyde Park) **F2**, 2207 Hillside Ave. (east of Wantagh
Pkwy.), 746-4898
(Wantagh) **F4**, 3266 Merrick Rd. (east of Wantagh Pkwy.),
785-3853
*U – Both the original New Hyde Park restaurant and the
new Wantagh sibling serve "very fine" "traditional" Japanese
specialties, including "great" "fresh" sushi; it's nothing
fancy, always "pleasant", "squeaky-clean" and "reliable."*

Sasaki*/S (Carle Place) **F3** | 22 | 15 | 21 | $23 |
540 Westbury Ave. (1 block east of Cherry Lane), 333-3434
U – This "quiet" neighborhood favorite "off the main drag" offers "traditional seating on the floor" and all-around "excellent" Japanese food; dining here may not be innovative, but it's always "very satisfying."

Sea Shanty/S (Northport) **D5** | 18 | 11 | 16 | $22 |
1416 Woodbine Ave. (bet. Scudder Ave. & Main St.), 261-8538
U – On weekends, Northport regulars line up at this "no-ambiance" shanty for "very fresh", "inexpensive seafood"; this "real neighborhood spot is small" but "convenient."

Seeda Thai/S (Valley Stream) **G3** | 18 | 13 | 18 | $22 |
28 N. Central Ave. (Merrick Rd.), 561-2626
U – A "decorless storefront" is the South Nassau setting for "spicy and delicious" bargain-priced Thai food served by a "helpful" staff; despite caveats that "it's good but should be better", most call this "Thai heaven."

SEMPRE VIVOLO (Hauppauge) **E6** | 24 | 22 | 22 | $39 |
696 Motor Pkwy. (Old Willets Path), 435-1737
U – The "suburban relation" of NYC's Vivolo and Anche Vivolo, this "refined", "jackets required" Northern Italian is a "really high-power business-lunch" destination by day and a coolly "romantic" trysting place at night; add "knowledgeable and unobtrusive service" and "consistently" "high-quality" food for a perfect "special-occasion" place.

Sergio's/S (Massapequa) **F4** | 16 | 8 | 18 | $27 |
5422 Merrick Rd. (bet. E. & W. Shore Drs.), 541-6554
M – "Good Italian food" and "white-glove service" are what this small storefront with zero decor delivers, but that's enough to bring in crowds; still, the appeal is lost on critics who say it's "much ado about nothing."

1770 HOUSE/S (East Hampton) **C12** | 22 | 24 | 21 | $43 |
143 Main St. (Dayton Lane), 324-1770
M – It seems more like Vermont than East Hampton at this Continental-Italian filled with "antiques" and "fine old-world charm"; the "quiet", smoke-free dining room is the setting for cuisine that most call "fresh" and "delicious", but others shrug off as "boring" and merely "ordinary."

75 Main/S (Southampton) **D12** | 17 | 16 | 14 | $37 |
75 Main St. (bet. Hampton Rd. & Job's Lane), 283-7575
M – So very "trendy", so very Southampton, this "creative" Eclectic bistro in the heart of the village does wonderful things with breakfast ("cappuccino and Le NY Times*") and also serves up "good pastas, pizzas" and "delicious grilled fish"; detractors say it's "seriously overpriced" and "the best service goes to regulars."*

Sfuzzi Southampton at Bowden | 18 | 19 | 18 | $38 |
Square/S (Southampton) **D12**
52 N. Sea Rd., 283-2800
M – Converts who can pronounce it think this "trendy"
Italian newcomer on the site of Herb McCarthy's
"doesn't feel like a chain"; they praise the "beautiful
Bellinis", "excellent pasta" and "good pizza"; the
unconvinced say they "expected more" than this
"overpriced, pretentious" mega-scene.

Siam Lotus/S (Bay Shore) **F6** | – | – | – | M |
1664 Union Blvd. (bet. Park & 4th Aves.), 968-8196
Near the Bay Shore LIRR station and off the beaten
track, this small, sparkling-new storefront Thai is the
best ethnic to hit South Suffolk in a long time; flavors
are intense, ingredients fresh, and prices make sense.

Siam Palace/S (Port Washington) **E3** | 17 | 11 | 15 | $25 |
24B Main St. (Maryland Ave.), 883-1082
U – One of the first LI Thais, this Intown spot is still
"dependable"; though a few say it's "lost some sparkle
over the years", most agree that "nice service" and
"spicy" food at "reasonable prices" offset "no decor."

Silver's/S (Southampton) **D12** | 20 | 13 | 15 | $26 |
15 Main St. (Job's Lane & Nugent St.), 283-6443
U – When an "old-time" "drugstore soda fountain"
serves eclectic Italianate cuisine of "unexpected
quality", the result comes off as "eccentric" and "fun";
though a few complain that it's "overpriced for a
luncheonette", this, after all, is the Hamptons.

Soho/S (Long Beach) **(CLOSED)** | 20 | 15 | 19 | $23 |
1034 West Beech St. (Georgia & Kentucky Sts.), 889-5992
U – A block from the beach, this "casual" South Shore
newcomer serves an "unusual" menu of Thai, Italian,
West Indian and Cajun delights; though a few feel the
kitchen's "trying to reach for the trend but not quite
making it", most like the "creative specials" and "reggae
music" as a welcome change of pace.

Sotto Luna/S (Roslyn Heights) **E3** | 17 | 13 | 16 | $26 |
367 Willis Ave. (Strathmore N. & S.), 621-2112
U – Respondents applaud this "rising star" on the North
Shore "pasta-pizza scene" and its cutting-edge Italian
menu pizza from the wood-burning oven", "super pastas"
and "well-prepared seafood"; the "small storefront" is
no great shakes, but a "convenient location" and
"reasonable prices" are.

Long Island

Southside Fish & Clam/SX | 16 | 6 | 10 | $18 |
(Lindenhurst) **F5**
395 W. Montauk Hwy. (bet. 4th & 5th Sts.), 226-3322
*U – For "cheap", "fast", "reliably fresh" seafood eaten off
"paper plates" with "plastic cutlery", this fish store with a
restaurant on the side can't be beat; South Shore stoics
wait in "long lines" for "cafeteria-style" "self-service";
"wear old clothes", "roll up sleeves" and just "enjoy."*

Spare Rib/S (Commack) **D5** | 19 | 11 | 15 | $21 |
2098 Jericho Tpke. (Indian Head Rd.), 543-5050
*U – "If you have the time to wait", this "no-pretense",
"great-value" "family restaurant" offers a "basic menu" of
"consistently good" "down-home" cooking"; it's no palace
and choruses of "'Happy Birthday' are drowned out by
screaming kids", but "it does what it's supposed to."*

Sri Lanka Gourmet/S | 16 | 12 | 17 | $22 |
(Oceanside) **G3**
Lincoln Plaza, 2901 Lincoln Ave. (Atlantic & Davison
Aves.), 764-4692
*M – Located in an "obscure shopping center", this
"small", "no-atmosphere" Sri Lankan (similar to Indian
but lighter) is called "very good" by some, "just ok" by
others; the owner and staff are gracious, and the price
is right; wine and beer only.*

Stango's/SX (Glen Cove) **D3** | 15 | 9 | 17 | $20 |
19 Grove St. (Cedar Swamp Rd.), 671-2389
*U – "Families have fun" at this bit of "Little Italy in Glen
Cove", where prices are low and the "food and decor"
are like "Mama's kitchen" "back in the '50s – we never
said "Mama" was a decorator, just a "good" cook.*

STARR BOGGS/S | 27 | 23 | 21 | $47 |
(Westhampton Beach) **E10**
Dune Deck Hotel, 379 Dune Rd., 288-5250
*U – A "beautiful" beachfront setting ("like being in the
Caribbean") does justice to the "excellent"
Contemporary American food at this new location of star
chef Starr Boggs's eponymous restaurant which many
call "the Hamptons' best"; the total package –
"delightful" food, "elite wine list", "great views", "friendly
service" – "rivals NYC's best", so book well in advance.*

Stresa (Manhasset) **E3** | – | – | – | E |
1524 Northern Blvd. (Shelter Rock Rd.), 365-6956
*It looks like another hit for the owners of Navona and Il
Tulipano, whose most recent venture on the North
Shore Northern Italian scene is already garnering praise
for well-prepared Tuscan specialties served in gracious
surroundings; check out the homemade desserts.*

Thai House (Huntington) **D5** | 19 | 17 | 18 | $23 |
273 New York Ave. (north of Main St.), 351-8424
*M – "For very spicy and flavorful Thai cuisine", Suffolk
County ethnic-food fanciers seek out this "lovely" little
eatery with its "good, fresh food" and "efficient service";
some say the kitchen is "inconsistent", but all agree
"don't exceed two peppers" without glottis insurance.*

THREE VILLAGE INN/S | 20 | 24 | 21 | $33 |
(Stony Brook) **D6**
150 Main St. (bet. Rte. 25A & Christian Ave.), 751-0555
*M – "Serving good old-fashioned American dishes" in a
"quaint", "Colonial" ambiance, this "Stony Brook
landmark" is an "American classic – updated and
dandy"; it may be "too Laura Ashley", but "if you must
eat at a tourist factory, this is as good as any" and ideal
for Mother's Day.*

To Fu/S | 19 | 14 | 17 | $20 |
(Farmingville) **E6**, 1260 Waverly Ave. (Portion Rd.),
698-6550
(Woodbury) **E4**, Jericho Plaza, 8025 Jericho Tpke. (west
of Woodbury Rd.), 921-7981
(Commack) **D5**, 2158 Jericho Tpke. (Sunken Meadow
Pkwy.), 499-2792
(Smithtown) **D6**, Smithaven Mall (Jericho Tpke. & Rte.
347), 360-2676
(Roslyn Heights) **E3**, 255 Willis Ave. (south of L.I.E.),
484-7456
*M – Reports are mixed on this new Chinese-Japanese
chainlet; some praise the "large portions" of "wonderful"
food "cooked with a light hand", citing "good, cheap,
reliable sushi" and "well-prepared vegetarian dishes";
others say that "neither" cuisine comes off well; each
location is a bit different, but all are "crowded."*

Tortilla Grill/SX (Huntington) **D5** | – | – | – | I |
335 New York Ave. (Rte. 25A), 423-4141
*With only six tables, this adorable new Huntington
Tex-Mex hot spot has its hands full keeping up with the
demand for ridiculously inexpensive, freshly grilled fare
wrapped in homemade tortillas; N.B. the 3 AM closing
time on weekends keeps it hopping.*

Trattoria di Meo/S (Roslyn) **E3** | 19 | 10 | 17 | $33 |
105 Northern Blvd. (bet. Port Washington Blvd. & Middle
Neck Rd.), 627-5515
*U – For "neighborhood eating", this "unpretentious" little
"old-fashioned" "Southern Italian" offers "very good food"
that "needs a better facility" and is "pricey for a local joint."*

Trattoria Tulipano/S (Huntington) **D5** | 22 | 19 | 19 | $36 |
(fka Il Tulipano)
92 E. Main St. (Ward Hill Rd.), 351-3663
*U – On a Saturday night, all of Huntington seems to be
dining at this "wonderful sister restaurant of Navona";
they come for "classy", "well-presented" Northern Italian
dishes in contemporary (some say "cold") dining rooms;
a few say this "current 'in' place" is "a little too full of
itself"; new lower prices and a family-style menu are
keeping with the times.*

Tung Ting/S (Centerport) **D5** | 19 | 18 | 18 | $25 |
23A Centershore Rd. (Rte. 25A), 261-7770
*M – Our surveyors say the "lovely" ambiance at this
"huge" Chinese overlooking Mill Pond places it "a cut
above" the usual Oriental; the food (including sushi) is
described as "excellent" and "gourmet" by some, merely
"so-so" by others.*

UB Loves Cafe & Grill/S | 16 | 16 | 16 | $20 |
(Hicksville) **E4**
Delco Plaza Shopping Ctr., 53 E. Old Country Rd.
(1 block east of Rte. 107), 938-5686
*M – The "fun menu" of this "casual" and "glitzy" new
mid-Nassau "entry in the pizza and pasta" sweepstakes
makes it a "good place to go with the kids", and good
"for a quick light meal"; still, to some surveyors it's "not
too special", BYO.*

Umberto's Pizza/S | 21 | 10 | 16 | $20 |
(New Hyde Park) **F2**
633 Jericho Tpke. (Lakeville Rd.), 437-7698
*U – Superlatives are the rule ("the best slice on LI!", "the
best Sicilian in the Tri-State area") at this "local" West
Nassau pizzeria; go for "large portions", "reasonable
prices" and "decor so bad it's good."*

Uncle Dai/S | 19 | 13 | 18 | $20 |
(Woodbury) **E4**, 7940 Jericho Tpke. (Peck's Lane), 364-8008
(Glen Cove) **D3**, 26 School St. (Glen St.), 671-1144
(Great Neck) **E2**, 148 Middle Neck Rd. (Kensington
Gate), 487-8460
*M – "Free wine" and "consistently good" "inexpensive"
Chinese fare explain the popularity of this expanding North
Nassau minichain (the Woodbury spot also does a buffet);
critics call them "Chinese greasy spoons", but "great value"
and "friendly service" keep all three "always busy."*

Veranda/S (Glen Cove) **D3** | 23 | 22 | 21 | $38 |
75 Cedar Swamp Rd. (north of Glen Cove Rd.), 759-0394
U – An entrenched North Shore crowd adores this
"well-appointed" Northern Italian that might not be on
the cutting edge but "consistently" delivers "excellent"
food and "quality service"; despite generally highish
prices, the $20 midweek dinner "is the best buy around."

Vespa/S (Great Neck) **D3** | – | – | – | E |
96 Northern Blvd. (Great Neck Rd.), 829-0005
This branch of a NYC Northern Italian looks like a
winner, offering unusual high-ticket homemade pastas
as well as fish, vegetarian, veal and chicken entrees;
antiques and memorabilia complete the setting.

Villa d'Este/S (Floral Park) **F2** | 22 | 18 | 19 | $36 |
146 Tulip Ave. (near Little Neck Pkwy.), 354-1355
M – With new owners, this "old-fashioned" Italian is
"really coming up again", thanks to "wholesome good
food" and "friendly" service; the less satisfied say it's
"pricey" and "both the menu and decor need updating."

Villa Doria/S (Bellmore) **F3** | 22 | 19 | 21 | $32 |
2565 Bellmore Ave. (2 blocks south of Merrick Rd.), 785-5353
U – The "balsamic vinegar on the table" is the first clue
that this South Nassau "find" is not your typical Italian –
that and its "inventive" Nuova Cucina cuisine; most call
the menu "super" and the garden ambiance "relaxed",
but a few question the food when the owner is
"vacationing in St. Bart's."

Villa Gattopardo (Roslyn) **E3** | 20 | 20 | 20 | $37 |
1441 Old Northern Blvd. (Skillman Rd.), 484-6730
M – Loyalists think this North Shore offspring of NYC's Il
Gattopardo "deserves more business than it gets", citing
"great veal chops and pasta dishes" served in a
"soothing atmosphere"; though critics say the place is
"not inspired", all agree that the midweek "pasta menu
is a great bargain."

Villa Testarossa*/S (Montauk) **B14** | 16 | 14 | 15 | $31 |
Main St. (center of town), 668-4505
M – This Montauk newcomer has attracted a following
with its "consistent" "light Northern Italian" fare, though
some say "there are better pasta places around"; patio
dining and a wine-and-cheese hour are pluses.

Violet's/S (East Hampton) **C12** | 13 | 19 | 14 | $35 |
341 Pantigo Rd., Rte. 27 (Spring Close Hwy.), 329-0600
M – Neither the "beautiful outdoor garden" nor the "pretty"
"country" decor compensates for the "expensive",
"uneven" Continental cuisine or "service slower than
USAir" at this East End yearling.

Von Leesen's*/X (Farmingdale) **F3** | 18 | 10 | 17 | $13 |
282 Main St. (Conklin St.), 531-9898
U – Run by Kord and Hannie Fick, this "comfy, folksy, friendly" 1950's-style ice cream parlor–luncheonette serves "the real thing" at low, low prices – "tuna on Wonder bread", homey German dishes and ice cream.

Wall's Wharf/S (Bayville) **D4** | 15 | 15 | 15 | $28 |
18 Greenwich Ave. (Bayview Ave.), 628-2291
U – "Go for the view" of LI Sound at this "no-fuss" seafooder with its "fresh", but only "average", fare; "huge" portions justify the prices, but "service is slow."

Watercolors Cafe/LS (Melville) **E4** | 16 | 20 | 15 | $27 |
Huntington Hilton Hotel, 598 Broad Hollow Rd. (Spagnoli Rd.), 845-1000
M – Folks are "pleasantly surprised" by the fairly priced Contemporary American food that's "not bad for a hotel" and "nicely served" in a very "pretty", "open lobby"; the "terrific brunch" is popular on Sundays.

Waterfront, The/S (Montauk) **B14** | 18 | 20 | 16 | $33 |
West Lake Dr. (Rte. 27), 668-1300
M – With "gorgeous views" of West Lake, this "beautifully redone" Continental's food can be "good" but may leave "something to be desired"; deck dining plus live entertainment and dancing on weekends keep it hopping, no reserving often means a wait.

West End Cafe/S (Carle Place) **F3** | 16 | 17 | 17 | $24 |
Clock Tower Shopping Center, 187 Glen Cove Rd. (½ mile north of Old Country Rd.), 294-5608
M – Newly redecorated and redefined, this "upscale" Contemporary International, "hidden in the back of a shopping mall", is considered "a gem" by devotees; more demanding diners find the fare "unremarkable", the service "shuffling" and the scene "too crowded" and "noisy."

White Sands/S (Plainview) **E4** | 18 | 14 | 17 | $29 |
Morton Village, 1040 Old Country Rd. (Rex St.), 931-6296
M – There's a "large selection" of "very fresh fish, properly prepared", at this "nouvelle" seafooder whose fare runs the gamut from Thai to Mexican; some call the shopping-center setting "stark", but most defend the place as a "reliable" "good value."

Wylie's Ribs/S (Amagansett) **C13** | 14 | 11 | 14 | $23 |
Montauk Hwy. (next to post office), 267-3388
M – This "NYC export" is very "un-Hampton", with ribs and chicken that most call "run-of-the-mill" and "a real disappointment"; "moderate prices" and a "kids-are-welcome" attitude may explain its popularity.

Yamaguchi/S (Port Washington) **E3** | 21 | 13 | 17 | $29 |

63 Main St. (next to LIRR station), 883-3500
*U – "Real sushi fans" like this "small neighborhood"
storefront and tout it a "first-class" place "where the
North Shore's Japanese executives dine"; however,
service and decor are "lacking."*

Yamato/S (Plainview) **E4** | 17 | 14 | 17 | $26 |

Citibank Ctr., 1115 Old Country Rd. (Plainview Rd.),
433-3277
*M – "Pleasant service" and "reasonable prices" in
"plain", "shopping-center" surroundings are what you'll
find at this "neighborhood Japanese" plus sushi and
other "good", if not extraordinary, dishes.*

Y.E. Coyote/S (Hicksville) **E4** | 17 | 14 | 17 | $27 |

355 S. Broadway (Old Country Rd.), 932-4310
*M – This "small", "cute" but "uncomfortable storefront"
serves "fresh SW" and "Tex-Mex" cuisine that's "rich
with flavor and color"; though a few say it's overrated,
chili-heads call it "spicy", "inexpensive" "fun."*

LONG ISLAND INDEXES

TYPES OF CUISINE

Long Island

Noodles
North Street Grill
Pasta Pasta
Petite Gourmet

Caribbean
Calabash
Chez Antoine
Nakisaki

Chinese
Calabash
Eye of the Tiger
Fu Ho
Hong Kong Seafood
Hunam
Hunan Gourmet East
Hunan Taste
Jade Garden
Jani
J.J. Hwang
Lotus East
Ming's HSF
Nakisaki
Oriental Grill
Tung Ting
Uncle Dai

Coffee Shops/Diners
Estia/Amagansett
Hildebrandt's
Honest Diner
Von Leesen's

Continental
Aegean East
B.K. Sweeney's
Boardwalk
Buckram Stables
56th Fighter Group
Fountaine's Beacon
Frederick's
George Washington
Gordon's
Gurney's Inn
Koenig's
La Grange Inn
La Pace
La Primavera
Lareira
La Tavernetta
L'Endroit
Locust Valley Inn
Mirko's
Panama Hattie's
Riverview
Rose Cottage
Sergio's
1770 House
Violet's

Waterfront
White Sands

Dim Sum
Fu Ho
Hong Kong Seafood
Lotus East
Ming's HSF
Oriental Grill

Eclectic
American Bistro
Barney's
Best of Both Worlds
Blue Parrot Cafe
Bruzell's
Courtyard Cafe
Franzi & Nell's
Harlequin Cafe
Millie's Place
Mim's
Palm Garden
Panama Hattie's
Pasta Pasta
Pasta's Cafe
Petite Gourmet
Rigatoni
Ross' North Fork
75 Main
Soho
Wall's Wharf
Watercolors Cafe

French Bistro
Alouette
Jonathan's
Rose Cottage

French Classic
Alouette
Capriccio
Chez Noelle
Fyodoroff
Giulia
La Coquille
La Mascotte
La Petite Msn. Russe
L'Endroit
Le Soir
Rose Cottage
Veranda

French Contemporary
Alouette
American Hotel
Chez Antoine
Chez Noelle
La Coquille
La Marmite

Long Island

La Mascotte
Mirabelle
Palm Garden

German
Koenig's
La Grange Inn
Pumpernickel's

Greek
Aegean East
Medit. Snack Bar
Old Stove Pub

Hamburgers
Rhumb Line
Robke's
Von Leesen's

Ice Cream Shops
Hildebrandt's
Von Leesen's

Indian
Akbar
Diwan

International
Garden City Grande
Hildebrandt's
Millie's Place
Peter's Inn
Petite Gourmet
Santosha
1770 House
Soho
Watercolors Cafe
West End Cafe

Irish/British
Dublin Delights
John Peel Room

Italian (Northern)
Aragosta–Blue Lobster
Bayport House
Benny's
Capriccio
Cirella's
Due Torri
Emilia
Franina's
Gaetano's
Giulia
Harlequin Cafe
Il Cappuccino
Il Garofano
I Santi
La Caravella
La Marmite
La Pace

La Piccolo Liguria
La Primavera
La Sila
La Tavernetta
Mario
Mirko's
Navona
Nick & Toni's
Palm Restaurant
Pappagallo
Piccolo
Ristorante Orlando
Sapore di Mare
Sfuzzi
Stresa
Trattoria Tulipano
Veranda
Vespa
Villa Gattopardo

Italian (Southern)
Calamari Kitchen
Chefs of New York
Eddie's Pizza
La Bussola
La Parma
Mama Lombardi's
Mother Kelly's
Piccola Bussola
Robke's
Stango's
Trattoria di Meo
Umberto's

Italian (North & South)
Alfredo's Pizza
Basilico
Cafe Girasole
Cafe Stefano
Cafe Testarossa
Caffe Baci
Caffe Spasso
Caffe Spuntino
Caracalla
Casa Rustica
Cirella's
Classico
Della Femina
Di Benardo's Bistro
DiMaggio's
Emilio's
Franina's
Il Pozzo
Il Sapore
James Lane Cafe
Jonathan's
La Dolce Sera
La Famiglia
La Ginestra

68

Long Island

La Vigna
La Viola
Main Street Pasta
Michael's – A Bistro
Navona
Pappagallo
Pasta-Eria
Pasta's Cafe
Pomodoro
Rachel's
Rigatoni
Romantico
Sempre Vivolo
Sergio's
Silver's
Sotto Luna
Stango's
Trattoria di Meo
Trattoria Tulipano
UB Loves Cafe
Villa d'Este
Villa Doria
Villa Testarossa

Japanese
Ashai Tokyo
Bonbori
Gasho of Japan
Hana
Kokura II
Kura Barn
Kurofune
Sapporo
Sasaki
To Fu
Yamaguchi
Yamato

Jewish
Colbeh*
(*Kosher)

Mediterranean
Ahrash Cafe
Nick & Toni's
Saffron
Sapore di Mare

Mexican/Tex-Mex
Baja
Casa Luis
Casa Margarita
El Tapatio
Little Rock Rodeo
Tortilla Grill

Middle Eastern
Ahrash Cafe
Colbeh
Kabul

Pizza
Alfredo's Pizza
Chefs of New York
DiMaggio's
Eddie's Pizza
Umberto's

Portuguese
Estoril Granada
Lareira

Russian
Fyodoroff
La Petite Msn. Russe

Seafood
Amagansett Fish
Aragosta–Blue Lobster
Armando's
Boardwalk
Calamari Kitchen
Canterbury Ales
Claudio's
Coast Grill
Crescent
Dar Tiffany
Dave's Downtown
Dave's Grill
Fish Net
Gordon's
Gosman's Dock
James Lane Cafe
Jolly Fisherman
Karen Lee's
Little Rock Yacht
Lobster Inn
Lobster Roll
Louie's Shore
Medit. Snack Bar
Mirko's
Oakland's
Paddy McGee's
Peter Luger
Pumpernickel's
Rhumb Line
Riverbay
Riverview
Robke's
Ross' North Fork
Sea Shanty
Silver's
Southside Fish/Clam
Violet's
Wall's Wharf
Waterfront
White Sands

Southern
Raay-Nor's Cabin

Long Island

Southwestern
Adam's Grill
Coyote Grill
Little Rock Rodeo
Y.E. Coyote

Spanish
Casa Luis
Casa Margarita
Estoril Granada
Iberian

Sri Lankan
Sri Lanka Gourmet

Steakhouses
Abel Conklin's
B.K. Sweeney's
Bryant & Cooper
Dar Tiffany
Frank's Steaks

Jimmy Hay's
Jolly Fisherman
Little Rock Rodeo
McCluskey's
Old Stove Pub
Palm Restaurant
Peter Luger
P.G. Steakhouse

Thai
Bangkok Palace
Seeda Thai
Siam Lotus
Siam Palace
Thai House

Vegetarian
(Most Chinese, Indian
and Thai restaurants)
Bangkok Palace
Santosha

LOCATION BY TOWN

Amagansett
  Amagansett Fish
  Estia/Amagansett
  Gordon's
  Honest Diner
  Lobster Roll
  Wylie's Ribs
Amityville
  Hong Kong Seafood
  Rose Cottage
  Santosha
Baldwin
  Calabash
  Chez Antoine
  Raay-Nor's Cabin
Bayport
  Bayport House
  Le Soir
Bay Shore
  Il Garofano
  Siam Lotus
Bayville
  Aragosta-Blue Lobster
  Crescent
  Wall's Wharf
Bellmore
  Bayou
  McCluskey's
  Villa Doria
Bellport
  Bellport
  J-Dave's Old Inlet
  Bohemia
  Courtyard Cafe
Bridgehampton
  C.J. Thorne
  Karen Lee's
  Ming's HSF
  One Ocean Road
Carle Place
  Caffe Spasso
  Emilia
  Fyodoroff
  Sasaki
  West End Cafe
Cedarhurst
  Eddie's Pizza
  La Viola
  Mother Kelly's
Centerport
  Tung Ting
Commack
  Di Benardo's Bistro
  Emilio's
  Kurofune
  La Mascotte
  Spare Rib

East Hampton
  Cafe Max
  Della Femina
  Fresno Place
  James Lane Cafe
  Laundry Restaurant
  Little Rock Rodeo
  Little Rock Yacht
  Maidstone Arms
  Nick & Toni's
  Palm Restaurant
  1770 House
  Violet's
East Hills
  L'Endroit
  La Primavera
East Meadow
  La Famiglia
East Northport
  Chefs of New York
  Peter's Inn
East Norwich
  Cafe Girasole
East Setauket
  Lotus II East
Farmingdale
  56th Fighter Group
  Von Leesen's
Farmingville
  To Fu
Floral Park
  Koenig's
  Villa d'Este
Garden City
  Akbar
  B.K. Sweeney's
  Garden City Grande
  Newport Grill
  Orchid
  Polo Grill
Glen Cove
  Ashai Tokyo
  La Bussola
  La Ginestra
  La Pace
  Pasta's Cafe
  Romantico
  Stango's
  Uncle Dai
  Veranda
Glen Head
  California Grille
  Pappagallo
Great Neck
  Great Neck
  Bruzell's
  Colbeh

71

Long Island

El Tapatio
Giulia
Millie's Place
Navona
North Street Grill
Peter Luger
Pomodoro
Uncle Dai
Vespa

Greenport
Claudio's
Rhumb Line

Greenvale
Dar Tiffany
Hunan Taste
La Vigna

Hampton Bays
Fish Net
Fountaine's Beacon
Oakland's

Hauppauge
Due Torri
Gasho of Japan
Il Pozzo
Jade Garden
Mario
Sempre Vivolo

Hempstead
Nakisaki

Hicksville
Aegean East
Eye of the Tiger
La Caravella
Pasta's Cafe
Pasta-Eria
UB Loves Cafe
Y.E. Coyote

Holbrook
Mama Lombardi's

Huntington
Abel Conklin's
Ahrash Cafe
Bonbori
Conrad's Bar/Grill
Iberian
Jonathan's
Kabul
Kura Barn
La Parma
Medit. Snack Bar
P.G. Steakhouse
Petite Gourmet
Piccolo
Pomodoro
Ristorante Orlando
Thai House
Tortilla Grill
Trattoria Tulipano

Huntington Station
Jani
Panama Hattie's

Inwood
La Sila

Island Park
Coyote Grill
Jimmy Hay's
Paddy McGee's

Jamesport
Elbow Room

Jericho
Frank's Steaks
Milleridge Inn

Kings Park
American Bistro

Levittown
Hunam

Lindenhurst
Southside Fish/Clam

Locust Valley
Barney's
Buckram Stables
Country Inn
Locust Valley Inn

Long Beach
Baja
Soho

Manhasset
La Coquille
Pasta's Cafe
Stresa

Massapequa
Sergio's

Mastic Beach
Eddie's Pizza

Melville
Alouette
Cirella's
Frederick's
Watercolors Cafe

Merrick
Hunan Gourmet East
J.J. Hwang
Oriental Grill

Miller Place
Dublin Delights

Mineola
Caffe Spuntino
Estoril Granada
Lareira

Montauk
Dave's Downtown
Dave's Grill
Gosman's Dock
Gurney's Inn
Villa Testarossa
Waterfront

Long Island

New Hyde Park
  Eddie's Pizza
  Sapporo
  Umberto's Pizza
Northport
  Pumpernickel's
  Robke's
  Sea Shanty
Oakdale
  Riverview
Oceanside
  La Parma
  Sri Lanka
Oyster Bay
  Calamari Kitchen
  Canterbury Ales
Patchogue
  Gaetano's
Plainview
  White Sands
  Yamato
Port Jefferson
  Danford's Inn
  Hana
  Harrington's
  Noodles
  Pasta Pasta
Port Washington
  Chez Noelle
  DiMaggio's
  Diwan
  La Piccolo Liguria
  Louie's Shore
  Pomodoro
  Siam Palace
  Yamaguchi
Quogue
  Inn at Quogue
  River Inn
Rockville Centre
  Country Pantry
  George Martin
  Gumbo Alley
  Rigatoni
Roslyn
  Blue Parrot Cafe
  Bryant & Cooper
  George Washington
  Jolly Fisherman
  Palm Garden
  Trattoria di Meo
  Villa Gattopardo
Roslyn Estates
  Classico
Roslyn Heights
  Adam's Grill
  Il Sapore
  Michael's
  Sotto Luna
  To Fu

Sagaponack
  Old Stove Pub
Sag Harbor
  American Hotel
  Il Cappuccino
Sea Cliff
  Harlequin Cafe
Selden
  Cafe Stefano
Shelter Island
  Ram's Head Inn
Smithtown
  Casa Luis
  Casa Margarita
  Casa Rustica
  Main Street Pasta
  To Fu
Southampton
  Basilico
  Coast Grill
  Lobster Inn
  Post House
  75 Main
  Sfuzzi
  Silver's
Southold
  Armando's
  Ross' North Fork
St. James
  Dublin Delights
  Lotus East
  Mirabelle
Stony Brook
  Franzi & Nell's
  Three Village Inn
Syosset
  Cafe Testarossa
  Capriccio
  Caracalla
  Franina's
  Fu Ho
  La Viola
  Mim's
  Rachel's
Uniondale
  Cody's
Valley Stream
  Seeda Thai
Wainscott
  Bruce's
  Sapore di Mare
Wantagh
  Boardwalk
  Sapporo
Water Mill
  I Santi
  Mirko's
Westbury
  Alfredo's Pizza
  Benny's

Long Island

Caffe Baci
John Peel Room
La Dolce Sera
Piccola Bussola
Westhampton
 Hampton Square
 Saffron
 Starr Boggs
West Islip
 La Grange Inn
Williston Park
 Best of Both Worlds
 Hildebrandt's
La Marmite
La Parma
Riverbay
Woodbury
 G.D. Graffiti
 Kokura II
 Pasta's Cafe
 To Fu
 Uncle Dai
Woodmere
 Bangkok Palace
 La Petite Maison Russe
 La Tavernetta

SPECIAL FEATURES AND APPEALS

Bar/Singles Scenes
Abel Conklin's
Bayou
Bruce's
Buckram Stables
California Grille
Canterbury Ales
Conrad's Bar/Grill
Country Inn
Crescent
Danford's Inn
56th Fighter Group
Fountaine's Beacon
Harlequin Cafe
Harrington's
John Peel Room
Laundry Rest.
Noodles
Oakland's
Paddy McGee's
Peter's Inn
Rhumb Line
Sfuzzi
Wall's Wharf
Waterfront

Breakfast
(All hotels and the
 following standouts)
Danford's Inn
Dave's Downtown
Dub. Delights (St. James)
Estia/Amagansett
Honest Diner
75 Main
Three Village Inn
Von Leesen's
Watercolors Cafe

Brunch
(Best of the many)
Boardwalk
Bruce's
C.J. Thorne
Conrad's Bar/Grill
Country Inn
Crescent
Danford's Inn
Di Benardo's Bistro
Due Torri
56th Fighter Group
Fyodoroff
George Washington
Gurney's Inn
I Santi
Jonathan's

Karen Lee's
Louie's Shore
Maidstone Arms
Milleridge Inn
Millie's Place
Nick & Toni's
North Street Grill
Oriental Grill
Paddy McGee's
Palm Garden
Panama Hattie's
Polo Grill
Ram's Head Inn
Riverbay
Riverview
75 Main
Sfuzzi
Three Village Inn
Uncle Dai
Violet's
Watercolors Cafe
Waterfront

Business Dining
Abel Conklin's
Alouette
American Hotel
Barney's
Basilico
Benny's
Best of Both Worlds
Bryant &and Cooper
Caracalla
Casa Rustica
Chez Noelle
Conrad's Bar/Grill
Courtyard Cafe
Crescent
Danford's Inn
Diwan
Due Torri
Frank's Steaks
Frederick's
Il Pozzo
Inn at Quogue
John Peel Room
Kokura II
La Caravella
La Coquille
La Dolce Sera
La Ginestra
Mario
Navona
Newport Grill
North Street Grill
Palm Garden

Long Island

Pappagallo
Peter Luger
Piccolo
Polo Grill
Ristorante Orlando
Riverbay
Sempre Vivolo
Sfuzzi
Starr Boggs
Stresa
Trattoria Tulipano
Veranda
Watercolors Cafe

Dancing
(Nightclubs and the
 following; check times)
Aragosta–Blue Lobster
California Grille
Colbeh
Danford's Inn
Due Torri
56th Fighter Group
Fyodoroff
Garden City Grande
Gurney's Inn
Harlequin Cafe
Inn at Quogue
John Peel Room
La Famiglia
Mim's
Nakisaki
Noodles
Ristorante Orlando
Starr Boggs
Waterfront

Delivers
(Call to check range
 and charges, if any)
Ahrash Cafe
Alfredo's Pizza
Aragosta–Blue Lobster
Bellport
Best of Both Worlds
Bruzell's
Caffe Baci
Caffe Spasso
Canterbury Ales
Cody's
Colbeh
Conrad's Bar/Grill
Country Inn
Courtyard Cafe
Di Benardo's Bistro
Diwan
Eye of the Tiger
Fresno Place
Hunan Gourmet East

Iberian
I Santi
La Bussola
La Viola
Michael's – A Bistro
Millie's Place
Mother Kelly's
One Ocean Road
Oriental Grill
Panama Hattie's
Pasta's Cafe
Piccola Bussola
Ristorante Orlando
Siam Palace
Silver's
Uncle Dai
Villa Testarossa
Violet's
Wall's Wharf
Yamato

Entertainment
(Check days, times
 and performers)
Aegean (guitar/vocalist)
American Hotel (piano)
Aragosta (piano/vocalist)
Bayou (varies)
Bruce's (piano)
California Grille (DJ)
Classico (accordion)
Cody's (jazz)
Colbeh (vocalists)
Crescent (piano)
Danford's Inn (vocalists)
Dar Tiffany (jazz)
Due Torri (vocalists)
El Tapatio (vocalists)
Estoril Granada (piano)
56th Fighter (bands, DJ)
Fountaine's (varies)
Franina's (guitar, violin)
Fyodoroff (cabaret, jazz)
Garden City (bands)
Gurney's Inn (bands)
Hampton Square (piano)
Harlequin (bands, blues)
Harrington's (jazz)
Inn at Quogue (piano)
J-Dave's Old Inlet (piano)
John Peel Room (bands)
Jolly Fisherman (piano)
La Famiglia (guitar)
La Grange Inn (piano)
La Tavernetta (piano)
Locust Valley Inn (piano)
Millie's Place (guitar)
Noodles (guitar)
Oakland's (guitar)

Long Island

Palm Garden (piano)
Piccolo (piano)
Polo Grill (piano)
Post House (bands)
Pumpernickel's (accordion)
Ram's Head Inn (jazz)
Rist. Orlando (piano)
Riverview (piano)
Sergio's (guitar)
Starr Boggs (varies)
Three Village Inn (piano)
Tung Ting (piano)
Watercolors Cafe (piano)
Waterfront (varies)

Palm Restaurant
Peter Luger
Post House
Ram's Head Inn
Rhumb Line
Riverview
Sapore di Mare
Sfuzzi
Starr Boggs
Three Village Inn
Veranda
Violet's
Wall's Wharf
Wylie's Ribs

Fireplaces

Abel Conklin's
Adam's Grill
American Hotel
Barney's
Bellport
B.K. Sweeney's
Bruce's
Bryant & Cooper
Casa Luis
Casa Rustica
Chez Antoine
Conrad's Bar/Grill
Country Inn
Coyote Grill
Danford's Inn
Della Femina
Diwan
56th Fighter Group
George Washington
Hampton Square
Il Sapore
Inn at Quogue
J-Dave's Old Inlet
John Peel Room
Jolly Fisherman
La Grange Inn
La Mascotte
La Pace
Lareira
Laundry Rest.
Locust Valley Inn
Louie's Shore
Maidstone Arms
Mario
Michael's – A Bistro
Milleridge Inn
Millie's Place
Mill River Inn
Mirko's
Noodles
North Street Grill
One Ocean Road
Paddy McGee's
Palm Garden

Health/Spa Menus

(Most places cook
to order to meet
any dietary request;
call in advance to
check; almost all
health food spots,
Chinese, Indian and
other ethnics have
health-conscious meals,
as do the following)
American Bistro
American Hotel
Best of Both Worlds
California Grille
Courtyard Cafe
Danford's Inn
Di Benardo's Bistro
Due Torri
Fu Ho
Gasho of Japan
Gurney's Inn
Hunan Gourmet East
Hunan Taste
Jade Garden
La Petite Msn. Russe
Lotus East
Lotus II East
Milleridge Inn
Mirabelle
Mother Kelly's
Romantico
Tung Ting

Historic Interest

Abel Conklin's
American Hotel
George Washington
Harrington's
Hildebrandt's
Inn at Quogue
La Grange Inn
La Viola
Louie's Shore
Maidstone Arms

Long Island

Milleridge Inn
Post House
Raay-Nor's Cabin
1770 House
Silver's
Three Village Inn
Villa Gattopardo

Hotel Dining

American Hotel
  American Hotel
Claremont Hotel
  Palm Garden
Comfort Inn
  La Famiglia
Dune Deck Hotel
  Starr Boggs
Garden City Hotel
  Polo Grill
Gurney's Inn
  Gurney's Inn
Hedges Inn
  James Lane Cafe
Huntting Inn
  Palm Restaurant
Inn at Quogue
  Inn at Quogue
Island Inn Hotel
  John Peel Room
Maidstone Arms
  Maidstone Arms
Ram's Head Inn
  Ram's Head Inn
1770 House
  1770 House

"In" Places

American Bistro
American Hotel
Barney's
Basilico
Bayou
Bellport
Cafe Testarossa
California Grille
Casa Rustica
C.J. Thorne
Coast Grill
Conrad's Bar/Grill
Coyote Grill
Crescent
Della Femina
Due Torri
Estia/Amagansett
Eye of the Tiger
Fresno Place
Garden City Grande
George Martin
Gordon's
Honest Diner

I Santi
James Lane Cafe
J.J. Hwang
Karen Lee's
La Pace
La Parma
Laundry Rest.
Little Rock Rodeo
Lobster Roll
Millie's Place
Mill River Inn
Mirko's
Navona
Nick & Toni's
North Street Grill
Old Stove Pub
Paddy McGee's
Peter Luger
Polo Grill
Saffron
Sapore di Mare
75 Main
Starr Boggs
Stresa
Trattoria Tulipano

Late Dining
(All hours after 11 PM)
Alfredo's Pizza (1)
Eddie's Pizza (2)
Harrington's (12)
Hong Kong Seafood (12)
Laundry Rest. (12)
North Street Grill (12)
Stango's (11:30)
Watercolors Cafe (24 hrs.)

Noteworthy Newcomers (49)
Adam's Grill
Alouette
Aragosta–Blue Lobster
Ashai Tokyo
Best of Both Worlds
Cafe Max
Calabash
Calamari Kitchen
California Grille
Conrad's Bar/Grill
Crescent
Dave's Downtown
Della Femina
Estia/Amagansett
Fyodoroff
Garden City Grande
G.D. Graffiti
Gumbo Alley
Honest Diner
Hong Kong Seafood
I Santi

Long Island

J.J. Hwang
Kabul
La Dolce Sera
La Viola (Syosset)
Newport Grill
Noodles
North Street Grill
Oakland's
One Ocean Road
Palm Garden
Piccola Bussola
Pomodoro
Rigatoni
Rose Cottage
Saffron
75 Main
Sfuzzi
Siam Lotus
Soho
Sotto Luna
To Fu (Roslyn Hts.)
Tortilla Grill
Vespa
Villa Testarossa
Violet's
Waterfront
Wylie's Ribs
Y.E. Coyote

Offbeat

Aegean East
Ahrash Cafe
Alouette
Amagansett Fish
Baja
Bayou
Best of Both Worlds
Blue Parrot Cafe
Calabash
Calamari Kitchen
California Grille
Conrad's Bar/Grill
Country Pantry
Coyote Grill
Dublin Delights
Estia/Amagansett
56th Fighter Group
Garden City Grande
Gasho of Japan
Gumbo Alley
Harlequin Cafe
Harrington's
Honest Diner
Hong Kong Seafood
Jonathan's
La Petite Msn. Russe
Little Rock Rodeo
Lobster Roll
Mother Kelly's
Nakisaki

Petite Gourmet
Raay-Nor's Cabin
Santosha
Soho
Sri Lanka Gourmet
Stresa
White Sands
Y.E. Coyote

Outdoor Dining
(G = Garden,
 S = Sidewalk,
 W = Waterside location)
Adam's Grill (G)
American Hotel (G)
Aragosta (W)
Bayport House (G)
Boardwalk (G,W)
Bonbori (G)
Bruce's (G)
Buckram Stables (G)
Cafe Girasole (G)
Claudio's (W)
Coast Grill (W)
Coyote Grill (G,W)
Crescent (G,W)
Danford's Inn (G)
Dave's Downtown (G,W)
Dave's Grill (G,W)
Dublin Delights (G,S)
56th Fighter Group (G)
Franzi & Nell's (G)
Garden City (G,S)
Gasho of Japan (G)
Gosman's Dock (G,W)
Gurney's Inn (G,W)
Hampton Square (G)
Harlequin Cafe (G)
Il Pozzo (G)
James Lane Cafe (G)
J-Dave's Old Inlet (G)
Jolly Fisherman (W)
Little Rock Rodeo (G)
Little Rock Yacht (G,W)
Lobster Roll (G)
Louie's Shore (W)
Maidstone Arms (G)
Mirko's (G)
Noodles (G)
Oakland's (G,W)
Paddy McGee's (G,W)
Post House (G)
Ram's Head Inn (G,W)
Riverview (G,W)
Sapore di Mare (G,W)
Sfuzzi (G)
Soho (G)
Starr Boggs (G,W)
Tung Ting (W)

Long Island

Villa Doria (W)
Villa Testarossa (G)
Violet's (G)
Wall's Wharf (G,W)
Waterfront (G)

Parties &
Private Rooms
(All major hotels,
 plus the following;
 best of the many)
Adam's Grill*
Barney's
Bayport House
Bellport*
Benny's
Bruce's*
Bryant & Cooper
Cafe Girasole
Caffe Spuntino
Calabash*
California Grille*
Capriccio*
Caracalla
Casa Rustica*
Chez Antoine*
Chez Noelle
Cirella's
C.J. Thorne
Coast Grill
Conrad's Bar/Grill
Country Inn*
Coyote Grill
Crescent*
Dar Tiffany*
Della Femina*
Di Benardo's Bistro
Due Torri*
Emilia
Eye of the Tiger*
56th Fighter Group*
Frederick's*
Fresno Place
Fyodoroff
Garden City Grande*
Gasho of Japan
George Martin*
George Washington*
Giulia*
Gosman's Dock*
Harrington's*
Hildebrandt's
Iberian*
Il Garofano
I Santi*
J-Dave's Old Inlet*
Jolly Fisherman*
Kabul
Karen Lee's*

La Bussola
La Caravella*
La Dolce Sera*
La Ginestra
La Marmite*
La Mascotte*
La Pace*
La Parma*
La Piccolo Liguria
La Primavera
Lareira*
La Sila*
La Viola
L'Endroit*
Le Soir*
Mario*
Michael's – A Bistro
Milleridge Inn*
Millie's Place (Gt. Neck)*
Mirabelle
Mirko's
Navona
Nick & Toni's
Noodles*
North Street Grill*
Oriental Grill
Pappagallo*
Peter Luger*
Peter's Inn
P.G. Steakhouse*
Piccola Bussola*
Piccolo
Pomodoro
Post House*
Ristorante Orlando*
Riverbay*
Romantico*
Ross' North Fork
Saffron
Sapore di Mare*
Three Village Inn*
Trattoria Tulipano*
Umberto's*
Veranda*
Villa d'Este*
Villa Doria*
Villa Gattopardo
Waterfront*
(*Private rooms)

People-Watching
American Hotel
Barney's
Basilico
California Grille
C.J. Thorne
Coyote Grill
Dar Tiffany
Della Femina

Long Island

Estia/Amagansett
Fyodoroff
Garden City Grande
George Martin
Gordon's
Honest Diner
I Santi
Karen Lee's
La Tavernetta
Millie's Place
Mill River Inn
Mim's
Mirko's
Nick & Toni's
North Street Grill
Old Stove Pub
One Ocean Road
Paddy McGee's
Palm Restaurant
Peter Luger
Polo Grill
Sapore di Mare
75 Main
Sfuzzi
Starr Boggs
Trattoria Tulipano

Power Scenes

American Bistro
American Hotel
Barney's
Basilico
Benny's
Bruzell's
Bryant & Cooper
Cafe Testarossa
Casa Rustica
Chez Noelle
C.J. Thorne
Conrad's Bar & Grill
Courtyard Cafe
Dar Tiffany
Della Femina
Due Torri
Gordon's
Honest Diner
Il Pozzo
I Santi
Karen Lee's
La Coquille
La Marmite
La Pace
La Primavera
La Tavernetta
La Viola
L'Endroit
Millie's Place
Mill River Inn
Mim's
Mirabelle

Mirko's
Navona
Nick & Toni's
North Street Grill
Old Stove Pub
Palm Restaurant
Peter Luger
Polo Grill
Sapore di Mare
Sempre Vivolo
1770 House
Starr Boggs
Stresa
Three Village Inn
Trattoria Tulipano
Veranda

Pre-Theater/ Early-Bird Menus
(Call to check
 prices and times)
American Bistro
American Hotel
Bayport House
Bonbori
Bruzell's
Cafe Stefano
C.J. Thorne
Dar Tiffany
Due Torri
56th Fighter Group
Frank's Steaks
Gurney's Inn
Harrington's
Iberian
John Peel Room
La Grange Inn
La Pace
La Petite Msn. Russe
Louie's Shore
Michael's – A Bistro
Milleridge Inn
Ming's HSF
Newport Grill
Piccolo
Post House
Rose Cottage
Ross' North Fork
Santosha
Sergio's
Southside Fish/Clam
Watercolors Cafe
White Sands

Prix Fixe Menus
(call to check
 prices and times)
Akbar
Alouette
American Hotel

Long Island

Barney's
Best of Both Worlds
Boardwalk
Bruzell's
Cafe Stefano
Chez Noelle
Classico
Claudio's
Colbeh
Courtyard Cafe
Dar Tiffany
Diwan
Due Torri
56th Fighter Group
Frank's Steaks
Franzi & Nell's
Fyodoroff
George Martin
Giulia
Gordon's
Gurney's Inn
Harlequin Cafe
Harrington's
Iberian
Il Sapore
John Peel Room
Jonathan's
Kokura II
La Mascotte
La Pace
La Petite Msn. Russe
Lareira
La Tavernetta
Locust Valley Inn
Michael's – A Bistro
Milleridge Inn
Mill River Inn
Mim's
Ming's HSF
Mirabelle
Nakisaki
Newport Grill
Nick & Toni's
Oriental Grill
Palm Garden
Peter Luger
Peter's Inn
Piccolo
Polo Grill
Post House
Ram's Head Inn
Riverbay
Riverview
Romantico
Rose Cottage
Ross' North Fork
Sergio's
1770 House
Sfuzzi

Sri Lanka
Stango's
Trattoria Tulipano
Veranda
Villa Testarossa
Watercolors Cafe

Pubs
Canterbury Ales
Rhumb Line

Quiet Conversation
Alouette
American Hotel
Basilico
Cafe Girasole
Danford's Inn
Di Benardo's Bistro
Fountaine's Beacon
Il Pozzo
Kokura II
La Caravella
La Coquille
La Mascotte
Mill River Inn
Mirabelle
Mirko's
Palm Garden
Pasta Pasta
Petite Gourmet
Piccolo
Polo Grill
Sapore di Mare
1770 House
Soho
Watercolors Cafe

Romantic Spots
American Hotel
Aragosta–Blue Lobster
Barney's
Basilico
Benny's
Bonbori
Cafe Girasole
Casa Rustica
Chez Antoine
Chez Noelle
Classico
Courtyard Cafe
Coyote Grill
Due Torri
Giulia
Gordon's
Il Pozzo
Inn at Quogue
La Caravella
La Coquille
La Mascotte

Long Island

La Pace
L'Endroit
Le Soir
Little Rock Yacht
Maidstone Arms
Michael's – A Bistro
Mill River Inn
Mirabelle
Mirko's
Navona
One Ocean Road
Palm Garden
Pappagallo
Petite Gourmet
Polo Grill
Rose Cottage
Ross' North Fork
Sapore di Mare
1770 House
Starr Boggs
Three Village Inn
Veranda
Villa Gattopardo
Violet's
Wall's Wharf
Waterfront

La Parma (Huntington)
Mill River Inn
Mirabelle
Petite Gourmet
Rachel's
Rigatoni
Santosha
Sea Shanty
1770 House
Tortilla Grill

Senior Appeal

Armando's Seafood
Benny's
Due Torri
Fountaine's Beacon
George Washington
Gurney's Inn
Il Garofano
Jolly Fisherman
La Ginestra
La Grange Inn
La Marmite
La Pace
La Vigna
Locust Valley Inn
Milleridge Inn
Palm Garden
Pappagallo
Post House
Pumpernickel's
Rose Cottage
Ross' North Fork
Sea Shanty
Three Village Inn
Villa d'Este
Villa Gattopardo
Violet's

Smoking Prohibited

Calamari Kitchen
California Grille
G.D. Graffiti

Teas

Gurney's Inn
Il Pozzo
Maidstone Arms
Palm Garden
Polo Grill
Starr Boggs

Teenagers & Other Youthful Spirits

Baja
Best of Both Worlds
Blue Parrot Cafe
Cafe Testarossa
Caffe Baci
Caffe Spasso
Calamari Kitchen
Coast Grill
Dublin Delights
Emilio's
Eye of the Tiger
56th Fighter Group
Fu Ho
Gasho of Japan
G.D. Graffiti
George Martin
Gumbo Alley
Hildebrandt's
Honest Diner
J.J. Hwang
John Peel Room
La Caravella
Little Rock Rodeo
Locust Valley Inn
Mother Kelly's
Noodles
Spare Rib
Tortilla Grill
UB Loves Cafe
Villa Doria
Violet's
Wylie's Ribs
Y.E. Coyote

Long Island

Wheelchair Access
(Check for bathroom
access; almost all hotels,
plus the following)
Abel Conklin's
Adam's Grill
Aegean East
Ahrash Cafe
Akbar
Alfredo's Pizza
Alouette
American Bistro
Armando's
Baja
Bangkok Palace
Basilico
Bayport House
Bellport
Benny's
Best of Both Worlds
B.K. Sweeney's
Blue Parrot Cafe
Boardwalk
Bonbori
Bruce's
Bruzell's
Bryant & Cooper
Buckram Stables
Cafe Girasole
Cafe Stefano
Cafe Testarossa
Caffe Baci
Caffe Spasso
Caffe Spuntino
Calabash
Calamari Kitchen
California Grille
Canterbury Ales
Capriccio
Caracalla
Casa Luis
Casa Margarita
Casa Rustica
Chez Antoine
Cirella's
C.J. Thorne
Classico
Coast Grill
Cody's
Colbeh
Conrad's Bar/Grill
Country Inn
Courtyard Cafe
Coyote Grill
Crescent
Danford's Inn
Dave's Grill
Della Femina
Di Benardo's Bistro

Dublin Delights
Due Torri
Eddie's Pizza
Elbow Room
El Tapatio
Emilia
Emilio's
Estia/Amagansett
Eye of the Tiger
56th Fighter Group
Franina's
Fresno Place
Fu Ho
Fyodoroff
Gaetano's
Garden City Grande
Gasho of Japan
G.D. Graffiti
George Martin
George Washington
Giulia
Gordon's
Gosman's Dock
Gumbo Alley
Hana
Harlequin Cafe
Hildebrandt's
Honest Diner
Hunam
Hunan Taste
Il Cappuccino
Il Garofano
Il Sapore
I Santi
Jani
Kabul
Koenig's
La Caravella
La Coquille
La Dolce Sera
La Marmite
La Mascotte
La Pace
La Parma
La Petite Msn. Russe
La Piccolo Liguria
La Primavera
Lareira
La Sila
La Tavernetta
Laundry Rest.
La Vigna
La Viola
L'Endroit
Little Rock Rodeo
Little Rock Yacht
Lobster Inn
Lobster Roll
Locust Valley Inn

Long Island

Main Street Pasta
Mama Lombardi's
McCluskey's
Michael's – A Bistro
Mill River Inn
Milleridge Inn
Millie's Place
Mim's
Ming's HSF
Nakisaki
Navona
Newport Grill
Nick & Toni's
Noodles
North Street Grill
Oakland's
Old Stove Pub
One Ocean Road
Oriental Grill
Paddy McGee's
Panama Hattie's
Pappagallo
Pasta-Eria
Pasta's Cafe
Pasta Pasta
Peter Luger
Peter's Inn
Piccola Bussola
Piccolo
Raay-Nor's Cabin
Rachel's
Rhumb Line
Rigatoni
Ristorante Orlando
Riverbay
Riverview
Robke's
Romantico
Rose Cottage
Ross' North Fork
Saffron
Sapporo
Sasaki
Sea Shanty
Seeda Thai
Sergio's
75 Main
Siam Lotus
Soho
Sotto Luna
Southside Fish/Clam
Sri Lanka Gourmet
Stango's
Stresa
Three Village Inn
To Fu
Trattoria di Meo
Trattoria Tulipano
UB Loves Cafe

Veranda
Villa d'Este
Villa Doria
Villa Testarossa
Watercolors Cafe
Waterfront
West End Cafe
White Sands
Wylie's Ribs
Yamato
Y.E. Coyote

Winning Wine Lists
American Bistro
American Hotel
Barney's
Cafe Girasole
Canterbury Ales
Casa Rustica
Conrad's Bar/Grill
Coyote Grill
Dar Tiffany
Dave's Downtown
Hampton Square
Il Pozzo
Karen Lee's
La Caravella
La Marmite
La Mascotte
La Pace
L'Endroit
Le Soir
Mill River Inn
Mirabelle
North Street Grill
Panama Hattie's
Polo Grill
Ross' North Fork
Sapore di Mare
Starr Boggs
Stresa
Trattoria Tulipano

Young Children
(Besides the normal
fast-food places)
Adam's Grill*
Aegean East*
Ahrash Cafe*
Armando's*
Best of Both Worlds*
Boardwalk*
Bruzell's*
Cafe Testarossa*
Caffe Baci
Calamari Kitchen*
Canterbury Ales*
Claudio's*
Coast Grill

Long Island

Conrad's Bar/Grill*
Danford's Inn*
El Tapatio*
Estia/Amagansett*
Eye of the Tiger
56th Fighter Group*
Fish Net*
Fu Ho
Gasho of Japan*
G.D. Graffiti*
George Martin*
George Washington*
Gosman's Dock*
Hildebrandt's
Honest Diner
Il Cappuccino*
J.J. Hwang
John Peel Room*
Jolly Fisherman*
Koenig's*
La Caravella
La Grange Inn*
La Vigna
Little Rock Rodeo*
Little Rock Yacht*
Lobster Roll*

Louie's Shore*
Mama Lombardi's*
McCluskey's*
Milleridge Inn*
Mim's*
Mother Kelly's
Noodles*
Oriental Grill
Paddy McGee's*
Pasta's Cafe*
Raay-Nor's Cabin*
Rigatoni*
Ross' North Fork*
Sapporo*
Sfuzzi*
Southside Fish/Clam*
Spare Rib*
Tortilla Grill
UB Loves Cafe
Villa Testarossa*
Violet's
Watercolors Cafe*
Wylie's Ribs*
Y.E. Coyote*
(*Children's menu served)

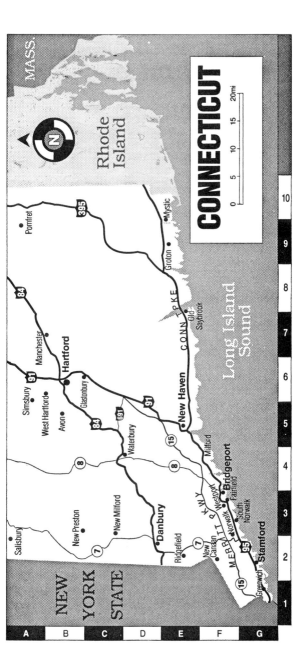

CONNECTICUT'S MOST POPULAR RESTAURANTS

Each of our reviewers has been asked to name his or her five favorite restaurants. The 40 spots most frequently named, in order of their popularity, are:

1. Bertrand
2. Jean-Louis
3. Homestead Inn
4. Robert Henry's
5. Amadeus
6. Da Pietro's
7. Sol e Luna
8. Bella Luna
9. Centro
10. Stonehenge
11. L'Abbee
12. Mayflower Inn
13. Boxing Cat Grill
14. Cafe du Bec Fin
15. Copper Beech Inn
16. Hopkins Inn
17. Inn at Ridgefield
18. Meson Galicia
19. West Street Grill
20. Restaurant du Village
21. Spazzi
22. Miche-Mache
23. Pasta Nostra
24. Manero's
25. The White Hart
26. Bee and Thistle Inn
27. Roger Sherman Inn
28. Frank Pepe Pizzeria
29. Fine Bouche
30. Scoozi Trattoria
31. Terra
32. Maria's Trattoria
33. Griswold Inn
34. Cavey's
35. La Strada
36. Le Chambord
37. Sally's Apizza
38. Doc's
39. Silvermine Tavern
40. Panda Pavilion

It's obvious that many of the restaurants on the above list are among the area's most expensive. However, all of New York City's surrounding areas have an abundance of bargain spots that are popular and worth noting. Connecticut's Best Buys are listed on page 92.

TOP RATINGS*

TOP 40 FOOD RATINGS
(In order of rating)

27 – Jean-Louis
Robert Henry's
Da Pietro's
26 – Fine Bouche
Restaurant du Village
Doc's
Frank Pepe Pizzeria
Bertrand
Cavey's
25 – Golden Lamb Buttery
Sally's Apizza
L'Abbee
Meson Galicia
Max-a-Mia
24 – Pasta Nostra
Stonehenge
Homestead Inn
Amadeus
Copper Beech Inn
Bee and Thistle Inn
Miche-Mache

Abbott's Lobster
West Street Grill
Cafe du Bec Fin
23 – Mayflower Inn
Il Falco
Max on Main
Scribner's
Maison le Blanc
Ruth's Chris
La Bretagne
La Strada
White Hart
Spazzi Trattoria
Apricot's
Le Chambord
Sol e Luna
Assaggio
Randall's Ordinary
Peppercorn's Grill

TOP SPOTS BY CUISINE

**Top American
(Contemporary)**
27 – Robert Henry's
25 – L'Abbee
24 – Miche-Mache
West Street Grill
23 – Mayflower Inn

**Top American
(Traditional)**
25 – Golden Lamb Buttery
24 – Bee and Thistle Inn
23 – Randall's Ordinary
19 – Elms Inn
MacKenzie's Old Ale

Top Continental
24 – Stonehenge
Amadeus
23 – Apricot's
22 – Inn at Ridgefield
Hopkins Inn

Top French Classic
26 – Fine Bouche
Restaurant du Village
24 – Homestead Inn
Copper Beech Inn
21 – Roger Sherman Inn

---

*Excluding restaurants with voting too low to be reliable.

French Contemporary
27 – Jean-Louis
26 – Bertrand
Cavey's
24 – Cafe du Bec Fin
23 – Maison le Blanc

Top Hotel Dining
24 – Stonehenge Inn
Homestead Inn
Copper Beech Inn
Bee and Thistle Inn
23 – Mayflower Inn

Top Italian (Northern)
27 – Da Pietro's
26 – Doc's
25 – Max-a-Mia
23 – Sol e Luna
Assaggio

Top Italian
(North & South)
24 – Pasta Nostra
23 – Il Falco
La Strada
Spazzi Trattoria
20 – 500 Blake St. Cafe

Top Newcomers/Rated
25 – Max-a-Mia
24 – Miche-Mache
West Street Grill
23 – Mayflower Inn
White Hart

Top Newcomers/Unrated
— Cafe Christina
— Chef Martin
— Fjord Fisheries
— Mona Lisa
— Sagebrush Cafe

Top Pizzerias
26 – Frank Pepe Pizzeria
25 – Sally's Apizza
20 – Prezzo
19 – Sunrise Pizza
16 – Bricks

Top Seafood
24 – Abbott's Lobster
Cafe du Bec Fin
23 – Scribner's
White Hart
19 – Capitol Fish House

Top Worth a Trip
25 – Golden Lamb Buttery,
Brooklyn
24 – Copper Beech Inn,
Ivoryton
Bee and Thistle Inn,
Old Lyme
Abbott's Lobster,
Noank
23 – Mayflower Inn,
Washington

TOP 40 OVERALL DECOR
(In order of rating)

28 – Golden Lamb Buttery
27 – Mayflower Inn/V
    Robert Henry's
26 – Homestead Inn
25 – Bertrand
    Copper Beech Inn/V
    Bee and Thistle Inn
    Randall's Ordinary
    Stonehenge/V
24 – Cavey's
    Restaurant du Village
    Cobb's Mill Inn/V
    Roger Sherman Inn
    Apricot's
    White Hart
    Hopkins Inn/V
23 – Old Lyme Inn
    Hop Brook
    Jean-Louis
    Silvermine Tavern/V
    Tollgate Hill Inn

    Boulders Inn/V
    Fine Bouche
    Il Forno
    Meson Galicia
22 – Griswold Inn
    Amadeus
    Inn at Ridgefield/V
    Sol e Luna
    Terra
    Avon Old Farms Inn
    Ragamont Inn
21 – Dolce/V
    La Strada
    Freshfields/V
    L'Abbee
    Inn on Lake Waramaug
    West Street Grill
    MacKenzie's Roadhouse
20 – Il Falco

TOP 40 OVERALL SERVICE
(In order of rating)

26 – Golden Lamb Buttery
25 – Robert Henry's
    Fine Bouche
    Jean-Louis
24 – Restaurant du Village
    Bertrand
    Da Pietro's
    Copper Beech Inn
    Homestead Inn
23 – Cavey's
    Stonehenge
    Bee and Thistle Inn
    Mayflower Inn
    L'Abbee
    Randall's Ordinary
    Meson Galicia
22 – Amadeus
    La Bretagne
    Maison le Blanc
    Inn at Ridgefield

    Il Falco
    Miche-Mache
    White Hart
21 – Apricot's
    Old Lyme Inn
    Tollgate Hill Inn
    Max-a-Mia
    Cafe du Bec Fin
    Rudy's
    La Strada
    Hopkins Inn
    Le Chambord
    Max on Main
    Roger Sherman Inn
    Le Bon Coin
    Gregory's
20 – Thai Orchid
    Ragamont Inn
    Morgan
    Freshfields

V = Also has an outstanding view.

BEST BUYS

TOP 40 BANGS FOR THE BUCK

This list reflects the best dining values in our *Survey*. It is produced by dividing the cost of a meal into the combined ratings for food, decor, and service.

1. Frank Pepe Pizzeria
2. Rein's
3. Sally's Apizza
4. Amarillo Grill
5. Bloodroot
6. Su Casa
7. Great American Cafe
8. Bertucci's
9. Congress Rotisserie
10. China Pavilion
11. Sunrise Pizza Cafe
12. Bricks
13. Panda Inn
14. Abbott's
15. Bangkok
16. Tiger Bowl
17. Thai Orchid
18. Little Kitchen
19. Gail's Station House
20. Max-a-Mia
21. Panda Pavilion
22. Pellicci's
23. Arizona Flats
24. Hot Tomato's
25. Harry's TX BBQ
26. Wild Scallion
27. Onion Alley
28. Hunan U.S. 1
29. Breakaway
30. Kotobuki
31. Pasa Vera
32. Bruxelles Brasserie
33. Mackenzie's
34. Tucson Cafe
35. Hay Day Cafe
36. Hacienda Don Emilio
37. Centro
38. Gates
39. Bali
40. Peppercorn's Grill

Additional Good Values

Abis
Alforno
Angelino's
Apulia
Backstreet
Bart's Paradise Cafe
Black Goose Grill
Bonani
Brookfield Bistro
Butterfield's
Capers
Chale Ipanema
Cobble Cookery
Costa del Sol
Derosa's
Di Fiore's
Diorio
Doc's
Fortune Village
Ganga
Heavenly Hog
Hot Tamales
Jetstream's Cafe
Kansas City Bar-B-Q

Lemon Grass
Li's Brothers Inn
Little Mark's
Lotus East
Maria's Trattoria
Mario's
Meera
Oasis Diner
Pantry
Parma
Ragamont Inn
Rumba
Saigon City
Sakura
Saybrook Fish House
Sesame Seed
Sheesh Mahal
Spazzi Trattoria
Taj Mahal
Thai Garden
Thataway Cafe
Truc Orient Express
Woodland

Connecticut
Area Code 203

F	D	S	C

ABBOTT'S LOBSTER IN THE ROUGH/S (Noank) **E9**

| 24 | 15 | 14 | $20 |

117 Pearl St. (off Main St.), 536-7719
U – Besides the "best lobster in Southern New England", this Noank landmark is "worth a drive from anywhere" for some of the state's freshest fish and best dining values; the "no-frills" outdoor picnic-table decor and casual service are offset by a "great view" of the water; open daily May – Labor Day, weekends-only through Columbus Day; BYO.

Abis/S (Greenwich) **G1**

| 17 | 15 | 17 | $25 |

381 Greenwich Ave. (Railroad Ave.), 862-9100
M – Surveyors split on this Greenwich Japanese: "very good food in a garden setting" vs. "unimpressive" and "minimally attractive"; the sushi and sashimi get kudos, but the rest of the menu is "rarely exciting"; the staff "treats children well", but do kids like raw fish?; BYO.

A Garden Cafe/S (Greenwich) **G1**

| 17 | 11 | 13 | $21 |

1191 E. Putnam Ave. (I-95, exit 5), 637-5474
M – Though primarily a catering company, this BYO Eclectic cafe offers a "limited menu" of "Jamaican specialties" and "good vegetarian food"; despite a garden, its decor is "low-budget" and service is only "well-meaning."

Al Dimarco's Dinner/Supper Club/S (Stamford) **G2**

| – | – | – | M |

222 Summer St. (Broad St.), 327-0030
If you think the good ol' days of dining and dancing are long gone, then you haven't tried this new supper club; its mid-priced food – steak Diane, veal Oscar, Caesar salad – complements the '40s and '50s theme, complete with Big Band music and polished dance floor.

Alforno Brick Oven Pizzeria Ristorante/S (Old Saybrook) **E8**

| – | – | – | M |

Brian Alden Shopping Ctr., 1654 Boston Post Rd. (Rte. 166), 399-4166
Good-looking quarters and snappy service keep this up-to-the-minute brick-oven pizzeria hopping; fans of this "NY wannabe" suggest you stick to the "Tuscan" pizzas, since the rest of the menu is "generic"; critics say "a bit pretentious – it's only a pizzeria."

	F	D	S	C

Allen's Clam | 17 | 16 | 16 | $30
& Lobster House/S (Westport) **F3**
191 Hillspoint Rd. (Greensfarms Rd.), 226-4411
M – It's been in business since 1930, but the consensus on this touristy, "classic" "real New England fish house" is "not what it once was", with some diners saying the "standard fare" "needs a new, young touch"; there's no denying the "great view" of the Sound; closed in winter.

Amadeo's Ristorante (Westport) **F3** | 22 | 18 | 19 | $33
1431 Post Rd. E. (bet. Maple Ave. & Turkey Hill Rd.), 254-9482
U – The "food is great", but the room is often "too noisy" at this homey but sophisticated regional Italian on the busy Boston Post Road; an "interesting, diversified menu" offers modern riffs of dishes that some call "comparable to NY's best", though less pricey.

AMADEUS RESTAURANT/S | 24 | 22 | 22 | $37
(Stamford) **G2**
201 Summer St. (Broad St.), 348-7775
U – In honor of Wolfgang Amadeus, the music played on the grand piano at this "elegant" Downtowner is mostly Mozart, and the "excellent" food is mostly Viennese; fans cite the "good schnitzels", "best duck ever" and "great desserts"; "big-city ambiance" and well-paced service make it "worth the $", "perfect for a special meal", and convenient to the Center for the Arts, BYO.

Amarillo Grill (Hartford) **B6** | 19 | 15 | 19 | $18
309 Asylum St. (Ann St.), 247-7427
U – A "fairly good representative of Texas BBQ" is high praise coming from picky rib-lovers; "cute but effective" and "nicely presented food" bring touches of urban class to a finger-licking experience that's as good for adults as it is for kids; reasonable prices make it all the better.

Angelino's/S (Westport) **F3** | – | – | – | I
Post Plaza, 1092 Post Rd. E. (Morningside St.), 227-0865
A real family restaurant, this amiable spot's a favorite for both its pizzas and large portions of red-sauce Italian classics; we missed it on our questionnaire, but many write-ins indicate that reasonable prices and good quality have built a loyal following.

Angsavanee East/S (Stamford) **G2** | 20 | 18 | 19 | $31
25 Bank St. (Atlantic Ave.), 324-3245
U – What seems like a mismatched marriage of Thai and Italian is actually more of a separate-but-equal live-in arrangement; the "delicate and exotic" Thai specialties get the kudos, but fans say the kitchen speaks fluent Italian too; "charming" decor spans the continents – a "strange mix that works."

Connecticut | F | D | S | C |

APRICOT'S/S (Farmington) **C5** | 23 | 24 | 21 | $36 |
1593 Farmington Ave. (Rte. 4), 673-5903
U – The "pretty-as-a-postcard" setting with a lovely view of the Farmington River from the patio outclasses the food – but only slightly – at this "delightful" American-Continental; though "pricey", "large portions", "old-world comfort" and romance are worth a trip; insiders dismiss the dark downstairs pub.

Apulia Restaurant | 20 | 13 | 17 | $27 |
(South Norwalk) **G2**
70 N. Main St. (Martin Luther King Blvd.), 852-1168
U – A recent renovation that added takeout plus an Italian bread bakery is not reflected in the scores for this "lively" SoNo Italian, which many call their "favorite spot"; a "well-prepared menu" at fair prices, appeals to foodies as well as families, despite waits and noise.

Arizona Flats/S (Bridgeport) **F3** | 18 | 15 | 16 | $21 |
3001 Fairfield Ave. (Gilman Ave.), 334-8300
M – Customers are not sure how to define the food, variously described as "standard Mexican", "upscale Tex-Mex" and "nouvelle" South of the Border; however, "ample" portions, modest prices and decor festooned with Mexican and cowboy artifacts make this "informal and fun."

Assaggio (West Hartford) **B6** | 23 | 18 | 20 | $29 |
904 Farmington Ave. (Troutbrook Rd.), 233-4520
U – Italian food with a "wood-fired" Tuscan touch and a bit of Californian flair is a mix that works well at this West Hartford spot "popular for a night out"; "sedate '30s supper club" ambiance, ok prices and staff with a "great attitude" are a winning mix.

Avon Old Farms Inn/S (Avon) **B5** | 18 | 22 | 19 | $31 |
Rte. 44 (Rte. 10), 677-2818
U – Lovingly preserved, this "charming" "18th-century home" is a "step back in time", but some respondents say the Continental food is "too fancy" and best for the "in-laws"; however, its "pretty" surroundings, "cheerful staff" and reasonable prices make for a "pleasant experience."

Azteca's (New Haven) **E5** | 21 | 19 | 20 | $31 |
14 Mechanic St. (bet. State & Lawrence Sts.), 624-2454
U – The "hip New Haven crowd" generally praises the "Nouvelle Mexican and American SW" food as well as the "funky" but "nice decor"; "attentive service" and "very unusual" specials are noted, but prices are highish for Mexican – at least by local college-kid standards.

Connecticut　　　　　　| F | D | S | C |

Bacci's Restaurant*/S　　| 23 | 22 | 20 |$34|
(Southbury) **D3**
900 Main St. S. (Rte. 172), 262-1250
*U – "True Tuscan cuisine" is its forte, but dishes from
other parts of Northern Italy are also featured at this
"real gem"; "pleasing, clean, simple decor" and a "young
staff" ("very friendly", if sometimes "overeager") lend a
measure of "charm" to this medium-priced spot where
the main complaint is it's "always crowded."*

Backstreet/S (Darien) **G2**　　| 17 | 16 | 17 |$25|
22 Center St. (Post Rd.), 655-9944
*M – "Good for lunch but not for a serious dinner", this
"Waspy watering hole" is where "tout Darien goes" to
see and be seen over trendy "American bistro" food that
fans call "dependable" "quality at reasonable prices", but
others find "bland" and "ordinary."*

Bagdon's/S (New Haven) **E5**　　| – | – | – | M |
9 Elm St. (State St.), 777-1962
*The fourth in a quick succession of restaurants in the
same location, this brand-new, modestly priced
Contemporary American may have staying power; its
inventive menu is a sharp but fitting contrast to the
stylish black-and-white modern decor and '40s music.*

Bali of Greenwich/S　　| 20 | 19 | 19 |$28|
(Greenwich) **G1**
55 Arch St. (Greenwich Ave.), 629-0777
*M – Offering a "great mix of Chinese and Indonesian"
food, this "attractive" ethnic also boasts "wonderful"
Oriental decor and "polite, unobtrusive" service in a
gracious setting; though some say the Chinese menu is
"too Americanized", this is the "place to go for rijstafel."*

Bangkok/S (Danbury) **D2**　　| 20 | 15 | 17 |$19|
Nutmeg Square, 72 Newtown Rd. (I-84, exit 8), 791-0640
*U – "Though in a shopping center", this Thai's "limited
menu" of "well-prepared" dishes is a welcome
"surprise"; "the owner always makes you feel at home",
and friendly service, not to mention modest prices,
warm our surveyors' hearts.*

Bart's Paradise Cafe*/S　　| 13 | 13 | 16 |$25|
(Greenwich) **G1**
18 W. Putnam Ave. (Greenwich Ave.), 869-8383
*M – For comfortable, "casual ambiance" and a "simple
meal" that's "not too expensive", this "plain-Jane"
Eclectic may fill the bill, but many say the "enormous
menu" is too "ambitious", with "so-so" food explaining
why you can "get in when other spots are booked."*

| F | D | S | C |

BEE AND THISTLE INN/S | 24 | 25 | 23 | $35 |
(Old Lyme) **E8**
Bee and Thistle Inn, 100 Lyme St. (Rte. 1), 434-1667
U – "Perfect in every season, from summer gardens to winter fireplaces"; this "wonderful", "romantic" "old" "bed-and-breakfast"–cum–restaurant is an ideal "place to stop on the way to Cape Cod, Newport or Boston" for "superb" Contemporary American cuisine served with plenty of "old Connecticut charm"; live music on weekends.

Bella Italia/S (Danbury) **D2** | 17 | 13 | 15 | $30 |
2 Padanaram Rd. (Hayes Town Ave.), 743-3828
M – Well-prepared "traditional Italian" at "moderate" prices makes this "gaudy" spot a "local favorite" but "not worth a detour"; they'll "make anything you want", but service can be "slow" at this "trying-to-go-upscale Italian."

Bella Luna Ristorante/S | 21 | 20 | 18 | $34 |
(Greenwich) **G1**
Old Post Rd. #3 (loop off Post Rd.), 862-9555
U – "Bustling" and "festive", this Italian newcomer is already such a "hot spot" that it can be "hard to get into" – and is "noisy and crowded" when you do; "country Italian" ambiance and "warm" service complement an "interesting Tuscan bistro menu" (designer pizzas, pastas, etc.) at high-side prices.

Bellini Restaurant* (Hartford) **B6** | 23 | 25 | 20 | $42 |
438 Franklin Ave. (Brown St.), 296-2100
U – Those few who know of this Contemporary French–Italian report an attractive, elegant setting and very "good food" plus consistent, professional service; stiff prices and "small portions" may be why response on this pretty, upscale place is so light.

BERTRAND (Greenwich) **G1** | 26 | 25 | 24 | $56 |
253 Greenwich Ave. (Arch St.), 661-4459
U – This "little bit of France" in tony Greenwich shows off chef-owner Christian Bertrand's "association with Lutece" in its "outstanding" Classic French food and first-class wine list, presented in a setting with "vaulted ceilings" and a "beautiful crowd"; a few say the "service lacks the warmth one expects when paying the price."

Bertucci's Brick Oven Pizzeria/S | 15 | 14 | 15 | $16 |
(Westport) **F3**, 833 Post Rd. E. (Sherwood Island connector), 454-1559
(West Hartford) **B6**, 330 N. Main St. (Asylum St.), 231-9571
(Orange) **E4**, 550 Boston Post Rd. (Peck Lane), 799-6828
(Darien) **G2**, 54 Boston Post Rd. (I-95, exit 13), 655-4299
M – Boston based, these "designer pie" outposts please most surveyors with "truly tasty" "brick-oven pizza" at "affordable" prices; however, critics say the food tastes like it "visited every other chain."

Connecticut

Black Goose Grill/S (Darien) **G2** | 15 | 17 | 16 | $25 |
972 Post Rd. (Center St.), 655-7107
*M – "Honest food and value" and a "cozy" bar setting
plus "great wines by the glass" and "beer on tap" keep
"yuppies" coming to this "unpretentious" American grill,
especially for a "quick weeknight" bite or brunch;
dissenters "yawn" at "spotty service" and "skimpy
portions" of "boring food."*

Black Rock Castle*/S | 19 | 15 | 20 | $27 |
(Bridgeport) **F3**
2895 Fairfield Ave. (Jetland St.), 336-3990
*U – "You don't have to be Irish to love this pub, a replica
of an Irish castle where the blarney is as thick as Irish
mist" but is "outrageously fun"; "Guinness on tap" and
"delicious food with friendly service" appeal to the
burghers who make this a "neighborhood hangout."*

Bloodroot/S (Bridgeport) **F3** | 18 | 14 | 12 | $15 |
85 Ferris St. (Fairfield Ave.), 576-9168
*M – "You either hate it or love it" describes reactions to
this "feminist organic Vegetarian stronghold" on the
water in Bridgeport; the "lesbian bookstore" section and
"militant service" can be a turnoff, but good vegetarian
fare at modest prices make it "worth a visit."*

Bluewater Cafe*/S | 18 | 16 | 17 | $30 |
(New Canaan) **F2**
15 Elm St. (Main St.), 972-1799
*M – This "tiny", trendy new New Canaanite strikes some
as "intimate" and others as "uncomfortably cramped",
but most agree it delivers "surprisingly good food",
especially the "pastas" and daily specials.*

Bombay's Authentic Indian | – | – | – | M |
Cuisine/S (Hartford) **B6**
89 Arch St. (Main St.), 724-4282
*Though few of our surveyors have discovered it, this
Indian is a welcome addition to Hartford's dining scene;
the bare-bones setting could be more appealing, but the
staff tries hard and the modestly priced food gets
applause for its authenticity and presentation; BYO.*

Bonani/S (Stamford) **G2** | 19 | 11 | 14 | $23 |
490 Summer St. (Bedford St.), 348-8138
*U – Even though "neither decor nor service" wins prizes,
"good cheap plentiful eats" make this Indian a "better-
than-average" choice; if "not up to NYC Little India
standards", it's still easy enough to "like this place."*

Connecticut | F | D | S | C |

Boulders Inn/S (New Preston) **B3** | 19 | 23 | 19 |$35 |
Boulders Inn, East Shore Rd., Rte. 45 (Rte. 202), 868-0541
M – The "charming, romantic setting" with a "great view"
of Lake Waramaug receives better mentions than the
Contemporary New England cuisine at this "classy"
country inn, but the food is decent enough to guarantee
"a nice escape"; add "gracious" service and "outdoor
dining" in summer and you have a "unique spot."

Boxing Cat Grill/S | 20 | 20 | 18 |$29 |
(Old Greenwich) **G1**
1392 E. Putnam Ave. (Sound Beach Ave.), 698-1995
U – "Buffy and Muffy rub elbows" with local businessmen at
this "always-crowded", "fun" and "funky" "watering hole"
dispensing "innovative" American fare, "Manhattanish"
ambiance, "upbeat" service and "great people-watching."

Breakaway/S (Fairfield) **F3** | 19 | 11 | 15 |$20 |
2316 Post Rd. (Sasco Hill Rd.), 255-0026
U – For years this "jam-packed" "hangout" has been a
"reliable" choice for a "good casual meal" (especially
with kids in tow), thanks to the "great salads, burgers
and sandwiches" at fair prices; even its staunchest fans
say the decor "needs freshening up."

Bricks, The/S (Norwalk) **G2** | 16 | 15 | 17 |$17 |
Bricks Plaza, 181 Main St. (Rte. 123), 847-8414
U – This lively new "brick-oven pizzeria" is a big hit with
the "family" trade – "kids love" getting "pizza dough to
play with", and the open cooking area provides lots of
distractions (and noise); prices are low.

Brookfield Bistro*/X (Brookfield) **D3** | 20 | 13 | 18 |$21 |
Colonial Square, 483 Federal Rd., Rte. 7 (Rte. 133),
740-9555
U – Known more for its "limited" but "well-executed"
Contemporary American menu than for its simple decor,
this small, friendly storefront is a "favorite", thanks to
affordable, "always consistent" food; the simple fare
includes outstanding homemade breads and desserts.

Bruxelles Brasserie | 20 | 19 | 19 |$27 |
and Bar/S (New Haven) **E5**
220 College St. (Crown St.), 777-7752
M – Proximity to the Shubert Theater and Yale makes
this "casual" American bistro, located in an "attractive"
converted townhouse, a trendy destination – "young in
spirit" and "good for people-watching"; despite a
well-priced, "light and varied menu", critics find "no
reason to return."

Bull's Head Diner/LS (Stamford) **G2** | – | – | – | I |
43 High Ridge Road (Summer St.), 961-1400
Fairfield County's biggest, glitziest and newest diner has been packed to the gills virtually 24 hours a day since it opened; big portions and low prices are part of the reason, plus a nine-page menu that warrants a Dewey decimal number on size alone; regulars say stick with the tried-and-true diner fare and Greek specialties.

Butterfield's* (West Hartford) **B6** | 20 | 20 | 19 | $25 |
971 Farmington Ave. (S. Main St.), 231-1922
U – With an Eclectic menu and well-prepared food, this West Hartford eatery is building a following for its "simple", "quality" food in a whimsical setting; reasonable prices, decent service and a patio for summer dining are pluses.

Cafe Christina/S (Westport) **F3** | – | – | – | M |
1 Main St. (Boston Post Rd.), 221-7950
Located in Westport's spectacularly renovated former town library, this newcomer takes on the chef-owner's original regional Italian food; breathtaking murals and decorative artwork serve as a backdrop; convenience and moderate prices help make this a hit.

CAFE DU BEC FIN | 24 | 18 | 21 | $41 |
(Old Greenwich) **G1**
199 Sound Beech Ave. (Arcadia Rd.), 637-4447
M – "Top-notch food", including "wonderful soups", "awesome seafood" and desserts, wins fans for this Contemporary French, with its relaxed Provençal "charm"; though a few feel it's "expensive" and "pretentious", most surveyors say the "interesting menu" and wine list make this "worth the price."

Cannery Cafe, The*/S (Canaan) **A2** | 23 | 16 | 19 | $27 |
85 Main St. (bet. Rtes. 7 & 44), 824-7333
U – A "gem in Connecticut's NW corner", this "unexpected find" is praised for its "imaginative" American menu with a slightly Southern slant, along with "cute" decor, "friendly" service and a "good selection of American wines"; though a "little spotty", it's "always a good value."

Capers*/S (Brookfield) **D3** | 15 | 17 | 16 | $24 |
Rolling Wood Plaza, 265 Federal Rd. (bet. Rte. 133 & White Turkey Rd.), 775-1625
M – The reasonably priced "Californian cuisine" can be either "pleasant" or "ordinary" here, but we hear "the chef is incredible when he chooses to be creative"; the "pretty Brookfield setting", "young, upbeat staff" and "fresh pesto pizza" get extra mentions.

Connecticut

Capitol Fish House | 19 | 17 | 18 | $29 |
Restaurant (Hartford) **B6**
391 Main St. (Capital Ave.), 724-3370
*U – The seafood at this convenient Downtowner is
"sometimes outstanding, other times just good", but prices
are always sensible; heads-up service complements "nice
surroundings" in a "restored 19th-century hotel."*

Carbone's Ristorante (Hartford) **B6** | 22 | 17 | 20 | $30 |
588 Franklin Ave. (Goodrich St.), 296-9646
*U – This family-owned "old-world Southern Italian" is a
50-year-old local "landmark", still offering "flashes of
brilliance" and a great "veal parmigiana"; though a few
grouse that they "need to shake things up", most cite
the "nice service", "pleasant" decor and "good typical"
"homestyle" food at "decent" prices.*

CAVEY'S (Manchester) **B7** | 26 | 24 | 23 | $44 |
45 E. Center St. (Main St.), 643-2751
*U – Two restaurants in one: a cellar-level "formal
French" with a prix fixe menu, and an upstairs "informal
Italian" with a "pleasant" Mediterranean mien; the
"consistently excellent", if "highly priced", French food
gets better notices, but "warm and gracious service", an
"excellent wine list" and "very good Italian" ain't bad,
either; stellar jazz on weekends wins cellar applause.*

Centro/S | 20 | 20 | 19 | $28 |
(Fairfield) **F3**, 1435 Post Rd. (Reef Rd.), 255-1210
(Greenwich) **G1**, 328 Pemberwick Rd. (Glenville Rd.),
531-5514
*U – "Lots of beautiful people" are even happier now that
they can make reservations at this "California-ish"
Fairfield trattoria and its younger Greenwich sister; our
surveyors like both of these "bright and lively" "gathering
places", where "chic" food is matched by "whimsical",
"informal" decor, "good value" and "friendly service."*

C'est Si Bon/S (Greenwich) **G1** | 19 | 16 | 17 | $28 |
151 Greenwich Ave. (Lewis St.), 869-1901
*M – A "nice bistro sort of place", this central Greenwich
"bakery and charcuterie" is a "classic ladies-who-lunch
spot", also handy for "snacks" and "dessert and coffee";
complaints focus on the "snooty" "all-French waiters",
and a few folks feel it's pricey for "small portions."*

Chale Ipanema Restaurant/S | – | – | – | M |
(Hartford) **B6**
452 Wethersfield Ave. (Meadow St.), 296-2120
*One of the few local sources of authentic Brazilian and
Portuguese cuisine, and a great addition to the ethnic
restaurant scene in Hartford; fans acknowledge the
"pleasant staff" and "great food" at moderate prices, but
dismiss the storefront decor.*

Charles Bistro*/S (New Milford) **C3** | 21 | 17 | 18 | $30 |
51 Bank St. (bet. Main & Railroad Sts.), 355-3266
U – "Surprisingly good" "French bistro food" in an offbeat storefront describes this attractive restaurant and its "good presentation" of such classic favorites as onion soup and roast duck; it's "charming for lunch" – and open for dinner Wednesday through Saturday.

Chart House, The/S | 16 | 20 | 17 | $29 |
(Greenwich) **G1**, 3 River Rd. (Post Rd.), 661-2128
(Chester) **D6**, 129 W. Main St. (Rte. 9), 526-9898
(Simsbury) **A5**, 4 Hartford Rd. (Rte. 10), 658-1118
M – "Great ambiance" and "beautiful settings" are the main attractions at these three locations of an "informal" national seafood-and-steak chain, but while the service is "enthusiastic" and the food's "good for a chain", most surveyors call the "basic" menu just "average."

Chef Martin/S (Branford) **F6** | – | – | – | M |
899 W. Main St., Rte. 1 (Shore Beach Rd.), 488-7668
The "unique menu", "attentive" service and a "sweet" setting make fans for this "attractive" little Contemporary American–Eclectic; prices are modest, and even those who find the cooking "uneven" agree "Martin tries hard."

Chez Pierre*/S (Stafford Spring) **A8** | 18 | 19 | 19 | $41 |
111 W. Main St. (bet. Rtes. 32 & 190), 684-5826
U – This longtime Tolland County Classic French combines "good food with good service" in a homey setting; "the greatest lamb dishes" get special mention; N.B. this Chez Pierre is not related to Westport's.

Chez Pierre Bistro (Westport) **F3** | 20 | 18 | 19 | $34 |
146 Main St. (bet. Elm & Myrtle Sts.), 227-5295
M – Any place that can offer "consistently good" French bistro food for 35 years "has to be admired", especially with the new less-expensive menu; whether it's "comfortable" or "fossilized" is your call, but loyalists say this "longtime favorite" offers "friendly service" and decent value in a "convenient" attractive Downtown location.

China Pavilion/S (Rocky Hill) **B7** | 20 | 17 | 17 | $19 |
1860 Silas Deane Hwy. (Rte. 91, exit 24), 257-9219
U – "Best Chinese for miles" sums up the sentiment on this suburban Hartford favorite; "very nice decor" and accommodating service are a foil for "good food at fair prices"; weekend dim sum is an added enticement.

Connecticut | F | D | S | C |

Christoper Martin's/S | 19 | 17 | 18 | $29 |
(New Haven) **E5**
860 State St. (Clark St.), 776-8835
M – "Light, bright and amiable", this "busy bar and restaurant" attracts a "faithful clientele" with a "consistent" American-Continental menu and "pleasant" service; critics say it's a "bar that should serve drinks only" – the food's "just ok."

Christopher's Restaurant/S | 17 | 18 | 18 | $28 |
(Brookfield) **D3**
834 Federal St., Rte. 7 (Rte. 25), 775-4409
M – The "wonderful, romantic atmosphere" in the "wilds of Connecticut" gets more huzzahs than the Contemporary American food, which ranges from "innovative" to "fair"; "cozy" fireplaces and access to "the Brookfield Craft Center" make this "nice old house" worth a visit.

Ciaobella/S (Greenwich) **G1** | – | – | – | M |
1309 E. Putnam Ave. (I-95, exit 5), 637-1155
A "brand-new" Italian along the Post Road north of town wins praise for "fresh, well-prepared pastas", plus "tasty" variations on Traditional Italian classics, at prices that won't break the bank; the building has been "tastefully remodeled and landscaped."

Cobble Cookery, The/S (Kent) **B2** | – | – | – | I |
Kent Green Shopping Ctr., Kent Green (off Rte. 7), 927-3393
Open only for lunch and informal tea, this delightful gourmet shop fronts a bright, blue-and-white French Provincial cafe that serves a small but appealing selection of light sandwiches and soups; a great place for a "good, simple lunch" or "takeout" – "try the cheeses"; BYO.

Cobb's Mill Inn/S (Weston) **E3** | 15 | 24 | 18 | $34 |
12 Old Mill Rd. (intersection Rtes. 53 & 57), 227-7221
M – Its New England cuisine is "old-fashioned" at best, but the "spectacular" pond-and-waterfall setting is the "real draw" for this rural "18th-century mill"; critics say "you can't eat the water wheel", but "sentimental" fans endure the "ordinary food" for the "dream location."

Columbus Park | 22 | 14 | 18 | $28 |
Trattoria Italiana (Stamford) **G2**
205 Main St. (Columbus Square), 967-9191
U – "Noise" and "long waits" come with the territory at this highly touted "Tuscan" that's "worth it for the food", especially the "fresh pasta specials"; a "friendly ambiance", like "being in Florence", makes this a "good place to take a date" or make a deal over lunch.

Conde's Club America | 19 | 18 | 18 | $33 |
(Old Greenwich) **G1**
Hyatt Regency Greenwich, 1800 E. Putnam Ave.
(Soundbeach Ave.), 637-1234 x56
*M – The glitzy Hyatt on the Stamford-Greenwich line
has "done a good job" proving that hotel restaurants can
be "better than you'd expect"; the old Italian menu in this
dinner-only dining room has been replaced by a Modern
Regional American and Continental one at slightly lower
prices, but the elegant decor remains the same.*

Congress Rotisserie/S | 22 | 16 | 18 | $20 |
(Hartford) **B6**
7 Maple Ave. (Jefferson St.), 560-1965
*U – "Always crowded" and "noisy" describes this
high-energy Downtown spot that does a land-office
lunch business, thanks to "staggering portions" of New
American fare; an upbeat black-and-white setting
backdrops well-prepared "great-value" food.*

COPPER BEECH INN/S | 24 | 25 | 24 | $41 |
(Ivoryton) **E7**
Copper Beech Inn, 46 Main St. (Rte. 9), 767-0330
*U – A "lovely location" near the Goodspeed Theater,
"white-glove service" and "delightful" Country French
food have made this "elegant, expensive" old landmark
a "retreat" and "a page out of dining history"; though
critics call it "stuffy", with "uneven" food, for most this is
a "sophisticated", "first-class restaurant."*

Costa del Sol*/S (Hartford) **B6** | 22 | 21 | 24 | $25 |
Monte Carlo Plaza, 901 Wethersfield Ave. (I-91), 296-1714
*U – "Very tasty" Spanish food, especially the tapas, and
exceptional service sum up this reasonably priced
Hartford eatery that's a culinary journey "back a couple
of centuries" to the grace and charm of old Spain – as
long as you overlook the shopping-plaza setting.*

DA PIETRO'S (Westport) **F3** | 27 | 19 | 24 | $46 |
36 Riverside Ave. (bet. I-95 & Post Rd.), 454-1213
*U – The "extraordinary" Northern Italian and Modern
French food served at this tiny "charmer" is "up to NYC
standards" (with prices to match), especially the
"fantastic risotto", "wonderful rack of lamb" and
"exceptional" service; complaints center on "small,
cramped quarters" and "high noise levels."*

Derosa's/S (Westport) **F3** | 17 | 13 | 17 | $24 |
577 Riverside Ave. (Rte. 1), 227-7596
*M – "Huge portions" of "well-priced", "better-than-
average" Italian food and proximity to the Westport
station account for the "commuter mobs" at this "busy,
noisy joint" whose fans "go for the veal Florentine",
pastas and garlic bread.*

Diana Restaurant/S (Groton) **E9** | – | – | – | M |

Fashion Plaza, 970 Fashion Plaza, Rte. 1 (Paquonnack Rd.), 449-8468

Lebanese food is rare enough in Connecticut, so when the food is "terrific" and reasonably priced, you've got a winner – even if there's "something missing in the ambiance" and service at this shopping-center ethnic.

Di Fiore's Ristorante*/S | 23 | 17 | 19 | $26 |
(Hartford) **B6**

395 Franklin Ave. (Preston St.), 296-2123

U – "Popular" even among many local Italians, this likable spot features chef-owner Don Di Fiore's "delicious food" served with style at reasonable prices; ok decor and a takeout menu are added attractions.

Diorio Restaurant and Bar* | 25 | 21 | 23 | $27 |
(Waterbury) **D4**

231 Bank St. (Grand St.), 754-5111

U – A local Holiday Inn seems an unlikely location for an "excellent" Northern Italian, but surveyors who find it give this promising yearling high marks for "fabulous fare", a "bright and airy" setting and top-notch service.

DOC'S/SX (New Preston) **B3** | 26 | 10 | 17 | $27 |

62 Flirtation Ave. (Rte. 45), 868-9415

U – There's "no pretense, no frills" at this "tiny shack", but Doc does "wonderful things with spices and fresh herbs" to make everything "excellent" – from his "antipasto bread and olives" to imaginative pizzas and other "homemade" Italian specialties; "everyone who is young should try it at least once"; BYO.

Dolce Italian Bistro/S (Stamford) **G2** | 19 | 21 | 17 | $34 |

78 Southfield Ave. (Greenwich Ave.), 325-2007

M – The drive through a dicey neighborhood rewards diners with "very good Italian food" ("lots of garlic"), "dramatic decor" and a "great view" through expansive windows "overlooking Stamford harbor"; but some think the food has "slipped" and is "a bit expensive."

Elms Inn, The/S (Ridgefield) **E2** | 19 | 20 | 20 | $40 |

The Elms Inn, 500 Main St. (Gilbert St.), 438-2541

M – "Location is everything" at this "elegant" old Colonial inn; though many think the Continental-American food "had its moments" years ago and is now "nothing to write home about", loyal fans still adore the "old-fashioned" cuisine, "friendly service" and "charming setting."

Fagan's Riverview (Stratford) **F4** | 18 | 17 | 18 | $28 |
946 Ferry Blvd. (Rte. 1), 378-6560
*U – Since 1955, this "old standard" has served seafood
and "American favorites" that "might be the best in the
area" – though "still not much" in the imagination
department; critics say the ambiance is "getting a little
tired", but the water view is excellent; its "weekday
early-bird specials are a real bargain."*

Fiddlers/S (Chester) **D6** | – | – | – | M |
4 Water St. (town center), 526-3210
*It wasn't on our questionnaire, but respondents clued us
in to this popular destination for dinner before a show at
the Goodspeed; the reasonably priced French-accented
menu features "good fresh fish" and shellfish;
weekdays, businesspeople find it a fine lunch stop too.*

FINE BOUCHE/S (Centerbrook) **E7** | 26 | 23 | 25 | $42 |
78 Main St. (off Rte. 9, exit 3), 767-1277
*U – "The chef is a master" at this "excellent" little French
restaurant near the Goodspeed, with "outstanding" service,
an "exceptional wine list" and "romantic" ambiance; there
are several small dining rooms in this restored old house;
there's even an "excellent" $22.50 pre-theater menu.*

500 Blake Street Cafe/LS | 20 | 18 | 18 | $31 |
(New Haven) **E5**
500 Blake St. (Whalley Ave.), 387-0500
*M – "Good but never great", this popular New Haven
Italian with its "20th-century saloon" decor is as much a
"watering hole" for the "noisy crowd at happy hour" as it
is a restaurant; fans like the "bright", "Victorian"
atmosphere and recommend the "great Sunday
brunch"; critics say "it takes itself too seriously"; BYO.*

5 Mile River Grille/S (Rowayton) **G2** | 18 | 17 | 17 | $28 |
148 Rowayton Ave. (Rte. 136), 855-0025
*M – "Nestled in the quaint boating village" of Rowayton is
this "neighborhood" place, with an "imaginative, simple"
Contemporary American menu; surveyors describe a
"quiet", "comfortable" setting and a "nice staff", but most
think the chef changes have made the food "hit or miss."*

Fjord Fisheries Restaurant/S | – | – | – | M |
(Stamford) **G2**
Sportsplex Health Club, 43 Brawnhouse Rd. (I-95, exit 6),
325-0255
*It's only logical that a store that sells superior seafood
should also do a good job cooking it, and this offshoot of
a Cos Cob retailer is doing brilliantly; you can't lose wth
such beautifully presented, moderate-priced Norwegian
classics as smorgasbord platter, but even prosaic
American specialties like clam chowder and fried fish
show expertise; call ahead for directions.*

	F	D	S	C

Connecticut

Fortune Village Chinese | – | – | – | M |
Restaurant/S (Branford) **E5**
120 N. Main St. (Cedar St.), 481-3568
Surveyors report "very good" Chinese food and "lots of it" at this attractive Branford ethnic; "fine" service and "good value" make this "something special."

FRANK PEPE | 26 | 11 | 13 | $15 |
PIZZERIA/SX (New Haven) **E5**
157 Wooster St. (Brown St.), 865-5762
U – New Haven residents, Yalies and most of the state call this "pizza-lover's nirvana" "the best in the world"; expect "surly waitresses" and "long lines", but also plan to enjoy "phenomenal pizza" with the "crispiest crust" around from "old-time coal-burning brick ovens"; some will argue that pizza was invented here.

Frank's Restaurant (Hartford) **B6** | 16 | 15 | 16 | $28 |
185 Asylum St. (Trumbull St.), 527-9291
U – An "old standard" for generations of diners, this Downtown Italian pleases most with its "lively" ambiance and "varied menu" of moderately priced traditional favorites; it's handy for "business dining", though "spotty service" can be a problem.

Freshfields/S (West Cornwall) **B2** | 20 | 21 | 20 | $32 |
Rte. 128 (Rte. 7), 672-6601
U – The name says it all: "fresh ingredients and a fresh approach" to Contemporary American cooking in a "delightful country" setting; it's somewhat "expensive" but "worth it" – "go in the summer and sit on the porch", "try brunch on the dock" or "stop on a day trip for lunch."

Gaetano's Restaurant (Hartford) **B6** | 17 | 18 | 19 | $29 |
Hartford Civic Ctr. Plaza (bet. Trumbull & Asylum Sts.), 249-1629
U – This Downtown Italian with its busy bar has become a popular, "chichi hangout" thanks to affordable "homestyle food", decent service and "nice" quarters.

Gail's Station House/S | 20 | 13 | 18 | $20 |
(Ridgefield) **E2**
378 Main St. (Barley Ave.), 438-9775
U – "Known far and wide" for the "best breakfast in Connecticut", this Ridgefield Eclectic also serves "adequate" to "yummy" lunches and dinners in a "simple" setting; with "huge portions" and "fabulous homemade baked goods", it's like "going to Grandma's on Sunday morning" – except she's less "disorganized."

F	D	S	C

Ganga*/S (Norwalk) G2
18	13	18	$25

41 Wall St. (Isaac St.), 838-0660
M – "If you like Indian food, this is the place to go" for a "diverse and widely varied menu" of "nicely prepared" vegetarian and "Northern and Southern" specialties; "attentive" service makes up for lack of atmosphere.

Gates Restaurant/S
18	18	17	$25

(New Canaan) **F2**
10 Forest St. (East Ave.), 966-8666
M – A "consistent favorite" with "ladies who lunch", it's the place for "New Wave salads" and "light American food" served in a garden setting; at night a "noisier", "terminally yuppie crowd" takes over, and service can be "erratic."

Giovanni's Sericus Steakhouse/S
–	–	–	M

(Stamford) **G2**, 1297 Long Ridge Rd. (Merritt Pkwy.), 322-8870
(Darien) **G2**, 2748 Boston Post Rd. (I-95), 325-9979
At both addresses, this Italian-style steakhouse offers simple grilled meats and fish plus large portions of pasta and American side dishes; try the "twin lobsters if you have a hearty appetite."

GOLDEN LAMB BUTTERY/X (Brooklyn) B10
25	28	26	$46

Bush Hill Rd. (Wolf Den Rd.), 774-4423
U – This "stylish converted barn" gets the highest decor rating in the state, but the "fabulous country dining" and well-paced service fare almost as well at this "romantic", "out-of-the-way" but "out-of-this-world" spot; the $55 prix fixe menu features "simply prepared" but delicious Classic American dishes and vegetables straight from the garden.

Great American Cafe/S
15	18	15	$17

(Glastonbury) **C6**
Somerset Sq., 140 Glastonbury Blvd. (Main St.), 657-8057
M – "A great happy hour crowd" frequents this "loud but fun" Glastonbury hangout where the "trendy" American food can be either "dreadful" or "interesting", and the service can seem stressed out; however, "patio dining" and a lively nightclub help its popularity.

Greenwich Harbor Inn/S
14	15	14	$28

(Greenwich)
(fka The Showboat) **G1**
Greenwich Harbor Inn, 500 Steamboat Rd. (Arch St.), 661-9800
M – Our surveyors wonder if this waterside hotel dining room, under new management, "can ever recover from its old reputation"; completely renovated, it now features a "beautiful outdoor patio" where "the view's the thing"; as for the Contemporary American food, improvements are noted, but it still has got a long way to go.

Gregory's (Fairfield) **F3** | 21 | 17 | 21 | $32 |
1599 Post Rd. (Beach Rd.), 259-7417
*M – Our respondents can't make up their minds about
this "creative" "American bistro" in a "small and plain"
"narrow storefront"; friends say the food is "always
good" for "feasting", and there's a "comfortable" setting
and "personalized service"; foes, on the other hand, call
it "too pricey" and say it's "solid but nothing special."*

Griswold Inn, The/S (Essex) **E7** | 18 | 22 | 19 | $31 |
The Griswold Inn, 36 Main St. (Rte. 9), 767-1776
*M – It's hard not to love "the Griz", a "quaint",
200-year-old Essex inn "steeped in nautical history";
"Sunday hunt breakfasts", entertaining "sea chanteys"
and Christmas festivities attract "history buffs" and
"tourists", but the "heavy" Traditional American food gets
mixed notices: from "so-so" to "surprisingly good."*

Hacienda don Emilio (Stamford) **G2** | 16 | 16 | 17 | $23 |
222 Summer St. (Main St.), 324-0577
*M – The recent arrival of a "terrific" new chef should
"greatly improve" the food at this "interesting" Mexican;
its "lively", "kitschy", "faux Mexican" decor and "intrusive
mariachi" music can still "get on your nerves."*

Harry's TX Barbecue & AZ Grill/S | 17 | 9 | 14 | $17 |
(Stamford) **G2**
934 Hope St. (Bennett St.), 348-7427
*M – "Harry tries hard" at this "busy" "BBQ joint" filled
with "families and lots of kids"; its fans would make a
detour for the "killer beans and Carolina pork", but the
less-convinced say that, though "cheap", it's "cramped",
"a bit of a dive" and "certainly not Texas."*

Hay Day Cafe/S (Ridgefield) **E2** | 21 | 18 | 18 | $27 |
21 Governor St. (Main St.), 438-2344
*M – This "cute" new cafe has been added to the retail
"country place" where Connecticut cognoscenti shop for
"pricey" but "high-quality" "gourmet" food; with somewhat
"reasonable" prices and "lovely, creative" American food,
it's "nifty" for a "pleasant lunch" or brunch.*

Hearthstone Restaurant* | 16 | 18 | 17 | $33 |
(Hartford) **B6**
678 Maple Ave. (Adelaide St.), 246-8814
*M – An institution for 50 years, this old-line Downtowner
still attracts a following with its Continental-style
steakhouse menu and attractive, traditional decor; to
some it "has seen better days."*

Heavenly Hog | 23 | 12 | 16 | $19 |
Restaurant*/S (Manchester) **B7**
520 Center St. (McKee St.), 649-1212
*M – BBQ fans for miles around are addicted to the
"good", spicy-hot ribs served at this no-frills "eat-with-
your-fingers place"; takeout and delivery take the sting
out of the indifferent decor and service.*

HOMESTEAD INN/S | 24 | 26 | 24 | $48 |
(Greenwich) **G1**
The Homestead Inn, 420 Field Point Rd. (Horse Neck
Lane), 869-7500
*U – "Classic French cuisine" in a "quintessential New
England country inn" makes this "consistently one of the
best" for a "special-occasion or expense-account"
dinner; though it's "expensive", the "romantic" setting,
"excellent" food and solid service justify the tab.*

Hop Brook Restaurant/S | 16 | 23 | 19 | $29 |
(Simsbury) **A5**
77 West St. (Rtes. 10 & 167), 651-0267
*U – The "romantic" location of this "charming"
"reincarnation of an old mill" is "worth a lot" – especially
if you snag a "window seat over the brook"; the
Regional American food may be "not so great", but the
"fabulous views" are really the main course.*

HOPKINS INN/SX (New Preston) **B3** | 22 | 24 | 21 | $34 |
Hopkins Inn, 22 Hopkins Rd. (Rte. 45), 868-7295
*U – A "beautiful natural setting" on Lake Waramaug and
"amiable service" make this inn one of the area's "nicest
dining experiences"; though its "well-executed" Swiss-
and Austrian-accented food may seem a "bit heavy",
"where else can you enjoy old-fashioned extravagant
desserts" along with a lakeside sunset.*

Hot Tamales* (Hartford) **B6** | 18 | 18 | 16 | $23 |
1 Union Place (Asylum St.), 247-5544
*U – Early reports on the spicy SW food and lively decor
at this new 'in' spot are positive, though it's not for the
faint of heart – "you can smell the garlic for miles"; but
sweet-tooths say it's "a great place for a big dessert";
add low prices, patio dining and live entertainment.*

Hot Tomato's/S (Hartford) **B6** | 21 | 17 | 17 | $23 |
1 Union Pl. (Asylum St.), 249-5100
*U – Related to Hot Tamales, this "hip" hot spot has fans
applauding its "great bistro-style Italian cooking" and
"contemporary setting"; the place has "unexpected
quality despite its cutesy name."*

Connecticut | F | D | S | C |

Hunan U.S. 1/S (Norwalk) **G2** | 16 | 12 | 16 | $19 |
80 Connecticut Ave. (U.S. 1), 838-9111
*U – Though there's "not much else around", the
consensus on this Szechuan is "ok" but "nothing
inspired"; "low prices and good service" make it a place
to "bring the kids" "when you're in the neighborhood."*

Il Falco (Stamford) **G2** | 23 | 20 | 22 | $37 |
59 Broad St. (bet. Summer St. & Washington Blvd.),
327-0002
*M – Holding its own against an onslaught of
competitors, this six-year-old Downtowner wins the
hearts of regulars with its "excellent Northern Italian
food", "solid" service and "lovely", "intimate" setting;
though a few think the "expensive", "ambitious" menu is
"unremarkable", most call it a "favorite."*

Il Forno Ristorante/S (Stamford) **G2** | 22 | 23 | 19 | $31 |
45 Atlantic St. (Broad St.), 357-8882
*M – "Spectacular decor", like "dining in an outdoor
piazza", draws "crowds" who like this Italian newcomer
for upscale business lunches, "homestyle" dinners and
late-evening pizzas; the "service still needs polishing",
but high scores confirm this as a "wonderful addition to
the dining scene."*

Il Mulino (Stamford) **G2** | 19 | 15 | 18 | $32 |
Springdale Shopping Ctr., 1078 Hope St. (Camp Ave.),
322-3300
*M – "Tucked away" in a nondescript plaza, this "not
fancy" Italian convinces loyal fans that it's "worth a trip"
with "basic" fare that "can be excellent", if "a bit
expensive"; critics warn that the cooking and service are
uneven – "you just never know."*

Inn at Gwyn Careg/S (Pomfret) **A9** | – | – | – | E |
Inn at Gwyn Careg, 426 Mashamoquett Rd. (Rte. 44),
928-7768
*This "idyllic" country inn deserves attention for its "lovely",
if pricey, Continental food and beautiful setting amidst
magnificent gardens in a carefully restored 1920s estate;
gracious service completes the elegant picture.*

Inn at Ridgefield, The/S | 22 | 22 | 22 | $44 |
(Ridgefield) **E2**
20 W. Main St., Rte. 35 (Rte. 33), 438-8282
*U – The town of Ridgefield makes a "peaceful" "Colonial
setting" for a "dignified" meal in this "charming old inn";
the traditional Continental cuisine with a "German
influence" is "consistently elegant", and the service
always "attentive"; critics who fault "stuffy" ambiance
and high prices are overwhelmingly outvoted.*

Connecticut | F | D | S | C |

Inn at Woodstock Hill/S | – | – | – | M |
(South Woodstock) **A9**
94 Plaine Hill Rd. (Rtes. 169 & 171), 928-0528
Located in a converted carriage house on a beautiful
rural estate, this little-known Continental–Traditional
American is best appreciated in summer, when visitors
can enjoy the outdoor deck; winter is for Sunday buffet
brunches in the fire-lit dining room.

Inn on Lake Waramaug/S | 17 | 21 | 19 | $34 |
(New Preston) **B3**
The Inn on Lake Waramaug, 107 North Shore Rd.
(Rte. 45), 868-0563
M – "Just the place" to enjoy an "autumn day or a
snowy evening", say those who love this "charming
country inn" and Contemporary American restaurant
"high above" Lake Waramaug; beyond that, our raters
can't agree if the food is "pedestrian" or "innovative."

JEAN-LOUIS (Greenwich) **G1** | 27 | 23 | 25 | $54 |
61 Lewis St. (bet. Mason St. & Greenwich Ave.), 622-8450
U – "First-class" "across the board" is this "fabulous"
Contemporary French, the "masterful" creation of
"chef's chef" Jean-Louis Gerin; an "intimate and
elegant" room is the setting for "light and exquisite"
food, "superb service" and a "top-flight" wine list; it's
"deluxe in every way" – including prices, but "worth it."

Jetstream's Cafe/S (Avon) | 15 | 20 | 16 | $16 |
(fka Airstream's Roadside Cafe) **B5**
52 E. Main St., Rte. 44 (Rte. 10), 677-9026
U – Upbeat, colorful decor is the highlight at this "great
family restaurant"; with its informal American food at
moderate prices and "wonderful patio" for
warm-weather dining, it's "welcoming to all ages."

Kansas City Bar-B-Q Heaven*/S | 16 | 8 | 14 | $22 |
(East Haven) **E5**
913 Foxon Rd. (Rose St.), 466-2222
M – Barbecue is always a hot topic, and this "pork
synthesizer" is no exception; fans ignore the decor and
go for the "superb" ribs and "delectable brisket", but
some suggest you "save for a ticket to KC instead."

Khan's Mongolian Garden/S | 15 | 12 | 14 | $20 |
(Stamford) **G2**
135 Bedford St. (bet. Broad & Spring Sts.), 975-0209
U – "Don't blame the cook since you did it yourself" at
this low-atmosphere Chinese where diners choose the
raw ingredients for a personalized "stir-fry" by showman
chefs; whether the concept is "silly" or "fun" is up to you,
but it's a "good value", "especially with hungry kids."

Kismet*/S (Ridgefield) **E2** | 21 | 14 | 18 |$22|
296 Ethan Allen Hwy. (Rte. 102), 431-1211
U – In an "unlikely location" in outer Ridgefield, this "very friendly", very "authentic" Indian pleases surveyors with its "excellent, well-priced" food and "wonderful sitar player"; the decor is just ok, but the $9.95 Sunday buffet "brunch is the best."

Kotobuki/S (Stamford) **G2** | 22 | 13 | 18 |$24|
457 Summer St. (Broad St.), 359-4747
U – In an easy-to-miss spot next to Caldor, this "no-atmosphere" "neighborhood-style" spot is arguably "the best Japanese in Stamford", and certainly a bargain for "authentic", "fresh and delicious" food.

Kujaku Japanese | 22 | 17 | 19 |$29|
Restaurant*/S (Stamford) **G2**
84 W. Park Pl. (Summer St.), 357-0281
U – "Fresh sushi", "very good hibachi" cooking and "clean, modern premises" add to the popularity of this Downtown Stamford Japanese, handy for a working lunch or shopping break; extra kudos for professional service and specials that are "always the best."

L'ABBEE/S (New Canaan) **F2** | 25 | 21 | 23 |$45|
62 Main St. (Locust Ave.), 972-6181
U – This "small gem" may be a "little too precious" even for New Canaan, but fans think "heaven has a kitchen like this" one, with its "delightful", "imaginative" New American food and suave service; "very tiny" but "lovingly decorated", it can be "stuffy and cramped" at peak times, so go during the week; "small portions" make it "rather pricey", but gourmet takeout saves tips.

La Bretagne (Stamford) **G2** | 23 | 16 | 22 |$39|
2010 W. Main St. (bet. Havermeyer Lane & West Ave.), 324-9539
M – Lots of loyal fans are aging right along with this popular Stamford French that still receives high marks for "authentic, consistent" food and "no surprises"; they overlook the "tired" decor that "needs updating" and concentrate on the "good old-fashioned" food and service at this "top suburban choice."

La Maison Indochine/S | 22 | 14 | 18 |$34|
(Greenwich) **G1**
107-109 Greenwich Ave., 2nd fl. (Lewis St.), 869-2689
U – "Hokey decor" and a "lousy" second floor location belie the "first-rate" Vietnamese food served here; despite prices judged "expensive" for an ethnic, "friendly service" and the subtly "exotic" mix of French technique and Oriental ingredients create an "interesting change of pace."

La Provence (South Norwalk) **F3** | 21 | 18 | 19 | $35 |
86 Washington St. (Main St.), 855-8958
M – A recent change in chef/ownership has caused the food to slip at this SoNo charmer that's "not quite Provence" but still an "excellent French bistro", with improved, "unpretentious" service; "it doesn't get any better than this for the money", since the prix fixe lunch is $12 and dinner is only $19.50 for "good French food in pleasant, country-style surroundings."

La Strada (Greenwich) **G1** | 23 | 21 | 21 | $46 |
48 W. Putnam Ave. (Greenwich Ave.), 629-8484
M – Supporters of this "very pricey" and "sophisticated" "Manhattan-like" Northern Italian "can't get over the fact" that it shares its parking lot with a bowling alley, but they praise the "excellent" food and "bright", "splashy" decor; to critics, however, "typical NYC" means "overpriced and pretentious" in a "cold and cavernous" room.

La Trattoria at the Redding | 19 | 21 | 19 | $34 |
Station*/S (West Redding) **D2**
4 Long Ridge Rd. (at the train station), 938-9160
M – Enthusiastic new owners have kept the "gorgeous" country Mediterranean look intact at this charming spot beside the West Redding station, but the transition from French to Italian has been less smooth; some report "good food" and a "very cheerful staff", while others say the "surroundings are better than the food."

La Villa Restaurant (Westport) **F3** | – | – | – | M |
3 Bay St. (Post Rd.), 454-1312
Located in a plain-Jane storefront, "this small, casual", newish Northern Italian hasn't attracted much of a following yet; food reports range from "surprisingly good" to "disappointing", but prices are moderate and the staff aims to please; wine and beer only.

Le Bistro des Amis (Westport) **F3** | – | – | – | M |
7 Sconset Square (Post Rd.), 226-2647
French bistro cooking has come to Westport with style and reasonable prices at this new Downtown spot; attractive decor and solid skills in the kitchen promise many friends who'll stick around; don't miss the desserts.

Le Bon Coin/S (New Preston) **B3** | 20 | 19 | 21 | $36 |
Rte. 202 (Rte. 47), 868-7763
M – "Country charm" and "Traditional French cooking" create a fine dining experience in this "lovely" little spot in Litchfield County; though a few have encountered "poor food" and would "pass it by", most say "good food and service" make this a local "favorite."

F	D	S	C

Le Chambord (Westport) **F3** | 23 | 19 | 21 |$40 |

1572 Post Rd. E. (Maple Ave.), 255-2654
*M – Not a place for innovation, this "formal", 23-year-old
"classic" specializes in "solid French food the old way",
including roast duck, Dover sole and Grand Marnier
soufflé; "hand-kissing" service and a $22.95 prix fixe
dinner that may be one of Westport's best bargains help
make up for a somewhat "shopworn dining room."*

Le Marmiton/S (New Milford) **C3** | – | – | – | E |

373 Litchfield Rd. (Rte. 7), 350-2884
*Boosters who have tried this Litchfield County
newcomer "hope they make it", because the Classic
French "food is as delightful as the owners", and the
country French quarters in a pretty little white-clapboard
house are just as charming.*

Lemon Grass Thai Cuisine*/S | 22 | 16 | 19 |$24 |
(West Hartford) **B6**

7 S. Main St. (Farmington Ave.), 233-4405
*M – This well-rated and relatively inexpensive Thai wins
fans for its exotic ethnic specialties and overall "good"
eating; however, service may be haphazard, and it
won't win any decor prizes; wine and beer only.*

Leon's/S (New Haven) **E5** | 21 | 12 | 16 |$29 |

321 Washington Ave. (Howard Ave.), 777-5366
*M – Crowds still form "long, noisy lines" for the "huge
portions" of "hearty" "Southern-style" Italian food served
up at this '40s-era "old-world institution"; though the
outdated decor is "tacky" and the service "casual in the
extreme", "there's a reason it's been here so long."*

Lily's/SX (Canton) **B5** | – | – | – | M |

Rte. 44 West (Rte. 177), 693-8558
*Delicious home-cooked American meals from a changing
blackboard menu, eccentric decor, caring service and a
fun setting attract diners from all over the state; abandon
dieting and try the to-die-for biscuits, home-fried
potatoes or any other of the many items; P.S. weekend
breakfasts are a mob scene so get there early; BYO.*

Li's Brothers Inn*/S (Darien) **G2** | 19 | 17 | 21 |$20 |

Goodwives Shopping Ctr., 25-48 Old Kings Hwy. N.
(Rte. 1), 656-3550
*U – "Former NYers" "yearning to find" "dependable", "good-
value" Chinese food exult in this large, "convenient",
unexpectedly "pleasant" newcomer in a strip mall;
"unrushed service" is another reason to try it.*

Connecticut | F | D | S | C |

Little Kitchen, The/S | 22 | 14 | 17 | $21 |

(New Canaan) **F2**, 64 Main St. (Elm St.), 972-6881
(Westport) **F3**, 47 Main St. (off Post Rd.), 454-5540
*U – Both the Westport "storefront" takeout location and
the "small", "no-frills" New Canaan restaurant offer
"yummy" "China Sea cuisine", with a "great variety of
dishes" that includes Indonesian and Thai specialties;
service plus low prices add to this duo's appeal.*

Little Mark's Big Bar-B-Que | – | – | – | I |
(Vernon) **A7**
226 Talcottville Rd. (bet. Rtes. 30 & 83), 872-1410
*Though few have heard of it, this casual BBQ can't be
beat for good, messy food at great prices; early-bird
specials and a patio for summer dining are pluses.*

Lotus East Chinese | 16 | 12 | 15 | $22 |
Restaurant/S (Greenwich) **G1**
64 Greenwich Ave. (Post Rd.), 661-4181
*M – "Good for Greenwich residents but not worth a trip
from afar", this "typical Connecticut" Chinese offers
"absolutely predictable" but generally "good food"; decor
is "discouraging" and service "needs help", but a handy
location and fair prices provide a little compensation.*

Lotus Restaurant (Vernon) **A7** | – | – | – | M |
497 Talcottville Rd. (Merline Rd.), 871-8962
*Away from big-city hassles in rural Vernon is this
little-known Vietnamese serving "fine food" at fair prices;
with its "very good staff" and comfortable premises, this
unusual ethnic is worth looking into.*

MacKenzie's Old Ale House*/S | 19 | 17 | 17 | $21 |
(Bethel) **D2**
12 Depot Place (Greenwood Ave.), 748-3662
*M – "Real pub atmosphere" and a "warm welcome"
make this remodeled 1830 Victorian house a convivial
place for "a great variety of drinks" and solid, simple
American food; stick to the specialties (like homemade
pot pies) and you'll enjoy this "up-to-date tavern."*

MacKenzie's Redding | 18 | 21 | 19 | $27 |
Roadhouse/S (Redding) **E3**
406 Redding Rd., Rte. 53 (Rte. 107), 938-3388
*M – This "cozy" rebuilt roadhouse is popular for drinks
and dinner or Sunday brunch; the broad menu of "pub
fare" and New England specialties is "fine" and the
service is friendly, but the real attraction is the
"picturesque setting" with its "fireplaces and rustic" charm.*

Magnificent J's*/S (Stamford) **G2** | 17 | 19 | 16 | $31 |
Sheraton Stamford Hotel, 1 First Stamford Pl. (I-95, exit 7), 967-2222
M – The posh and "pretty" dining room of the Sheraton in Stamford has survived several cuisine changes, and now offers seafood and Contemporary American items; early reports on the latest incarnation are good.

Maison le Blanc (New Milford) **C3** | 23 | 20 | 22 | $37 |
218 Kent Rd., Rte. 7 (1 mile north of Rte. 202), 354-9931
U – Make a "pilgrimage from the city" to this charming restored circa-1775 "country inn" serving "delicious" "creative" French food in a "reasonable prix fixe format"; "good service" and a "warm setting" surrounded by gardens are why "word of mouth" on this place is strong.

Manero's Restaurant/S | 16 | 11 | 16 | $27 |
(Greenwich) **G1**
559 Steamboat Rd. (Railroad Ave.), 869-0049
M – Our surveyors differ on this "noisy" kid-crowded "landmark steakhouse"; fans love the "heapings" of "great steaks and chops", super "gorgonzola salad" and "real garlic bread" at this "value" for "the whole hungry family"; foes fault the "boring" food and "awful atmosphere" and say it "peaked in the '60s."

Mansion Clam House/S | 17 | 12 | 16 | $25 |
(Westport) **F3**
541 Riverside Ave. (Bridge St.), 454-7979
M – Three decades later, this "reliably good" standby near the Westport train station still offers "very New England" seafood in a "plain, informal setting"; though some grumble the "food isn't that great", loyalists clamor for "superb clam chowder", reasonably priced lobsters and the old-fashioned "fish fry" and say it's a "good place to take guests", especially in summer for patio dining.

Maria's Trattoria (Norwalk) **G2** | 22 | 11 | 17 | $17 |
172 Main St. (Rte. 123), 847-5166
M – A local "hole in the wall" with "excellent, fresh homestyle Italian food" that's so popular that "a wait in line" is the weekend rule; "variety with quality" and "good food for the money" are the draws; as Yogi Berra once said, "nobody goes there anymore – it's too crowded."

Mario's/S (Westport) **F3** | 18 | 11 | 16 | $25 |
36 Railroad Ave. (at the railroad station), 226-0308
U – "Commuters right off the train" pop across the street for drinks, prime rib and "well-prepared basic Italian food in extra-large portions", but it's just as "noisy and busy" on weekends thanks to "friendly service" and "reasonable prices" that make it "perfect for what it is": a "popular" "local hangout."

F	D	S	C

Mario The Baker (Stamford) **G2**　| – | – | – | I |
864 High Ridge Rd., Turn-of-River, 329-0440
Plain as plain can be, this pizzeria is one of the best in America with perfectly baked thin crusts and absolutely fresh ingredients drawing crowds at peak hours.

MAX-A-MIA/S (Avon) **B5**　| 25 | 19 | 21 | $26 |
Fairway Shops, 70 E. Main St., 677-6299
U – Upbeat, "fun atmosphere" and lively decor make this an informal, "favorite local place"; the "great focaccia and roasted garlic, pastas, and wood-fired oven-baked pizza" from the light, Contemporary Italian menu "can't be beat"; there's "always a wait" but "worth it."

Max on Main (Hartford) **B6**　| 23 | 20 | 21 | $33 |
205 Main St. (bet. Buckingham & Park Sts.), 522-2530
U – "A dressed-up version" of its relative, Max-A-Mia, this "sophisticated bistro" offers "more inventive and experimental" food that some rate "about the best north of NYC"; an "eager-to-please" staff and "good values" mean this "yuppie heaven" is among Hartford's finest.

MAYFLOWER INN/S　| 23 | 27 | 23 | $43 |
(Washington Depot) **C3**
Mayflower Inn, Rte. 47, 868-9466
U – The "proprietors haven't forgotten a thing" in renovating this fabulous 28-acre property, which may be "the best inn in Connecticut"; chef John Farnsworth's "imaginative food with an early American feeling", "attentive service", an "excellent wine list" and "picture-pretty grounds" make this "too beautiful to miss."

Meera*/S (Stamford) **G2**　| 18 | 11 | 16 | $20 |
227 Summer St. (bet. Main & Broad Sts.), 975-0477
U – Our surveyors split ranks on this Downtown Indian: "wonderfully prepared" vs. "not bad"; ultimately, this "inexpensive", "lower-end" storefront is "friendly but not fiery" and more convenient than driving all the way to NYC for something better.

MESON GALICIA/S (Norwalk) **F3**　| 25 | 23 | 23 | $35 |
10 Wall St. (East Ave.), 866-8800
U – The state's highest-rated Spaniard, this "sophisticate" in a renovated trolley house is a "dazzler", offering "la comida España as it should be"; "sensational" tapas, "excellent Spanish wines" and seafood, and "extremely friendly" service make this the place for a "top-notch" Iberian experience.

Mhai Thai/S (Greenwich) **G1** | 19 | 18 | 17 |$28 |
280 Railroad Ave. (Arch St.), 625-2602
M – "Tasty Thai food in a Buddha's garden" impresses
our surveyors, who report "succulent specials", a "good
variety of unusual dishes" and "fresh ingredients" in an
"interesting" setting; "reasonable prices" and pleasant, if
"slow", service make locals glad there's been a "Thai
invasion" in Greenwich.

MICHE-MACHE (South Norwalk) **G2** | 24 | 19 | 22 |$33 |
18 S. Main St. (Washington Ave.), 838-8605
U – "One of the best new restaurants around" is this
"hip", "trendy"-and-"knows-it" "hot spot" whose "cute
name" is a good indication of the "inventive"
Contemporary American food prepared by its "talented"
young chef-owner; "very popular with upwardly mobile
types", this attractive storefront has "good prices", a
"diverse wine list" and "lots of grilled specialties."

Mona Lisa/S (Stamford) **G2** | – | – | – | M |
133 Atlantic St. (Broad St.), 348-1070
Relocating to the 'burbs after several years in the Big
Apple, the owners of this promising newcomer have
turned a former jewelry store into an intimate, attractive
Italian restaurant; prices are modest and everything,
including breads and desserts, is homemade.

Monica's Restaurant | – | – | – | I |
(Stamford) **G2**
323 Shippan Ave. (Hanover St.), 359-0678
Not much on decor, this dinerlike Family place hidden
behind "Fish and Chips" serves up tasty home-cooking –
excellent homemade pasta, sandwiches, woups and the
best cheesecake in town; a real bargain, Monica's is
worth searching for.

Mooring, The/S (Mystic) **E10** | 14 | 17 | 15 |$29 |
Mystic Hilton, 20 Coogan Blvd. (off Rte. 27), 572-0731
U – Disgruntled patrons say this "great location" on the
river in historic Mystic "just misses", with so-so service
and "average seafood preparations"; fans say it "still hits
the mark for brunch", or just "go for drinks and the view."

Morgan/S (Greenwich) **G1** | 20 | 18 | 20 |$32 |
265 Glenville Rd. (Riversville Rd.), 531-5100
M – "Upbeat" and "New Yorky", this "trendy American
bistro" is "still fine", offering "consistently good food and
service" in a "lively", "noisy" setting; though detractors
say it's "cramped" and "unruly" and has "run out of
steam", solid scores are the bottom line.

Murasaki Japanese Restaurant/S | – | – | – | M |
(Simsbury) **A6**
Federal Green, 10 Wilcox St. (Rte. 10), 651-7929
*Those few who know of this likable little storefront
Japanese call it a "very friendly spot", with a "nice sushi
bar" plus "big portions" of well-prepared specialties; a
patio for summer dining is an extra; wine and beer only.*

Nistico's Red Barn (Westport) **F3** | 15 | 18 | 16 |$28 |
292 Wilton Rd. (Merritt Pkwy.), 222-9549
*M – This renovated "Yankee barn", "right off the Merritt", is
a "serious family noshing factory" and a "nice place to
meet someone"; large portions and "good value" can't
disguise the fact that the "meat-and-potatoes" Continental
food, though "always palatable", is "hardly haute cuisine."*

Oasis Diner* (Hartford) **B6** | 15 | 18 | 18 |$16 |
271 Farmington Ave. (Laurel St.), 241-8200
*M – Upstairs in this Hartford fixture is a "top-drawer diner"
with a "traditional '50s look" and "good-size portions" of
typical American-retro food; downstairs is Club Comet, an
energetic nightclub, leading one surveyor to suggest it's
"more of a meet, than meat, market."*

Old Lyme Inn/S (Old Lyme) **E6** | 22 | 23 | 21 |$38 |
Old Lyme Inn, 85 Lyme St. (I-95, exit 70), 434-2600
*U – "Very charming", "romantic" and "comfortable" aptly
describe this 19th-century clapboard inn where the
American and French food is as "lovely" as the "great
ambiance"; "don't miss the game and the sweetbreads,
but save room for a chocolate dessert."*

Ondine*/S (Danbury) **D2** | 24 | 19 | 22 |$35 |
Rte. 37 (Wheeler Dr.), 746-4900
*U – Danburyites are blessed with elegant "gourmet dining"
and "impeccable service" at this handsome, Contemporary
French; it's not cheap, but the "creative" prix fixe menu
offers "good value" for dinner or Sunday brunch.*

Onion Alley/S (Westport) **F3** | 16 | 15 | 15 |$20 |
42 Main St. (Post Rd.), 226-0794
*U – A central location and "service with a smile" make
this "old standby" Eclectic-American a handy "respite
after a shopping binge"; on weekends the "younger set"
comes for the live music and "good burgers, salads and
gourmet pizzas."*

Panda Inn/S (West Hartford) **B6** | 21 | 19 | 19 |$22 |
West Hartford Ctr., 964 Farmingdale Ave. (N. Main St.),
233-5384
*U – "If you need a Chinese fix", some call this the "best
Chinese" in West Hartford; comfortable decor and
professional service are inviting, but for real aficionados,
the "food is even good enough to take home."*

Panda Pavilion/S　　　　| 18 | 15 | 17 | $21 |

(Greenwich) **G1**, 137 W. Putnam Ave. (bet. Dearfield & Broadside Drs.), 869-1111
(Norwalk) **F3**, 370 Main Ave. (near Linden St.), 846-4253
(Westport) **F3**, 1300 Post Rd. E. (off Morningside Dr.), 255-3988
(Fairfield) **F3**, 923 Post Rd. (Grand Union Shopping Ctr.), 259-9777
M – Now there are four in this "reliable" Fairfield County minidynasty, serving "large portions" of "good" "Chinese food that rivals NYC" and "efficient" (some say "too quick") service; though "there are better Chinese restaurants", these are "consistently pleasant."

Pantry, The* (Washington Depot) **C3** | 23 | 19 | 17 | $22 |
5 Titus Rd. (Rte. 47), 868-0258
U – You can "shop and eat" at this "great little" gourmet shop–cum–restaurant, a "comfortable spot" for breakfast, lunch or a tea; whoever "makes the soups is a genius", but "imaginative sandwiches" and "fresh pastas" also get kudos; wine and beer only.

Parma Restaurant (Glastonbury) **B6** | – | – | – | M |
21 Rankin Rd. (Main St.), 659-9657
U – Reliable Northern and Southern Italian cooking has been coming out of this Glastonbury kitchen for years; though few of our surveyors know of it, comfortable quarters and welcoming service make this worth a stop.

PASTA NOSTRA　　　　| 24 | 14 | 16 | $31 |
(South Norwalk) **F2**
116 Washington St. (bet. Water & Main Sts.), 854-9700
U – This "minimalist" SoNo storefront keeps devotees coming back, with "food so good it makes you wanna cry"; yes, it's pricey for homemade pasta, but the good news is they finally take reservations and credit cards; open Tuesday to Friday lunch, Thursday to Saturday dinner.

Pasta Vera/SX (Greenwich) **G1**　　| 22 | 10 | 17 | $22 |
Putnam Plaza, 88 E. Putnam (Greenwich Ave.), 661-9705
U – "Unfortunately, this gem is no longer hidden", so "expect a wait" for "generous portions" of "excellent homemade pasta", "creatively" sauced; what do "slow service", a setting "like a hospital", "no credit cards" and "no elbow room" matter? – it's "cheap and oh, so good"; takeout lets you avoid the crush.

Pellicci's/S (Stamford) **G2**　　　| 18 | 14 | 19 | $21 |
96 Stillwater Ave. (Spruce St.), 323-2542
M – "Huge portions" of "reliable" "old-time family Italian" food have been satisfying loyal locals for 45 years at this low-atmosphere but comfortable "standby"; there's a reason it's always crowded: "great value"; the pizzas and family-style dinners are definite kid-pleasers.

Connecticut

	F	D	S	C

Peppercorn's Grill (Hartford) **B6** | 23 | 19 | 20 | $29 |

357 Main St. (Capital Ave.), 547-1714
*U – An "interesting Italian menu" and a "very nice dining
atmosphere" make this a Hartford "favorite"; "frantic"
service at peak times is a downside, a "good Italian
wine list" is a booster; P.S. it "helps if they know you."*

Peppermill Restaurant/S | 15 | 13 | 16 | $24 |
(Westport) **F3**

1700 Post Rd. E. (Maple Ave.), 259-8155
*M – This "pleasant" steakhouse "hasn't changed in 15
years", offering "fair prices" and "simple, decent
American cuisine", including a "very good salad bar";
complaints of being "boring" and a "senior-citizen
saltless and tasteless scenario" don't bother the throngs
at "Sunday dinner with the kids."*

Pequot Grill/LS (Ledyard) **D10** | – | – | – | E |

Foxwood Casino, Ledyard Indian Reservation, 885-3176
*It's safe to say that no one comes here only for the food;
however, this Traditional American has had a "rising
reputation" as the fanciest of the casino eateries with
decent food and a pretty setting making up for losses at
those other tables.*

Pierpont's*/S (Hartford) **B6** | 22 | 22 | 20 | $33 |

Goodwin Hotel, 1 Haynes St. (bet. Asylum & Anne Sts.),
522-4935
*U – Located in Downtown Hartford's historic Goodwin
Hotel, built by J.P. Morgan, this inventive Continental-
American keeps an old tradition alive with "superb
service" and a lovely setting for "quiet dining."*

Pompano Oyster Bar and | 18 | 19 | 17 | $28 |
Seafood Grill/S (Westport) **F3**

1460 Post Rd. E. (Maple Ave.), 259-1160
*M – The old Pompano Grill has become a lower-priced
seafood spot with whimsical nautical decor; "yups" and
"middle-aged suburbanites" clamor for the "well-prepared"
"interesting menu", but critics call it "mediocre" and "noisy"
and "wonder why they changed it."*

Post and Beam, The/S (Chester) **D6** | 21 | 23 | 21 | $37 |

Inn at Chester, 318 W. Main St. (3.2 miles west of Rte. 9),
526-9541
*U – "A change in ownership" brings a "fresh" twist to the
sophisticated "classic New England fare" served at this
"charming and welcoming inn"; gracious service and a
lovely rural setting make it a local favorite for special
occasions and a destination for food-loving tourists.*

Prezzo*/S (New Canaan) **F2** | 20 | 16 | 15 |\$31 |
2 Forest St. (East Ave.), 972-7666
*M – New and rather "racy" (an upended motorcycle is
its "centerpiece"), this "slick" but "romantic" black-and-
white Italian serves "excellent pastas" with "fresh, delicate
flavors"; "service can lag at times", but fans say despite
highish prices it's "usually worth it."*

Prince of Wales/S (Norwich) **D9** | – | – | – | M |
Norwich Inn and Spa, Rte. 32 (I-395, exit 79A), 886-2401
*You don't have to be a designated dieter to enjoy the
"tasty, healthy" Contemporary American cuisine at this
"luxurious" inn and health spa in NE Connecticut; set in
a remodeled 19th-century estate, the restaurant serves
breakfast, lunch and dinner to the public; our surveyors
call it a "must-trip."*

Radisson Arrowhead | – | – | – | E |
(Southbury) **D4**
Southbury Hotel, 1284 Strongtown Rd., 598-7600
*Only the name changed when the Ramada
Renaissance was recently reflagged; the $37.50 prix
fixe at the White Oak Room (open for weekend dinner
only) is still an intriguing and creative, if a little pricey,
Contemporary American and the same talented kitchen
staff is on hand for breakfast, lunch and dinner daily at
the equally good, but informal, Arrowhead Cafe.*

Ragamont Inn/S (Salisbury) **A2** | 19 | 22 | 20 |\$30 |
Ragamont Inn, 8 Main St. (Rte. 44), 435-2372
*M – "The environs are lovely" at this early 19th-century
antique-filled inn, especially on the "terrace in the
summer" or in the "cozy dining room in autumn"; the
food is Traditional Continental with a "strong Austrian
touch" – roesti, sweetbreads and other "Swiss-German"
favorites; a few critics say it's "lost some of its spark."*

RANDALL'S ORDINARY/S | 23 | 25 | 23 |\$34 |
(North Stonington) **D10**
Randall's Ordinary, Rte. 2 (I-95, exit 92), 599-4540
*U – For a "trip back in time" to "a Colonial experience"
of "open-hearth cooking", try this "wonderful" restored
1685 inn and restaurant; the "limited menu" is "interesting
and delicious", and the intimate dining rooms "make for
great conversation."*

Rattlesnake Bar | – | – | – | M |
& Grill/S (South Norwalk) **F3**
2-4 S. Main St. (Washington St.), 852-1716
*Lively quarters and a trendy, upbeat crowd make this
SoNo location under the railroad trestle the right address
for a busy bar serving Mexican beers and reasonably
priced SW food; though not on our questionnaire, its fans
wrote us in droves.*

| | F | D | S | C |

Rein's New York Style Deli Restaurant/LSX (Vernon) **A7** | 18 | 10 | 16 | $14 |

Shops of 30, 435 Hartford Tpke. (I-84, exit 65), 875-1344
M – "Carnegie Deli it's not", but fans still call this bargain-priced pastrami palace "outstanding and without equal north of NYC", or at least "good for CT" with "standard sandwiches" and a "diverse menu" – plus no decor.

RESTAURANT DU VILLAGE/S (Chester) **D6** | 26 | 24 | 24 | $48 |

59 Main St. (Maple St.), 526-5301
U – "You can't ask for much more" than this "lovely" French "bistro in the village of Chester"; "impeccable service" and a "charming country house", complete with lace curtains and "gracious hosts", complement the "authentic French country cooking"; sure, it's expensive, but quality and charm don't come cheap.

River Club Cafe* (Wilton) **F2** | 20 | 19 | 19 | $27 |

Wilton Exec. Complex, 15 River Rd. (Rte. 7), 762-0694
M – What some fans call "CT's best-kept secret" is this "elegant" American "luncheon place" (also open for dinner on Saturday) with a "country club setting" in an unlikely office-building location; "small" but "pretty", it's "good" for "exotic salads" and other "innovative" light fare.

ROBERT HENRY'S (New Haven) **E5** | 27 | 27 | 25 | $51 |

1032 Chapel St. (bet. College & High Sts.), 789-1010
U – "Save your pennies and splurge" on what surveyors call "probably the best formal dining in the state", a "très chic" Contemporary American that earns our highest overall rating for food, decor and service and ranks No. 1 in popularity; solid service, a "fine wine cellar" and "elegant dining, artfully presented" combine to create a "night to remember."

Roger Sherman Inn/S (New Canaan) **F2** | 21 | 24 | 21 | $41 |

Roger Sherman Inn, 195 Oenoke Ridge Rd. (Homewood Lane), 966-4541
M – Recently refurbished, this "charming Colonial country inn" is "prettier than ever"; the French and Mediterranean "food is not the best thing about it", but a meal here is "always very good", if a little "expensive."

Rudy's Restaurant/SX (New Milford) **C3** | 23 | 18 | 21 | $32 |

122 Litchfield Rd. (Rte. 102), 354-7727
U – This "stick-to-your-ribs Swiss" wins raves from those who "love those potato pancakes, roesti and Toblerone dessert", served in a solarium setting with a "beautiful pond and lovely grounds"; "tell them it's your birthday and they'll ring the bells."

Connecticut | F | D | S | C |

Rumba*/S (Danbury) **D2** | 20 | 14 | 21 | $21 |
52 Pembroke Rd. (Rte. 37 N.), 746-7093
*U – Widely known for its "terrific Cuban fare", this
"funky" spot with a "great staff" produces wonderful
"paella", but fans of this unusual and "always consistent"
ethnic say "don't miss the cassava fingers"; BYO.*

Ruth's Chris Steak House/S | 23 | 17 | 19 | $37 |
(Newington) **C6**
2513 Berlin Tpke. (Robins Ave.), 666-2202
*M – Part of a nationwide chain, this Hartford-area
outpost is "the place to go for steak" plus "fabulous
prime rib and martinis", "great baked potatoes and
salad" in "huge portions"; critics call it "ordinary" except
for the high prices.*

Sagebrush Cafe/S (Georgetown) **E3** | – | – | – | M |
6 Main St. (off Rte. 7), 544-9660
*In a prime spot beside a locally famous saloon, this
newcomer offers tasty SW cuisine in a stylish but
delightfully informal atmosphere; the usual salsas,
enchiladas and other old favorites are joined by
ambitious dishes like mole – all reasonably priced.*

Saigon City*/S (New Haven) **E5** | 19 | 14 | 22 | $22 |
1180 Chapel St. (Park St.), 865-5033
*U – "Good food and pleasant service" are the hallmarks
of this busy Vietnamese storefront with a large,
authentic menu; be sure to try the "special soups",
vegetarian spring rolls, and the shrimp and noodles.*

Sakura/S (Westport) **F3** | 19 | 17 | 18 | $27 |
680 Post Rd. E. (Hills Point Rd.), 222-0802
*M – "Inexpensive lunches", "good sushi" and "polite
service" plus a visible location explain the success of this
somewhat glitzy Japanese; if "the best Japanese around",
it's "one of the only ones", and kids love its hibachi bar.*

SALLY'S APIZZA/SX | 25 | 9 | 14 | $15 |
(New Haven) **E5**
237 Wooster St. (Olive St.), 624-5271
*U – Zounds! Sally's has slipped a notch, now running
"second only to Pepe's" in the great Pizza Wars; still,
"Sally's people" find it "hard to believe pizza can be this
ambrosial", with "fresh tomato pies" (in summer) that are
"one of the best foods of all time"; it's nothing to look at
and the servers "act like they're doing you a favor" when
you finally reach the head of the line, but don't miss it!*

Connecticut | F | D | S | C |

Saybrook Fish House/S | 19 | 15 | 17 | $25 |
(Old Saybrook) **E6**
99 Essex Rd. (Sunrise Dr.), 388-4836
M – A handy place for "dinner with the family" or "lunch after a ride in the country", this seafood house offers an "abundance of food" plus a free "bowl of fruit for dessert"; more demanding types think it's "pedestrian" citing mundane ambiance and a "no-reservations policy" as drawbacks.

Scoozi Trattoria & Wine Bar/S | 21 | 19 | 19 | $29 |
(New Haven) **E5**
1104 Chapel St. (York St.), 776-8268
U – "The feel of a NY trattoria" is yours at this "local New Haven gathering spot" with "consistently wonderful" Italian food and a "fresh", "informal" setting; "boutique pizza", "pleasant pasta" and "concerned service" make this a "new favorite."

Scribner's/S (Milford) **F4** | 23 | 16 | 19 | $28 |
31 Village Rd. (Merwin Ave.), 878-7019
U – A "quality experience" "for the money" is why fans flock to this shore-town seafooder; the informal ambiance is "nothing to rave about" and service can be "uneven", but "fabulously fresh fish", a "nice wine list" and "great chocolate pecan pie" offset its shortcomings.

Sesame Seed* (Danbury) **D2** | 18 | 13 | 16 | $19 |
68 W. Wooster St. (Division St.), 743-9850
U – "Even if you're not a flower child", you might want to try this offbeat California-meets–Middle East hangout, which attracts a cross-generational following for its "fresh, delicious, healthy and inexpensive" vegetarian meals and "simple" lunch-type fare.

Sheesh Mahal/S (Westport) **F3** | – | – | – | M |
256 Post Rd. E. (Imperial St.), 454-0737
The handful of surveyors who have found this storefront BYO Indian "can't say enough about the food", especially the unusual vegetarian dishes; though it's nothing to look at and service can be spotty, good food at modest prices makes it "well worth trying."

Shish Kebab House | – | – | – | M |
of Afghanistan (Hartford) **B6**
360 Franklin Ave. (bet. Prestin & Otis Sts.), 296-0301
Virtually without competition in the area, this authentic Afghan with its intricately spiced, but not fiery hot, food appeals to adventurous diners who like to try exotic cuisines; low prices and friendly character help compensate for its rather ordinary storefront decor.

Silvermine Tavern/S (Norwalk) **F3** | 16 | 23 | 17 | $31 |

Silvermine Tavern, 194 Perry Ave. (Silvermine), 847-4558
*M – "A dreamy country setting that seems worlds away
from suburbia" describes this landmark Yankee inn with
a view of the Five Mile River; longstanding complaints
that it serves the "worst food in a lovely setting" may
soon change, thanks to a capable "new chef."*

Simsbury 1820 House/S | – | – | – | E |
(Simsbury) **A6**

731 Hopmeadow St., Rte. 10 (Rte. 44), 658-7658
*A country inn during the first part of the century, this old
landmark fell into disrepair until its renovation in the
mid-'80s; now it has 34 pretty guest rooms and a pricey
Continental restaurant with Northern Italian flair.*

Sol e Luna Ristorante Toscana/S | 23 | 22 | 18 | $37 |
(Westport) **F3**

25 Powers Court (Post Rd.), 222-3837
*U – For "truly solar dining", this "classy" newcomer
"delivers on its Tuscan promises" with "excellent" food
and "accommodating" service; a few complain that it's
"overpriced" and "disorganized", but most applaud
"unusual dishes" such as "stuffed zucchini flowers" and
"quail on polenta."*

Spazzi Trattoria and Wine Bar/S | 23 | 20 | 18 | $30 |
(Fairfield) **F3**

Brick Walk Plaza, 1229 Post Rd. (Beach Rd.), 256-1629
*U – "If you love garlic, you'll love this place" where the
fragrant bulb is idolized in "fabulous Contemporary
Italian dishes" on the "creative Californian"-influenced
menu; behind its strip-mall facade is an "informal" and
"usually crowded" trattoria where no-reserving can
mean "infuriating waits."*

Spinning Wheel Inn/S | 17 | 20 | 18 | $32 |
(Redding Ridge) **E3**

107 Black Rock Tpke., Rte. 58 N. (Merritt Pkwy., exit 45),
938-2511
*U – Many of our raters report "overpriced" "airline-style
food" at this wedding-intensive former estate – what "a
shame", because the circa-1742 building in a garden is
exceptionally alluring; at best, it's a vintage New
England rest stop after a day in the country.*

Standish House* | 21 | 23 | 20 | $37 |
(Old Wethersfield) **C6**

222 Main St. (Marsh St.), 721-1113
*U – "Good ambiance combined with good food" in a
French-American vein make this a popular destination;
though a few say the seasonally changing menu can be
"hit or miss" at a stiff price, solid scores and a delightful
setting tell the real story here.*

STONEHENGE/S (Ridgefield) **E2** | 24 | 25 | 23 | $45 |
Stonehenge Inn, Rte. 7 (1 mile south of Rte. 35), 438-6511
M – A "beautiful" setting, skilled service and "excellent"
Contemporary French–Continental cuisine add up to a
totally satisfying dining experience at this "elegant" inn;
sure, a few find it "stuffy" and "overpriced", but high
ratings confirm the majority view that Stonehenge is
perfect for a special occasion.

Su Casa/S (Branford) **E5** | 18 | 16 | 17 | $18 |
400 E. Main St. (Rte. 139), 481-5001
U – The "best Mexican food in town", "good margaritas"
and "dark beer" get the nod at this Branford "standby"
dispensing "fun and festive" south-of-the-border
favorites; despite a "dark dining room" and "too long a
wait", fair prices make this a "local 'in' spot."

Sunrise Pizza Cafe/S | 19 | 11 | 16 | $16 |
(Norwalk) **F3**, 211 Liberty Sq. (Rte. 136), 854-1676
(Stamford) **G2**, 299 Long Ridge Rd. (High Ridge), 356-0006
M – An "eccentric array" of "innovative designer pizzas"
is the mainstay of these "casual", "cheap" "Californian-style"
cafes that even fans admit are "like eating in someone's
basement"; at the newer Stamford location, you'll also
find pastas, burgers and salads.

Taj Mahal/S (Greenwich) **G1** | – | – | – | M |
Howard Johnson's Motor Lodge, 1114 E. Putnam Ave.
(I-95, exit 5), 698-2952
In an unlikely location, the Howard Johnson's Motor
Lodge, this new, authentic and beautifully decorated
Northern Indian is serving delicious dishes rarely seen
in these parts; from the uniformed sikh at the door to the
white wicker chairs and Indian puppets inside, the stage
is set for a satisfying meal at a sensible price.

Terra Ristorante Italiano/S | 22 | 22 | 14 | $35 |
(Greenwich) **G1**
156 Greenwich Ave. (Lewis St.), 629-5222
M – Instant "popularity ruined the service" and "crammed"
the "crowds" in "like sardines" at this "trendy" new trattoria,
but it still serves "excellent" "Italian grilled chicken", perfect
"fried calamari" and "innovative pastas"; this "'in' scene" is
"noisier than La Guardia", but some people measure
success by decibel levels.

Thai Orchid/S (New Haven) **E5** | 22 | 14 | 20 | $22 |
1027 State St. (Lawrence St.), 624-7173
U – Once considered a "well-hidden secret", this "small,
unassuming" "storefront" attracts a following for "tasty
Thai cuisine" that uses "reliably fresh ingredients and
interesting spices"; its "diner decor" hardly matters in
light of the "attentive service" and "good food."

Thataway Cafe/S (Greenwich) **G1** | 14 | 13 | 16 | $21 |
409 Greenwich Ave. (Railroad Ave.), 622-0947
M – A lower Greenwich Avenue address makes this
"burgers, etc." American a "good stop after the flicks",
but the "young singles crowd" is more attuned to the
"bar scene with jazz" than the "marginal", albeit
"inexpensive", "pub food."

Three Bears, The/S (Westport) **F3** | 17 | 19 | 18 | $30 |
333 Wilton Rd. (Newtown Tpke.), 227-7219
M – This "traditional old Connecticut country restaurant"
in a "sweetly charming", "antique-filled" setting offers
"consistently satisfactory" but "unexciting" "New
England" "grandma food": steaks, "double lamb chops",
"good fish" and "early-bird dinners"; but critics say "this
place should go into hiding."

Tiger Bowl/S (Westport) **F3** | 22 | 6 | 16 | $16 |
Child World Shopping Ctr., 1872 Post Rd. E. (I-95, exit 19),
255-1799
U – "Don't tell anybody" about the "excellent food" at
this "bargain-priced", "no-ambiance" "storefront" that
happens to serve "some of the very best" "high-quality
Chinese food" in the area; try the "terrific Shanghai
noodles", and don't forget it's BYO.

**Tollgate Hill Inn
and Restaurant**/S (Litchfield) **B4** | 21 | 23 | 21 | $36 |
Tollgate Hill Inn, Rte. 202 (Tollgate Rd.), 567-4545
U – This New American offers "all you could want in a
country inn", a charming "setting for Sunday dinner" and
"worth a drive for lunch" – unless you make this "romantic
bed-and-breakfast" your "weekend oasis"; "it's a surprise
to find such good food" in such a "quiet, remote" spot.

Truc Orient Express* /S
(Hartford) **B6** | 24 | 15 | 19 | $24 |
735 Wethersfield Ave. (South St.), 296-2818
U – "Ethnic food up to NYC standards" and "friendly,
helpful" service explain why this first-rate Vietnamese
has gained a loyal following; decor is "basic", but the
food is "imaginative and faithful to this cuisine's
French-influenced flavors."

Tucson Cafe/S (Greenwich) **G1** | 17 | 15 | 16 | $22 |
130 E. Putnam Ave. (Millbank Ave.), 661-2483
M – The "good-times bar" of this Southwestern is a
"mecca for young singles" drawn to the "pickup scene"
and the "best margaritas in town"; foodies, conversely,
say the nuevo-wavo "Tex-Mex food is in abundant
supply" but "sloppy"; even fans suggest you "request a
table near a waiter" and make "the appetizers a meal."

1249 West Restaurant*/S | 23 | 18 | 21 | $31 |
(Waterbury) **D4**
1249 W. Main St. (Ravin St.), 756-4609
*U – Though it's been around for years, this little-known
Waterbury Italian in a rehabbed Downtown building
"often surprises" with a "tasty meal" from an interesting
menu served with savvy and style; prices are a bit on
the high side, but the specials are "outstanding."*

Under Mountain Inn* (Salisbury) **A2** | 19 | 23 | 19 | $33 |
Under Mountain Inn, 482 Under Mountain Rd., Rte. 41
(4 miles north of village ctr.), 435-0242
*U – "Exactly what an inn should be", this "picturesque"
little B&B is open to the public for dinner on Fridays and
Saturdays; its British-born chef-owner's American food
with an English accent is "secondary" to the bucolic
scenery and "gracious", fire-lit ambiance.*

Vernon Stiles Inn/S | – | – | – | M |
(Thompson) **A10**
Rtes. 193 & 200 (I-395, exit 99), 923-9571
*This lovingly restored 1814 building is the "elegant
setting" for owner Joseph Silberman's "beautifully
presented" American-Continental cuisine; Sunday
brunch, a $14.95 Friday-night buffet, and special pre-
and post-theater menus (the Bradley Playhouse is
nearby) make this mid-priced option appealing.*

Versailles Rotisserie | 21 | 14 | 16 | $28 |
Restaurant/S (Greenwich) **G1**
315 Greenwich Ave. (Arch St.), 661-6634
*U – Long known to locals for its "bakery with wonderful
French pastries and quiches", this tiny storefront "bistro"
also serves affordable, "good, if somewhat skimpy,
authentic brasserie meals"; "arrogant service" is
authentic, too, but don't let it spoil your enjoyment of a
"first-rate cappuccino and dessert."*

Vicolo Ristorante/S (Stamford) **G2** | – | – | – | E |
20 Summer St. (Main St.), 978-1489
*Surveyors say this pricey Downtown Contemporary
Italian is "not bad, but with so many others that are
much better, why go back?"; there's "ok" food in a
greenhouse setting, but the service, too, seems green.*

WEST STREET GRILL (Litchfield) **B4** | 24 | 21 | 19 | $34 |
43 West St. (on the green), 567-3885
*U – "Too bad it's been discovered", say Litchfield County
glitterati who come "to dine and people-watch" at James
O'Shea's "trendy" CT version of the "Upper East Side";
the "imaginative combinations" and "ultrafresh ingredients"
produced by this American Contemporary kitchen
appeal to culinarians who suggest that you "go during
the week" if "noise" and "snobby clientele" bother you.*

Connecticut | F | D | S | C |

WHITE HART, THE/S (Salisbury) **A2** | 23 | 24 | 22 | $35 |
The White Hart, Village Green (Rtes. 41 & 44), 435-0030
M – Recently "renovated" and "restored to prominence",
this "lovely New England inn" sports a new name for its
main dining room – Julie's New American Sea Grill –
and a new Contemporary American menu that most find
"interesting" and "exciting"; critics warn "ok if you crave
a country setting, but don't expect anything terrific"; the
Tap Room is oustanding at "half the price."

Whitehouse Restaurant, The*/S | 17 | 16 | 16 | $30 |
(Old Saybrook) **E6**
1687 Boston Post Rd. (Spencer Plains Rd., Rte. 154),
399-6291
M – Open for dinner only, this "elegant restaurant in a
beautiful setting" sparks mixed reviews for its traditional
Continental-American menu, relatively moderate prices
and service – from very "good" to "very ordinary."

White Oak, The (Southbury) **D4** | – | – | – | M |
Radisson Hotel, 1284 Strongtown Rd., (Rte. 84, exit 16),
598-7600
This upscale hotel restaurant serves mid-priced
Contemporary German–Italian fare in an intimate spot
with only six tables dedicated chandeliers and mirrors;
dinner only, Friday and Saturday – reservations required.

Wild Scallion, The/S (Norwalk) **F3** | 16 | 14 | 16 | $20 |
480 Westport Ave. (Strawberry Hill Rd.), 849-9411
M – The strip-mall section of the Post Road between
Norwalk and Westport is an unlikely location for this
"preppy bar" with "informal" SW food, that's "good for a
quick bite"; though barely rising above "ordinary", it's
"friendly" and "dependable."

Woodland, The/S (Lakeville) **B2** | 20 | 15 | 18 | $26 |
192 Sharon Rd., Rte. 41 (Rte. 112), 435-0578
M – "Bear-size portions" of "good-value" SW food create
"long waits" at this popular, "no-atmosphere" spot; fans
insist it's a "pleasant surprise", a "lovely evening in
every way", but critics say "bring salt and pepper" and
beware of "moody" service.

Woods/S (Old Greenwich) **G1** | – | – | – | M |
148 Sound Beach Ave. (I-95, exit 5), 637-3604
This new American grill is attracting fans of food cooked
over hardwood – from soups and salads to appealing
main courses, nearly every dish has at least one element
finished on the grill; moderate prices and attractive
gray-and-mauve decor complete a promising scene.

CONNECTICUT INDEXES

TYPES OF CUISINE

Connecticut

Californian
Capers
Max on Main

Chinese
China Pavilion
Fortune Village
Khan's Mongolian
Lotus East
Panda Inn
Panda Pavilion
Tiger Bowl

Continental
Al Dimarco's
Amadeus
Apricot's
Avon Old Farms Inn
Black Rock Castle
Brookfield Bistro
Christopher Martin's
Cobb's Mill Inn
Elms Inn
Griswold Inn
Hearthstone
Hopkins Inn
Inn at Gwyn Careg
Inn at Ridgefield
Inn at Woodstock Hill
Miche-Mache
Nistico's Red Barn
Pierpont's
Radisson Arrowhead
Ragamont Inn
Simsbury 1820 House
Stonehenge
Vernon Stiles Inn
Whitehouse

Cuban
Rumba

Delis
Rein's

Dim Sum
China Pavilion

Diners
Bull's Head Diner
Oasis Diner

Eclectic
A Garden Cafe
Bart's Paradise Cafe
Brookfield Bistro
Butterfield's
Chef Martin
Cobble Cookery
Congress Rotisserie
Gail's Station House

Gates
Lily's
Miche-Mache
Onion Alley
Pantry
Post and Beam
River Club Cafe

French Bistro
C'est Si Bon
Charles Bistro
Chez Pierre (Wstpt.)
La Provence
Le Bistro des Amis
Versailles

French Classic
Bertrand
Chez Pierre (Staf. Spg.)
Copper Beech Inn
Fine Bouche
Homestead Inn
La Bretagne
Le Bon Coin
Le Chambord
Le Marmiton
Restaurant du Village
Standish House

French Contemporary
Bellini
Bertrand
Cafe du Bec Fin
Cavey's
Copper Beech Inn
Da Pietro's
Fine Bouche
Jean-Louis
Maison le Blanc
Ondine
Restaurant du Village
Roger Sherman Inn
Stonehenge

German
White Oak

Greek
Bull's Head Diner

Hamburgers
Breakaway

Health Food
Prince of Wales

Indian
Bombay's
Bonani
Ganga

Connecticut

Kismet
Meera
Sheesh Mahal
Taj Mahal

Indonesian
Bali of Greenwich
Little Kitchen

Irish/British
Black Rock Castle
MacKenzie's Old Ale
Under Mountain Inn

Italian (Northern)
Alforno
Amadeo's
Assaggio
Bacci's
Bella Luna
Cavey's
Ciaobella
Da Pietro's
Diorio
Doc's
Dolce Italian Bistro
Hot Tomato's
La Villa
Max-a-Mia
Peppercorn's Grill
Prezzo
Scoozi
Simsbury 1820 House
Terra Ristorante
1249 West

Italian (North & South)
Amadeo's
Angelino's
Angsavanee East
Apulia
Bella Luna
Bella Italia
Bellini
Bertucci's
Bricks
Cafe Christina
Carbone's
Centro
Columbus Park
Derosa's
Di Fiore's
500 Blake St. Cafe
Frank's
Gaetano's
Il Falco
Il Mulino
Il Forno
La Strada

La Trattoria
Leon's
Maria's Trattoria
Mario's
Mario The Baker
Mona Lisa
Parma
Pasta Nostra
Pasta Vera
Pellicci's
Spazzi Trattoria
Vicolo
White Oak

Italian (Nuova Cucina)
Assaggio
Doc's
Max-a-Mia
Peppercorn's Grill
Sol e Luna

Japanese
Abis
Kotobuki
Kujaku
Murasaki
Sakura

Jewish
Rein's

Mediterranean
Bella Italia
Roger Sherman Inn

Mexican/Tex-Mex
Azteca's
Hacienda don Emilio
Su Casa

Middle Eastern
Diana
Sesame Seed

Mongolian
Khan's Mongolian

Norwegian/Scandinavian
Fjord Fisheries

Pizza
Alforno
Angelino's
Bertucci's
Bricks
Frank Pepe Pizzeria
Prezzo
Sally's Apizza
Sunrise Pizza

Connecticut

Seafood
Abbott's
Allen's Clam House
Cafe du Bec Fin
Capitol Fish House
Ciaobella
Fagan's Riverview
Fiddlers
Fjord Fisheries
Giovanni's
Mansion Clam House
Pompano Oyster Bar
Saybrook Fish House
Scribner's
White Hart

Southwestern
Arizona Flats
Azteca's
Harry's TX BBQ
Hot Tamales
Pierpont's
Tucson Cafe
Sagebrush Cafe
Wild Scallion

Spanish
Costa del Sol
Meson Galicia
Rumba

Steakhouses
Chart House
Giovanni's
Hearthstone

Manero's
Mario's
Peppermill
Ruth's Chris

Swiss
Hopkins Inn
Rudy's

Thai
Angsavanee East
Bangkok
Lemon Grass
Mhai Thai
Thai Orchid

Vegetarian
(Most Chinese, Indian
and Thai restaurants)
A Garden Cafe
Bloodroot
Ganga
Sesame Seed
Sheesh Mahal

Viennese
Amadeus

Vietnamese
La Maison Indochine
Little Kitchen
Lotus Restaurant
Saigon City
Truc Orient Express

LOCATION BY TOWN

Avon
    Avon Old Farms Inn
    Jetstream's Cafe
    Max-a-Mia
Bethel
    MacKenzie's Old Ale
Branford
    Chef Martin
    Fortune Village
    Su Casa
Bridgeport
    Arizona Flats
    Black Rock Castle
    Bloodroot
Brookfield
    Brookfield Bistro
    Capers
    Christopher's
Brooklyn
    Golden Lamb Buttery
Canaan
    Cannery Cafe
Canton
    Lily's
Centerbrook
    Fine Bouche
Chester
    Chart House
    Fiddlers
    Post and Beam
    Restaurant du Village
Danbury
    Bangkok
    Bella Italia
    Ondine
    Rumba
    Sesame Seed
Darien
    Backstreet
    Bertucci's
    Black Goose Grill
    Giovanni's
    Li's Brothers Inn
East Haven
    Kansas City Bar-B-Q
Essex
    Griswold Inn
Fairfield
    Breakaway
    Centro
    Gregory's
    Panda Pavilion
    Spazzi Trattoria
Farmington
    Apricot's
Georgetown
    Sagebrush Cafe

Glastonbury
    Great American Cafe
    Parma
Greenwich
    Abis
    A Garden Cafe
    Bali of Greenwich
    Bart's Paradise Cafe
    Bella Luna
    Bertrand
    C'est Si Bon
    Centro
    Chart House
    Ciaobella
    Greenwich Harbor Inn
    Homestead Inn
    Jean-Louis
    La Maison Indochine
    La Strada
    Lotus East
    Manero's
    Mhai Thai
    Morgan
    Panda Pavilion
    Pasta Vera
    Taj Mahal
    Terra Ristorante
    Thataway Cafe
    Tucson Cafe
    Versailles
Groton
    Diana
Hartford
    Amarillo Grill
    Bellini
    Bombay's
    Capitol Fish House
    Carbone's
    Chale Ipanema
    Congress Rotisserie
    Costa del Sol
    Di Fiore's
    Frank's
    Gaetano's
    Hearthstone
    Hot Tamales
    Hot Tomato's
    Max on Main
    Oasis Diner
    Peppercorn's Grill
    Pierpont's
    Shish Kebab House
    Truc Orient Express
Ivoryton
    Copper Beech Inn
Kent
    Cobble Cookery

Connecticut

Lakeville
  Woodland
Ledyard
  Pequot Grill
Litchfield
  Tollgate Hill Inn
  West Street Grill
Manchester
  Cavey's
  Heavenly Hog
Milford
  Scribner's
Mystic
  Mooring
New Canaan
  Bluewater Cafe
  Gates
  L'Abbee
  Little Kitchen
  Prezzo
  Roger Sherman Inn
New Haven
  Azteca's
  Bagdon's
  Bruxelles Brasserie
  Christopher Martin's
  500 Blake St. Cafe
  Frank Pepe Pizzeria
  Leon's
  Robert Henry's
  Saigon City
  Sally's Apizza
  Scoozi
  Thai Orchid
Newington
  Ruth's Chris
New Milford
  Charles Bistro
  Le Marmiton
  Maison le Blanc
  Rudy's
New Preston
  Boulders Inn
  Doc's
  Hopkins Inn
  Inn/Lake Waramaug
  Le Bon Coin
Noank
  Abbott's
North Stonington
  Randall's Ordinary
Norwalk
  Bricks
  Ganga
  Hunan U.S. 1
  Maria's Trattoria
  Meson Galicia
  Panda Pavilion
  Silvermine Tavern

Sunrise Pizza
Wild Scallion
Norwich
  Prince of Wales
Old Greenwich
  Boxing Cat Grill
  Cafe du Bec Fin
  Conde's
  Woods
Old Lyme
  Bee and Thistle Inn
  Old Lyme Inn
Old Saybrook
  Alforno
  Saybrook Fish House
  Whitehouse
Old Wethersfield
  Standish House
Orange
  Bertucci's
Pomfret
  Inn at Gwyn Careg
Redding
  MacKenzie's Roadhse.
Redding Ridge
  Spinning Wheel Inn
Ridgefield
  Elms Inn
  Gail's Station House
  Hay Day Cafe
  Inn at Ridgefield
  Kismet
  Stonehenge
Rocky Hill
  China Pavilion
Rowayton
  5 Mile River Grille
Salisbury
  Ragamont Inn
  Under Mountain Inn
  White Hart
Simsbury
  Chart House
  Hop Brook
  Murasaki
  Simsbury 1820 House
Southbury
  Bacci's
  Radisson Arrowhead
  White Oak
South Norwalk
  Apulia
  La Provence
  Miche-Mache
  Pasta Nostra
  Rattlesnake Bar
South Woodstock
  Inn at Woodstock Hill

Connecticut

Stafford Spring
 Chez Pierre
Stamford
 Al Dimarco's
 Amadeus Restaurant
 Angsavanee East
 Bonani
 Columbus Park
 Dolce Italian Bistro
 Giovanni's
 Hacienda don Emilio
 Harry's TX BBQ
 Il Falco
 Il Forno
 Il Mulino
 Khan's Mongolian
 Kotobuki
 Kujaku
 La Bretagne
 Magnificent J's
 Mario The Baker
 Meera
 Mona Lisa
 Pellicci's
 Sunrise Pizza
 Vicolo Ristorante
Stratford
 Fagan's Riverview
Thompson
 Vernon Stiles Inn
Vernon
 Little Mark's
 Lotus Restaurant
 Rein's
Washington Depot
 Mayflower Inn
 Pantry
Waterbury
 1249 West
 Diorio

West Cornwall
 Freshfields
West Hartford
 Assaggio
 Bertucci's
 Butterfield's
 Lemon Grass
 Panda Inn
Weston
 Cobb's Mill Inn
Westport
 Allen's Clam House
 Amadeo's
 Angelino's
 Bertucci's
 Cafe Christina
 Chez Pierre
 Da Pietro's
 Derosa's
 La Villa
 Le Chambord
 Little Kitchen
 Mansion Clam House
 Mario's
 Nistico's Red Barn
 Onion Alley
 Panda Pavilion
 Peppermill
 Pompano Oyster Bar
 Sakura
 Sheesh Mahal
 Sol e Luna
 Three Bears
 Tiger Bowl
West Redding
 La Trattoria
Wilton
 River Club Cafe

SPECIAL FEATURES AND APPEALS

Bar/Singles Scenes
Amarillo Grill
Apricot's
Arizona Flats
Bart's Paradise Cafe
Bertucci's
Black Rock Castle
Boxing Cat Grill
Breakaway
Butterfield's
Centro
Christopher Martin's
Derosa's
500 Blake St. Cafe
5 Mile River Grille
Great American Cafe
Greenwich Harbor Inn
Hacienda don Emilio
Hot Tamales
Jetstream's Cafe
Mario's
Miche-Mache
Oasis Diner
Onion Alley
Sagebrush Cafe
Spazzi Trattoria
Tucson Cafe
White Oak
Wild Scallion

Breakfast
(All hotels and the
following standouts)
C'est Si Bon
Gail's Station House
Pantry
Pequot Grill
Rein's
Versailles

Brunch
(Best of the many)
Apricot's
Avon Old Farms Inn
Bacci's
Backstreet
Bee and Thistle Inn
Black Goose Grill
Black Rock Castle
Bloodroot
Boulders Inn
Boxing Cat Grill
Bruxelles Brasserie
C'est Si Bon
Charles Bistro
China Pavilion

Christopher's
Cobb's Mill Inn
Dolce Italian Bistro
Elms Inn
500 Blake St. Cafe
Freshfields
Gates
Griswold Inn
Hay Day Cafe
Homestead Inn
Hop Brook
Inn at Gwyn Careg
Inn at Ridgefield
Inn at Woodstock Hill
Inn/Lake Waramaug
Jetstream's Cafe
L'Abbee
MacKenzie's Rdhse.
Max-a-Mia
Nistico's Red Barn
Old Lyme Inn
Ondine
Pierpont's
Post and Beam
Prince of Wales
Ragamont Inn
Roger Sherman Inn
Rudy's
Silvermine Tavern
Simsbury 1820 House
Spinning Wheel Inn
Stonehenge
Three Bears
Tollgate Hill Inn
Vernon Stiles Inn
Versailles
West Street Grill
White Hart

Business Dining
Abis
Al Dimarco's
Alforno
Amadeus
Amarillo Grill
Apricot's
Apulia
Assaggio
Avon Old Farms Inn
Bacci's
Bella Luna
Bellini
Bertrand
Black Goose Grill
Black Rock Castle
Boxing Cat Grill

Connecticut

Butterfield's
Cafe Christina
Capitol Fish House
Carbone's
Cavey's
Chale Ipanema
Chart House
Chef Martin
Chez Pierre (Staf. Spg.)
Chez Pierre (Wstpt.)
Christopher Martin's
Christopher's
Columbus Park
Conde's
Diana
Di Fiore's
Diorio
Dolce Italian Bistro
500 Blake St. Cafe
5 Mile River Grille
Frank's
Gaetano's
Ganga
Great American Cafe
Gregory's
Hacienda don Emilio
Hearthstone
Homestead Inn
Hop Brook
Hot Tomato's
Il Forno
Il Falco
Inn at Gwyn Careg
Inn at Ridgefield
Inn/Lake Waramaug
Kotobuki
Kujaku
La Bretagne
La Provence
La Strada
Lemon Grass
Leon's
Lotus Restaurant
MacKenzie's Rdhse.
Magnificent J's
Manero's
Mario's
Max on Main
Mayflower Inn
Meera
Meson Galicia
Mona Lisa
Morgan
Nistico's Red Barn
Ondine
Panda Inn
Parma
Pellicci's
Peppercorn's Grill

Peppermill
Pierpont's
Pompano Oyster Bar
Post and Beam
Prince of Wales
Restaurant du Village
River Club Cafe
Robert Henry's
Roger Sherman Inn
Ruth's Chris
Saybrook Fish House
Scribner's
Sol e Luna
Standish House
Stonehenge
Truc Orient Express
Whitehouse
Wild Scallion

Dancing
(Nightclubs and the
following; check times)
Al Dimarco's
Boxing Cat Grill
Bricks
Dolce Italian Bistro
5 Mile River Grille
Gates
Great American Cafe
Greenwich Harbor Inn
Mayflower Inn
Mooring
Oasis Diner
Onion Alley
Pellicci's
Whitehouse

Delivers
(Call to check range
 and charges, if any)
Angelino's
Angsavanee East
Assaggio
Avon Old Farms Inn
Backstreet
Bali of Greenwich
Bart's Paradise Cafe
Bertucci's
Bombay's
Cobble Cookery
Congress Rotisserie
Di Fiore's
Diorio
Dolce Italian Bistro
Gates
Giovanni's
Gregory's
Hacienda don Emilio
Harry's TX BBQ

Connecticut

Heavenly Hog
Kansas City Bar-B-Q
Kismet
Kujaku
L'Abbee
La Provence
Little Kitchen
Little Mark's
Lotus East
Mario The Baker
Meera
Onion Alley
Panda Pavilion
Pantry
Pellicci's
Peppermill
Rein's
Sesame Seed
Sol e Luna
Sunrise Pizza
Thataway Cafe

Entertainment
(Check days, times
and performers)
Al Dimarco's (varies)
Apricot's (piano)
Avon Old Farms (varies)
Bacci's (varies)
Bart's (varies)
Bee/Thistle (varies)
Black Rock Castle (varies)
Boxing Cat Grill (bands)
Butterfield's (piano)
Cavey's (varies)
Charles Bistro (guitar)
Chef Martin (varies)
Chris Martin's (varies)
Dolce Italian Bistro (piano)
Fagan's (varies)
5 Mile River Grille (varies)
Gail's (varies)
Gates (blues, jazz)
Golden Lamb (vocalist)
Great American Cafe (DJ)
Griswold Inn (varies)
Hac don Emilio (guitar)
Harry's TX BBQ (jazz)
Hop Brook (guitar, jazz)
Hot Tamales (guitar)
Inn/Gwyn Careg (varies)
Inn at Ridgefield (piano)
Kismet (varies)
MacKenzie's (piano)
Mayflower Inn (piano)
Meson Galicia (guitar)
Miche-Mache (bands)
Mooring (DJ, piano)
Oasis Diner (DJ, bands)

Old Lyme Inn (guitar)
Pellicci's (jazz, piano)
Post and Beam (piano)
Rad Arrowhead (bands)
Randall's (varies)
Roger Sherman (piano)
Su Casa (guitar)
Thataway Cafe (jazz)
Tollgate Hill Inn (piano)
Tucson Cafe (jazz)
Whitehouse (varies)
White Oak (DJ)

Fireplaces
Assaggio
Avon Old Farms Inn
Bacci's
Bee and Thistle Inn
Bertrand
Black Goose Grill
Boulders Inn
Bricks
Capers
Chart House
Chez Pierre (Staf. Spg.)
Christopher's
Cobb's Mill Inn
Elms Inn
Giovanni's
Golden Lamb Buttery
Griswold Inn
Homestead Inn
Hop Brook
Hopkins Inn
Il Forno
Inn at Gwyn Careg
Inn at Ridgefield
Inn at Woodstock Hill
Inn/Lake Waramaug
Kismet
MacKenzie's Rdhse.
Maison le Blanc
Mayflower Inn
Mooring
Nistico's Red Barn
Old Lyme Inn
Post and Beam
Prince of Wales
Ragamont Inn
Randall's Ordinary
Robert Henry's
Rudy's
Rumba
Sakura
Saybrook Fish House
Silvermine Tavern
Simsbury 1820 House
Sol e Luna

Connecticut

Spazzi Trattoria
Spinning Wheel Inn
Standish House
Stonehenge
Su Casa
Three Bears
Tollgate Hill Inn
Under Mountain Inn
Vernon Stiles Inn
Wild Scallion

Health/Spa Menus

(Most places cook
to order to meet
any dietary request;
call in advance to
check; almost all
health food spots,
Chinese, Indian and
other ethnics have
health-conscious meals,
as do the following)
Avon Old Farms Inn
Bloodroot
Gaetano's
Hop Brook
Le Bon Coin
Pantry
Prince of Wales
Rein's

Historic Interest

Allen's Clam House
Avon Old Farms Inn
Bee and Thistle Inn
Boulders Inn
Cafe Christina
Carbone's
Christopher's
Cobb's Mill Inn
Copper Beech Inn
Elms Inn
Frank Pepe Pizzeria
Freshfields
Golden Lamb Buttery
Griswold Inn
Homestead Inn
Hop Brook
Hopkins Inn
Inn at Gwyn Careg
Inn at Ridgefield
Inn at Woodstock Hill
Inn/Lake Waramaug
MacKenzie's Old Ale
MacKenzie's Rdhse.
Maison le Blanc
Mayflower Inn
Meson Galicia
Old Lyme Inn
Pierpont's

Post and Beam
Prince of Wales
Ragamont Inn
Randall's Ordinary
Roger Sherman Inn
Silvermine Tavern
Spinning Wheel Inn
Standish House
Three Bears
Tollgate Hill Inn
Vernon Stiles Inn
White Hart

Hotel Dining

Bee and Thistle Inn
  Bee and Thistle Inn
Boulders Inn
  Boulders Inn
Copper Beech Inn
  Copper Beech Inn
Elms Inn
  Elms Inn
Goodwin Hotel
  Pierpont's
Greenwich Harbor Inn
  Greenwich Harbor Inn
Griswold Inn
  Griswold Inn
Holiday Inn Waterbury
  Diorio
Homestead Inn
  Homestead Inn
Hopkins Inn
  Hopkins Inn
Howard Johnson's
  Taj Mahal
Hyatt Reg. Greenwich
  Conde's
Inn at Chester
  Post and Beam
Inn at Gwyn Careg
  Inn at Gwyn Careg
Inn at Woodstock Hill
  Inn at Woodstock Hill
Inn/Lake Waramaug
  Inn/Lake Waramaug
Mayflower Inn
  Mayflower Inn
Mystic Hilton
  Mooring
Norwich Inn and Spa
  Prince of Wales
Old Lyme Inn
  Old Lyme Inn
Radisson Arrowhead
  White Oak
Ragamont Inn
  Ragamont Inn
Randall's Ordinary
  Randall's Ordinary

Connecticut

Roger Sherman Inn
   Roger Sherman Inn
Salisbury Inn
   Salisbury Inn
Sheraton Stamford Hotel
   Magnificent J's
Silvermine Tavern
   Silvermine Tavern
Simsbury 1820 House
   Simsbury 1820 House
Stonehenge Inn
   Stonehenge
Tollgate Hill Inn
   Tollgate Hill Inn
Under Mountain Inn
   Under Mountain Inn
West Hartford Inn
   Assaggio
White Hart
   Julie's Tap Room

"In" Places

Arizona Flats
Bacci's
Bella Luna
Bloodroot
Boxing Cat Grill
Bull's Head Diner
Cafe Christina
Centro
Derosa's
Frank Pepe Pizzeria
Great American Cafe
Hot Tamales
Hot Tomato's
Le Bistro des Amis
Max-a-Mia
Miche-Mache
Pasta Nostra
Robert Henry's
Sol e Luna
Spazzi Trattoria
Su Casa
Terra Ristorante
Truc Orient Express

Late Dining
(All hours after 11 PM)
Oasis Diner (12)
Pequot Grill (24 hrs.)
Rein's (12)

Noteworthy Newcomers (50)
Abis
A Garden Cafe
Al Dimarco's
Alforno
Amadeo's
Amarillo Grill

Bagdon's
Bart's Paradise Cafe
Bella Luna
Bertucci's
Bluewater Cafe
Bombay's
Bricks
Bull's Head Diner
Butterfield's
Cafe Christina
Chef Martin
Ciaobella
Diorio
Fjord Fisheries
Gail's Station House
Greenwich Harbor Inn
Hay Day Cafe
Hot Tamales
Il Forno
Jetstream's Cafe
Kansas City Bar-B-Q
Kujaku
La Trattoria
Le Bistro des Amis
Le Marmiton
Lemon Grass
Li's Brothers Inn
MacKenzie's Old Ale
Magnificent J's
Max-a-Mia
Mayflower Inn
Mona Lisa
Miche-Mache
Oasis Diner
Pequot Grill
Pompano Oyster Bar
Post and Beam
Prezzo
Rattlesnake Bar
Sagebrush Cafe
Sol e Luna
Taj Mahal
Terra Ristorante
Vicolo
West Street Grill
White Hart
Woods

Offbeat
Al Dimarco's
Angsavanee East
Arizona Flats
Bali of Greenwich
Black Rock Castle
Bloodroot
Bombay's
Bonani
Diana
Harry's TX BBQ
Heavenly Hog

Connecticut

Khan's Mongolian
Kansas City Bar-B-Q
La Maison Indochine
Little Mark's
Miche-Mache
Prince of Wales
Rumba
Sagebrush Cafe
Shish Kebab House
Spazzi Trattoria
Taj Mahal
Truc Orient Express

Outdoor Dining

(G = Garden,
 S = Sidewalk,
 W = Waterside location)
Abbott's (G,W)
A Garden Cafe (G)
Allen's (W)
Amadeo's (G)
Amadeus (S)
Apricot's (G,W)
Apulia (G,S)
Arizona Flats (G)
Bacci's (G)
Backstreet (G,S)
Bella Luna (G)
Bellini (G)
Black Rock Castle (G)
Black Goose Grill (G)
Bloodroot (G,W)
Bluewater Cafe (G)
Boulders Inn (G,W)
Bricks (G)
Butterfield's (G)
Centro (G,S)
Chart House (S,W)
Chez Pierre (Wstpt.) (G)
Chop Chop (G)
Cobble Cookery (G)
Cobb's Mill Inn (W)
Doc's (W)
Dolce (W)
Fagan's (W)
Freshfields (G,W)
Gail's Station (G,S)
Golden Lamb (G,W)
Great Amer Cafe (G,S)
Greenwich Harbor (G)
Hacienda don Emilio (G)
Homestead Inn (G)
Hop Brook (G,W)
Hopkins Inn (G)
Hot Tamales (G,S)
Hot Tomato's (G)
Inn at Woodstock Hill (G)
Inn/Gwyn Careg (G,W)
Inn/Waramaug (G,W)

Jetstream's Cafe (G)
Kansas City Bar-B-Q (G)
Kismet (G)
La Trattoria (G)
Le Bistro des Amis (G)
Little Mark's (G)
MacKenzie's Old Ale (G)
MacKenzie's Rdhse. (G)
Mansion Clam House (G)
Mayflower Inn (G)
Meson Galicia (G,S)
Mhai Thai (G)
Murasaki (G)
Panda Pavilion (G)
Prince of Wales (G)
Ragamont Inn (G)
River Club Cafe (G)
Roger Sherman Inn (G)
Rumba (G)
Sakura (G)
Scoozi (G,S)
Silvermine Tav (G,W)
Simsbury 1820 House (G)
Sol e Luna (G)
Spinning Wheel Inn (G)
Stonehenge (W)
Su Casa (G)
Terra Ristorante (G)
Thataway Cafe (G)
Tollgate Hill Inn (G)
Tucson Cafe (G,S)
White Hart (G)
Wild Scallion (G)

Parties & Private Rooms

(All major hotels, plus
 the following; best of
 the many)
Abbott's*
Allen's Clam House
Amadeo's*
Amadeus
Apricot's*
Apulia
Arizona Flats
Avon Old Farms Inn*
Azteca's
Bacci's*
Bella Luna
Bellini
Bertrand*
Black Rock Castle*
Boxing Cat Grill*
Bruxelles Brasserie*
Butterfield's
Cafe du Bec Fin
Cannery Cafe
Carbone's*

144

Connecticut

Cavey's*
Centro*
Chez Pierre (Wstpt.)
Christopher's*
Cobb's Mill Inn*
Columbus Park
Congress Rotisserie
Costa del Sol
Da Pietro's
Di Fiore's*
Dolce Italian Bistro
Fine Bouche*
500 Blake St. Cafe*
5 Mile River Grille
Freshfields*
Golden Lamb Buttery
Gregory's
Hacienda don Emilio*
Heavenly Hog
Hop Brook*
Hot Tomato's
Il Falco*
Il Forno
Inn at Ridgefield*
Jean-Louis
Jetstream's Cafe
Khan's Mongolian
L'Abbee
La Bretagne*
La Strada
Le Bon Coin*
Le Chambord*
Le Marmiton*
Leon's*
MacKenzie's Old Ale*
MacKenzie's Rdhse.*
Maison le Blanc*
Max on Main
Meson Galicia
Miche-Mache*
Morgan*
Oasis Diner
Ondine*
Pellicci's*
Peppercorn's Grill
Rattlesnake Bar*
River Club Cafe*
Robert Henry's
Rudy's*
Scoozi
Scribner's*
Sol e Luna*
Spinning Wheel Inn*
Standish House*
Three Bears*
Vernon Stiles Inn*
West Street Grill*
White Hart*
Whitehouse*
(* Private rooms)

People-Watching
Amadeus
Bellini
Bertrand
Bloodroot
Boxing Cat Grill
Bruxelles Brasserie
Bull's Head Diner
Cafe Christina
Centro
Congress Rotisserie
Derosa's
Frank Pepe Pizzeria
Gail's Station House
Great American Cafe
Hearthstone
Homestead Inn
Hot Tomato's
Le Chambord
Mario's
Max on Main
Onion Alley
Pasta Nostra
Pierpont's
Robert Henry's
Sol e Luna
West Street Grill

Power Scenes
Amadeus
Bellini
Bertrand
Homestead Inn
Jean-Louis
Max on Main
Pierpont's
Robert Henry's
Sol e Luna

Pre-Theater/ Early-Bird Menus
(Call to check
  prices and times)
Amadeus
Assaggio
Bagdon's
Capers
Charles Bistro
Chart House
Cobb's Mill Inn
Copper Beech Inn
Diorio
Fagan's Riverview
Fine Bouche
Hearthstone
Hop Brook
Little Mark's
MacKenzie's Rdhse.
Nistico's Red Barn
Peppermill

Connecticut

Rumba
Saybrook Fish House
Scribner's
Three Bears
Tiger Bowl
Vernon Stiles Inn
Versailles
Whitehouse

Prix Fixe Menus
(Call to check
 prices and times)
Abis
A Garden Cafe
Amadeus
Avon Old Farms Inn
Bacci's
Bagdon's
Bella Italia
Bertrand
Bluewater Cafe
Boulders Inn
Cafe du Bec Fin
Carbone's
Cavey's
C'est Si Bon
Charles Bistro
Copper Beech Inn
Da Pietro's
Diana
Dolce Italian Bistro
Fine Bouche
500 Blake Street Cafe
Ganga
Griswold Inn
Harry's TX BBQ
Hop Brook
Inn at Ridgefield
Inn/Lake Waramaug
Jetstream's Cafe
Khan's Mongolian
Kismet
Kujaku
La Provence
La Trattoria
Le Chambord
MacKenzie's Roadhse.
Magnificent J's
Maison le Blanc
Meera
Mona Lisa
Mooring
Nistico's Red Barn
Ondine
Peppermill
Prince of Wales
Radisson Arrowhead
Randall's Ordinary
Jean-Louis

Roger Sherman Inn
Rumba
Sakura
Scoozi
Sheesh Mahal
Shish Kebab House
Silvermine Tavern
Stonehenge
Truc Orient Express
Vernon Stiles Inn
Versailles
Wild Scallion

Pubs
Apricot's
Black Rock Castle
500 Blake St. Cafe
Hop Brook
MacKenzie's Old Ale
Whitehouse

Quiet Conversation
Amadeo's
Amadeus
Avon Old Farms Inn
Bali of Greenwich
Bee and Thistle Inn
Bella Luna
Bellini
Bertrand
Cafe du Bec Fin
Chale Ipanema
Chez Pierre (Staf. Spg.)
Christopher's
Cobb's Mill Inn
Copper Beech Inn
Da Pietro's
Diorio
Elms Inn
Fine Bouche
5 Mile River Grille
Ganga
Hay Day Cafe
Homestead Inn
Hopkins Inn
Il Falco
Inn at Gwyn Careg
Inn at Ridgefield
Inn at Woodstock Hill
Inn/Lake Waramaug
L'Abbee
La Provence
La Strada
La Trattoria
La Villa
Le Bon Coin
Le Chambord
Le Marmiton
Maria's Trattoria

Connecticut

Max on Main
Mayflower Inn
Meson Galicia
Mona Lisa
Morgan
Nistico's Red Barn
Old Lyme Inn
Ondine
Post and Beam
Ragamont Inn
Restaurant du Village
Robert Henry's
Roger Sherman Inn
Silvermine Tavern
Standish House
Stonehenge
Su Casa
Three Bears
Tollgate Hill Inn
1249 West
Vernon Stiles Inn
White Hart

Romantic Spots

Avon Old Farms Inn
Bee and Thistle Inn
Bella Luna
Cafe du Bec Fin
Chez Pierre (Staf. Spg.)
Christopher's
Cobb's Mill Inn
Copper Beech Inn
Elms Inn
Fine Bouche
Homestead Inn
Hopkins Inn
Il Forno
Inn at Gwyn Careg
Inn at Ridgefield
Inn at Woodstock Hill
Inn/Lake Waramaug
L'Abbee
La Trattoria
Le Bon Coin
Mona Lisa
Nistico's Red Barn
Old Lyme Inn
Post and Beam
Roger Sherman Inn
Silvermine Tavern
Spinning Wheel Inn
Standish House
Stonehenge
Su Casa
Three Bears
Tollgate Hill Inn
White Hart

Senior Appeal

Abbott's
Al Dimarco's
Allen's Clam House
Assaggio
Bull's Head Diner
Capers
Cobb's Mill Inn
Fagan's Riverview
Hopkins Inn
Le Chambord
Little Mark's
MacKenzie's Rdhse.
Manero's
Maria's Trattoria
Oasis Diner
Pellicci's
Peppermill
Randall's Ordinary
Rein's
Rudy's
Rumba
Saybrook Fish House
Scribner's
Silvermine Tavern
Spinning Wheel Inn
Wild Scallion

Smoking Prohibited

Bee and Thistle Inn
Bloodroot
Bluewater Cafe
China Pavilion
Cobble Cookery
Doc's
Golden Lamb Buttery
Hay Day Cafe
Inn at Gwyn Careg
Kansas City Bar-B-Q
Lemon Grass
Little Kitchen
Murasaki
Pantry
Saybrook Fish House
White Hart

Teas

Bee and Thistle Inn
Cobble Cookery
Inn at Woodstock Hill
Pantry
Simsbury 1820 House
Versailles

Teenagers & Other Youthful Spirits

Abbott's
Alforno
Bertucci's

Connecticut

Breakaway
Bricks
Bull's Head Diner
Butterfield's
Centro
Frank Pepe Pizzeria
Gail's Station House
Great American Cafe
Heavenly Hog
Jetstream's Cafe
Kansas City Bar-B-Q
Mooring
Oasis Diner
Onion Alley
Pellicci's
Prezzo
Randall's Ordinary
Sally's Apizza
Sunrise Pizza
Tucson Cafe

Wheelchair Access

(Check for bathroom access, almost all hotels, plus the following)

Abbott's
Abis
A Garden Cafe
Alforno
Al Dimarco's
Allen's Clam House
Amadeo's
Amarillo Grill
Angsavanee East
Apricot's
Apulia
Arizona Flats
Avon Old Farms Inn
Azteca's
Bacci's
Backstreet
Bagdon's
Bart's Paradise Cafe
Bella Italia
Bella Luna
Bertucci's
Black Rock Castle
Black Goose Grill
Bloodroot
Bluewater Cafe
Bombay's
Bonani
Boxing Cat Grill
Breakaway
Bricks
Brookfield Bistro
Bruxelles Brasserie
Bull's Head Diner
Butterfield's
Cafe Christina

Cafe du Bec Fin
Cannery Cafe
Capers
Carbone's
Cavey's
C'est Si Bon
Charles Bistro
Chart House
Chef Martin
Christopher Martin's
Ciaobella
Cobble Cookery
Columbus Park
Congress Rotisserie
Costa del Sol
Diana
Di Fiore's
Doc's
Dolce Italian Bistro
Fagan's Riverview
Fine Bouche
Fiddlers
500 Blake St. Cafe
5 Mile River Grille
Fjord Fisheries
Frank's
Gaetano's
Ganga
Gates
Giovanni's
Golden Lamb Buttery
Great American Cafe
Gregory's
Hacienda don Emilio
Harry's TX BBQ
Hay Day Cafe
Heavenly Hog
Hop Brook
Hot Tamales
Hot Tomato's
Il Falco
Il Forno
Il Mulino
Jean-Louis
Jetstream's Cafe
Khan's Mongolian
Kansas City Bar-B-Q
Kismet
Kujaku
L'Abbee
La Bretagne
La Strada
La Trattoria
La Villa
Le Bistro des Amis
Le Bon Coin
Le Chambord
Lemon Grass
Leon's
Li's Brothers Inn

Connecticut

Little Kitchen
Little Mark's
Lotus East
Lotus Restaurant
MacKenzie's Old Ale
MacKenzie's Rdhse.
Manero's
Mario's
Max-a-Mia
Max on Main
Meera
Meson Galicia
Mhai Thai
Miche-Mache
Mona Lisa
Morgan
Murasaki
Nistico's Red Barn
Ondine
Onion Alley
Panda Inn
Panda Pavilion
Parma
Pasta Nostra
Pasta Vera
Pellicci's
Peppercorn's Grill
Peppermill
Pequot Grill
Pompano Oyster Bar
Prezzo
Rattlesnake Bar
Rein's
River Club Cafe
Robert Henry's
Rudy's
Ruth's Chris
Saigon City
Sagebrush Cafe
Sally's Apizza
Saybrook Fish House
Scoozi
Scribner's
Sesame Seed
Shish Kebab House
Sol e Luna
Spazzi Trattoria
Spinning Wheel Inn
Standish House
Su Casa
Sunrise Pizza
Thataway Cafe
Three Bears
Tiger Bowl
Tucson Cafe
1249 West
Versailles
Vicolo
West Street Grill

White Hart
Whitehouse
Wild Scallion
Woodland
Woods

Winning Wine Lists
Amadeus
Bacci's
Bertrand
Chez Pierre (Staf. Spg.)
Pasta Nostra
Robert Henry's

Young Children
(Besides the normal
fast-food places)
Abbott's*
Alforno*
Allen's Clam House
Amarillo Grill*
Angelino's*
Arizona Flats*
Avon Old Farms Inn*
Backstreet*
Bart's Paradise Cafe*
Breakaway
Bricks*
Bull's Head Diner*
Butterfield's*
Cannery Cafe*
Capers*
Carbone's*
Centro*
Chart House*
Christopher's*
Diana*
Di Fiore's*
Diorio*
Fiddlers*
500 Blake St. Cafe*
Fjord Fisheries*
Frank Pepe Pizzeria
Frank's*
Gail's Station House*
Gates*
Great American Cafe*
Griswold Inn*
Hacienda don Emilio
Harry's TX BBQ*
Heavenly Hog
Hop Brook*
Hot Tamales*
Inn at Woodstock Hill*
Inn/Lake Waramaug*
Jetstream's Cafe*
Khan's Mongolian*
Kansas City Bar-B-Q*
Kujaku*

149

Connecticut

Le Bon Coin*
Leon's*
Li's Brothers Inn*
Little Mark's*
MacKenzie's Old Ale*
MacKenzie's Rdhse.*
Manero's*
Maria's Trattoria
Mario's*
Max-a-Mia*
Mooring*
Murasaki*
Nistico's Red Barn*
Oasis Diner*
Onion Alley
Panda Inn
Pantry
Parma*
Pellicci's*
Peppermill*
Pompano Oyster Bar*

Ragamont Inn*
Randall's Ordinary*
Rein's
Rudy's*
Ruth's Chris
Sagebrush Cafe*
Sakura*
Sally's Apizza
Saybrook Fish House*
Shish Kebab House*
Silvermine Tavern*
Simsbury 1820 House
Standish House*
Su Casa*
Sunrise Pizza
Three Bears*
1249 West*
Vernon Stiles Inn*
Whitehouse*
Woodland*
(*Children's menu served)

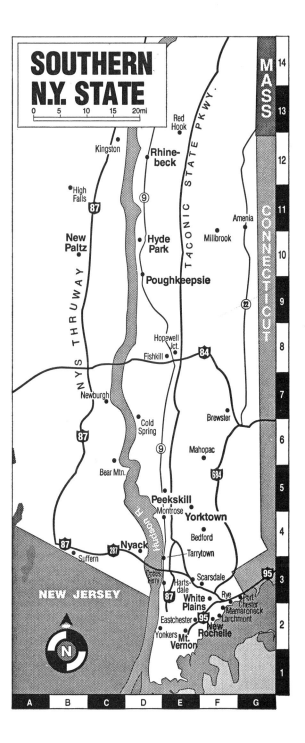

SOUTHERN NEW YORK STATE'S MOST POPULAR RESTAURANTS

Each of our reviewers has been asked to name his or her five favorite restaurants. The 40 spots most frequently named, in order of their popularity, are:

1. La Panetiere
2. Xaviar's in Piermont
3. Livanos
4. Harrald's
5. Freelance Cafe
6. Box Tree
7. American Bounty
8. Bully Boy's
9. Buffet de la Gare
10. L'Hostellerie Bres.
11. Escoffier Room
12. Auberge Maxime
13. Xaviar's in Garrison
14. Pinocchio
15. La Camelia
16. Arch
17. Inn at Pound Ridge
18. Dudley's
19. Le Chateau
20. Bistro Twenty-Two
21. Chart House
22. Old Drover's Inn
23. Dawat
24. Valentino's
25. Malabar Hill
26. Depuy Canal House
27. Willett House
28. Cobble Creek Cafe
29. Plumbush Inn
30. Auberge Argenteuil
31. Bird & Bottle Inn
32. Bistro Maxime
33. Troutbeck Inn
34. Eastchester Fish
35. Mulino's
36. Goldie's
37. Maxime's Brasserie
38. Ichi Riki
39. Il Cigno
40. 1766 Tavern

It's obvious that many of the restaurants on the above list are among the area's most expensive. However, all of New York City's surrounding areas have an abundance of bargain spots that are popular and worth noting. Southern New York State's Best Buys are listed on page 156.

TOP RATINGS*

TOP 40 FOOD RATINGS
(In order of rating)

29 – Xavier's in Piermont
28 – Xavier's in Garrison
　　　La Panetiere
27 – Harrald's
26 – Freelance Cafe
　　　Caterina de Medici
　　　Buffet de la Gare
　　　L'Hostellerie Bressane
　　　Auberge Maxime
　　　Escoffier Room
25 – Zeph's
　　　Box Tree
　　　American Bounty
　　　Marcello's
24 – Maxime's Brasserie
　　　Inn at Osborne Hill
　　　Sushi Raku
　　　Troutbeck Inn
　　　La Camelia
　　　L'Europe
　　　St. Andrew's Cafe

　　　Bistro Twenty-Two
23 – Arch
　　　Pinocchio
　　　Cafe Tamayo
　　　Depuy Canal House
　　　Les Bons Copains
　　　Inn at Pound Ridge
　　　Guida's
　　　Siam Sea Grill
　　　King & I
　　　Le Chateau
　　　Le Chambord
　　　Paul Ma's/Shanghai
22 – Hudson House (Nyack)
　　　Hunan Village
　　　Old Drover's Inn
　　　Thierry's Relais
　　　Il Cigno
　　　Il Portico

TOP SPOTS BY CUISINE

**Top American
(Contemporary)**
29 – Xavier's in Piermont
28 – Xavier's in Garrison
26 – Freelance Cafe
25 – Zeph's
　　　American Bounty

Top Chinese
23 – Paul Ma's/Shanghai
22 – Hunan Village
19 – Pagoda Restaurant
　　　Hunan Wok
　　　Hunan Manor

**Top American
(Traditional)**
23 – Inn at Pound Ridge
22 – Country Manor
21 – Bird & Bottle Inn
　　　Bully Boy's
18 – Old '76 House

Top Continental
27 – Harrald's
24 – Inn at Osborne Hill
23 – Arch
　　　Depuy Canal House
22 – Old Drover's Inn

---

*Excluding restaurants with voting too low to be reliable.

Top French
28 – La Panetiere
26 – Buffet de la Gare
     L'Hostellerie Bress.
     Auberge Maxime
     Escoffier Room

Top Hotel Dining
24 – Troutbeck Inn
22 – Old Drover's Inn
     Mulino's,
        La Reserve Hotel
21 – Bird & Bottle Inn
20 – 1766 Tavern,
        Beekman Arms

Top Indian
22 – Dawat
     Malabar Hill
21 – India House
19 – Bengal Tiger
18 – Abhilash

Top Italian (Northern)
22 – Il Cigno
     Il Portico
     Emilio's
     Mona Trattoria
21 – Giulio's of Tappan

Top Italian
(North & South)
26 – Caterina de Medici
25 – Marcello's
23 – Pinocchio
     Guida's
22 – Valentino's

Top Japanese
24 – Sushi Raku
22 – Ichi Riki
20 – Satsuma-ya
19 – Mount Fuji
18 – Sakura

Top Newcomers
23 – Les Bons Copains
20 – 1776 Tavern
—   Marichu
—   Maxime's La Petite
—   McKinney & Doyle

Top Seafood
22 – Il Portico
     Dudley's
     Caravela
21 – Eastchester Fish
20 – Salerno's

Top Steakhouses
21 – Willett House
20 – Salerno's
19 – Hudson's Rib/Fish
     Gregory's
18 – Jason's Ltd.

Top Worth a Trip
29 – Xaviar's, Piermont
28 – Xaviar's, Garrison
27 – Harrald's,
        Stormville
26 – Freelance Cafe,
        Nyack
     Buffet de la Gare,
        Hastings-on-Hudson

TOP 40 OVERALL DECOR
(In order of rating)

27 – La Panetiere
Le Chateau**

26 – Box Tree
Harrald's

25 – Troutbeck Inn/V
Xaviar's in Garrison/V
Inn at Pound Ridge
L'Hostellerie Bressane
Auberge Maxime/V

24 – Old Drover's Inn
Le Chambord
Escoffier Room
Plumbush Inn/V
American Bounty
St. Andrew's Cafe
Bird & Bottle Inn/V
Xaviar's in Piermont

23 – Depuy Canal House
Maxime's Brasserie
Arch

1766 Tavern
Bully Boy's
Bistro Twenty-Two
Mount Fuji

22 – Capriccio /V
Old '76 House
Penfield's /V
Caterina de Medici/V
Giulio's of Tappan
Thierry's Relais
Il Portico
Chart House/V

21 – Traveler's Rest
Hudson House/V(Nyack)
Livanos
Heathcote Crossing
L'Europe
Country Manor
Mona Trattoria

TOP 40 OVERALL SERVICE
(In order of rating)

27 – Harrald's

26 – Xaviar's in Piermont
Xaviar's in Garrison
La Panetiere

24 – Box Tree
St. Andrew's Cafe
Freelance Cafe
American Bounty
Caterina de Medici
Escoffier Room
Zeph's
Troutbeck Inn
Arch
Auberge Maxime

23 – L'Hostellerie Bressane
Bistro Twenty-Two
Country Manor
Buffet de la Gare
Depuy Canal House
L'Europe

22 – Le Chateau
Old Drover's Inn
Giulio's of Tappan
Auberge Argenteuil

21 – Plumbush Inn
Inn at Pound Ridge
Dudley's
Armadillo
Le Chambord
Susan & Bad Bill's
Sushi Raku
King & I
Cascade Mtn. Winery
Bully Boy's
Maxime's Brasserie
Bistro Maxime
Hudson House (Nyack)
Thierry's Relais
Cafe Tamayo
Guida's

V = Also has an outstanding view.

BEST BUYS

TOP 40 BANGS FOR THE BUCK

This list reflects the best dining in our *Survey*. It is produced by dividing the cost of a meal into the combined ratings for food, decor and service.

1. Red Rooster
2. Hunan Village
3. India House Rest.
4. St. Andrew's Cafe
5. King & I
6. Imperial Wok
7. Paul Ma's/Shanghai
8. Good Enough to Eat
9. Santa Fe (Tarrytown)
10. Armadillo
11. Grandma's Country
12. Malabar Hill
13. Foster's Coach Hse.
14. Hunan Manor
15. Nanuet Hotel
16. Sushi Raku
17. Khan's Mongolian
18. Susan/Bad Bill's Bar
19. Abhilash
20. Caterina de Medici
21. Hudson House (Nyack)
22. Pagoda
23. Hartsdale Garden
24. Hunan Wok
25. Cascade Mtn. Winery
26. Horsefeathers
27. Cafe Tamayo
28. Bengal Tiger
29. Dawat
30. Freelance Cafe
31. Siam Orchid
32. Ichi Riki
33. Haciendo Don Emilio
34. Ciao
35. Reef 'n Beef
36. Siam Sea Grill
37. Corridos Mexicanos
38. Louie's
39. Pancho Villa's
40. American Bounty

Additional Good Values

Aria
Bambina
Banta's
Benny's
Brass Anchor
Camino Real
Cantina
Casa Miguel
Chef Antonio
China Echo
Daniel's
Dynasty
Eastchester Fish G'rmet
Green and Bresler
Greenbaum/Gilhooly's
Gus's Franklin Park
Huckleberry's
Hudson's Ribs and Fish
John Richard's
Kit 'N Caboodle
La Fonda del Sol
La Mandas
La Scala
Le Shack

Mariner's Harbor
McKinney & Doyle
Orchid Garden
Owl's Nest
Palmer House Inn
Pars
Priya
Reka's Thai
Rockwell's
Royal Siam
Sam's
Santa Fe (Tivoli)
Schemmy's
Schneller's
Seasons
Silver Spoon Cafe
Slattery's
Szechuan Flower
Temptations
Trio's Cafe
Turning Point
Valentino's
Via Appia
Westchester Trawler

Southern
New York State
Area Code 914
Unless Otherwise Noted

F	D	S	C

Abhilash India Cuisine/S | 18 | 13 | 16 | $22 |
(New Rochelle) **F2**

30 Division St. (bet. Main & Huguenot Sts.), 235-8390
*M – The "plain-Jane", "dingy location" is not what
attracts surveyors to this Indian – it's the "huge" portions
of "good food" ("ask for hot") at "depression prices";
critics say there's "nothing to recommend now that the
sitar music is gone", and service is inconsistent; though
it's "pricey", two-for-one coupons ease the pain.*

Abis/S (Mamaroneck) **F2** | 18 | 15 | 16 | $29 |

406 Mamaroneck Ave. (near RR station), 698-8777
*M – "Underrated", say sushi lovers, though some demur
that this Downtown spot is "run of the mill"; recent
renovations (not yet reflected in scores), "friendly"
service and decent value attract a following, including "a
lot of Japanese people" – always a hopeful sign.*

Allyn's/S (Millbrook) **F10** | 21 | 19 | 19 | $32 |

Rte. 44 (4 miles east of Millbrook), 677-5888
*M – Located in a 200-year-old Dutchess County
farmhouse, this "nice countryside restaurant" is "hard to
find" but worth seeking out for its "creative" American
food ("great specials") and "casual yet elegant" setting;
critics say service is "lackadaisical."*

AMERICAN BOUNTY, THE | 25 | 24 | 24 | $36 |
(Hyde Park) **D10**

Culinary Institute of America, 651 S. Albany Post Rd.,
Rte. 9 (north of E. Dorsey Lane), 452-9600
*U – Accolades pile up for this Contemporary American
where you can see "tomorrow's culinary stars today";
boosters say it's an "eating education", with "superior
food", "nice ambiance" and servers who do an
"outstanding job"; despite "awfully expensive" prices,
plan on making weekend reservations well in advance.*

An American Bistro (Tuckahoe) **E2** | – | – | – | M |

174 Marbledale Rd. (Fisher Ave.), 793-0807
*Denise and Robert Horton finally opened their own
Contemporary American restaurant in Westchester
County, and they're capitalizing on the opportunity; the
mid-priced seasonal menu and energetic service keep
this charmer's 44 seats full.*

Angsavanee/S (Port Chester) **F3** | 21 | 17 | 19 | $36 |
163 N. Main St. (Highland St.), 937-2727
*M – Comments about this Westchester Northern Italian
(named for the owner's Thai wife) range from "top-notch" to
"boring", though the numbers say "consistently good"; the
staff gets mixed reviews; "high prices" are also faulted.*

Anthony's Uptown (Kingston) **C12** | – | – | – | E |
33 Crown St. (John St.), 339-2184
*It's located on the so-called oldest corner in America – all
four buildings date back to the 1700s; though few of our
surveyors are familiar with this Ulster County Contemporary
American, service is attentive, the decor comfortable, and
piano music on the weekends is a plus.*

ARCH, THE/S (Brewster) **F7** | 23 | 23 | 24 | $49 |
Rte. 22 N (north end of Rte. 684), 279-5011
*M – "Wonderful from escargot to soufflé" is the supportive
reaction to this Classic French favorite, with its pampering
servers in black-tie and "warm", "romantic" ambiance in a
wooded setting; but many dismiss it as "faux NYC" and
"disappointing at the price."*

Aria*/S (Yonkers) **D2** | 19 | 14 | 16 | $25 |
2375 Central Park Ave. (Jackson Ave.), 779-9888
*U – The place for Korean BBQ; it's "huge", "crowded",
"noisy" and smoky from the do-it-yourself barbecuing of
marinated beef, chicken, pork and shrimp; "fun for kids" and
"worth a try"; don't count on your waiter speaking English.*

Armadillo/S (Kingston) **C12** | 21 | 18 | 21 | $26 |
97 Abeel St. (bet. Wurtz & Hone Sts.), 339-1550
*U – This "lively", "authentic" Mexican "with a twist" of SW
style "perks up sleepy Kingston"; "fun waiters" and "lots of
food" at good prices make it a "hangout" the "locals love."*

Auberge Argenteuil/S | 22 | 21 | 22 | $48 |
(Hartsdale) **F3**
42 Healy Ave. (Central Park Ave.), 948-0597
*M – Respondents who love this "old-fashioned" Classic
French consider it "still worthy after all these years";
they praise the "romantic setting" in a hilltop Victorian
manor, "wonderful food" and "excellent" staff; critics
lambast "skimpy portions", "tired decor" and "sporadic
service"; most agree the prices are high.*

AUBERGE MAXIME/S | 26 | 25 | 24 | $52 |
(North Salem) **G4**
Rte. 116 (Rte. 121), 669-5450
*U – Duck (prepared seven different ways) is the word at
this "up-country sanctuary" with its "excellent", if "pricey",
French cuisine, "beautiful setting" and "accommodating"
service; it's "the closest the New York metro area has to a
culinary superstar."*

Southern New York State | F | D | S | C |

Azuma Sushi/S (Hartsdale) **F3** | – | – | – | E |
219 E. Hartsdale Ave. (near Hartsdale Station), 725-0660
You'll find "impeccable Japanese food in an austere setting" at this Westchester sushi-and-sashimi spot; it's always packed, thanks to serving "the best sushi in Westchester", even "better than NYC", but you'll have to pay the price.

Bambina (Armonk) **F3** | – | – | – | I |
(fka Covington)
45 Main St. (between School Lane & Maple Ave.), 273-5700
The old Covington is a "new, lively neighborhood gathering spot" specializing in gourmet pizza and pasta; with "friendly" service and modest prices, it's casual dining and good for families.

Banta's Steak & Stein/S | 13 | 14 | 15 | $24 |
(Wappingers Falls) **E8**, 9 Mall Plaza (Rte. 9), 297-6770
(New Windsor) **C7**, Union Ave. (Rte. 17K), 564-7678
M – Not a place for the culinary elite, but surveyors in general like these low-key steakhouses (despite the "tacky atmosphere") for their "simple fare and salad bar"; "good" burgers and "fair" prices make them "wise choices for families" at least "if you're in the area."

Bear Mountain Inn/S | 11 | 17 | 13 | $27 |
(Bear Mountain State Park) **C6**
Bear Mountain Inn, 786-2731
U – The American-Continental food at this rambling, "rustic" hunting lodge is "institutional" and "ordinary" at best, but that's not what the Inn is about; the park "compensates", with its "scenic" views, zoo and hiking trails; it may be a "tourist trap", but what choice is there?

Bengal Tiger/S (White Plains) **F3** | 19 | 16 | 17 | $24 |
144 E. Post Rd. (bet. Mamaroneck Ave. & Court St.), 948-5191
U – Reviewers appreciate this sensibly priced Westchester Indian whose "earthy food makes you feel like a native"; the "exotic" setting includes authentic art, a Sikh doorman and a glassed-in tandoori oven; if "slooow" service is a pain, then the lunch buffet "is a great opportunity to try several things" at a faster pace.

Benny's/SX (Irvington) **E3** | 16 | 7 | 14 | $24 |
6 S. Broadway (Main St.), 591-9811
M – "Crowded" and "noisy" with "long lines" describes this "no-atmosphere" institution, where schools of diners migrate for heaping portions of "good plain fish" at "bargain prices"; detractors say they've "lost their touch" and the food is "unexciting."

BIRD & BOTTLE INN/S | 21 | 24 | 21 | $41 |
(Garrison) **D6**
Old Albany Post Rd. (off Rte. 9), 424-3000
*U – "Like Thanksgiving dinner always", this country inn
located in an "intimate" tavern dating to 1761 pleases
fans with "romantic" colonial candlelit ambiance that
outshines the Traditional American and Continental fare.*

Bistro Maxime (Chappaqua) **E3** | 22 | 20 | 21 | $38 |
136 N. Greeley Ave. (near King St.), 238-0362
*M – This "casual" mid-Westchester bistro is run by
Maxime Ribera, whom fans describe as "the master
cooking for his friends"; though some say it "doesn't live
up to expectations" and warn that it's "not inexpensive",
most of our respondents praise its "consistently" "fine"
food and "charming" setting.*

BISTRO TWENTY-TWO/S | 24 | 23 | 23 | $45 |
(Bedford) **F4**
Rte. 22 (east of Rte. 684), 234-7333
*U – A menu change from Traditional French to a lighter,
more international style has produced "innovative" and
"interesting" results; with muted lighting and attentive
service, this Bedford bistro is still a good "place to
surprise out-of-town guests" with how sophisticated the
'burbs can be – even if prices are high.*

Black Bass Grill/S (Rye) **F2** | 19 | 18 | 17 | $27 |
2 Central Ave. (Post Rd.), 967-6700
*M – The skill of chef Bradley Barnes, who represented
the U.S. at the 1992 Culinary Olympics in Frankfurt, is
evident in the "creative cooking" served at this "casual"
American bistro in a Victorian home; though critics call it
"trendy, smoky, Waspy and stock-brokery", its admirers
just "sit by the fireplace" and enjoy.*

BOX TREE/S (Purdys) **F4** | 25 | 26 | 24 | $56 |
Box Tree Hotel, Rte. 22 (Rte. 116), 277-3677
*U – Surveyors rave about this "precious jewel" of a
Classic French country inn, located in an "elegant",
"romantic" 18th-century farmhouse in northern
Westchester; as breathtaking prices reflect, jewels cost
money, but few complain given the "superb atmosphere",
"fabulous food" and service that's "hard to beat."*

Brass Anchor*/S | 16 | 19 | 18 | $25 |
(Poughkeepsie) **D10**
31 Riverpoint Rd. (off Rte. 9), 452-3232
*U – A "beautiful" waterfront location overlooking the
Hudson River endears this "decent" seafooder to our
voters; modest prices and dependable service along
with the view make it "great for a summer evening."*

Brasserie Swiss (Ossining) **D4** | 17 | 13 | 18 | $30 |
118 Croton Ave. (bet. 9th St. & Rte. 9A), 941-0319
*M – Swiss-Continental food and "attentive service" are
the calling cards at this mid-Westchester spot, but
surveyors disagree on chef-owner Rolf Baumgartner's
food, with responses ranging from "nothing special" to
"fine"; many think the decor needs "some help."*

BUFFET DE LA GARE | 26 | 19 | 23 | $47 |
(Hastings-on-Hudson) **D3**
155 Southside Ave. (opposite RR station), 478-1671
*U – Forget the cramped quarters and "uncomfortable
chairs": the "superb" Classic French food served in this
mid-Westchester "bistro" is worth any discomfort – and
price; "gracious" service and "traditional, homey" food
make this like visiting "a bit of France."*

Bully Boy's/S (Congers) **D4** | 21 | 23 | 21 | $37 |
117 Rte. 303 (NY Twy., exit 12), 268-6555
*U – A Rockland County standby for 30 years, this merry
"old English" inn, complete with a duck pond, offers
"bountiful" Continental-American fare accompanied by
complimentary fruit, scones and honey; the country
setting, "attentive service" and "well-prepared food"
make high-side prices seem fair.*

Cafe Tamayo/S (Saugerties) **E14** | 23 | 18 | 21 | $29 |
89 Partition St. (Main St.), 246-9371
*U – Chef-owners Ricki and James Tamayo bring a
"sophisticated" Contemporary American menu at "New
York prices" to this "out-of-the-way" Hudson River
community; located in a renovated 19th-century
bar/restaurant, it has a "well-earned reputation" for
palate- and "eye-pleasing food" and "comfortable",
"informal" atmosphere; N.B. it's also a B&B.*

Camino Real/S (Pleasantville) **E3** | 17 | 15 | 18 | $25 |
160 Marble Ave. (bet. Stanley Ave. & Irvington St.),
769-6207
*U – While not a gourmet's delight, this low-frills "family
place" serves "huge portions" of moderately priced,
"fresh", though "not inspiring", Mexican and Spanish
food; service is friendly, and the "Friday-night bonus" of
foot-stompin' country music and two-stepping is fun.*

Cantina Restaurant/S (Ardsley) **E3** | 12 | 15 | 15 | $23 |
Saw Mill River Pkwy. (south of I-287), 693-6565
*M – You can't miss this "middle-of-the-road" Tex-Mex in
the median of the Saw Mill River Parkway; it's "better for
a road stop than a destination", especially for "sangria
on the outdoor patio" on a "warm summer evening."*

Capriccio/S (Brewster) **F7** | 21 | 22 | 20 | $41 |
Rte. 22 N (north end of Rte. 684), 279-2873
*M – The view from the terrace overlooking the reservoir
is undeniably "gorgeous, especially in the fall", at this
Northern Italian on the Putnam-Dutchess border, but
respondents are mixed in their opinions of the food:
some call it "excellent" and others "ordinary"; service
receives equal waffling -- from "super" to "lackluster" –
but solid numbers suggest giving it a try.*

Caravela/S (Tarrytown) **D3** | 22 | 15 | 19 | $33 |
53 N. Broadway (Main St.), 631-1863
*M – "Interesting", "unusual" seafood prepared with
Portuguese flair is an "excellent" "change of pace" at
this "warm" but "dreary" storefront; cognoscenti say
"stick to the Portuguese dishes and the captain's
suggestion for fish."*

Carl's/S (Larchmont) **F2** | 19 | 16 | 17 | $31 |
121 Myrtle Blvd. (Chatsworth Ave.), 834-1244
*U – The "straightforward" steakhouse menu draws an
upscale clientele to this small, "crowded" neighborhood
haunt; the "no-reservations" policy is a sore point, but
the fact that there are people who are willing to face a
"one- to two-hour wait on weekends says it all."*

Carolina House/S (Kinderhook) **E14** | – | – | – | M |
59 Broad St. (Rte. 9 & Albany Ave.), 518-758-1669
*Located in a Columbia County village, this log cabin
attracts in-the-know sightseers from Albany, who enjoy
a hearty mid-priced Southern menu of baby-back ribs,
blackened prime rib, seafood and fried chicken; the
decor is a match for the generous country cooking.*

Casa Miguel/S (Mount Kisco) **E4** | 19 | 12 | 16 | $24 |
222 E. Main St. (5 miles east of Saw Mill River Pkwy.),
666-7588
*M – Some consider this "loud and crowded" Tex-Mexer
"the best in the area", but others say it's "the usual
plates overloaded with gringo pabulum"; fans cite the
fajitas, margaritas, and salsa and chips as favorites;
decor is bland, but portions are large and prices fair.*

Cascade Mountain Winery/S | 22 | 18 | 21 | $28 |
(Amenia) **G11**
Flint Hill Rd. (3 miles north of Rte. 22), 373-9021
*U – It's "a long trip from just about anywhere", but this
simple, "rustic", weekends-only "American restaurant on
an unpaved road" can be "great" for "Sunday brunch", a
"picnic-type lunch" or an "innovative" meal of "all fresh
ingredients"; you can also tour the winery.*

CATERINA DE MEDICI | 26 | 22 | 24 | $32 |
(Hyde Park) **D10**
Culinary Institute of America, 651 S. Albany Post Rd.,
Rte. 9 (north of E. Dorsey Lane), 452-9600
U – "Best of the CIA choices", this "splendid Nouvelle
Italian" might be "the best buy in all of America" thanks
to the $24, seven-course prix fixe menu (at the 6:30
seating only); a "lovely room", "wonderful" student
servers and terrific food make for an experience that
"shouldn't be missed"; reserve in advance.

Chart House/S (Dobbs Ferry) **E3** | 15 | 22 | 16 | $32 |
High St. (near RR station), 693-4130
M – "Too bad you can't eat the views", because a
"great" Hudson River location overlooking the Tappan
Zee Bridge and the Palisades is the main attraction at
this chain outlet; "spectacular sunsets" from the terrace
make up for a steakhouse menu that most find merely
"reliable" and service that seems "inexperienced."

Chef Antonio/S (Mamaroneck) **F2** | 15 | 11 | 16 | $26 |
551 Halstead Ave. (Beach St.), 698-8610
M – Surveyors either love or hate this "seedy"-
looking neighborhood "soul Southern" Italian, praising
the "sturdy, generous" food or calling it "typical" and
"mediocre"; the bottom line: "good value" makes it ok for
families or for an "informal weeknight dinner."

Chelsea on the Hudson/S | 18 | 16 | 18 | $30 |
(Nyack) **D4**
65 Main St. (bet. B'way & Piermont Rd.), 358-1973
M – This Contemporary American–Continental gets
average marks for its deco-inspired ambiance and
congenial service; it's rated by some as "a good place to
eat after an afternoon of antiquing", but others say it's
"not up to expectations"; one respondent questions its
name, suggesting "Chelsea on the Parking Lot" instead.

China Echo*/LS (New City) **C4** | 19 | 17 | 17 | $21 |
253 Littleton Rd. (Palisades Pkwy. exit 10), 638-4333
M – "One of the better Rockland Chinese", this friendly
"neighborhood" spot in a converted old house is known for
its "consistently good", affordable food (try the "lobster
and scallions" or "China Echo chicken") and decent
service; a few raters rant that it's "come way down."

Ciao Restaurant/S (Eastchester) **E2** | 16 | 15 | 16 | $23 |
5 John Albanese Pl. (Main St.), 779-4646
M – "Good for family night", this "frenetic" mid-
Westchester "yuppie pizza parlor" pulls decent marks
for its "pizza, pasta and prices", but demanding diners
say it's "more fun to watch" the chef make the pies and
the "pastas are underwhelming"; expect "lots of kids."

Clarksville Inn/S (West Nyack) **C4** | 15 | 15 | 18 | $28 |
1 Strawtown Rd. (W. Nyack Rd.), 358-8899
*M – The owner "tries hard to please" at this quaint Civil
War–era Rockland County inn, which for some makes
up for a reasonably priced Continental menu that
doesn't always hit the spot; this place "has an
interesting history", but it's "not worth a long drive."*

Cobble Creek Cafe/S (Purchase) **F3** | 20 | 20 | 19 | $36 |
578 Anderson Hill Rd. (bet. King & Purchase Sts.),
761-0050
*M – The "California setting", Contemporary American
food and a location "convenient to SUNY-Purchase
concerts and shows" make this "small, cozy" cafe
"praiseworthy"; however, it can be "hectic for
pre-theater" and "too cramped for comfort", and some
find "prices high for tiny portions."*

Corner Bakery/S (Pawling) **E8** | – | – | – | M |
10 Charles Colman Blvd. (E. Main St.), 855-3707
*This quaint cafe/bakery cooks up moderately priced
Traditional American dishes, including grilled swordfish,
roast quail and pasta ribbons with salmon; its wood
floors, brick walls and candlelit tables create a relaxed,
homey atmosphere; wine and beer only.*

Cornetta's Seafood/S (Piermont) **D3** | 14 | 11 | 15 | $29 |
641 Piermont Ave. (Rte. 9W), 359-9852
*U – Lauded for its Hudson River location, this casual
seafooder, popular with boaters, "has had its heyday"; a
"basic Piermont staple", it's ok for "summer fare" on the
patio with the family, but "pretty pedestrian" otherwise.*

Corridos Mexicanos/S | 19 | 15 | 17 | $25 |
(Yonkers) **D2**
High Ridge Plaza Shopping Ctr., 1771 Central Park Ave.
(2 blocks north of Tuckahoe Rd.), 779-0990
*U – This "good-value" shopping-strip spot serves
"imaginative", "authentic", "well-seasoned" Mexican
cuisine; despite less inspiring decor, "pleasant staff" and
a "strolling minstrel" on Saturdays might make you
"think you're in Mexico."*

Country Manor, The/S | 22 | 21 | 23 | $34 |
(Poughkeepsie) **D10**
221 Dutchess Tpke. (DeGarmo & Burnett Rds.), 471-1246
*M – Located in a "lovely" 160-year-old farmhouse, this
casual Continental offers "everything from a basic
turkey dinner" to "elaborate entrees"; the "nice drive up"
the turnpike is rewarded by good food and service that's
appropriate for a country manor.*

Southern New York State | F | D | S | C |

Crabtree's Kittle House/S | – | – | – | E |
(Chappaqua) **E3**
Crabtree's Kittle House Country Inn, 11 Kittle Rd. (Rte.
117 & Reader's Digest Rd.), 666-8044
*Located in a 200-year-old Colonial mansion surrounded
by gardens, this inn with 12 charming guest rooms
offers an "innovative" Contemporary American menu
and one of the largest wine lists in the Tri-State area.*

Crystal Bay/S (Peekskill) **E5** | – | – | – | M |
Charles Point Landing (Rte. 9, Louisa St. exit), 737-8332
*An "excellent view in new quarters" is drawing attention
since Crystal Bay moved to the historic Fleischmann's
Gin building; the rustic setting features floor-to-ceiling
windows and a deck overlooking the Hudson; seafood's
the star, but the menu has enough to satisfy everyone.*

Daniel's/S (Eastchester) **E2** | 16 | 13 | 17 | $26 |
434 White Plains Rd. (Mill Rd.), 337-1883
*U – The painted flowers on this "comfortable" Northern
Italian's 11 tables create a charming setting for "good"
homemade pasta and other "reasonably priced" dishes.*

Dawat/S (White Plains) **F3** | 22 | 20 | 19 | $28 |
230 E. Post Rd. (near old Alexander's Mall), 428-4411
*U – "Clearly the class act of Westchester Indian fare",
offering "excellent" authentic food ("when the menu says
spicy, believe it!") and "better service than most"; the
buffet lunch is "among the best deals in Westchester."*

Depuy Canal House/S | 23 | 23 | 23 | $46 |
(High Falls) **B11**
Rte. 213 (Lucas Ave.), 687-7700
*M – Once a Colonial tavern, now a charming Contemporary
American; one diner's "innovative" and "creative" food is
another's "weird" and "hit or miss"; though expensive and
not for everyone, loyal fans say "don't change a thing."*

Dockside Harbor/S (Tarrytown) **D3** | 14 | 17 | 15 | $28 |
Tarrytown Boat Club, White St. (across from Tarrytown
RR station), 631-2888
*M – A "drop-dead" Hudson River view partly makes up for
"ordinary" Continental food at this local standard; popular
with commuters, it also attracts boaters with its docking
spaces; the patio is a plus, but service could improve.*

Dudley's Restaurant/S | 22 | 20 | 21 | $34 |
(Ossining) **D4**
6 Rock Ledge Ave. (Rte. 9), 941-8674
*U – Once a speakeasy, this tiny, off-the-beaten-path
New American changes its "terrific" menu four times a
year; though "ungenerous portions" make it seem "a bit
pricey", it's generally well-regarded for its "pretty decor",
"attentive service" and upbeat piano bar.*

Dynasty*/S (Wappingers Falls) **E8** | 16 | 14 | 17 | $24 |
Old Post Rd. (Rte. 9), 298-0023
M – This hard-to-find Chinese attracts Oriental clients drawn to its fresh, not-too-spicy food; Occidentals, on the other hand, appreciate the staff's eagerness to help with the menu; it's not a looker, but comfortable.

Eastchester Fish Gourmet/SX | 21 | 10 | 16 | $26 |
(Scarsdale) **E2**
837 White Plains Rd. (Brooks St.), 725-3450
U – Don't go here for decor or ambiance – the appeal of this no-frills "storefront" linked to a retail fish market is "fresh fish, simply prepared"; the "no-reservations policy" and "good value" means long lines.

Edenville Inn*/S (Warwick) **A4** | 26 | 23 | 20 | $36 |
4 Blooms Corner Rd. (County Rd. 1), 986-8500
U – "Interesting" "high-quality" Northern Italian cuisine is served at this "pleasant country setting" in a circa-1794 Orange County house; surveyors say the "warm atmosphere" and "charming" staff make this "one of our favorites for a day in the country."

Edmundo's Too/S (White Plains) **F3** | 20 | 15 | 19 | $36 |
141 E. Lake St. (B'way), 287-0220
U – "Not for gourmets", this "old-style Italian" pleases instead with "large portions" of good food in "typical suburban" surroundings; people-watchers find it "a good place to spot local politicos" – watch out for prices, though.

Emilio's/S (Harrison) **F2** | 22 | 18 | 20 | $36 |
1 Colonial Pl. (Harrison Ave.), 835-3100
U – "Emilio and his wife are the gracious" hosts who preside over this Northern Italian in a "beautiful old house" in Westchester; the restaurant has a "typical" but often "delightful" menu and "friendly" service.

Enzo's/S (Mamaroneck) **F2** | 18 | 13 | 18 | $33 |
451 Mamaroneck Ave. (near RR station), 698-2911
U – "Regulars return" to this Northern Italian "hangout" for "good, consistent" food and the amiable chef-owner Enzo, who "knows everyone"; it's "loud", "crowded" and "not particularly pretty", it's "like eating at Enzo's home."

ESCOFFIER ROOM | 26 | 24 | 24 | $41 |
(Hyde Park) **D10**
Culinary Institute of America, 651 S. Albany Post Rd., Rte. 9 (north of E. Dorsey Lane), 452-9600
U – The CIA's flagship student-run restaurant is a "luxurious" Classic French that's "top drawer all the way"; though it may be "too fancy and ornate" for some tastes, most surveyors "love the beautiful room", "ultimate gourmet" food and "deluxe" service; reserve early for "the best school lunch ever" and "get a table by the glassed-in kitchen."

Foster's Coach House/S | 13 | 15 | 16 | $19 |
(Rhinebeck) **D12**
9193 Montgomery St. (Rte. 9), 876-8052
U – "Everyone goes" to this family-owned "converted barn" with booths that look like horse stalls and an "inexpensive but not memorable" menu of burgers, steaks and other Traditional American fare; it's a "local favorite" for a "quick bite."

FREELANCE CAFE & WINE | 26 | 20 | 24 | $33 |
GARDEN/SX (Piermont) **D3**
506 Piermont Ave. (Rte. 9W Business District exit), 365-3250
U – The younger sibling of Xavier's next door, this bustling, "casual" cafe has "wonderful" Nouvelle American food that's "almost as good" and certainly "cheaper"; those in the know say it's a prime place to "watch for celebrities", but some carp about long waits and "too many Manhattanites."

Fritz's/S (Granite Springs) **F4** | 22 | 19 | 20 | $40 |
Old Tomahawk St. (Rte. 118), 248-7100
M – On the northern edge of Westchester, this "charming" Contemporary American "country inn" is called "wonderful" by some, "not memorable" by others; ratings suggest that you can expect "interesting food" and "solicitous" service albeit at a hefty tab.

Gasho of Japan/S | 17 | 20 | 18 | $29 |
(Hawthorne) **E3**, 2 Saw Mill River Rd. (Hawthorne Circle), 592-5900
(Central Valley) **C5**, Rte. 32 (NY Twy., exit 16), 928-2277
M – Purists bypass these typical Japanese hibachi-style steakhouses set in the "authentic atmosphere" of a "Japanese farmhouse", but many dig the "knife-wielding chefs" and kitschy "drinks with umbrellas"; it's "fun for kids", first dates and dinner with the in-laws.

Giardino/S (Briarcliff Manor) **E3** | – | – | – | E |
53 N. State Rd. (bet. Rtes. 9A and 100), 923-3100
A sister restaurant to NYC's Fino, Giardino is already attracting attention; owned by the former chef at Pinocchio Ristorante, this pricey Northern Italian specializes in homemade pasta and features mushrooms from around the world.

Giulio's of Tappan/S (Tappan) **D3** | 21 | 22 | 22 | $36 |
154 Washington St. (Rte. 303), 359-3657
U – Located in a "cozy" and "beautiful Victorian home", surveyors still call this 20-year-old "red-velvet Italian" "better-than-average", even "consistently excellent"; the food may be a little "heavy" for some, but service is reliable and high-side prices aren't out of control.

Golden Duck, The/SX | – | – | – | M |
(Scarsdale) **E2**
102 Garth Rd. (Great Rock Rd.), 723-1886
This small, not very well-known Chinese suburbanite,
near the station, features interesting multi-regional food
at a moderate price; comfortable (if plain) quarters and
competent service complete the picture.

Goldie's/S (North Tarrytown) **D3** | 20 | 13 | 19 |$31|
226 Beekman Ave. (Hudson St.), 631-9794
U – "A true find", this small, "plain" neighborhooder with
"great" river views features chef-owner Deborah
Goldstein's "fresh market", "imaginative" and "unusually
good" New American cuisine; a very few say the menu's
"too ambitious."

Good Enough to Eat/S | 21 | 18 | 19 |$25|
(High Falls) **B11**
Rte. 213 (Lucas Ave.), 687-9003
U – "Not worth a special trip", but certainly "good
enough" to stop for when you're in the area and crave
"Mom's cooking": chicken pot pie, stews, pot roast,
waffles and biscuits; prices are fair, and the setting
reminds some of a "Vermont retreat."

Good Life, The/S (Mamaroneck) **F2** | 18 | 12 | 17 |$28|
1422 E. Boston Post Rd. (Mamaroneck Ave.), 698-3956
M – Some call this reasonably priced Contemporary
American "cozy", while others deem it "cramped";
they're just as split on the menu ("imaginative and
healthful" vs. "just ok"), which focuses on chicken, fish,
vegetables and cheese – Italian focaccia is a specialty;
no atmosphere to speak of, but service is "pleasant."

Grandma's Country Pie | 14 | 11 | 15 |$17|
Restaurant/SX (Yorktown) **E5**
Rte. 202 (4 miles west of Taconic Pkwy.), 739-7770
M – This low bugdet "family-style" restaurant with a
"quaint" country feeling features 30 types of "great"
homemade pies; as for the rest of the Traditional
American menu, some find it dependable, others advise
"fast bite only"; best strategy: go for breakfast, then "buy
the pie and bring it home."

Green and Bresler*/S | 23 | 11 | 18 |$27|
(Red Hook) **E12**
29 W. Market St. (off B'way), 758-5992
U – It may look "like a luncheonette", but the creative
Contemporary American food "far surpasses the decor"
at this "simple storefront"; though best known for its
catering, regulars say it's a "gem" for the price and
"worth a detour if you're anywhere near Red Hook."

Greenbaum and Gilhooly's*/S | 14 | 13 | 15 | $25 |
(Wappingers Falls) **E8**
1400 Rte. 9 (Old Hopewell and Meyers Corners Rds.),
297-9700
*M – Some call this "crowded, noisy", no-reservations
steakhouse a "meat-lover's dream", but more
demanding types would "rather eat at home";
impersonal service and boring decor won't win any
prizes, but prices are "reasonable."*

Gregory's/S (White Plains) **F3** | 19 | 15 | 19 | $34 |
324 Central Ave. (½ mile south of Rte. 119), 684-8855
*M – Convenient to the Westchester County Center, this
"old-fashioned Italian" receives mixed reviews; on
balance, the decor's somewhat "ordinary", but "good
service" and "ample portions" of "better-than-average"
food have created a following.*

Grouper Cafe/S (Mount Kisco) **E4** | 19 | 18 | 17 | $33 |
251 Lexington Ave. (Moore Ave.), 241-8969
*M – Seafood is the specialty at this "lively" (read,
"noisy") watering hole; though a few say the cooking is
"inconsistent" and the service needs "work", the majority
view is "fresh" and "well prepared", but "expensive."*

Guida's Italian Restaurant/S | 23 | 19 | 21 | $34 |
(Ossining) **D4**
199 Main St. (Rte. 9), 941-2662
*M – Some rave about this Italian, calling it "NYC food in
Ossining" and insisting "oh! what a find!", but others call
the "theatrical" presentation "stuffy"; it has a loyal
following, despite prices being somewhat high for Italian.*

Guidetti's Lodge*/S (Wingdale) **G9** | 20 | 21 | 21 | $34 |
Pleasant Ridge Rd. (Rte. 22 & Rte. 55), 832-6721
*U – Though few surveyors know of it, this '50s-era "old
hunting lodge", located in a Dutchess County hamlet,
serves a well-rated, high end Continental menu; good
food and deft service add appeal to "a wonderful setting
for a romantic evening."*

Gus's Franklin Park/S (Harrison) **F2** | 18 | 8 | 17 | $27 |
126 Halstead Ave. (Franklin St.), 835-9804
*M – Everybody knows one another at this circa-1929
Cheers-type "joint" that's a good place for "eating, not
dining" on "seafood and gemütlichkeit"; the wait can be
"long", but on a good night "the fish is great and so is
the Key lime pie" at this landmark that's short on decor
but long on value.*

Hacienda Don Emilio/S | 17 | 16 | 18 | $24 |
(Larchmont) **F2**
1266 Boston Post Rd. (bet. Weaver St. & Richbell Rd.),
834-2738
*M – Kids "love the mariachis" at this "attractive"
Mexican, and grown-ups like the "lively bar" dispensing
"frozen blue margs" and "friendly" service, but there's a
split on the food: "bland and ordinary", vs. "a cut above
most Westchester Mexicanos" with "authentic dishes
that are very unusual."*

HARRALD'S/SX (Stormville) **E8** | 27 | 26 | 27 | $57 |
Rte. 52 (5½ miles east of Taconic Pkwy.), 878-6595
*M – Stormville, in Dutchess County, may not be close to
anyplace, but aficionados travel from afar for "fabulous"
"three-hour dining" at this "quaint", timbered country
"cottage" with its varied, "formal" Continental menu
noted for in-season game dishes, "civilized" setting and
"wonderful" service; dissenters say it's "stuffy" and
skiing "downhill", but high numbers, including cost, tell
the story.*

Hartsdale Garden/S (Hartsdale) **F3** | 15 | 12 | 15 | $19 |
Westchester Square, 285 N. Central Ave., 683-1611
*M – One of many Chinese on Central Avenue, this
"good-value" spot offers food that's "well-prepared and
basic" or "so-so", depending whom you ask; "run-down
decor" is a bummer, but "attentive service" is applauded.*

Heathcote Crossing/S | 18 | 21 | 19 | $30 |
(Scarsdale) **E2**
2 Weaver St. (Five Corners), 723-1333
*M – This "lovely" Tudor manor "has seen many
restaurants" come and go before this "comfortable"
Continental-American opened in 1991; while opinions
are mixed, there's a vibe that "this one has potential."*

Hilltop Restaurant/LSX (Nyack) **D4** | 16 | 11 | 16 | $23 |
312 Main St. (Rte. 9W & Rte. 59), 358-2728
*M – A "casual", "informal" Rockland County old-timer
that "isn't much to look at", but most agree is a "great
place to drop in at the last minute" for Italian and
seafood; it's "not memorable", but "good value" makes
this a "second kitchen" for many locals.*

Hope and Anchor/S | 17 | 16 | 20 | $28 |
(Larchmont) **F2**
141 Chatsworth Ave. (Railroad Way), 833-0340
*U – A "husband and wife team" turn out pleasant
seafood and light International cooking at this basic,
"homey" storefront; surveyors call it an "acceptable,
courteous local place", although a few up anchor.*

F	D	S	C

Horsefeathers/S (Tarrytown) **D3** | 14 | 14 | 15 | $20 |

94 N. Broadway, Rte. 9 (2 blocks north of Main St.), 631-6606
*M – Locals say this "bright", "youthful fill-up stop" is a
"reliable place" for burgers, beer, etc. in a "pubby",
"neighborhood" setting; detractors say it's "aptly named
and that's being polite."*

Huckleberry's/S | 13 | 14 | 13 | $22 |
(Yorktown Heights) **E5**

355 Kear St. (off Rte. 118), 245-1984
*M – "Yuppies love it", but the "perpetual happy hour is
guaranteed to depress anyone who cares about food" at
this trendoid American that walks, talks, tastes and
looks "like a chain restaurant"; modest prices make it
"good for families" and "ok for a quick bite."*

Hudson House/S (Cold Spring) **D7** | 18 | 20 | 19 | $32 |

Hudson House, 23 Main St. (Market St.), 265-9355
*U – Located in a picturesque Putnam County village,
the best thing about this Continental-style country inn is
its panoramic view of the Hudson, but word is that the
food and service are "much improved with new owners";
with 15 guest rooms, you can "make a weekend of it."*

Hudson House/S (Nyack) **D4** | 22 | 21 | 21 | $29 |

131 Main St. (Franklin St.), 353-1355
*U – New chef Daniel Coon "works wonders" with the
New American food at this up-and-comer whose
"imaginative", "NYC-type menu", "friendly" service and
"reasonable" prices have diners who found it
"disappointing" before, now reporting a "great new find."*

Hudson's Ribs and Fish*/S | 19 | 14 | 18 | $26 |
(Fishkill) **D8**

Rte. 9 (1½ miles from Rte. 84), 297-5002
*M – The "popovers with strawberry butter are divine" at
this "busy" Dutchess County BBQ where portions are
"plentiful" and prices are fair; it's popular with families –
apparently including their "screaming infants."*

Huff House/S (Roscoe) **A12** | – | – | – | M |

Huff House, off County Rd. 94 (5½ miles south of Rte. 17),
482-4579
*Though few surveyors have sampled it, this Sullivan
County inn deep in a Catskills trout-fishing area is "great
when fly-fishing on the Delaware"; owned by the same
family for generations, it has 47 guest rooms plus an
inviting dining room serving Continental and Traditional
American favorites.*

Hunan Manor/S (Hartsdale) **F3** | 19 | 14 | 18 | $22 |
149 S. Central Ave. (Hartsdale Plaza), 997-0204
*M – Located on a congested Downtown thoroughfare,
this storefront Chinese elicits mixed comments: "the
best in Central Westchester" and "always reliable" vs.
"standard", "nothing special", and "quality has declined."*

Hunan Village/S (Yonkers) **D2** | 22 | 17 | 21 | $22 |
1828 Central Park Ave. (State St.), 779-2272
*U – "In a sea of Chinese restaurants", this "consistently
good" place "stands out"; its fans cite "freshest
vegetables" and "imaginative presentation" from an
"interesting menu out of Chinatown", plus low prices
and a staff that "can't do enough to please."*

Hunan Wok/S (Hartsdale) **F3** | 19 | 11 | 16 | $21 |
415 N. Central Park Ave. (1 mile north of Hartsdale Ave.),
684-6505
*M – One of many Hunan-monikered eateries on Central
Park Avenue, this "reliable" Chinese keeps fans "going
between trips to Chinatown"; it's "crowded", and a "solid
value", but detractors call it "ordinary."*

Ichi Riki/S | 22 | 17 | 20 | $28 |
(Nyack) **D4**, 110 Main St. (bet. B'way & Franklin St.),
358-7977
(Elmsford) **E3**, 1 E. Main St. (Rtes. 119 & 9A), 592-2220
*U – All the "Japanese businessmen eating here can't be
wrong", which must be why so many rate these as the
"best sushi" around; be aware that the tab for "sushi can
add up" quickly.*

Il Cenacola*/S (Newburgh) **C7** | 28 | 23 | 26 | $41 |
152 Rte. 52 (near Rte. 300), 564-4494
*U – A real find in an otherwise inauspicious Orange
County Hudson River town, this little-known Northern
Italian inspires raves: "best Tuscan kitchen outside of
Italy"; it's "dignified", with "homey", "authentic Italian
ambiance", suave service and prices that surveyors
don't mind paying.*

Il Cigno Ristorante/S | 22 | 17 | 18 | $40 |
(Scarsdale) **E2**
Colonial Village Shopping Ctr., 1505 Weaver St. (near
Hutchinson Pkwy.), 472-8484
*U – "This is where you dine when the market is up" – on
"inventive Italian", including "excellent risotto and
pastas" and "the best pomodoro sauce anywhere"; a
recent remodeling should nullify gripes about "shabby"
decor; tuxedoed waiters are seen as "professional" and
"attentive" by most, "snooty" and "snobbish" by a few.*

Il Portico/S (Tappan) **D3** | 22 | 22 | 20 | $38 |

89 Main St. (off Palisades Pkwy.), 365-2100
U – Serving up "uniformly excellent Northern Italian fare" in a restored 1850s hotel, this high-end "tiny gem across the river" in Rockland County "tries very hard", with "attentive service", "warm" atmosphere and "constantly improving" food; fans say "close your eyes and you could be eating in Milan."

Imperial Wok/S | 19 | 15 | 18 | $21 |

(Yorktown) **E5**, 1940 Commerce St. (Rte. 35), 245-3840
(Thornwood) **E3**, 851 Franklin Ave. (Commerce St.), 747-3111
(Somers) **F4**, 13 Heritage St. (Rte. 202 Shopping Ctr.), 277-8900
M – This popular "family-oriented" Chinese minichain originated in Yorktown and recently franchised; while some say they offer "nothing special", the verdict is generally "good solid Chinese food", with "nice-sized portions" and "fair prices."

India House Restaurant/S | 21 | 17 | 21 | $22 |
(Montrose) **E4**

199 Albany Post Rd. (near Rte. 9), 736-0005
U – With "plentiful", "consistently good" Indian food and "always smiling" servers, this colorful younger sister to White Plains's Bengal Tiger is "just as good" – if not better – than her sibling in the eyes of our respondents.

INN AT OSBORNE HILL | 24 | 18 | 21 | $38 |
(Fishkill) **D8**

150 Osborne Hill Rd. (5 miles from Rte. 84), 897-3055
U – A Culinary Institute–trained husband-and-wife team "try hard and succeed" at this "quaint" out-of-the-way but "worth-the-trip" Dutchess County Continental country inn; "innovative" food, an "extraordinary wine list" and "responsive" service all draw praise.

INN AT POUND RIDGE/S | 23 | 25 | 21 | $44 |
(Pound Ridge) **F3**

Rte. 137 (end of Rte. 172), 764-5779
U – After a "wonderful renovation job", this old inn made a dramatic "comeback", offering a "classy" setting for "excellent" Traditional American food plus "warm, courteous" service; fans say the food's "improving all the time", but remains "pricey for its market."

Japan Inn/S (Bronxville) **E2** | 19 | 12 | 20 | $26 |

28 Palmer Ave. (Paxton Rd.), 337-1296
M – "Stick with sushi" at this Downtown Japanese – the other specialties are "good but expensive"; "friendly" service compensates for the "touristy" surroundings, though detractors say it's "seen better days."

Jason's Ltd./S (Eastchester) **E2** | 18 | 15 | 19 | $29 |
478 White Plains Rd. (Mill Rd.), 961-5717
*U – This "publike" steakhouse "standby" draws
"repeaters" with its "limited menu" of "chop-house" fare,
"good seafood" and "homey", if "heavy", Continental
dishes – it's "nothing special", but a "reliable" value
popular with "businessmen."*

John Richard's/S (Dobbs Ferry) **E3** | 15 | 12 | 15 | $24 |
39 Chestnut St. (Main St.), 693-6404
*M – An "informal" pub, this "friendly" place has become
a hangout, thanks to affordable steaks and seafood
from the grill, live jazz and a "great selection of beers."*

Khan's Mongolian/S (Blauvelt) **D3** | 15 | 13 | 16 | $19 |
21 Rte. 303 (NY Twy., exit 12), 359-8004
*U – "Good for the price", "great for kids" and
"satisfactory for hungry adults willing to sacrifice
comfort", this all-you-can-eat Mongolian-style BBQ is –
how do we put it? – "a little different."*

King & I/S (Nyack) **D4** | 23 | 19 | 21 | $25 |
91-93 Main St. (bet. Franklin St. & B'way), 353-4208
*U – This "favorite Thai restaurant" recently tripled in
size, adding a bar and live entertainment; "friendly
service" and "great food" at "reasonable" prices make
for a "wonderful" ethnic experience.*

Kit 'N Caboodle/S (Mount Kisco) **E4** | 16 | 16 | 16 | $24 |
443 Lexington Ave. (near Rte. 117), 241-2440
*M – "A good staple from burgers to roast beef to nachos
to fish", this "crowded, informal bar"–cum–restaurant
attracts a "yuppie crowd"; some say it's a "great casual
place", others say "ok, nothing special."*

LA CAMELIA/S (Mount Kisco) **E4** | 24 | 20 | 21 | $41 |
234 N. Bedford Rd. (Saw Mill River Pkwy., Kisco Ave.
exit), 666-2466
*U – Fans say they've "never had a bad meal" at this
high-end "Spanish standout" specializing in dishes from
the maritime province of Galicia; located in a "nice old
house" atop a hill, its only negative is its "cramped
quarters"; try the "great" tapas on Sunday afternoon,
and imagine strolling the gardens of the Alhambra as
you listen to a classical guitarist.*

La Fonda del Sol/S | 15 | 14 | 15 | $24 |
(Wappingers Falls) **E8**
100 Old Rte. 9 (Rte. 28), 297-5044
*M – Fun is the emphasis at this Tex-Mex spot "for Anglo
tastes", with eclectic entertainment: an open mike,
country and western, rock 'n' roll, and Irish music; it's a
friendly family spot that's "pleasant for a quick bite", but
not much more.*

Lago di Como/S (Tarrytown) **D3** | 21 | 17 | 18 | $39 |
27 Main St. (off Rte. 9), 631-7227
M – At this "comfortable", classic Northern Italian, besides homemade pasta you'll find "exciting" dishes such as seasonal fresh white truffles and suckling pig; fans gush that it "puts to shame all the other Italians" in Sleepy Hollow country, but critics call it "costly" – "Tarrytown is not Manhattan."

La Mandas*/S (White Plains) **F3** | 17 | 7 | 17 | $20 |
251 Tarrytown Rd. (I-287), 684-9228
M – The "best dive ever", this 50-year-old Southern Italian on a busy street has zip decor but lots of "yummy" old-style food, including what one enthusiast calls "the best pizza outside of Italy", all at modest prices; dissenters label it "noisy" and "ordinary."

LA PANETIERE/S (Rye) **F2** | 28 | 27 | 26 | $57 |
530 Milton Rd. (Oakland Beach Ave.), 967-8140
U – The "gorgeous" decor, "sophisticated" service and "flawless" French food at this "country-style inn" come at steep prices, but without complaints, since the food cops the third-highest rating in the Tri-State area; for most surveyors, it's "worth a trip from anywhere" for a memorable "first-class" dining experience.

La Riserva/S (Larchmont) **F2** | 19 | 14 | 18 | $34 |
2382 Boston Post Rd. (1 mile south of Larchmont Ave.), 834-5584
M – "Large portions" of "robust" food are the draw at this "old-time Italian" with a "typical red-sauce" menu and "attentive" service; opinions on the decor vary – "warm" and "comfortable" vs. "tacky" – but most agree it's out of sync with the "pricey" tab.

La Rive*/S (Catskill) **D14** | 24 | 20 | 22 | $36 |
All Kings Rd. (Dedrich Rd.), 518-943-4888
U – It's a "long way" up the Hudson, but surveyors don't mind venturing to this Classic French "treasure" in a 200-year-old farmhouse down a dirt road; ample servings and "dreamy" setting make this a major attraction; open May–Sept. only; N.B. call for directions.

La Scala*/S (Armonk) **F3** | 16 | 15 | 19 | $27 |
386 Main St. (1 mile west of Rte. 684), 273-3508
M – Our reviewers have mixed feelings about this "neighborhood"-type Armonk Italian; some call the "basic Italian" food "good" and "fresh", but detractors say "so-so"; it's "crowded, smoky, and noisy" downstairs but "quieter in the upstairs dining room."

LE CHAMBORD/S | 23 | 24 | 21 | $44 |
(Hopewell Junction) **E8**
2075 Rte. 52 (off Taconic Pkwy.), 221-1941
*M – In a "gorgeous" circa-1860 mansion full of antiques
and art, this highly rated but expensive Hudson River
French makes a "pretty place for a formal dinner"; even
so, mixed opinion on the food has some calling it
"elegant" and others "mediocre"; its party space for up
to 300 is "good for weddings."*

LE CHATEAU/S (South Salem) **G4** | 23 | 27 | 22 | $50 |
Rte. 35 (intersection Rte. 123), 533-6631
*M – Built in 1907, J.P. Morgan's "beautiful" castle on 32
wooded acres overlooking a valley is a "splendid"
setting for "gracious" service and Classic French food
that "almost matches the views" and the prices; though
it's well-loved, many find the place "factorylike" – on
weekends you can find yourself in the middle of
someone else's wedding.*

Le Pavillion* (Poughkeepsie) **D10** | 25 | 21 | 26 | $37 |
230 Salt Point Tpke. (bet. N. Grand Ave. & Vedell Rd.),
473-2525
*U – Cozy and romantic, this French country inn just
outside Poughkeepsie offers candlelight, classical
music, delicious food and "charming" service; an
"always-fine dining experience", it's not cheap, but the
$27.50 prix fixe dinner is a value.*

Le Petit Bistro*/S (Rhinebeck) **D12** | 23 | 18 | 23 | $38 |
8 E. Market St. (center of village), 876-7400
*U – "Just like a Paris bistro", this petite eatery serves
"well-done" Classic French cuisine in a "charming"
historic village; the "limited" menu and stiff prices don't
faze its well-heeled local regulars.*

Les Bons Copains/S (Suffern) **B4** | 23 | 19 | 20 | $36 |
150 La Fayette Ave. (Rte. 59), 368-1112
*U – A seasonal menu of French and International dishes
(e.g. grilled Moroccan chicken with dates) adds up to a
"wonderful" experience for surveyors who call this
"pleasant", tapestried newcomer "a real find"; "friendly"
service and an "uncrowded" setting complete the picture.*

Le Shack/S (White Plains) **F3** | 17 | 14 | 18 | $27 |
68 Gedney Way (Mamaroneck Ave.), 428-1264
*M – Les folks can't make up their minds about this
"informal" "standby", serving Frenchified American food
("fromage burgers", "onion soup", etc.) from a
blackboard menu; les fans say "always steady" and
"good"; les critics say "only if you must."*

L'EUROPE/S (South Salem) **G4**　| 24 | 21 | 23 | $48 |
Rte. 123 (½ mile from New Canaan border), 533-2570
*U – "Excellent" French food and "gracious hospitality"
define this "quiet", "wonderfully traditional" South Salem
"country inn"; though it's "somewhat pricey", diners are
undeterred, in light of its many "charms."*

L'HOSTELLERIE BRESSANE/SX　| 26 | 25 | 23 | $47 |
(Hillsdale) **G14**
Rtes. 22 & 23, 518-325-3412
*M – Set in rolling Columbia County on the way to the
Berkshires, this "old-school French" country inn inspires
many: "magnifique", "excellent", "amazing"; however,
critics call its "formal" atmosphere "dated", "stuffy" and
"too high-priced"; still, "fine" service and the fireplaces
ignite plenty of "charm" and get high ratings.*

Livanos/S (White Plains) **F3**　| 21 | 21 | 20 | $35 |
200 Central Ave. (Rte. 119), 428-2400
*M – This busy, "stylish" Contemporary American sparks
controversy: for every critic who calls the "glitzy" decor
"plastic" and the food "mediocre", there's a fan who
thinks it's "pretty" and "the only restaurant in
Westchester – or should be"; scores suggest that it's
"worth the price", and a try.*

Locust Tree Inn*/S (New Paltz) **B10**　| 21 | 22 | 22 | $30 |
215 Huguenot St. (off Rte. 299), 255-7888
*U – Situated in an "historic" restored (1700s) stone
house overlooking a golf course, this "lovely old inn"
provides an "exciting" Eclectic menu and a welcome
respite from strolling the streets of New Paltz; "save
some bread to feed the ducks."*

Long Pond Inn/S (Mahopac) **F6**　| 22 | 22 | 19 | $37 |
708 Long Pond Rd. (bet. Rte. 6 & Rte. 6N), 628-0072
*U – "Hard to find but worth the hunt", this "secluded"
"log cabin on the lake" serves inventive Contemporary
American food (e.g. barbecued scallops wrapped in
leeks with Cambodian fire paste, duck crêpes with
crème fraîche and scallions); the "casual" setting is
especially "cozy" by the "fireplace on a cold night."*

Louie's Italian/S (Yonkers) **D2**　| 17 | 15 | 18 | $24 |
187 S. Broadway (Herriot St.), 969-8821
*U – "Good food for the money" explains the popularity
of this "unassuming" Italian in a down-at-the-heels
neighborhood; set in a Victorian house, it's "homey" and
"intimate", a "nice place to go for drinks" as well as food.*

Maison Lafitte/S | 15 | 18 | 16 |$38|
(Briarcliff Manor) **E3**
Chappaqua Rd. (off Rte. 9A), 941-5787
*U – Diners are unimpressed with this Westchester
Classic French located in a "Tara"-style mansion: many
call the food "so-so" and the service "sloppy"; most
lament it's "gone with the wind" – "Westchester's
answer to Mamma Leone's."*

Malabar Hill (Elmsford) **E3** | 22 | 16 | 18 |$24|
145 E. Main St. (Old Rd.), 347-7890
*U – A relative newcomer, this "wholesome" Indian is
building a consensus that it serves "better than average"
or even "the best" Indian food around; the only
complaints: "inattentive" service and long waits – "why
no reservations?"*

Manzi's/S (Hastings-on-Hudson) **D3** | 15 | 10 | 16 |$26|
17-19 Main St. (Warburton Ave.), 478-0404
*M – "Heavy on calories and garlic", this low-atmosphere
"traditional" Italian "offers no surprises", just friendly
service and "good but not great" Italian food; even folks
who say it serves "mediocre food in mediocre
surroundings" appreciate that "the price is right."*

MARCELLO'S/S (Suffern) **B4** | 25 | 18 | 20 |$36|
2121 Lafayette Ave. (Rte. 59), 357-9108
*U – A standout menu sets this "class-act" Rockland
County storefront Italian apart; "Marcello takes pride" in
"superb" food that's "on a par with East Side Italian
restaurants"; a few complain that the service, though
good, "is not as good as the food."*

Marichu* (Bronxville) **E2** | 18 | 17 | 15 |$39|
104 Kraft Ave. (across from RR station), 961-2338
*U – The instant success of this "interesting", "expensive
for Bronxville" Basque has caused service to suffer –
"somewhat disorganized", and waits that can be long
even with reservations; still, the "unusual" menu has
adventurous diners "excited" and eager to return; N.B.
regulars will be glad to hear that they lowered prices
after our survey was conducted.*

Mariner's Harbor/S (Highland) **C10** | 15 | 18 | 16 |$27|
46 River Rd. (Grand St.), 691-6011
*U – Across the Hudson from Poughkeepsie, this
seafooder "at the river's edge" boasts extraordinary
views, which help make up for just "ok" food; "noisy,
informal" and popular with locals, it "will do if you can't
go to City Island."*

MAXIME'S BRASSERIE/S | 24 | 23 | 21 | $45 |
(Granite Springs) **F4**
Old Tomahawk St. (Rte. 118), 248-7200
U – "NYC comes to the suburbs" at this remodeled landmark with its new brasserie menu, lower prices and younger clientele; still operated by the venerable Maxime Ribera, it offers "some of the best French food around" and "now one of the best deals, too."

Maxime's La Petite Affaire/S | – | – | – | E |
(Briarcliff Manor) **E3**
(fka La Petite Affaire)
Rte. 9 (north of Rte. 117), 941-5556
Maxime Ribera is on a roll with this bistro, which he took over in 1992 (after our survey was conducted) and revamped; the word is spreading that the Mediterranean menu is "a great improvement."

McKinney & Doyle*/S (Pawling) **E8** | 23 | 18 | 21 | $27 |
10 Charles Colman Blvd. (E. Main St.), 855-3875
U – Peevish "locals regret the day NYC discovered" this "light-hearted" International-style "cafe" – "shhhh, secret of the country"; perhaps "not for a special occasion", but it pleases with a bakery that turns out notable cakes.

Meson Castellano (White Plains) **F3** | 18 | 15 | 18 | $33 |
135 E. Post Rd. (Rte. 118), 428-8445
M – "Viva España!" cry fans of this Downtown Spaniard, but are nearly outshouted by dissenters blaring "surly waiters and tasteless food"; it's about "the best in the area", however, and a "good value", especially "if you can't make it to Spain or Manhattan."

Mohonk Mountain House/S | 13 | 19 | 17 | $31 |
(New Paltz) **B10**
Mountain Rest Rd. (Rte. 299), 255-1000
U – The Traditional "mess-hall" American chow at this timbered Catskills resort reminds some of "sleepaway camp", but that's "not the issue": the hotel is "a genuinely great place" for a "romantic" getaway, and after an invigorating hike they "won't let you go hungry."

Mona Trattoria/S (Croton Falls) **F4** | 22 | 21 | 18 | $41 |
Rte. 22 (Hardscrabble Rd.), 277-4580
U – Most agree that the Northern Italian food, especially the homemade pasta, at this "beautiful" old house in Putnam County is "good" to "excellent", if "overpriced"; complainers say quality of service "depends on the waiters' moods."

Mount Fuji/S (Hillburn) **B4**　| 19 | 23 | 19 | $32 |
Rte. 17 (2 miles north of Mahwah, NJ), 357-4270
*U – "Japanese food with glitz" sizzles at this
mountaintop Nippon-style steakhouse with its "kitschy"
decor and "exciting views" of NYC; though most
surveyors like the food, it's the knife-wielding teppanyaki
"show" that makes this "an experience."*

Nanuet Hotel/LSX (Nanuet) **C3**　| 17 | 6 | 14 | $16 |
Nanuet Hotel, 132 Main St. (Middletown Rd.), 623-9600
*U – Though this Rockland County hotel pizzeria may be
a "dump" with "decor less than zero", it makes the "best
pizza in the county"; patient service and tolerable prices
create "the perfect place for young families."*

Nino's/S (Bedford) **F4**　| 19 | 18 | 19 | $43 |
Rte. 121 (bet. Rtes. 22 & 35), 234-3374
*M – "This old gray mare ain't what she used to be" is
the consensus of those who claim this once-great
Westchester Northern Italian "standby" is "riding on its
reputation"; even so, "long waits at a noisy bar" confirm
that many still enjoy the high net worth food and
atmosphere – or because it's handy to Caramoor.*

Off Broadway Restaurant/S　| 22 | 15 | 20 | $33 |
(Dobbs Ferry) **E3**
17 Ashford Ave. (B'way), 693-6170
*M – Respondents say the food is first-run at this
"innovative" American with its "weekend guitar-playing",
"industrial styling" and "interesting" combinations ("duck
salad", "blueberry banana cheesecake", etc.); to critics
it's "long on noise, short on atmosphere."*

OLD DROVER'S INN/S　| 22 | 24 | 22 | $46 |
(Dover Plains) **F10**
Old Drover's Inn, Old Post Rd. (Rte. 22), 832-9311
*U – "The drovers would be amazed" at what has
become of this "charming" Colonial inn that offers
"innovative" American food, "huge drinks" and seductive
"fireplaces in every room"; it's the newest member of
the elite Relais & Chateaux group and, with four
bedrooms, is "worth a trip" to Dutchess County.*

Old '76 House/S (Tappan) **D3**　| 18 | 22 | 20 | $32 |
110 Main St. (Washington Ave.), 359-5476
*U – "History buffs" will recall that Major Andre was
imprisoned here during the Revolutionary War (it's been
in operation since 1776); as for the gustatory
experience, the "acceptable" Traditional American food
and "cozy fireside" ambiance add up to a winning "Early
American" experience; "inexpensive specials" offset
highish prices.*

Southern New York State | F | D | S | C |

Old Stonehouse Inn/S | 18 | 20 | 19 | $30 |
(Orangeburg) **D3**
15 Kings Hwy. (Rte. 303), 359-5665
U – Located in an 18th-century Dutch sandstone building, this Rockland County Continental offers "quaint atmosphere with good food" of the old school, e.g., roast duckling, filet of beef and rack of lamb; improved scores since our last Survey *suggest that this "rustic Early American" is worth a return visit.*

Orchid Garden/S (Nyack) **D4** | 18 | 16 | 17 | $19 |
(fka Hunan Empire)
132 Main St. (Franklin St.), 353-3113
U – The former Hunan Empire, under new ownership, has a spiffy contemporary look (not yet reflected in the scores), plus a sushi bar and free delivery; its Intown location makes it handy for a quick lunch or takeout.

Owl's Nest/X (High Mount) **B14** | – | – | – | I |
The Clubhouse Rd., 254-5917
High Mount, on the Ulster-Delaware County border, is so tiny the buildings don't have addresses; still, this "good roadside inn" serving Italian-accented steak and seafood was brought to our attention by plenty of write-ins; open Friday and Saturday nights only.

Pagoda Restaurant/S | 19 | 16 | 18 | $24 |
(Eastchester) **E2**
701 White Plains Rd. (Willmot Rd.), 472-1600
M – Surveyors mostly praise the "decent" mid-priced fare served at this "roomy" Downtown White Plains Chinese, though some feel the dining room "could use a renovation" and the food is forgettable.

Painter's Tavern/S | – | – | – | M |
(Cornwall-on-Hudson) **C6**
8 Idlewild Ave. (next to Fanning Memorial Bandstand), 534-2109
If you're near West Point, plan a stop in this scenic hamlet; primarily a tavern, Painter's also offers a fair-priced Eclectic menu of Japanese, Mexican and Italian specialties; the decor consists of brick walls, parquet floors, a brass-trimmed bar, and the works of local artists.

Palmer House Inn/S (Amenia) **G11** | – | – | – | M |
Palmer House Inn, Cascade Rd. (Rte. 22), 373-7870
"Good" American country food is the stock-in-trade of this little-known rural inn; "friendly service", "reasonable" prices and "comfortable" quarters make it a handy stop on a wine-tasting or apple-picking foray; the outdoor patio and working fireplace are seasonal attractions.

Pancho Villa's/S (Larchmont) **F2** | 15 | 14 | 16 | $22 |
145 Larchmont Ave. (Boston Post Rd.), 834-6378
*U – Crowds pack this lower Westchester Mexican for the
"best margaritas anywhere"; "portions are large and
satisfying", though critics call it "fast food."*

Papa-Razzi/LS (White Plains) **F3** | – | – | – | M |
1 N. Broadway (Main St.), 949-3500
*Pasta, salad and pizza from the wood-burning display
oven are the attractions at this new Downtown eatery;
the trattoria-style decor features lots of "paparazzi"
photos;* N.B. *kids eat free Saturday and Sunday.*

Pars/S (Armonk) **F3** | 12 | 13 | 13 | $24 |
A & P Shopping Center, 454 Main St., 273-8811
*U – "Move over Sizzler!"; this "basic" steakhouse has a
"nice pub" feel and "fair" prices for "steak and potatoes";
"you get your money's worth", so "bring the family"; the
$7.95 weekday buffet lunch buffet is a "bargain."*

Paul Ma's/Shanghai/S | 23 | 10 | 19 | $21 |
(Yorktown) **E5**
Rte. 35 (Rte. 202), 962-7996
*U – "Innovative Chinese cuisine" served "by the master
chef himself" is why numerous surveyors call this the
"best Chinese food in the metro area"; it has a "dreadful
storefront setting", but "friendly staff", "great value" and
"interesting" food are far more important.*

Pearl of the Atlantic/S | 19 | 12 | 16 | $32 |
(Port Chester) **F3**
Fox Island Rd. (Grace Church St.), 939-4227
*M – "Almost impossible to find" at the end of a dirt road
by the water's edge, this seafooder specializes in "heavy
duty" portions of lobster and "Portuguese fishing-village
fare"; the plain dining room is often "crowded" and "noisy."*

Penfield's (Rye Brook) **F3** | 20 | 22 | 20 | $37 |
Rye Town Hilton, 699 Westchester Ave. (5 miles south of
I-287), 939-6300
*U – "For hotel food, this is surprisingly good", say
surveyors of the seasonal Contemporary American;
though a few naysayers call this attractive spot "nothing
out of the ordinary", most diners praise the "fresh and
tasty" cuisine and "polite, efficient" service.*

Peter Pratt's Inn*/S (Yorktown) **E5** | 22 | 22 | 21 | $34 |
Croton Heights Rd. (near Rte. 118), 962-4090
*U – In the winter, dinner is served in the stone-walled
cellar of this secluded 18th-century farmhouse, and in
the summer the scene shifts to the porch; though some
think "decor is the strong point", equally high scores for
the Contemporary American cuisine (crab cakes, lamb,
salmon) promise a complete success.*

Piermont on the Hudson/S | 17 | 19 | 17 | $33 |
(Piermont) **D3**
701 Piermont Ave. (Rte. 9W), 365-1360
M – "Location" is everything at this Northern Italian with a deck overlooking the Hudson – "have a drink outside in summer and watch the sunset"; the food earns mixed reviews, from "satisfying" to "average"; most agree that "high prices" diminish the experience.

Pinocchio Ristorante/S | 23 | 16 | 20 | $39 |
(Eastchester) **E2**
309 White Plains Rd. (Highland Ave.), 337-0044
M – Many say it serves "the best Italian food in Westchester" with "excellent" specialties; however, a few complain about "snooty" service, "tired decor" and dishes that "cost like NYC."

PLUMBUSH INN/S (Cold Spring) **D7** | 22 | 24 | 21 | $40 |
Rte. 9D (8 miles north of Bear Mtn. Bridge), 265-3904
U – This "stunning" Victorian's "exquisite setting" on five wooded acres inspires more fervor than the old-style Swiss-Continental fare, but the numbers show "excellent food" and "attentive service" as well; it comes at a price, but it's a "wonderful" place to stop when antiquing.

Pondfield's/S (Bronxville) **E2** | 19 | 17 | 20 | $29 |
124 Pondfield Rd. (Cedar St.), 337-3330
M – Despite "several changes in owners" and though there are "other better places", this "unpretentious", moderately priced, Swiss-accented Continental "cafe" keeps 'em "coming back"; "comfortable" ambiance, "efficient" service and the ability to "handle Saturday night crowds well" explains its success.

Priya Indian Cuisine*/S (Suffern) **B4** | 14 | 11 | 16 | $23 |
36 Lafayette Ave., Rte. 59 (bet. Chestnut St. & Rte. 22), 357-5700
U – "Not-too-spicy" Northern Indian at "good prices" sums up this well-liked Rockland Countyite that could benefit from "more decor."

Provare at Arrowwood/S | 18 | 19 | 18 | $32 |
(Rye Brook) **F3**
Arrowwood Conference Ctr., Anderson Hill Rd., 939-4554
M – A real "kick", this "high-tech pizza parlor" boasts a demonstration pizza oven and an antipasto bar plus a "breezy, innovative" Italian menu; but many people find the funky-modern decor "hard on the eyes", and the place "cramped" and "noisy when crowded."

Quarropas/S (White Plains) **F3** | 20 | 17 | 18 | $33 |
478 Mamaroneck Ave. (Shapham Pl.), 684-0414
U – Words like "unusual", "imaginative" and "innovative"
abound regarding the Contemporary American food at
this "plain" but "comfortable" storefront; a few complain
of "spotty" quality and "confused" service, especially on
Saturday nights, but all agree "the price is right."

Red Rooster, The/SX (Brewster) **F7** | 16 | 10 | 16 | $14 |
Rte. 22 (3 miles north of Rte. 84), 279-8046
U – This incredibly popular old-fashioned drive-in has a
huge American "fast food" menu: hot dogs, burgers,
"fried everything", shakes, sundaes, etc.; it's an
inexpensive "one-of-a-kind" stop "on the way" to the
Berkshires, and the "kids" can play miniature golf on an
adjoining course.

Reef 'n Beef/S (Peekskill) **E5** | 14 | 14 | 15 | $21 |
Rte. 9, Annsville Circle (east of Bear Mtn. Bridge), 737-4959
U – Foodies love to hate this steakhouse, but crowds
still herd to it for "substantial" portions of "good-value"
"standard" American fare; expect "lots of tacky weddings
and junior proms", and come "early before the crowds
start" (especially "after an Army game").

Reka's Thai Restaurant/S | 17 | 15 | 17 | $28 |
(White Plains) **F3**
2 Westchester Ave. (bet. Main St. & Rte. 22), 949-1440
M – Everyone agrees that Reka's a real "character", but
opinions differ on the Thai food – "wonderful" and
"interesting" vs. "mediocre" and "erratic"; opinions also
contrast on the service: "friendly" vs. "awful."

River Club/S (Nyack) **D4** | 17 | 20 | 17 | $29 |
11 Burd St. (1 block south of Main St.), 358-0220
M – Right "on the river", this casual Continental garners
many more favorable comments about the "great
location" than the "ordinary food" (although scores
improved since our last Survey); most still say "such a
shame" – "really pretty" but "spotty at best."

Rockwell's/S | 12 | 12 | 14 | $19 |
(Bedford Hills) **F4**, 728 Bedford Rd. (Green Lane), 666-0099
(Tuckahoe) **E2**, 16 Depot Sq. (Main St.), 961-7744
(Scarsdale) **E2**, 718 Central Ave. (3 miles north of
Jackson Ave.), 725-8240
M – Westchester's answer to "TGI Friday's" – these
havens for "permissive parents" go all out for the family
trade; "bless Rockwell's", say moms and dads, but the
unencumbered say it's "like eating in a school cafeteria."

Romolo's/S (Congers) D4
| 21 | 17 | 20 | $33 |

77 Rte. 303 (3½ miles north of NY Twy.), 268-3770
M – This recently renovated Italian, in business since 1978, tallies a split vote: "mediocre" or "Rockland County's best"; the traditional menu offers "plenty to eat with fair prices", and much "better-than-average" service.

Royal Siam* (Pearl River) C3
| 15 | 11 | 15 | $22 |

22 E. Center Ave. (near Rte. 304), 735-5906
M – "Bargain prices" are the main attraction at this Rockland County Thai; fans cite "reasonably authentic" food from a "diverse menu", but others say it's "very average"; decor definitely isn't royal.

Rudy's Beau Rivage/S
| 10 | 15 | 14 | $31 |

(Dobbs Ferry) E3
19 Livingston Ave. (B'way), 693-3192
U – "What a waste of a view!" is the consensus on this "High Tacky"–style Continental in a once-noble mansion overlooking the Hudson; though a few feel that it "does have a certain charm", most say "eat before you go."

Sakura/S (Scarsdale) E2
| 18 | 15 | 17 | $28 |

56 Garth Rd. (across from RR station), 723-7767
M – Loyal "locals like it", but opinions vary on this "friendly and pleasant" spot that "can't decide if it's Chinese or Japanese", from "weak on all counts" to "above average"; N.B. there's a children's sushi menu.

Salerno's Old Town/S
| 20 | 13 | 18 | $33 |

(Tuckahoe) E2
100 Main St. (Terrace St.), 793-1557
U – Although the "old-fashioned" "steak-and-potatoes" menu shows "little or no imagination", this "solid, not spectacular" performer churns out heaps of good, "simple food"; the "grubby setting" may turn some people off, but "year after year", fans "keep going back."

Sam's/LS (Dobbs Ferry) E3
| 15 | 13 | 16 | $23 |

128 Main St. (B'way), 693-9724
U – This "decent local haunt" serving Northern Italian specialties and pizza; though some confuse this with a similarly named spot, and "wish the food were better", it's clear that for fans, it's "a neighborhood necessity."

Santa Fe/S (Tarrytown) D3
| 18 | 16 | 16 | $22 |

5 Main St. (off Rte. 9), 332-4452
M – This "cheerful" Tarrytown cantina wins applause from a "lively" crowd for "better-than-average" Mexican food at "moderate prices"; "spotty" service and "tight" quarters get boos.

Santa Fe*/S (Tivoli) **D12** | 21 | 16 | 19 | $24 |
52 Broadway (bet. Montgomery St. & North Rd.), 757-4100
*U – "No gloppy refried beans here" – this upscale
"authentic" Mexican serves dishes made with
"wonderful fresh ingredients"; "fair" prices, "courteous"
service and "imaginative" food justify the trip to this
interesting old Northern Dutchess town.*

Satsuma-ya/S (Mamaroneck) **F2** | 20 | 14 | 18 | $31 |
576 Mamaroneck (1 block north of RR station), 381-0200
*U – The "French-inspired Japanese food" makes for
"unusual combinations that work" at this "diner"-like
Westchester "nouvelle" Oriental with "European
undertones"; service is "excellent" and "kid-friendly",
though prices are "above average."*

Sawpit/S (Port Chester) **F3** | 14 | 10 | 16 | $30 |
25 S. Regent St. (bet. Westchester Ave. & Boston Post
Rd.), 939-1360
*M – "Welcome to the '50s" at this "down-to-earth" Port
Chester landmark; the "old-fashioned" decor "could be
improved", but it's "always packed with regulars" who like
the "predictable" menu; critics just say "what a mess."*

Schemmy's Ltd./S (Rhinebeck) **D12** | – | – | – | I |
19 E. Market St. (Rte. 9), 876-6215
*This good old-fashioned ice cream parlor–cum–
sandwich shop is a local favorite and a handy place to
take a break when visiting Rhinebeck; prices are low,
and families are welcome.*

Schneller's*/S (Kingston) **C12** | 21 | 16 | 16 | $22 |
61 John St. (Wall St.), 331-9800
*U – "Best for lunch" while strolling through historic
Kingston, this über German tavern serves up hearty
fare, e.g., delicious, homemade schnitzels and wursts,
to a background of live polka music in a mammoth
outdoor beer garden; having started as a market, it uses
fresh produce, meat, and locally made wine and beer.*

Season's*/S (Harrison) **F2** | 14 | 9 | 16 | $25 |
385 Halstead Ave. (near RR station), 835-6868
*U – Reasonable prices and convenience for shoppers
are the best points about this otherwise "very average"
health-oriented American cafe; families "with children"
come often, and "older people" enjoy splitting the "large
portions"; decor is strictly "coffee shop."*

Sergio's (Hartsdale) **F3** | 19 | 18 | 17 | $40 |
18 N. Central Ave. (Rtes. 100 & 100A), 949-1234
*M – Surveyors either love or hate this "pricey" 30-year-old
Italian in a Tudor-style building; fans say the homemade
pasta, seafood and veal are "above average", but critics
say this "standard-issue" place has seen better days.*

1766 Tavern at Beekman Arms/S | 20 | 23 | 19 | $36 |
(Rhinebeck) **D12**
Beekman Arms Inn, 4 Mill St. (Rtes. 9 & 308), 871-1766
M – This "historic" circa-1766 inn, under the aegis of celebrity chef Larry (An American Place) Forgione, sports a "much improved" American menu and attractive "country-tavern" decor; apart from service that's a little "s-l-o-w", it "makes a wonderful day trip."

Siam Orchid I & II/S | 20 | 15 | 18 | $24 |
(Yonkers) **D2**, 750 Central Park (Ardsley Rd.), 723-9131
(Tarrytown) **D3,** 49 Main St. (Rte. 9), 631-8674
M – Considered "the best Thais in Westchester" by some, they even "rival NYC's best"; the staff is friendly and the decor "is not your typical basic Oriental design."

Siam Sea Grill/S (Port Chester) **F3** | 23 | 16 | 18 | $27 |
134 N. Main St. (Willie Ave.), 939-0477
U – "The owners are sweet and caring" at this Westchester Thai that serves "interesting", "enjoyable", "unusual" food; fans call it an "undiscovered jewel", but service sometimes slips; another drawback is the "war-zone" location in Downtown Port Chester.

Silvano's/S (Somers) **F4** | 18 | 17 | 18 | $43 |
Rte. 100 (Rte. 684, exit 6), 232-8080
M – Seafood's the catch at this "old-fashioned" Northern Italian; most say the food is "very good", the $12.95 lunch special is a "real bargain", and the staff "really cares"; critics say "it should be better after all these years."

Silver Spoon Cafe/S (Harrison) **F2** | 18 | 17 | 16 | $26 |
301 Halstead Ave. (across from RR station), 835-2609
U – An old diner converted into a "new wave" American cafe, this "crowded" "yuppie" spot sports a snazzy "art deco look" and a light menu with lots of pasta specials; it's "good for lunch" or "before the movies", and ideal for "families", though prices may be a bit high.

Slattery's/S (Nyack) **D4** | 17 | 13 | 19 | $25 |
9 N. Broadway (Main St.), 358-1135
U – "Large" portions and a convivial crowd are the attractions at this "everyday" publike place that serves a "standard" Continental menu; surveyors say it's "nothing fancy" but "convenient", and Irish singers add to the "lively" atmosphere.

Sonoma Restaurant & Cafe/S | – | – | – | M |
(Croton-on-Hudson) **D4**
Rte. 9A (Baltic Pl.), 271-4100
An "excellent" and "imaginative" menu and "carefully chosen wine list" set the tone of this airy Californian-style eatery in upper Westchester; it collected many write-in votes as a satisfying, "well-run" restaurant.

Spaccarelli's/S (Millwood) **E4** | 22 | 15 | 18 | $32 |
Intersection Rtes. 100 & 133, 941-0105
*M – This is another love-it-or-leave-it place; while the
Italian food draws accolades, service can be problematic
("bad attitude if you are not known") and there's "no
atmosphere" in the "tight" surroundings.*

ST. ANDREW'S CAFE | 24 | 24 | 24 | $28 |
(Hyde Park) **D10**
Culinary Institute of America, 651 S. Albany Post Rd.,
Rte. 9 (north of E. Dorsey Lane), 452-9600
*U – "Gourmet health food" is the lesson learned at this new
CIA student-run restaurant where you get a post-meal
nutritional analysis; "superbly prepared" Contemporary
American cuisine "minus the fat and rich sauces" results
in "amazingly good low-fat, low-cholesterol" meals.*

Stefini Trattoria*/S (Irvington) **E3** | 25 | 18 | 22 | $36 |
50 S. Buckout St. (Main St.), 591-7208
*U – "A real find", this Westchester "gem" serves
imaginative Northern Italian specialties in a relaxed,
"charming" environment; service is "a delight", pastas
are "great", but the prices aren't so charming.*

Stewart House/LS (Athens) **D13** | – | – | – | M |
2 N. Water St. (Second St.), 518-945-1357
*This cozy up-the-Hudson restaurant-cum-inn north of
the town of Catskill serves Contemporary American fare
spiced with fresh garden herbs; two menus are featured
– bistro and formal – in this pretty Victorian-style spot.*

Susan's & Bad Bill's Bar | 21 | 20 | 21 | $28 |
(Peekskill) **E5**
12 N. Division St. (Main St.), 737-6624
*M – This "comfortable" "local pub" "fills the bill", serving
"good" "Californian-style" cuisine in a "cute" "country
setting"; it's especially popular "after the movies",
though some label the food and service "erratic."*

SUSHI RAKU/S | 24 | 19 | 21 | $28 |
(North Tarrytown) **D3**
279 N. Broadway (Beekman Ave.), 332-8687
*U – "Excellent" "fresh sushi" and "shabu-shabu" served
in a "simple" setting by "friendly owners" make this so
much a "favorite" for Japanese food in Westchester that
regulars "park their chopsticks" in "special boxes."*

Sweetwaters/S (White Plains) **F3** | 18 | 17 | 18 | $30 |
577 N. Broadway (Fisher Lane), 328-8920
*U – Located near the train station, this "pretty", often
crowded, American bistro is, above all, "convenient";
beyond that, regulars find it "good" but "unexceptional",
with inconsistent service.*

Swiss Hutte Inn & Restaurant/S | – | – | – | M |
(East Hillsdale) **G14**
Rte. 23 at Catamount Ski Area, 518-325-3333
*Simple good Swiss Continental food in a comfortable
chalet setting distinguishes this restaurant at the foot of
the Catamount slopes; it tastes best after skiing, but in
summer, it's a good pit stop on the way to the Berkshires.*

Szechuan Flower/S | 16 | 12 | 15 | $22 |
(Greenburgh) **E4**
365 Central Ave. (Rte. 119), 472-1370
*M – Views range from "the best Szechuan in
Westchester" to "the worst", so it must be somewhere in
between; basically, this is "an old-fashioned Chinese
restaurant, fancy drinks and all", with a "no-ambiance
dining room" and "indifferent" service.*

Temptations*/SX (Nyack) **D4** | 23 | 18 | 19 | $12 |
80½ Main St. (bet. S. B'way & Franklin St.), 353-3355
*U – "Forget your diets" all ye who enter this "incredible
dessert shop"–cum–cafe specializing in "great ice cream"
and "outrageous" sweets, plus sandwiches, espresso and
cappuccino; celeb-watchers note: recent sightings of
Brooke Shields, Bill Murray and Helen Hayes.*

Thierry's Relais/S (Bedford) **F4** | 22 | 22 | 21 | $41 |
352 N. Bedford Rd. (Rte. 117), 666-9504
*U – Two new chefs recruited from restaurants in Europe
are changing the menu at this "charming" Classic
French with Belgian flair, a fact that's yet to be reflected
in the scores; the "wonderful Belgian couple" (Mr. &
Mrs. Thierry Van Dyke) who run the "comfortable"
19th-century house provide "a lot of TLC."*

Tony La Stazione/S (Elmsford) **E3** | 16 | 14 | 16 | $32 |
15 Saw Mill River Rd. (Rtes. 9A & 119), 592-5980
*M – Many wonder why this "place is always mobbed",
what with "average" Italian food, "disorganized" service
and only "fair" decor; those doing the mobbing insist that
the staff is "outgoing", portions are "huge" and they've
"never had a bad meal."*

Tony's Lobster & Steakhouse/S | 16 | 13 | 16 | $29 |
(Sparkill) **D3**
Rte. 340 (Rte. 9W), 359-7380
*M – This "longtime standby" is admittedly "lacking in
ambiance", but it serves "large portions" of "good,
honest" American food at "digestible prices"; the varied
steak and lobster menu "offers something for everyone."*

Towne Crier*/S (Pawling) **E8** | 18 | 16 | 17 | $28 |
62 Rte. 22 (Rte. 311), 855-1300
*U – The New Orleans–style food is "surprisingly good",
but the main lure here is live folk, jazz and Cajun music
that incites foot-stompin' fun; fans say "the food is as
good as the entertainment", citing "outstanding
desserts" and specialty coffees, but the SW decor, left
over from a prior incarnation, seems out of place.*

Traveler's Rest/SX (Millwood) **E4** | 19 | 21 | 21 | $37 |
Rte. 100 (2 miles north of Millwood), 941-7744
*U – "Ample" portions of "hearty" German and Continental
food distinguish this northern Westchester institution, in
business since 1890, with its stream, pond, waterfall and
outdoor walkways; it's "a wonderful special-occasion
restaurant" – "schmaltzy but enjoyable in small doses."*

Trio's Cafe/S (Scarsdale) **E2** | – | – | – | I |
1096 Wilmot Rd. (Weaver St.), 725-8377
*Affordable well-prepared Traditional American food in a
storefront location is "a big surprise in Scarsdale" for
those expecting to come here and eat out, not dine;
"elegance", "quality" and "originality" compose the
winning trio here.*

TROUTBECK INN/S (Amenia) **G11** | 24 | 25 | 24 | $47 |
Troutbeck Inn, Leedsville Rd. (Rte. 343), 373-9681
*U – In a '20s-era stone manor house on a Dutchess
County estate, this "corporate Camelot" serves
business groups from Sunday afternoon till Thursday,
and the general public on weekends; surveyors say that
the "imaginative" Contemporary American food,
"perfect" service and "lovely" surroundings make this
"heavenly" place a "hidden treasure."*

Turning Point, The/S (Piermont) **D3** | 17 | 17 | 16 | $26 |
468 Piermont Ave. (Rte. 9W, Business District exit),
359-1089
*U – This Continental with a downstairs "blues club"
offers "good food" in a "relaxed" atmosphere; although
"unremarkable", it's a "casual spot for a drink or light
supper"; the big draw is the entertainment, and
"stargazing" when celebrities visit.*

Two Moons/S (Port Chester) **F3** | – | – | – | M |
179 Rectory St. (Willett Ave.), 937-9696
*New to Westchester, this au courant Eclectic features
Native American artwork, making it "visually the most
sophisticated restaurant" around; the "different" menu
with a contemporary twist is also attractive.*

Umberto's (Rye) **F2** | 21 | 15 | 19 |$38|
92 Purchase St. (bet. Bordy Ave. & RR station), 967-1909
M – Surveyors can't agree on this "long-lived"
Downtown Northern Italian; fans admit there's "no
decor", but say the "food will bring you back" to "feast"
every time; foes call it a "run-of-the-mill trattoria" that's
"expensive" and "cramped" when busy.

Underhill Inn*/S (Hillsdale) **G14** | 21 | 20 | 22 |$35|
Rte. 22 (½ mile south of Rte. 23), 518-325-5660
U – This "cozy" Columbia County country inn, located in
a 150-year-old farmhouse, serves a "nice menu" of
Continental favorites; service is "attentive", and Sunday
brunch on the outdoor deck is a pleasure; P.S. they also
give cooking classes.

Valentino's/SX (Yonkers) **D2** | 22 | 11 | 17 |$28|
132 Bronx River Rd. (2 blocks north of McLean Ave.),
776-6511
U – "Who needs Arthur Avenue or Little Italy?" with this
popular, "noisy", "crowded", mid-price Italian around; it's
small and has the ambiance of a "dry cleaner", but it's
"big on food"; no reserving means waits on weekends.

Via Appia/S (White Plains) **F3** | 15 | 10 | 14 |$23|
9 Taylor Sq. (across from Silver Lake Park), 949-5810
U – "Your basic family-style Italian", this "old-fashioned"
"red-sauce" joint is a "longtime favorite" despite "hideous
decor"; it's "inexpensive" and "kinda like Little Italy."

Vintage Cafe/S (Cold Spring) **D7** | – | – | – | M |
91 Main St. (near the river), 265-4726
This likable cafe has been building a sterling reputation that
inspired write-ins; the creative chef-owner serves up an
eclectic New American menu in a small, cozy, "weathered"
room featuring hand-painted game-board tables.

Westchester Trawler/S | 13 | 8 | 13 |$25|
(Elmsford) **E3**
12 W. Main St. (next to Saw Mill River Pkwy.), 592-6799
U – Reviewers say this fish market/restaurant has been
"going downhill", with "tacky decor" and "boring" food
that's a "throwback to the '50s"; the faithful like the
"good fish, no dress code" and easy-on-the-wallet prices.

Whitecaps/LS (Ossining) **D4** | – | – | – | M |
Westerly Rd. (north of train station), 941-3311
Opened by a former Marriott executive chef and his
brother, this brand-new spot has been packed since day
one; the draws are the spectacular Hudson River view
from a location right on the marina, a substantial
steak-and-seafood menu, late-night hours and a busy
bar scene – plus 200 channels on the TV so you won't
ever miss a game.

Willett House/S (Port Chester) **F3** | 21 | 19 | 19 | $42 |
20 Willett Ave. (1 block from RR station), 939-7500
*M – This pricey Westchester steakhouse is trying to be
"Peter Luger North" – whether it is successful depends
on whom you ask ("terrific steak" vs. a "slide to
mediocrity"); either way, its "ample portions" and
"masculine decor" appeal to local big-eaters.*

XAVIAR'S IN GARRISON/SX | 28 | 25 | 26 | $53 |
(Garrison) **D6**
Highlands Country Club, Rte. 9D (south of Rte. 403),
424-4228
*U – For a "truly great experience" with a "spectacular"
"country-club setting" and "exquisite" New American
food; open only on weekends, owner Peter Kelly and
staff treat guests to "flawless service" and "classy,
stylish" dining awash in candlelight and fresh flowers;
it's a "special place for a special occasion" – but don't
forget to bring cash.*

XAVIAR'S IN PIERMONT/SX | 29 | 24 | 26 | $51 |
(Piermont) **D3**
506 Piermont Ave. (Rte. 9W, Business District exit),
359-7007
*U – Also owned by Peter Kelly, reviewers can't find
sufficient superlatives to describe this "superb"
Contemporary American that gets the top food rating in
this Survey; "perfection in food, ambiance and service"
is the norm, with "stellar service", a tiny "jewel" box of a
setting and "wonderful food" that "never disappoints";
make reservations far ahead, then be "pampered"; yes,
it's pricey, but "worth it."*

ZEPH'S (Peekskill) **E5** | 25 | 19 | 24 | $36 |
638 Central Ave. (bet. Nelson & Water Sts.), 736-2159
*U – Located in a "charming renovated building" in an
"urban renewal area", this pricey up-and-coming
Eclectic sports an "imaginative", "sophisticated" menu
and a "young, eager" staff in an "interesting" setting;
some feel it could one day "rival Xaviar's."*

SOUTHERN NEW YORK STATE INDEXES

TYPES OF CUISINE

American (Contemporary)
Allyn's
American Bounty
An American Bistro
Anthony's Uptown
Black Bass Grill
Cafe Tamayo
Carl's
Cascade Mtn. Winery
Chelsea on Hudson
Cobble Creek Cafe
Corner Bakery
Crabtree's
Depuy Canal House
Dudley's
Freelance Cafe
Fritz's
Goldie's
Good Enough to Eat
Good Life
Green and Bresler
Huckleberry's
Hudson House
John Richard's
Kit 'N Caboodle
Le Shack
Livanos
Long Pond Inn
Off Broadway
Old Drover's Inn
Penfield's
Peter Pratt's
Pondfield's
Quarropas
Season's
1766 Tavern
Silver Spoon Cafe
Sonoma
St. Andrew's Cafe
Susan's & Bad Bill's
Sweetwaters
Temptations
Troutbeck Inn
Vintage Cafe
Xaviar's Garrison
Xaviar's Piermont

American (Traditional)
Bird & Bottle Inn
Bully Boy's
Country Manor
Foster's Coach House
Grandma's
Heathcote Crossing
Horsefeathers
Huff House
Inn at Pound Ridge
Mariner's Harbor
Mohonk Mountain Hse.
Old '76 House
Old Stonehouse Inn
Palmer House Inn
Red Rooster
Reef 'n Beef
Rockwell's
Salerno's
Stewart House
Trio's Cafe
Two Moons
Whitecaps

Bar-B-Q
Aria
Hudson's

Basque
Marichu

Cajun/Creole
Towne Crier

Chinese
China Echo
Dynasty
Golden Duck
Hartsdale Garden
Hunan Manor
Hunan Village
Hunan Wok
Imperial Wok
Pagoda
Paul Ma's/Shanghai
Sakura
Szechuan Flower

Continental
Anthony's Uptown
Arch
Bear Mountain Inn
Bird & Bottle Inn
Brasserie Swiss
Bully Boy's
Chelsea on Hudson
Clarksville Inn
Country Manor
Dockside Harbor
Guidetti's Lodge
Harrald's
Heathcote Crossing
Hudson House
Huff House
Inn at Osborne Hill
Jason's
Manzi's
Meson Castellano
Nino's
Old Drover's Inn
Old Stonehouse Inn
Penfield's
Plumbush inn
Pondfield's
River Club
Rudy's Beau Rivage
Sawpit
Season's
Slattery's
Swiss Hutte
Traveler's Rest
Turning Point
Underhill Inn

Eclectic
Bistro Twenth-two
Depuy Canal House
Kit 'N Caboodle
Locust Tree Inn
Off Broadway
Painter's Tavern
Stewart House
Two Moons
Vintage Cafe
Zeph's

French Bistro
Bistro Maxime
Le Shack
Maxime's Brasserie

French Classic
Arch
Auberge Argenteuil
Box Tree
Buffet de la Gare
Escoffier Room
La Panetiere
La Rive
Le Chambord
Le Chateau
Le Pavillion
Le Petit Bistro
Les Bons Copains
L'Europe
L'Hostellerie Bressane
Maison Lafitte
Slattery's
Thierry's Relais

French Contemporary
Arch
Auberge Maxime
Le Chambord
Le Pavillion
Les Bons Copains
L'Europe

German
Schneller's
Traveler's Rest

Ice Cream Shops
Schemmy's

Indian
Abhilash
Bengal Tiger
Dawat
India House
Malabar Hill
Priya

International
Hope and Anchor
McKinney & Doyle

Italian (Northern)
Angsavanee
Capriccio
Daniel's
Edenville Inn
Edmundo's Too
Emilio's
Enzo's
Giardino
Giulio's
Guidetti's Lodge
Il Cenacola
Il Cigno
Il Portico
Lago di Como
La Riserva
Mona Trattoria
Nino's
Papa-Razzi

Piermont on Hudson
Provare
Sam's
Spaccarelli's
Stefini
Tony La Stazione
Umberto's

Italian (Southern)
Guida's
La Mandas
La Scala
Louie's
Via Appia

Italian (North & South)
Bambina
Caterina de Medici
Chef Antonio
Ciao
Cornetta's
Gregory's
Hilltop
Manzi's
Marcello's
Nanuet Hotel
Owl's Nest
Pinocchio
Romolo's
Sergio's
Silvano's
Slattery's
Valentino's

Japanese
Abis
Azuma Sushi
Gasho of Japan
Ichi Riki
Japan Inn
Mount Fuji
Orchid Garden
Sakura
Satsuma-ya
Sushi Raku

Korean
Aria

Mediterranean
Maxime's La Petite

Mexican/Tex-Mex
Armadillo
Camino Real
Cantina
Casas Miguel
Corridos Mexicanos
Hacienda Don Emilio

La Fonda del Sol
Pancho Villa's
Santa Fe

Mongolian
Khan's Mongolian

Pizza
Bambina
Ciao
La Mandas
Papa-Razzi

Portuguese
Caravela
Pearl of the Atlantic

Seafood
Banta's
Benny's
Brass Anchor
Caravela
Cornetta's
Crystal Bay
Dockside Harbor
Dudley's
Eastchester Fish
Foster's Coach House
Greenbaum/Gilhooly's
Gregory's
Grouper Cafe
Gus's Franklin
Hilltop
Hudson's
Il Portico
Jason's
John Richard's
Marichu
Mariner's Harbor
Pancho Villa's
Pars
Pearl of the Atlantic
River Club
Rockwell's
Salerno's
Silvano's
Tony's
Westchester Trawler
Whitecaps

Southern
Carolina House

Southwestern
Casa Miguel
Santa Fe

Spanish
Camino Real
La Camelia

Southern New York State

La Fonda del Sol
Meson Castellano

Steakhouses
Armadillo
Banta's
Carl's
Chart House
Cornetta's
Foster's Coach House
Greenbaum/Gilhooly's
Gregory's
Hudson's
Jason's
John Richard's
Owl's Nest
Pars
Reef 'n Beef

Rockwell's
Salerno's
Tony's
Whitecaps
Willett House

Swiss
Brasserie Swiss
Plumbush Inn
Swiss Hutte

Thai
King & I
Reka's
Royal Siam
Siam Orchid
Siam Sea Grill

LOCATION BY TOWN

Amenia
  Cascade Mtn. Winery
  Palmer House Inn
  Troutbeck Inn
Ardsley
  Cantina
Armonk
  Bambina
  La Scala
  Pars
Athens
  Stewart House
Bear Mountain
  State Park
  Bear Mountain Inn
Bedford
  Bistro Twenty-Two
  Nino's
  Thierry's Relais
Bedford Hills
  Rockwell's
Blauvelt
  Khan's Mongolian
Brewster
  Arch
  Capriccio
  Red Rooster
Briarcliff Manor
  Giardino
  Maison Lafitte
  Maxime's Brasserie
Bronxville
  Japan Inn
  Marichu
  Pondfield's
Catskill
  La Rive
Central Valley
  Gasho of Japan
Chappaqua
  Bistro Maxime
  Crabtree's
Cold Spring
  Hudson House
  Plumbush Inn
  Vintage Cafe
Congers
  Bully Boy's
  Romolo's
Cornwall-on-Hudson
  Painter's Tavern
Croton Falls
  Mona Trattoria
Croton-on-Hudson
  Sonoma
Dobbs Ferry
  Chart House

John Richard's
Off Broadway
Rudy's Beau Rivage
Sam's
Dover Plains
  Old Drover's Inn
Eastchester
  Ciao
  Daniel's
  Jason's
  Pagoda
  Pinocchio
East Hillsdale
  Swiss Hutte
Elmsford
  Ichi Riki
  Malabar Hill
  Tony La Stazione
  Westchester Trawler
Fishkill
  Hudson's
  Inn at Osborne Hill
Garrison
  Bird & Bottle Inn
  Xaviar's Garrison
Granite Springs
  Fritz's
  Maxime's Brasserie
Greenburgh
  Szechuan Flower
Harrison
  Emilio's
  Gus's Franklin
  Season's
  Silver Spoon Cafe
Hartsdale
  Auberge Argenteuil
  Azuma Sushi
  Hartsdale Garden
  Hunan Manor
  Hunan Wok
  Sergio's
Hastings-
  on-Hudson
  Buffet de la Gare
  Manzi's
Hawthorne
  Gasho of Japan
High Falls
  Depuy Canal House
  Good Enough to Eat
Highland
  Mariner's Harbor
High Mount
  Owl's Nest
Hillburn
  Mount Fuji

Southern New York State

Hillsdale
  L'Hostellerie Bressane
  Underhill Inn
Hopewell Junction
  Le Chambord
Hyde Park
  American Bounty
  Caterina de Medici
  Escoffier Room
  St. Andrew's Cafe
Irvington
  Benny's
  Stefini
Kinderhook
  Carolina House
Kingston
  Anthony's Uptown
  Armadillo
  Schneller's
Larchmont
  Carl's
  Hacienda Don Emilio
  Hope and Anchor
  La Riserva
  Pancho Villa's
Mahopac
  Long Pond Inn
Mamaroneck
  Abis
  Chef Antonio
  Enzo's
  Good Life
  Satsuma-ya
Millbrook
  Allyn's
Millwood
  Spaccarelli's
  Traveler's Rest
Montrose
  India House
Mount Kisco
  Casa Miguel
  Grouper Cafe
  Kit 'N Caboodle
  La Camelia
Nanuet
  Nanuet Hotel
Newburgh
  Il Cenacola
New City
  China Echo
New Paltz
  Locust Tree Inn
  Mohonk Mtn. Hse.
New Rochelle
  Abhilash India
New Windsor
  Banta's
North Salem
  Auberge Maxime

North Tarrytown
  Goldie's
  Sushi Raku
Nyack
  Chelsea on Hudson
  Hilltop
  Hudson House
  Ichi Riki
  King & I
  Orchid Garden
  River Club
  Slattery's
  Temptations
Orangeburg
  Old Stonehouse
Ossining
  Brasserie Swiss
  Dudley's
  Guida's
Pawling
  Corner Bakery
  McKinney & Doyle
  Towne Crier
Pearl River
  Royal Siam
Peekskill
  Crystal Bay
  Reef 'n Beef
  Susan's & Bad Bill's
  Zeph's
Piermont
  Cornetta's
  Freelance Cafe
Piermont-on-Hudson
  Turning Point
  Xaviar's Piermont
Pleasantville
  Camino Real
Port Chester
  Angsavanee
  Pearl of the Atlantic
  Sawpit
  Siam Sea Grill
  Two Moons
  Willett House
Poughkeepsie
  Brass Anchor
  Country Manor
  Le Pavillion
Pound Ridge
  Inn at Pound Ridge
Purchase
  Cobble Creek
Purdys
  Box Tree
Red Hook
  Green and Bresler
Rhinebeck
  Foster's Coach House
  Le Petit Bistro

Southern New York State

Schemmy's
1766 Tavern
Roscoe
  Huff House
Rye
  Black Bass Grill
  La Panetiere
  Umberto's
Rye Brook
  Penfield's
  Provare
Saugerties
  Cafe Tamayo
Scarsdale
  Eastchester Fish
  Golden Duck
  Heathcote Crossing
  Il Cigno
  Rockwell's
  Sakura
  Trio's Cafe
Somers
  Imperial Wok
  Silvano's
South Salem
  L'Europe
  Le Chateau
Sparkill
  Tony's
Stormville
  Harrald's
Suffern
  Les Bons Copains
  Marcello's
  Priya
Tappan
  Giulio's
  Il Portico
  Old '76 House
Tarrytown
  Caravela
  Dockside Harbor
  Horsefeathers
  Lago di Como
  Santa Fe
  Siam Orchid
Thornwood
  Imperial Wok

Tivoli
  Santa Fe
Tuckahoe
  An American Bistro
  Rockwell's
  Salerno's
Wappingers Falls
  Banta's
  Dynasty
  Greenbaum/Gilhooly's
  La Fonda del Sol
Warwick
  Edenville Inn
West Nyack
  Clarksville Inn
White Plains
  Bengal Tiger
  Dawat
  Edmundo's Too
  Gregory's
  La Mandas
  Le Shack
  Livanos
  Meson Castellano
  Mulino's
  Quarropas
  Reka's
  Sweetwaters
  Via Appia
Wingdale
  Guidetti's Lodge
Yonkers
  Aria
  Corridos Mexicanos
  Hunan Village
  Louie's
  Siam Orchid
  Valentino's
Yorktown
  Grandma's
  Imperial Wok
  Paul Ma's/Shanghai
  Peter Pratt's Inn
Yorktown Heights
  Huckleberry's

SPECIAL FEATURES AND APPEALS

Bar/Singles Scenes
Cantina
Corridos Mexicanos
Crabtree's
Dockside Harbor
Freelance Cafe
Grouper Cafe
Huckleberry's
John Richard's
King & I
La Fonda del Sol
Les Bons Copains
Le Shack
Livanos
Penfield's
Tony's
Turning Point
Whitecaps

Breakfast
(All hotels and the
following standouts)
Grandma's
McKinney & Doyle
Season's
Turning Point

Brunch
(Best of the many)
Allyn's
Arch
Bear Mountain Inn
Bird & Bottle Inn
Black Bass Grill
Box Tree
Brass Anchor
Cafe Tamayo
Capriccio
Chart House
Country Manor
Crabtree's
Depuy Canal House
Edenville Inn
Fritz's
Goldie's
Green and Bresler
Hudson House
Inn at Pound Ridge
La Camelia
L'Europe
Livanos
Locust Tree Inn
Long Pond Inn
Marcello's
McKinney & Doyle
Old '76 House

Old Drover's Inn
Painter's Tavern
Palmer House Inn
Plumbush Inn
1766 Tavern
Thierry's Relais
Troutbeck Inn
Underhill Inn
Vintage Cafe
Xaviar's Garrison
Xaviar's Piermont

Business Dining
An American Bistro
Angsavanee
Arch
Bird & Bottle Inn
Bistro Maxime
Bistro Twenty-two
Black Bass Grill
Box Tree
Brasserie Swiss
Buffet de la Gare
Bully Boy's
Capriccio
Caravela
Carl's
Chart House
Chelsea on Hudson
Clarksville Inn
Cobble Creek Cafe
Corridos Mexicanos
Country Manor
Dawat
Dudley's
Edmundo's Too
Giardino
Green and Bresler
Gregory's
Guida's
La Camelia
Lago di Como
La Panetiere
La Scala
Le Chambord
Le Chateau
Le Pavillion
Les Bons Copains
Livanos
Locust Tree Inn
Manzi's
Maxime's La Petite
Nino's
Old Stonehouse Inn
Penfield's
Peter Pratt's

Southern New York State

Piermont on Hudson
Pondfield's
Provare
Quarropas
Reka's
Sergio's
Silvano's
Spaccarelli's
Susan's & Bad Bill's
Sweetwaters
Thierry's Relais
Tony La Stazione
Tony's
Traveler's Rest
Troutbeck Inn
Umberto's
Underhill Inn
Via Appia
Westchester Trawler
Willett House
Xaviar's Garrison
Xaviar's Piermont

Dancing
(Nightclubs and the following; check times)
Armadillo
Bear Mountain Inn
Ciao
Crabtree's
Crystal Bay
Dockside Harbor
Hudson House
King & I
La Fonda del Sol
Penfield's
Towne Crier

Delivers
(Call to check range and charges, if any)
Corner Bakery
Dynasty
Green and Bresler
Sakura

Entertainment
(Check days, times and performers)
Anthony's Uptown (piano)
Bear Mtn. Inn (varies)
Camino Real (bands)
Cascade Mtn. (bands)
Ciao (piano)
Clarksville Inn (piano)
Corner Bakery (varies)
Corridos Mex. (bands)
Crabtree's (bands, jazz)
Crystal Bay (varies)

Depuy Canal (varies)
Dockside Harbor (jazz)
Dudley's (piano)
Good Enough (varies)
Haci Don Emilio (bands)
Huckleberry's (bands)
Hudson House (varies)
John Richard's (bands)
King & I (jazz, piano)
La Fonda del Sol (bands)
McKinney & Doyle (guitar)
Mount Fuji (DJ, piano)
Off Broadway (guitar)
Old '76 House (piano)
Old Stonehouse (bands)
Painter's Tavern (jazz)
Penfield's (varies)
River Club (guitar, piano)
Rockwell's (comedy)
Schneller's (bands)
1766 Tavern (jazz)
Slattery's (vocalists)
Sonoma (jazz)
Tony's (piano)
Towne Crier (bands)
Turning Point (blues)
Whitecaps (varies)

Fireplaces
Allyn's
Arch
Auberge Argenteuil
Bear Mountain Inn
Bird & Bottle Inn
Black Bass Grill
Box Tree
Bully Boy's
Cafe Tamayo
Cantina
Capriccio
Caravela
Carolina House
Cascade Mtn. Winery
Chart House
Country Manor
Crabtree's
Crystal Bay
Depuy Canal House
Edenville Inn
Heathcote Crossing
Hudson House
Kit 'N Caboodle
La Camelia
Le Chambord
Le Chateau
L'Hostellerie Bressane
Locust Tree Inn
Long Pond Inn
Maison Lafitte

Maxime's Brasserie
Maxime's La Petite
Nino's
Old Drover's Inn
Old '76 House
Old Stonehouse Inn
Palmer House Inn
Peter Pratt's
Piermont on Hudson
Plumbush Inn
River Club
Salerno's
Silvano's
St. Andrew's Cafe
Tony's
Traveler's Rest
Troutbeck Inn
Turning Point
Xaviar's Garrison

Health/Spa Menus

(Most places cook to order to meet any dietary request; call in advance to check; almost all health food spots, Chinese, Indian and other ethnics have health-conscious meals, as do the following)
Season's
St. Andrew's Cafe

Historic Interest

Allyn's
Anthony's Uptown
Armadillo
Auberge Argenteuil
Bird & Bottle Inn
Black Bass Grill
Box Tree
Cafe Tamayo
Clarksville Inn
Country Manor
Depuy Canal House
Dudley's
Edenville Inn
Foster's Coach House
Gregory's
Gus's Franklin
Heathcote Crossing
Hudson House
Huff House
Il Portico
Inn at Pound Ridge
La Rive
Le Chambord
Le Chateau

Les Bons Copains
Locust Tree Inn
Mohonk Mountain Hse.
Nanuet Hotel
Old Drover's Inn
Old '76 House
Old Stonehouse Inn
Palmer House Inn
Peter Pratt's
Schneller's
1766 Tavern
Thierry's Relais
Tony's
Traveler's Rest
Troutbeck Inn
Underhill Inn
Willett House

Hotel Dining

Arrowwood Conf. Ctr.
  Provare
Bear Mountain Inn
  Bear Mountain Inn
Beekman Arms Inn
  1766 Tavern
Bird & Bottle Inn
  Bird & Bottle Inn
Hudson House
  Hudson House
Huff House
  Huff House
Le Chambord
  Le Chambord
Nanuet Hotel
  Nanuet Hotel
Old Drover's Inn
  Old Drover's Inn
Palmer House Inn
  Palmer House Inn
Rye Town Hilton
  Penfield's
Troutbeck Inn
  Troutbeck Inn

"In" Places

Freelance Cafe
Off Broadway
Papa-Razzi
Santa Fe
1766 Tavern
Slattery's
Turning Point
Whitecaps

Late Dining

(All hours after 11 PM)
China Echo (11:30)
Hilltop (11:30)
Nanuet Hotel (12)

Southern New York State

Papa-Razzi (12)
Sam's (12)
Whitecaps (1)

Noteworthy Newcomers (14)

An American Bistro
Bambina
Crystal Bay
Dynasty
Giardino
Les Bons Copains
Marichu
Maxime's La Petite
McKinney & Doyle
Orchid Garden
Papa-Razzi
1766 Tavern
Two Moons
Whitecaps

Offbeat

Abhilash
Abis
Aria
Armadillo
Bengal Tiger
Caravela
Casa Miguel
Cascade Mtn. Winery
Corridos Mexicanos
Daniel's
Dawat
Gasho of Japan
Ichi Riki
India House
Japan Inn
Khan's Mongolian
King & I
Malabar Hill
Marichu
Mount Fuji
Off Broadway
Orchid Garden
Owl's Nest
Pancho Villa's
Pearl of the Atlantic
Priya
Reka's
Royal Siam
Sakura
Satsuma-ya
Schneller's
Season's
Siam Sea Grill
Silver Spoon Cafe
Sushi Raku
Temptations
Towne Crier

Outdoor Dining

(G = Garden,
 S = Sidewalk,
 W = Waterside location
Allyn's (G)
Arch (G)
Armadillo (G)
Auberge Maxime (G)
Bird & Bottle Inn (G)
Bistro Maxime (G)
Brass Anchor (G,W)
Cafe Tamayo (G)
Cantina (G)
Capriccio (G,W)
Carolina House (G)
Cascade Mtn. Winery (G)
Chart House (G,W)
Chelsea on Hudson (G)
Cornetta's (G,W)
Country Manor (G)
Crabtree's (G)
Crystal Bay (G,W)
Depuy Canal House (G)
Dockside Harbor (G,W)
Gasho of Japan (G)
Good Enough to Eat (G)
Good Life (S)
Green and Bresler (G)
Grouper Cafe (G)
Gus's Franklin (G)
Horsefeathers (S)
Hudson House (G,W)
Huff House (G)
Inn at Osborne Hill (G)
Le Chambord (G)
Le Pavillion (G)
Locust Tree Inn (G)
Long Pond Inn (G)
Maison Lafitte (G)
Mariner's Harbor (G,W)
Old Drover's Inn (G)
Painter's Tavern (S)
Palmer House Inn (G)
Papa-Razzi (S)
Peter Pratt's (G)
Piermont on Hudson (G,W)
Plumbush Inn (G)
Pondfield's (G)
Red Rooster (G)
River Club (G,W)
Santa Fe (G)
Schneller's (G)
1766 Tavern (G)
St. Andrew's Cafe (G)
Temptations (G)
Thierry's Relais (G)
Towne Crier (G,S)
Troutbeck Inn (G)
Turning Point (G)

Underhill Inn (G)
Whitecaps (G)
Willett House (W)
Xavier's Garrison (G)
Zeph's (G)

Parties & Private Rooms

(All major hotels, plus the following; best of the many)
Allyn's*
American Bounty*
Angsavanee*
Anthony's Uptown*
Arch
Auberge Argenteuil*
Auberge Maxime*
Bistro Maxime*
Bistro Twenty-two*
Black Bass Grill
Box Tree*
Brass Anchor
Buffet de la Gare*
Bully Boy's*
Cafe Tamayo*
Capriccio*
Caravela
Cascade Mtn. Winery*
Chart House
Clarksville Inn*
Cobble Creek Cafe
Country Manor*
Crabtree's*
Crystal Bay*
Depuy Canal House*
Dockside Harbor*
Dudley's*
Edenville Inn*
Emilio's
Escoffier Room*
Fritz's
Gasho of Japan*
Giulio's*
Goldie's*
Good Enough to Eat*
Guida's
Guidetti's Lodge*
Harrald's
Heathcote Crossing
Il Portico*
Inn at Osborne Hill*
Inn at Pound Ridge*
La Camelia*
Lago di Como
La Panetiere*
La Rive
Le Chateau*
Le Pavillion*

Les Bons Copains*
L'Europe*
L'Hostellerie Bressane
Livanos*
Locust Tree Inn*
Long Pond Inn*
Maison Lafitte*
Malabar Hill
Marcello's*
Maxime's Brasserie*
Maxime's La Petite*
McKinney & Doyle
Mohonk Mountain Hse.*
Mona Trattoria*
Off Broadway
Old '76 House*
Old Stonehouse Inn*
Owl's Nest*
Papa-Razzi
Pearl of the Atlantic*
Peter Pratt's*
Piermont on Hudson*
Pinocchio*
Plumbush Inn*
Quarropas
River Club*
Romolo's*
Rudy's Beau Rivage*
Schneller's*
Stefini
Stewart House*
Susan's & Bad Bill's
Thierry's Relais*
Towne Crier
Traveler's Rest*
Umberto's*
Underhill Inn*
Vintage Cafe
Whitecaps*
Willett House*
Xaviar's Garrison
Xaviar's Piermont
(*Private rooms)

People-Watching

Chart House
Freelance Cafe
Papa-Razzi
Provare
Santa Fe
Slattery's
Temptations
Turning Point

Power Scenes

Auberge Argenteuil
Bistro Maxime
La Panetiere
L'Hostellerie Bressane

Southern New York State

Maxime's Brasserie
Xaviar's Garrison
Xaviar's Piermont

Pre-Theater/ Early-Bird Menus
(Call to check prices and times)
Anthony's Uptown
Cobble Creek Cafe
Crystal Bay
Daniel's
King & I
Livanos
Off Broadway
Satsuma-ya
Sawpit
Slattery's
Stefini
Tony's
Towne Crier
Whitecaps

Prix Fixe Menus
(Call to check prices and times)
Allyn's
Anthony's Uptown
Arch
Auberge Argenteuil
Auberge Maxime
Bird & Bottle Inn
Bistro Twenty-two
Box Tree
Brass Anchor
Bully Boy's
Cafe Tamayo
Caterina de Medici
Chelsea on Hudson
Cobble Creek Cafe
Country Manor
Depuy Canal House
Edenville Inn
Fritz's
Hacienda Don Emilio
Harrald's
Hudson House (Nyack)
Imperial Wok
La Camelia
La Panetiere
La Rive
Le Chateau
Le Pavillion
L'Europe
Livanos
Maison Lafitte
Marichu
Maxime's Brasserie
Nino's
Old '76 House

Penfield's
Plumbush Inn
Priya
Satsuma-ya
Sawpit
Silvano's
Slattery's
Thierry's Relais
Tony's
Towne Crier
Troutbeck Inn
Umberto's
Underhill Inn
Xaviar's Garrison
Xaviar's Piermont

Pubs
Carl's
Gus's Franklin
John Richard's
Sam's

Quiet Conversation
Allyn's
Anthony's Uptown
Arch
Auberge Argenteuil
Auberge Maxime
Bird & Bottle Inn
Bistro Twenty-two
Brasserie Swiss
Buffet de la Gare
Cafe Tamayo
Cascade Mtn. Winery
Chelsea on Hudson
Daniel's
Fritz's
Giardino
Harrald's
Inn at Osborne Hill
La Camelia
La Panetiere
La Riserva
La Rive
Le Chateau
Le Pavillion
Le Petit Bistro
L'Europe
L'Hostellerie Bressane
Locust Tree Inn
Long Pond Inn
Manzi's
Nino's
Old Stonehouse Inn
Penfield's
Piermont on Hudson
Plumbush Inn
Quarropas
1766 Tavern
Thierry's Relais

Southern New York State

Traveler's Rest
Troutbeck Inn
Xaviar's Garrison
Xaviar's Piermont

Romantic Spots

Allyn's
Anthony's Uptown
Arch
Auberge Argenteuil
Auberge Maxime
Bird & Bottle Inn
Bistro Maxime
Bistro Twenty-two
Box Tree
Brasserie Swiss
Buffet de la Gare
Cafe Tamayo
Caravela
Cascade Mtn. Winery
Chelsea on Hudson
Clarksville Inn
Crabtree's
Giardino
Harrald's
La Camelia
La Panetiere
La Riserva
La Rive
Le Chambord
Le Chateau
Le Pavillion
Le Petit Bistro
L'Europe
L'Hostellerie Bressane
Locust Tree Inn
Long Pond Inn
Maison Lafitte
Mariner's Harbor
Nino's
Old Stonehouse Inn
Penfield's
Peter Pratt's
Piermont on Hudson
Plumbush Inn
Pondfield's
Romolo's
1766 Tavern
Thierry's Relais
Traveler's Rest
Troutbeck Inn
Turning Point
Vintage Cafe
Xaviar's Garrison
Xaviar's Piermont

Senior Appeal

Cantina
Casa Miguel
Ciao

Cornetta's
Country Manor
Dawat
Good Enough to Eat
Horsefeathers
Le Shack
Mariner's Harbor
Pondfield's
Red Rooster
Reef 'n Beef
Rockwell's
Season's
Silver Spoon Cafe
Stefini
Valentino's

Smoking Prohibited

Bistro Twenty-two
Depuy Canal House
Eastchester Fish
India House
Le Pavillion
McKinney & Doyle
Mohonk Mountain Hse.
Siam Sea Grill
Temptations
Troutbeck Inn
Whitecaps
Zeph's

Teas

Mohonk Mountain Hse.

Teenagers & Other Youthful Spirits

Armadillo
Camino Real
Cantina
Casa Miguel
Ciao
Cornetta's
Enzo's
Gasho of Japan
Good Enough to Eat
Grandma's
Hilltop
Horsefeathers
Huckleberry's
King & I
Le Shack
Pancho Villa's
Red Rooster
Rockwell's
Royal Siam
Sakura
Santa Fe
Satsuma-ya
Schemmy's
Schneller's
Season's

Southern New York State

Silver Spoon Cafe
Towne Crier
Valentino's
Via Appia

Wheelchair Access
(Check for bathroom access; almost all hotels, plus the following)
Abhilash
Abis
American Bounty
Angsavanee
Anthony's Uptown
Aria
Auberge Maxime
Bambina
Bengal Tiger
Benny's
Bistro Twenty-two
Black Bass Grill
Brasserie Swiss
Buffet de la Gare
Bully Boy's
Camino Real
Caravela
Carolina House
Casa Miguel
Caterina de Medici
Chef Antonio
Chelsea on Hudson
Ciao
Clarksville Inn
Corner Bakery
Corridos Mexicanos
Country Manor
Crabtree's
Crystal Bay
Daniel's
Dawat
Depuy Canal House
Dockside Harbor
Dudley's
Eastchester Fish
Edmundo's Too
Emilio's
Enzo's
Escoffier Room
Foster's Coach House
Gasho of Japan
Giardino
Good Enough to Eat
Grandma's
Green and Bresler
Greenbaum/Gilhooly's
Gregory's
Grouper Cafe
Hacienda Don Emilio
Harrald's
Hartsdale Garden

Heathcote Crossing
Hilltop
Hope and Anchor
Huckleberry's
Hudson's
Hunan Manor
Hunan Village
Hunan Wok
Ichi Riki
Il Cigno
India House
Inn at Osborne Hill
Inn at Pound Ridge
Japan Inn
Jason's
Khan's Mongolian
King & I
La Riserva
La Scala
Le Shack
L'Europe
L'Hostellerie Bressane
Livanos
Long Pond Inn
Louie's
Maison Lafitte
Malabar Hill
Manzi's
Marcello's
Mariner's Harbor
Maxime's Brasserie
Maxime's La Petite
Meson Castellano
Mohonk Mountain Hse.
Mona Trattoria
Mount Fuji
Old '76 House
Orchid Garden
Owl's Nest
Painter's Tavern
Pancho Villa's
Pars
Paul Ma's/Shanghai
Pearl of the Atlantic
Piermont on Hudson
Pinocchio
Plumbush Inn
Pondfield's
Quarropas
Reef 'n Beef
River Club
Rockwell's
Romolo's
Royal Siam
Sam's
Santa Fe
Satsuma-ya
Sawpit
Schemmy's
Schneller's

Season's
Sergio's
Silvano's
Silver Spoon Cafe
Slattery's
Sonoma
Spaccarelli's
St. Andrew's Cafe
Stewart House
Susan's & Bad Bill's
Szechuan Flower
Temptations
Towne Crier
Traveler's Rest
Two Moons
Umberto's
Underhill Inn
Valentino's
Via Appia
Westchester Trawler
Whitecaps
Willett House
Zeph's

Winning Wine Lists

Allyn's
American Bounty
Anthony's Uptown
Arch
Buffet de la Gare
Bully Boy's
Capriccio
Cascade Mtn. Winery
Depuy Canal House
Dockside Harbor
Dudley's
Escoffier Room
Freelance Cafe
Goldie's
Huff House
Il Cenacola
Il Cigno
Inn at Osborne Hill
Inn at Pound Ridge
La Camelia
La Panetiere
La Riserva
Le Chambord
Le Pavillion
Le Petit Bistro
Les Bons Copains
L'Europe
L'Hostellerie Bressane
Locust Tree Inn
Long Pond Inn
Maxime's Brasserie
Nino's
Penfield's
Piermont on Hudson

Plumbush Inn
Sergio's
Sonoma
Spaccarelli's
St. Andrew's Cafe
Traveler's Rest
Xaviar's Garrison
Xaviar's Piermont
Zeph's

Young Children
(Besides the normal
fast-food places)
Armadillo
Bambina*
Banta's*
Bear Mountain Inn*
Benny's*
Camino Real
Cantina*
Caravela*
Casa Miguel
Cascade Mtn. Winery
Chart House*
Chef Antonio*
Ciao
Cornetta's*
Corridos Mexicanos*
Crystal Bay*
Depuy Canal House*
Eastchester Fish*
Enzo's
Foster's Coach House*
Gasho of Japan*
Good Enough to Eat
Grandma's*
Greenbaum/Gilhooly's*
Grouper Cafe*
Hilltop
Horsefeathers*
Huckleberry's*
Hudson's
Huff House*
Ichi Riki*
King & I
Kit 'N Caboodle*
La Mandas
Le Shack
Mariner's Harbor*
McKinney & Doyle*
Mohonk Mountain Hse.
Mount Fuji*
Owl's Nest*
Painter's Tavern*
Pancho Villa's
Papa-Razzi*
Pars*
Penfield's*
Pondfield's

Southern New York State

Red Rooster
Reef 'n Beef*
Rockwell's*
Royal Siam
Sakura*
Sam's*
Santa Fe
Satsuma-ya
Sawpit*
Schemmy's
Schneller's

Season's*
Silver Spoon Cafe*
Temptations*
Tony's*
Towne Crier*
Trio's Cafe*
Valentino's
Via Appia*
Westchester Trawler
(*Children's menu served)

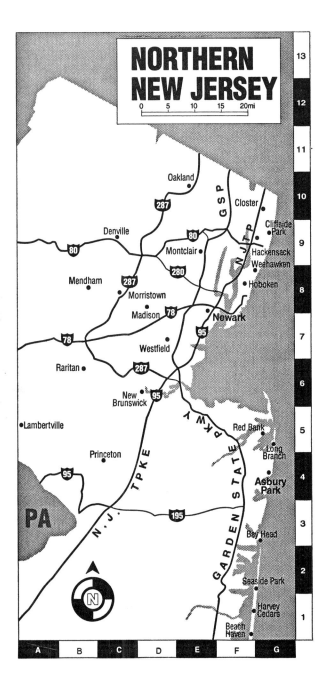

NORTHERN NEW JERSEY'S MOST POPULAR RESTAURANTS

Each of our reviewers has been asked to name his or her five favorite restaurants. The 40 spots most frequently named, in order of their popularity, are:

1. Saddle River Inn
2. Park & Orchard
3. Cafe Panache
4. The Manor
5. Highlawn Pavilion
6. Frenchtown Inn
7. Claude's Ho-Ho-Kus
8. Chez Madeleine
9. Frog and the Peach
10. Union Place
11. Dennis Foy's
12. Il Tulipano
13. Stony Hill Inn
14. Baumgart's Cafe
15. 40 Main Street
16. River Palm Terrace
17. Nanina's in the Park
18. Culinary Renaissance
19. Chengdu 46
20. Ken Marcotte
21. Doris and Ed's
22. Chez Andre
23. Chez Catherine
24. Jamie's
25. Beaugard's
26. Grand Cafe
27. Fromagerie
28. Le Chateau
29. Arthur's Landing
30. Ryland Inn
31. Archer's Ristorante
32. Bernard's Inn
33. Arthur's Tavern
34. Don Pepe
35. Girafe
36. Park One Eleven
37. Casa Dante
38. Il Capriccio
39. Yves
40. La Petite Auberge

It's obvious that many of the restaurants on the above list are among the area's most expensive. However, all of New York City's surrounding areas have an abundance of bargain spots that are popular and worth noting. New Jersey's Best Buys are listed on page 215.

TOP RATINGS*

TOP 40 FOOD RATINGS
(In order of rating)

27 – Saddle River Inn
    Farmingdale House
26 – Union Place
    Chez Catherine
    Chez Madeleine
    Fromagerie
    Culinary Renaissance
    Cafe Panache
25 – Yves
    River Palm Terrace
    Le Delice
    Ruga
    La Fontana
    Il Tulipano
24 – Dennis Foy's
    Le Petit Chateau
    Doris and Ed's
    Fresh Fields Cafe
    Sestri
    Frenchtown Inn
    Nanina's in the Park

    Frog and the Peach
    Casa Dante
    Dining Room
    Ryland Inn
    Mumfords'
    Il Mondo Vecchio
    Le Chateau
23 – Grand Cafe
    Park & Orchard
    Ken Marcotte
    Claude's Ho-Ho-Kus
    Joe & Maggie's
    Chengdu 46
    40 Main Street
    Pappardelle
    Girafe
    Jamie's
    Sergeantsville Inn
    Hamilton's Grill Room

TOP SPOTS BY CUISINE

Top American
(Contemporary)
26 – Culinary Renaissance
25 – Ruga
24 – Dennis Foy's
    Fresh Fields Cafe
    Frog and the Peach

Top American
(Traditional)
19 – Brass Rail
    Breakers
18 – Brielle Yacht Club
    Black Horse Inn
    Bluffs Hotel

Top Chinese
23 – Chengdu 46
21 – Phoenix Garden Too
20 – Mr. Tong
    Cathay 22
19 – Peking Duck House

Top Continental
27 – Saddle River Inn
26 – Fromagerie
23 – Jamie's
    Sergeantsville Inn
22 – Black Orchid

*Excluding restaurants with voting too low to be reliable.

Top "Down the Shore"
27 – Farmingdale House
26 – Fromagerie
24 – Doris and Ed's
        Mumfords'
23 – Joe & Maggie's

Top French Classic
26 – Chez Catherine
        Chez Madeleine
        Fromagerie
24 – Le Petite Chateau
        Le Chateau

French Contemporary
26 – Union Place
        Cafe Panache
25 – Yves
        Le Delice
24 – Frenchtown Inn

Top Hotel Dining
26 – Chez Catherine
        Westfield Manor
24 – Dining Room,
        Hilton at Short Hills
22 – Black Orchid,
        Headquarters Plaza
        Bernard's Inn
        Inn at Millrace Pond

Top Italian (Northern)
27 – Farmingdale House
25 – Il Tulipano
23 – Pappardelle
        Il Capriccio
        La Catena

Top Italian
(North & South)
25 – La Fontana
24 – Sestri
        Nanina's in the Park
        Casa Dante
        Il Mondo Vecchio

Top Newcomers/Rated
26 – Culinary Renaissance
24 – Il Mondo Vecchio
23 – Joe & Maggie's
19 – East Hill Grill
        Neelam

Top Newcomers/Unrated
—   Azteca
—   Cliff House Grill
—   Rosemary and Sage
—   Sonoma Grill
—   Stage Left

Top Seafood
24 – Doris and Ed's
23 – Hamilton's Grill Room
20 – Sea Shack
        Sinclaire's
18 – Bluffs Hotel

Top Spanish/Portuguese
21 – Casa Vasca
20 – Spanish Tavern
        Spain
        Fornos of Spain
19 – Tony da Caneca

Top Steakhouses
25 – River Palm Terrace
22 – Sammy's
21 – Ruth's Chris
19 – East Hill Grill
        Arthur's Tavern

Top Worth a Trip
24 – Frenchtown Inn,
        Frenchtown
        Ryland Inn,
        Whitehouse
23 – Girafe, Basking Ridge
        Sergeantsville Inn,
        Seargeantsville
        Hamilton's Grill Room
        Lambertville

TOP 40 OVERALL DECOR
(In order of rating)

28 – Dining Room
27 – Bluffs Hotel /V
    Highlawn Pavilion/V
25 – Grenville Restaurant
    Saddle River Inn
    La Fontana
24 – Bernard's Inn
    Inn at Millrace Pond
    Ryland Inn/V
    Black Orchid
    Pratos
    Sergeantsville Inn
    Frenchtown Inn/V
    Stony Hill Inn
23 – Yves
    Jamie's
    Manor
    Fromagerie
    Arthur's Landing/V
    Le Chateau

    Dennis Foy's
    Girafe
    Le Delice
    Le Petit Chateau
    Il Tulipano
    Shadowbrook/V
    Shinwa
22 – Claude's Ho-Ho-Kus
    Rudolfo
    Shanghai Red's/V
    Pronto Cena
    Grand Cafe
    Farmingdale House
    Hunt Club
    Lantana
21 – Frog and the Peach
    Breakers/V
    Armory/V
    Cucina di Roma
    Villa Amalfi

TOP 40 OVERALL SERVICE
(In order of rating)

25 – Saddle River Inn
24 – Fromagerie
    Dining Room
    Le Delice
    Union Place
    La Fontana
23 – Yves
    Farmingdale House
    Le Chateau
    Il Tulipano
    Grand Cafe
    Jamie's
    Le Petit Chateau
    Sestri
    Culinary Renaissance
22 – Frenchtown Inn
    Grenville Restaurant
    Rudolfo
    Chez Catherine
    Fresh Fields Cafe

    Frog and the Peach
    Black Orchid
    Sergeantsville Inn
    Ryland Inn
    Manor
    Cafe Panache
    La Catena
    Black Swan
    Doris and Ed's
    Dennis Foy's
21 – Nanina's in the Park
    Chez Madeleine
    Bernard's Inn
    Panico's
    Girafe
    Ruga
    Casa Dante
    Stony Hill Inn
    Chez Andre
    Ken Marcotte

V = Also has an outstanding view.

BEST BUYS

TOP 40 BANGS FOR THE BUCK

This list reflects the best dining values in our *Survey*. It is produced by dividing the cost of a meal into the combined ratings for food, decor and service.

1. Casa Comida
2. Chand Palace
3. Baumgart's Cafe
4. Casa Maya
5. Tuptim
6. Priory
7. Casa Vasca
8. Arthur's Tavern
9. Four Seas
10. Farm House
11. Don's
12. Mr. Tong
13. Cafe "Z"
14. Cathay 22
15. East
16. Neelam
17. Chengdu 46
18. Memphis Pig Out
19. Peking Duck House
20. Panevino
21. Olive Branch Cafe
22. Chatfield's
23. Park & Orchard
24. Black Forest Inn
25. Lady Jane's
26. East L.A.
27. Khiva
28. North Sea Village
29. Breakers
30. Il Mondo Vecchio
31. Spanish Tavern
32. Cafe Main
33. Pamir
34. Old Mill Inn
35. Fornos of Spain
36. Cucina di Roma
37. Haulout
38. Stadium
39. Mumfords'
40. Max's

Additional Good Values

Abin's Ristorante
Aldo & Gianni
Bangkok City
Brass Rail (downstairs)
Cafe Louis
Casa Dante
Cella Luna
Charles' Seafood
China 17
Clam Broth House
Court Street
Crab's Claw
De Angelo's
Don Manuel
Don Pepe
Eggiman's
Evelyn's Fish Mkt.
Fresh Fields Cafe
Golden Ko Shing
Grenville Restaurant
Hong Nung Kalbi
Jade Ho
Lafayette House

Laico's
Markers
Michael's Backstreet
Mike Doolan's
Net Lane's Fisherman
Pals Cabin
Peking Pavilion
Phoenix Garden Too
P.J. Clarke's
Ray's
Sergio's
Sirin Thai
Sorrento's
Spain
Squan Tavern
Taj Palace
Terra Cotta
Tony da Caneca
Turkish Kitchen
Tuzzio's
Vic's

Northern New Jersey
Area Code 201
Unless Otherwise Noted

	F	D	S	C

Abin's Ristorante*/S (Newark) **E8** | 26 | 25 | 23 | $23 |

184 Elm St. (Jefferson St.), 589-3349
U – Cognoscenti are "glad to see this" "delightful" little Italian "tucked away in the Ironbound section of Newark" added to the Survey; behind a streetside deli, the "attractive" dining room serves generous portions of first-rate Neapolitan favorites – "excellent food" at "good prices."

Adelitas (Montclair) **E9** | – | – | – | M |

716 Bloomfield Ave. (bet. N. Mountain Ave. & Valley Rd.), 744-4833
Brand new and worth a try, this cheerful Regional Mexican BYO storefront specializes in carnitas, mole, barbacoa and lots of spicy stuff that you can't get anywhere else but in Mexico; if service is a little disorganized, it's certainly willing, and prices are reasonable.

Alchemist & Barrister/LS | 16 | 17 | 16 | $29 |
(Princeton) **C4**

28 Witherspoon St. (Nassau St.), 609-924-5555
M – A "hangout" for students – "and their parents" – this "quaint", "historic" Princeton pub may be "better for drinking" than eating, with food that can be "tasty" or "ordinary", depending on whom you ask; its "friendly", "informal" atmosphere and "decent" eats keeps it "crowded."

Al Dente/S (Piscataway) **D6** | 19 | 17 | 19 | $30 |

1665 Stelton Rd. (Ethel Lane), 908-985-8220
M – Ratings suggest you give this "noisy", lively trattoria a try, despite its "outrageous" approach to decor ("like eating in an Italian grape arbor"); surveyors can't agree whether the all-pasta menu is "creative" and "superb" or "pretentious" and "overpriced."

Aldo & Gianni/S (Montvale) **E11** | 22 | 17 | 20 | $32 |

A&P Shopping Plaza, 108 Chestnut Ridge Rd. (Grand Ave.), 391-6866
U – "You'll be greeted like a member of the family" at this Bergen County shopping-center storefront Italian where "Aldo is the charming host and Gianni is in the kitchen cooking"; despite a few complaints of "too much oil" and "one sauce fits all", this "gem" packs 'em in, thanks to "terrific" food at fair prices and "top-notch service"; N.B. "long lines on weekend nights."

Anton's at the Swan*/S | 22 | 23 | 20 | $38 |
(Lambertville) **A5**
Swan Hotel, 43 S. Main St. (Swan St.), 609-397-1960
*M – Behind what could be one of the most atmospheric
"early Victorian" bars in the world, "creative" chef Anton
Dodel crafts his seasonally changing Contemporary
American food in a "charming", romantic setting; though
not cheap, it's priced right.*

Aranka's/S (Franklin Park) **C5** | – | – | – | M |
3185 Rte. 27 (Delar Pkwy.), 908-297-8060
*Practically all that's left of a once-thriving Hungarian
community, this homey, likable but low-atmosphere
spot serves hearty portions of Magyar specialties:
goulash, spaetzle and strudel; Saturday-night gypsy
music helps set the tone for an evening of fun mit
good food; BYO.*

Archer's Ristorante/S (Fort Lee) **F8** | 22 | 20 | 20 | $42 |
1310 Palisade Ave. (bet. Forest & Bellemeade Rds.),
224-5652
*M – "Pinkie-rings and big cars" shape the scene at
this symbol of "old-time Bergen County elite";
"elegant" (if overblown) atmosphere and "wonderful"
Italian food ("heavy but well-prepared") have kept this
"'in'-place" 'in' for almost 25 years; any place having
"waits" this long, with such steep prices, must be
doing something right.*

Armory, The/S (Perth Amboy) **E6** | 15 | 21 | 17 | $34 |
200 Front St. (Gordon St.), 908-826-6000
*U – A "lovely view" but "disappointing" food and service
sum up the sentiment on this "expensive", "hard-to-find"
Continental in a renovated armory on Raritan Bay;
downstairs, the Stars & Stripes cafe, with live jazz in the
bar, serves light fare and Sunday brunch; upstairs is the
"calm and elegant" dining room.*

Arthur's Landing/S | 17 | 23 | 18 | $37 |
(Weehawken) **F8**
Pershing Circle (Boulevard East), 867-0777,
(from NY: 800-835-6060)
*M – "If only the food were as good as the view",
this "romantic" New American across the Hudson
from Lower Manhattan might be more than just "a
novelty"; at $35 per person for pre-theater dinner,
ferry and jitney to the NYC theater district, it's "the
only civilized approach to Broadway"; critics cite
"uneven" quality due to chef changes and a feeling
of being in "a tourist trap."*

Arthur's Tavern/S | 19 | 12 | 16 | $21 |

(Morris Plains) **D8**, 700 Speedwell Ave. (Franklin Place),
455-9705/X
(Hoboken) **F8**, 237 Washington St. (3rd St.), 656-5009
(North Brunswick) **D6**, 644 George's Rd. (bet. Rtes. 1 &
130), 908-828-1117

Arthur's St. Moritz/S

(Sparta) **B10**, 9 White Deer Plaza (Rte. 181), Lake
Mohawk, 729-5677
*U – "How can they sell steak so cheap?"; "you don't
leave hungry" – or poor – from these "noisy", casual,
"formula" (but atmospheric) pubs where a plate-filling
24-ounce Delmonico is $10.95; sure, they're "crowded",
but "when you need a steak", "Arthur's does the job";
Arthur's St. Moritz serves an expanded menu in a
genteel lakeside setting.*

Assaggia Ristorante*/S | 25 | 21 | 22 | $32 |

(Wood-Ridge) **F9**
187 Hackensack St. (Moonachie Ave.), 933-0330
*U – "Sicilian gourmet food" is the stock-in-trade of this
sophisticated Bergen County newcomer that's a
refreshing change from standard Jersey Italianate;
besides affording cordial service, owner Ciro Santoro
has pieced together a stylish menu of "interesting",
"authentic" dishes that "almost always work."*

Auberge Swiss/S | 18 | 17 | 19 | $30 |

(Berkeley Heights) **D7**
331 Springfield Ave. (Snyder St.), 908-665-2310
*M – Whether you find this Union County Swiss-
Continental "fuddy-duddy" or "classic" probably depends
on your age, but the "country inn" atmosphere is friendly
and very "mittle European"; philes say the "hearty" food
is "comforting" and "tasty", but phobes find it
"unexciting" and "bland."*

Azteca/S (Berkeley Heights) **D7** | – | – | – | M |

579 Springfield Ave. (Plainfield Ave.), 908-665-8565
*Too nuevo to rate, Casa Maya's little Berkeley Heights
BYO sibling is attracting its own following with authentic
Mexican food (cactus enchiladas, chicken in mole, etc.),
a casual, cheerfully tiled setting and easy-to-take prices.*

Baci/S (Englewood) **F9** | 19 | 15 | 18 | $29 |

47 N. Dean St. (Palisade Ave.), 568-3173
*M – "Always crowded" and "lively", this Bergen County
"storefront" Italian throngs with "older yuppies" in search
of a "relaxing environment", "friendly service" and
"imaginative" food at "reasonable prices."*

Bahrs/S (Highlands) **G5** | 13 | 14 | 13 | $27 |
2 Bay Ave. (Rte. 36), 908-872-1245
U – "Not what it used to be", but still drawing crowds, this "run-of-the-mill NJ Shore restaurant" is known for a "great Sandy Hook view" and "basic seafood, almost"; given the "tired" decor and "rough" service, surveyors recommend Moby's, their outdoor "self-service" cafe; open Mother's Day through September.

Bangkok City*/S (Hoboken) **F8** | 21 | 14 | 15 | $20 |
335 Washington St. (bet. 3rd & 4th Sts.), 792-6613
U – For "good Thai in an unlikely place", try this Hoboken storefront that serves jewel-like portions of fragrant, intriguing cuisine at fair prices; be advised: service, though smiling, can be "slow."

Baumgart's Cafe/S (Englewood) **F9** | 21 | 13 | 18 | $22 |
45 E. Palisade Ave. (bet. Engle & Dean Sts.), 569-6267
M – "Crazy!"; this "quirky" Bergen County spot is an "old-fashioned" "'50s" diner by day, "nouveau" California Chinese by night; day or night, dig the "retro" "ice-cream-parlor setting", tuxedo-clad service and "delicious" food at prices that won't break the bank; BYO.

Beaugard's/S (Dumont) **F9** | 22 | 16 | 21 | $34 |
48 W. Madison Ave. (Washington Ave.), 387-8657
M – Inconsistency plagues this "unique" Northern Bergen storefront whose "up-to-date", "bistro-type" Italian food can be "innovative" and "superb" one day and "overrated" and "disappointing" the next; the "spare" but "serene" premises and serious prices don't quicken the pulse; BYO.

Bel'vedere/S (Clifton) **E9** | 17 | 15 | 18 | $31 |
247 Piaget Ave. (Main St.), 772-5060
M – "The waiters are in tuxedos, but the food is in cutoffs" at this "conventional" Northern Italian that gets brickbats for its "stuffy" staff and "retro-'50s Italian-mezza-Mediterranean decor"; still, it has a loyal cadre, for whom it remains "a favorite."

BERNARD'S INN (Bernardsville) **C7** | 22 | 24 | 21 | $38 |
The Bernard's Inn, 27 Mine Brook Rd., Rte. 202 (Mt. Airy Rd.), 908-766-0002
U – "A special place for a special evening"; for once, the "decor doesn't upstage the food" at this "sophisticated", meticulously restored inn that attracts a "conservative", slightly older clientele; chef Edward Stone's gently "progressive" American cuisine is a first-class treat, although the service could use some polish; a fine choice when you've got the money to spend.

Black Forest Inn/S (Stanhope) **C9** | 22 | 21 | 21 |$32|
249 Rte. 206 (I-80, exit 25), 347-3344
U – "Gourmet German food" may be "an oxymoron", but this rejuvenated Western NJ roadhouse, with its half-timbered architecture and old-world feel, manages it well, with "friendly" service and "well-prepared", reasonably priced Continental and German specialties.

Black Horse Inn/S (Mendham) **B8** | 18 | 20 | 19 |$32|
1 W. Main St., Rte. 24 (Mountain Ave.), 543-7300
U – The "country setting" and "rustic", "congenial" atmosphere are more widely praised than the "simple" American fare at this Morris County historic inn; though the food is just "a step up from satisfactory", this "cozy", popular spot with "friendly" service makes a "great country stopping place"; N.B. some folks prefer the "bustling", informal and "cheaper" Pub.

BLACK ORCHID, THE | 22 | 24 | 22 |$42|
(Morristown) **C8**
Headquarters Plaza Hotel, 3 Headquarters Plaza (Speedwell Ave.), 898-9100, x141
M – Nobody faults the "intimate", "romantic" ambiance and "sophisticated" decor (and stiff prices) of this formal, even "stuffy", Morris County hotel Continental, but as for the food, respondents can't decide: "superb" and "beautifully prepared" vs. "prissy" and unimpressive.

Black Swan, The (Princeton) **C4** | 22 | 20 | 22 |$42|
Scanticon Princeton, 100 College Rd. E. (Rte. 1), 609-452-7800
M – This "comfortably hotelish" Classic French in a high-tone conference center is an "intimate setting for good cuisine"; though some call it "a disappointment", for most, its sophisticated dining and "super" service are worth the price.

BLUFFS HOTEL, THE/S | 18 | 27 | 18 |$38|
(Bay Head) **G3**
The Bluffs Hotel, 575 East Ave. (bet. Mount & Chadwick Sts.), 908-892-1114
U – "One of the most romantic" rooms in New Jersey, with a "terrific" wraparound ocean view that invariably "surpasses the Continental cuisine" – but that's no disrepect to the moderately priced food.

Brass Rail, The/S (Hoboken) **F8** | 19 | 17 | 17 |$34|
135 Washington St. (bet. 1st & 2nd Sts.), 659-7074
M – The atmospheric downstairs "gin mill"/"jazz bar" fares better than the more formal upstairs dining room, but a recent menu change has lowered prices (not yet reflected in the ratings) and installed a similar mix of Continental, Italian and American standards on both levels.

Breakers, The/S (Spring Lake) **G3** | 19 | 21 | 18 | $30 |
Breakers Hotel, 1507 Ocean (Newark Ave.), 908-449-7700
*U – "Dining at the Shore exemplified"; no one seems to
mind highish prices in light of the "consistently good",
Italian-accented Continental food and the "upscale"
setting in a "well-kept Victorian" seaside hotel; try the
$11.95 early-bird.*

Brielle Yacht Club/S (Brielle) **G3** | 18 | 22 | 17 | $35 |
1 Ocean Ave. (on the Manasquan River), 908-528-7000
*U – On a "sunny winter day", sitting on the second floor
watching the river can be "unforgettable" at this
"thoroughly enjoyable" Traditional American restaurant in
a tony Shoreside marina; the lavish Sunday brunch buffet
gets extra nods; for a lighter meal, try Donny's downstairs.*

Cafe Louis*/S (Hoboken) **F8** | 18 | 14 | 17 | $25 |
505 Washington St. (5th St.), 659-9542
*U – "Cozy" is the operative word at this "tiny" Hoboken
storefront that serves an ever-changing but consistently
good Eclectic menu – "French one month, Italian the
next"; "courteous" service and reasonable prices
contribute to the cafe's appeal.*

Cafe Main/LS (Millburn) **E7** | 15 | 14 | 16 | $23 |
42 Main St. (Millburn Ave.), 467-2222
*M – When you can't bear the formality of 42 Main next door,
or want a "quick, inexpensive bite" before the Paper Mill
Playhouse, this "sprightly" Essex County storefront
American bistro may fill a need; "barely a step up from
Friday's", it trades on a mix of "fun atmosphere", "moderate
prices" and a "trendy" menu heavy on "yuppie burgers."*

CAFE PANACHE/S (Ramsey) **E11** | 26 | 19 | 22 | $40 |
130 E. Main St. (Franklin Tpke.), 908-934-0030
*U – A Top Spot in our Survey, this "delightful", BYO, "NYC-
type" modern French-Italian is "worth a detour" to northern
Bergen County; "housed in a former pancake house",
today it's an "upscale" setting for up-to-the-minute food
that earns an "A for creativity" and "warm and friendly"
service; it's "sublime for a special occasion", but not for
bargain-hunters.*

Cafe "Z"/S | 18 | 14 | 15 | $22 |
(Union) **F8**, Ideal Plaza, 2333 Morris Ave. (next to Union
High School), 908-686-4321
(East Hanover) **E8**, Castle Ridge Plaza, 360 Rte. 10
(next to Top's), 884-4600
*U – Only in Jersey could you find "SoHo" style "in a
shopping mall"; some think these pastarias are "cramped"
and "weird-looking", with their faux Italian "underground
cafe" decor; others call them "unique"; the made-fresh-daily
pastas and other casual fare is "surprisingly tasty" at a
"reasonable price", BYO.*

F	D	S	C

Capri Mia (South Hackensack) **F9** | – | – | – | M |

268 Huyler St. (Troast St.), 489-0743
Despite an odd location in an industrial area, this "noisy but excellent" Northern Italian inspired plenty of write-ins; regulars say "don't bother with the menu, just ask for the specials"; it's a welcoming little spot where the friendly "chef-owner knows everybody"; BYO.

Carijon's Middleville Inn*/S | 26 | 23 | 19 | $47 |
(Middleville) **B11**

901 Rte. 521 (Middleville Rd.), 383-9189
U – "In the middle of nowhere, but worth the trip" for chef-owner Steve Deren's "superb", "innovative" Contemporary American food served in a "relaxing country" setting; though expensive, this end-of-the-road "oasis" is ideal for a romantic dinner or a summer lunch on the patio.

Casa Comida/S (Long Branch) **G5** | 19 | 14 | 15 | $19 |

336 Branchford Ave. (Rte. 36), 908-229-7774
M – Calling this "one of New Jersey's best Mexicans" may be faint praise, but ratings suggest that this popular ("a two-hour wait is normal on weekends"), Victorianate Shore hacienda is "better than most", and the large vegetarian selection is a plus; critics moan "another Velveeta Mexican" with "Chi-Chi's decor."

CASA DANTE (Jersey City) **F8** | 24 | 18 | 21 | $34 |

737 Newark Ave. (Kennedy Blvd.), 795-2750
U – The "wiseguys have taste", if the crowds at this "elegant Italian" near Journal Square are any indication; the "traditional" Italian food "never disappoints", with service so smooth "the waiters are at your elbow before you know you want anything"; all this and prices considered "reasonable" for the "abundant" portions add up to a deal you shouldn't refuse.

Casa Maya/S (Meyersville) **D7** | 19 | 16 | 16 | $22 |

615 Meyersville Rd. (Bellmont Ave.), 908-580-0799
M – "Fun Mexican food" is yours at this colorful country casa located in "an old gas station" in an upscale "one-horse town"; don't expect refined Tex-Mex or reservations, just "authentic Mexican" that's "a cut above the standard" and also fairly cheap; BYO.

Casa Vasca/S (Newark) **E8** | 21 | 14 | 17 | $23 |

141 Elm St. (Prospect St.), 465-1350
U – Catch that "Basque macho feeling" at this Ironbound "favorite" that's heavy on "homey", hearty Spanish and Basque specialties and "Portuguese fishing village" atmosphere; sure, it's "cramped" and the service can be "inconsistent", but we're talking "great clams, shrimp and lobster" and "great value", too.

Cathay 22/S (Springfield) **E7** | 20 | 15 | 19 | $25 |
124 Rte. 22 W. (Hillside Ave.), 467-8688
U – "Elegant Chinese" that's "a cut" (or three) "above the routine"; "inspired", "innovative", fresh food (try the "unusual" "Hong Kong–style" specials) and "fine service" belie the pedestrian Union County location.

Cella Luna/S (Hoboken) **F8** | – | – | – | M |
221 Washington St. (bet. 2nd & 3rd Sts.), 420-0222
Popular and priced right, this Hoboken trattoria pleases diners with large portions of flavorful, family-style Southern Italian standards; the attractive, brick-walled storefront premises and a casual ambiance attract a convivial crowd, but takeout is also popular.

Chand Palace/S | 19 | 13 | 18 | $20 |
(Morristown) **C8**, 79 Washington St. (Atno St.), 539-7433
(Parsippany) **D8**, 257 Littleton Rd. (Parsippany Rd.), 334-5444
U – Unadventurous souls daunted by the downscale appearance of these Morris County storefronts are missing out on some of "the best Indian food in New Jersey"; the "all-you-can-eat" $5.95 lunch buffet is a megabargain; service is "fairly good" and the food's "intense – spicy when it should be"; BYO.

Charles' Seafood Garden | 17 | 16 | 16 | $27 |
(Beach Haven Crest) **F1**
8611 Long Beach Ave. (bet. 86th & 87th Sts.), 609-492-8340
M – Fans say "no vacation on Long Beach Island is complete" without a trip to this "solid seafood" standby with its cheerful "old Hollywood garden setting"; critics carp about just "adequate" service, but there are few alternatives; BYO; open May through mid-October.

Chatfield's Grill & Bar/S | 18 | 17 | 16 | $25 |
(Gladstone) **C7**
273 Main St. (Pottersville Rd.), 908-234-2080
M – This "casually clubby" American grill is located in a restored 1840s farmhouse in a charming old Hunt Country town; it draws a sophisticated "NY transport" crowd with its "relaxing atmosphere" and reasonable prices, though even fans say "stick to the burgers."

Chengdu 46/S (Clifton) **E9** | 23 | 19 | 21 | $30 |
1105 Rte. 46 E. (bet. Valley Rd. & Van Houton Ave.), 777-8855
M – Incongruously located along busy Route 46, this "elegant" Szechuan offers "excellent food" and tuxedoed service; though a few feel it's "resting on its egg rolls" and "not worth the price", most consider this "as good as Chinese gets."

Chez Andre/S (Maplewood) **E7** | 22 | 16 | 21 | $35 |

1844 Springfield Ave. (bet. Yale & Rutgers Sts.), 762-9191
*U – Travel to Provence via this "excellent French bistro",
the provenance of "attentive" chef-patron Emile Andre;
surveyors consider it an "amazing find in a nondescript
location", "quaint" and "charming", with "friendly" service
and "truly French" food; cheers too for the "great patio"
and the BYO policy.*

CHEZ CATHERINE (Westfield) **D6** | 26 | 20 | 22 | $47 |

Westfield Motor Inn, 431 North Ave. W. (bet. Central Ave.
& Broad St.), 908-232-1680
*U – This longtime bastion of "NY-priced" Classic French
food is widely praised as "excellent", "interesting",
"top-drawer" and "still a treat", but a few fault-finders
lament that "weird spicing has taken over"; solid ratings
indicate that the ayes have it.*

CHEZ MADELEINE (Bergenfield) **F9** | 26 | 15 | 21 | $40 |

4 Bedford Ave. (Washington Ave.), 384-7637
*U – "All the better for being such a surprise", this
"friendly" little BYO Bergen County storefront feels like a
"bistro on the Left Bank"; the food is "consistently
excellent" and a "great value", but the "claustrophobic"
"quarters" provide "no place to wait."*

China 17*/S (Paramus) **F9** | 20 | 13 | 16 | $21 |

177 Rte. 17 S. (Midland Ave.), 262-3699
*U – "Terrific Chinese food without Chengdu prices";
despite its "lousy location" and decor that makes it look
"like a takeout", this "excellent" Bergen County
newcomer is attracting fans for its "unusual" and
"well-prepared" dishes; daily dim sum is a plus; BYO.*

Clam Broth House/S | 12 | 9 | 11 | $25 |

(Hoboken) **F8**, 34 Newark St. (River St.), 659-2448
(West New York) **F8**, 540 55th St. (bet. Bergenline Ave.
& Kennedy Blvd.), 866-9599
*M – "It's famous" – why else would anyone go to this
"noisy", "crowded" Hoboken seafood "institution" (with a
newer branch upriver); for every diner who enjoys the
food and "turn-of-the-century" charm, there are three who
think it's "past its prime" and "living off its reputation."*

Claude's Ho-Ho-Kus Inn/S | 23 | 22 | 20 | $44 |
(Ho-Ho-Kus) **E9**

E. Franklin Tpke. (bet. Maple & Sheridan Aves.), 445-4115
*M – Fans of Claude Baills's "pricey" Bergen County
"landmark" praise his "Classical French food", top wine
list and the "family feeling" of this "elegant" 18th-century
inn; they also like the "superb value" prix fixe menus
and the "fireplace in the Tap Room in winter"; however,
detractors call it all "overstuffed" and think the chef
"should take a very long vacation."*

Cliff House Grill/S | – | – | – | E |
(Cliffside Park) **F9**
790 Anderson Ave. (Columbia Ave.), 943-4930
Villa Amalfi's new little brother sports an all-American steakhouse menu and a clubby, manly ambiance; though it's off to a rough start, with service that can be disorganized, it's worth considering when you crave meat and potatoes.

Colligan's Stockton Inn/S | – | – | – | M |
(Stockton) **A4**
1 Main St. (Rte. 29), 609-397-1250
This romantic 18th-century country inn boasts six dining rooms (five have fireplaces) and a locally famous wishing well; the Continental-American food and service can be problematic, but moderate prices and historical decor add appeal.

Court Cafe (Somerville) **D6** | 18 | 18 | 19 |$36|
18 E. Main St. (Northbridge St.), 908-725-7979
M – Ups and downs have plagued this cool, clubby "American Nouvelle" across from the Somerset County Courthouse, but new owner Bob Fallon promises improvement, including a lower-priced menu and comfortable new banquette seating; on weeknights, it's usually "busy with a legal crowd" – insiders prefer it for "weekend nights."

Court Street*/S (Hoboken) **F8** | 18 | 16 | 19 |$25|
(fka Talbot's)
61 Sixth St. (bet. Hudson & Washington Sts.), 795-4515
M – Some think this "quiet" American "bar/bistro" "tucked away on a Hoboken back street" was "more enjoyable" as the formal old Talbot's French restaurant, but those who appreciate a "good yuppie setting" laud the "neighborhood" atmosphere, "good service" and the "best cheeseburger in town."

Crab's Claw/S (Lavallette) **G2** | 17 | 13 | 15 |$24|
601 Grand Central Ave. (President Ave.), 908-793-4447
M – Reasonable prices, a decent seafood selection (try the lobster), 130 kinds of beer and a casual, homey setting near the beach draw crowds in "Bermuda shorts and T-shirts", but a no-reservations policy cause some to save it for "off-season."

Creations/S (Madison) **D8** | – | – | – | E |
(fka Cook Plaza Cafe)
54 Main St. (bet. Central Ave. & Waverly Pl.), 966-0252
Sometimes "the jazz is better than the food" at this pricey, bustling new Morris County American bistro–cum–supper club; savvy surveyors say "it's too new to take seriously", and it's "too bad they couldn't create a waiter to serve the food in a timely fashion."

Cucina di Roma/S (Red Bank) **F5** | 22 | 21 | 20 |$33|
6 Linden Place (Broad St.), 908-747-5121
*U – Two years after moving from Little Silver, this
well-rated Italian is "finally growing into its grand new
home" – an imposing red-brick Victorian-style building;
fans like the atmosphere and feel the creative
Northern-style food justifies the price.*

CULINARY RENAISSANCE/S | 26 | – | 23 |$38|
(Metuchen) **D8**
12 Center St. (Rte. 27), 908-548-9202
*U – A "much-needed" move to larger, more "comfortable"
quarters has made this Middlesex County Contemporary
American even more of a "find"; "exciting", "innovative"
food and "thoroughly professional staff" make this
"pricey" "jewel in Metuchen" "worth the trip"; N.B. it's
BYO, but there's a 10 percent discount at the liquor
store across the street.*

Cypress Inn/S (Wanamassa) **F4** | 18 | 18 | 18 |$29|
803 Rte. 35 N. (north of Asbury Park Circle), 908-775-8907
*M – Our surveyors divide over this longtime favorite for
"solid American" fare; it's "always reliable", and the
$8.95 early-bird is "one of the best bargains along the
Shore", but critics say "deadly dull" and "going downhill."*

De Angelo's*/S (Cliffside Park) **F9** | 20 | 13 | 17 |$31|
354 Lawton Ave. (Anderson Ave.), 945-3496
*U – "Not much on ambiance" and little known outside
the neighborhood, but "generous portions" of "excellent",
"homestyle" Italian food, including "wonderful specials",
and friendly service make this Bergen County "saloon"
-cum-restaurant popular with locals.*

De Anna's/X (Lambertville) **A5** | – | – | – | M |
18 S. Main St. (near Bridge & Main Sts.), 609-397-8957
*Though few surveyors know about this cozy BYO Italian
and its pretty garden in season, the friendly attention of
chef-owner De Anna Menzel and a limited, though
interesting, menu of homemade specialties make this a
worthy spot for lunch or supper.*

DENNIS FOY'S TOWNSQUARE/S | 24 | 23 | 22 |$46|
(Chatham) **D8**
Townsquare Mall, 6 Roosevelt Ave. (near Rte. 24), 701-0303
*U – Manhattan's loss was Morris County's gain when
Dennis Foy (ex Mondrian) returned to NJ and this
"inventive", "attractive" Contemporary American, "one of
the very best in the area"; Foy's cooking highlights the
freshest "high-quality" seasonal ingredients, served by a
polished staff; only the prices give diners pause before
enjoying this "treat."*

DINING ROOM, THE (Short Hills) **D8** | 24 | 28 | 24 | $52 |
Hilton at Short Hills, 41 JFK Pkwy. (off Rte. 78),
379-0100, ext. 7937
*U – "The most beautiful hotel dining room anywhere" – or at
least in NJ – is "coming on strong", with smooth service and
"excellent" Contemporary American food under new chef
Anthony Demes (ex La Caravelle and Maxime's); yes, it's
expensive, but a "superb" wine list and a comfortable,
mahogany-paneled setting help ease the pain.*

Don Manuel*/S (Newark) **E8** | 18 | 13 | 18 | $24 |
130 Main St. (Kossuth St.), 344-3614
*U – "One portion can feed a family" at this bare-bones
Ironbound bar-restaurant offering "good Spanish food"
at "bargain prices"; it does a land-office trade in three-,
four- and even-more-pound lobsters and its Sunday
afternoon tapas draws an interesting local crowd.*

Don Pepe/S | 18 | 13 | 16 | $26 |
(Newark) **E8**, 844 McArthur Hwy. (Raymond Blvd.), 623-4662
(Pine Brook) **G9**, 18 Old Longfield Ave. (Rte. 46), 882-6757
*U – The "granddaddy of the Newark Spanish restaurant
scene" has a new outpost in Pine Brook; either way,
"you won't go hungry" on "huge, huge portions" of "good
food with solid ethnic taste", "especially if you like garlic"
and "enormous" – no, make that "mutant" – lobsters;
though a few critics complain of "quantity not quality",
these "loud and noisy" Spaniards are "great fun", and
you "can't beat the prices."*

Don's/S (Livingston) **E8** | 14 | 11 | 13 | $17 |
650 S. Orange Ave. (W. Hobart Gap Rd.), 992-4010
*M – Not a destination, "not even a diner", this "casual
family" spot is the "hamburger hangout" in Essex
County, an "institution" where "abrupt service" and no
atmosphere pale in the face of "great burgers, onion
rings and hot dogs" – "don't order anything else."*

DORIS AND ED'S/S (Highlands) **F5** | 24 | 18 | 22 | $36 |
348 Shore Dr. (Hwy. 36 & Sandy Hook Park), 908-872-1565
*U – "Seafood supreme" and a top wine list characterize
this "real find off the beaten path" on the Jersey Shore;
"no-nonsense fresh fish", "attentive staff" and "imaginative"
specials make this comfortable, "airy" roadhouse with its
Sandy Hook Bay view "worth the trip"; "be prepared to
wait in high season", especially on Saturday night, when
no reservations are taken.*

Dove Island Inn (Stillwater) **B10** | – | – | – | E |

West Shore Dr., Rte. 521 (Rte. 622), Swartzwood Lake, 383-3336

"Surprising elegance in a remote spot" sparks this "gorgeous" Contemporary American on sylvan Swartzwood Lake, featuring the "imaginative, loving cookery" of chef Alfred Santasiere and the "engaging" welcome of his wife, Jayne; it's open on Friday and Saturday nights only – so reserve early.

East/S (Teaneck) **F9** | 22 | 19 | 17 | $27 |

1405 Teaneck Rd. (Rte. 4), 837-1260

U – "Take off your shoes" and hang out awhile at this sleek, airy Bergen County Japanese that specializes in a "great variety" of sushi and other "authentic" fare, including a formal keiseki dinner if you special-order; it's "mobbed with local Japanese" who aren't bothered by an "expensive" tab for "the best fresh sushi" around.

East Hill Grill/S (Englewood) **F9** | 19 | 16 | 17 | $35 |

36 Engle St. (Palisade Ave.), 568-HILL

M – Baci's newer sibling offers a "top NYC-style steakhouse menu" that attracts a considerable following, but some find it "disappointing"; it's "noisy" and "somewhat plain", with soaring ceilings and wooden floors, but has "good beef and fish" and heads-up service.

East L.A./S (Hoboken) **F8** | 15 | 12 | 12 | $20 |

508 Washington St. (bet. 5th & 6th St.), 798-0052

M – "Bring earplugs" to this "small", "raucous" storefront taqueria where the waiters say mañana and the "mediocre" food is "cheap and filling"; it's "tons of fun", with "great margaritas" – "sometimes that's enough."

Eccola/S (Parsippany) **D8** | – | – | – | M |

1082 Rte. 46 West (Beverwyck Rd.), 334-8211

Bustling, noisy and reasonably priced, this year-old trattoria sports a wood-burning oven behind the bar and a Milanese-style menu with a clutch of creative specialties – roast oysters with basil and leek, salmon ravioli, roast salt cod – along with all the old favorites; well-modulated service and a well-priced wine list add to the experience.

Eggiman's*/S | 16 | 14 | 18 | $20 |

(Spring Lake Heights) **F3**

2031 Hwy. 71 (Allare Rd.), 908-449-2626

M – A "basic dinner with some real local atmosphere" sums up this "tavern"-style American that serves "good old favorites"; it's not much to look at, but low prices and a "casual" mien make it popular with the "old guard."

Europa South/S | 18 | 15 | 17 | $29 |
(Point Pleasant Beach) **F3**
521 Arnold Ave. (Richmond Ave.), 908-295-1500
M – "Huge portions" of "paella", "sangria" and other
Spanish and Portuguese favorites ("heavy on the
garlic") make this "dark, comfortable" Iberian invariably
busy on "summer weekends"; still, there are critics who
say the food's only "so-so" and "not worth the trip."

Evelyn's Fish Market/S (Belmar) **G3** | 17 | 12 | 15 | $24 |
507 Main St. (Third Ave.), 908-681-0236
U – After several management changes, this Shore-
town seafooder is back on track under the stewardship
of its original owner, Joe Amiel, who has refurbished it
and "returned it to the original successful formula" –
"nothing fancy, just fresh fish, simply cooked"; it
deserves higher ratings.

Evergreen Restaurant/S | – | – | – | M |
(Upper Montclair) **E9**
594 Valley Rd. (Bellevue Ave.), 744-4120
This well-liked Essex County storefront inspired
surveyors to write in about its "savory, natural", trendy
American food (heavy on the vegetarian specialties)
and "all-around charming" decor and service; BYO.

Farm House, The/S (Little Silver) **E6** | 18 | 16 | 18 | $24 |
438 Branch Ave. (Markham Place), 908-842-5017
M – A "quaint", restored 100-year-old house and a
"gigantic salad bar" complete with "great U-peel shrimp"
are highlights of this slightly "out-of-the-way"
Continental-American; it's an "old standby" serving the
kind of "plain food" that "Grandma made"; BYO.

FARMINGDALE HOUSE/S | 27 | 22 | 23 | $39 |
(Farmingdale) **E3**
105 Academy St. (bet. Railroad & Bourd Aves.),
908-938-7951
U – What some call "the best Italian food in NJ" makes
this "elegant", "cozy" country inn "worth the trip from
anywhere"; though prices are a bit "out of sight" for "the
wilds" of Monmouth County, customers laud the
"professional service", "top-drawer" food and "great
decor" at this "winner" where "dining is an occasion."

Ferraro's Restaurant/S | 18 | 13 | 17 | $30 |
(Westfield) **D6**
8 Elm St. (across from train station), 908-232-1105
M – Side-by-side in this dual-personality Italian are a
"casual" pizzeria–cum–family restaurant (where "kids
feel at home" and parents can enjoy a "beer and a bowl
of pasta") and a more formal dining room serving "solid
Italian fare"; most surveyors stick to the "family side" for
"good value" and "reliable", "homey food."

F	D	S	C

Fornos of Spain/S (Newark) **E8** | 20 | 14 | 16 | $26 |

47 Ferry St. (Union St.), 589-4767

M – Fans shout "olé!" for the "huge portions" of "super Spanish food" served at this "popular" Ironbound "favorite"; despite a recent expansion, it's still "crowded" and "tacky" (red-vinyl chairs, Iberian murals, etc.), but for "good and plenty", "this is the place."

Forsgate Country Club/S | 17 | 20 | 19 | $33 |
(Jamesburg) **E5**

Forsgate Dr., Rte. 32 (NJ Tpke., exit 8A), 908-521-0070

M – This glamorous American overlooking the 18th green is an "impressive choice" if you want to "dress up and go out for supper"; but critics say the "unimaginative", "wedding-type" food "doesn't match" the setting or the price; the Sunday buffet brunch is the best bet.

40 Main Street (Millburn) **E7** | 23 | 19 | 21 | $42 |

40 Main St. (bet. Essex St. & Millburn Ave.), 376-4444

M – The "innovative" Contemporary American cooking works well at this "storefront" handy to the Paper Mill Playhouse; though "fairly expensive", its well-paced service, decent wine list and "relaxing" setting with "charming" country artifacts make it a "pleasant surprise."

Four Seas/S (Madison) **D8** | 19 | 17 | 18 | $25 |

24 Main St. (bet. Central Ave. & Green Village Rd.), 822-2899

M – "High prices" and "upscale" ambiance (for Chinese) are themes that unite comments on this Morris County old-timer; it's "one of the few Chinese restaurants" with "innovative food" and "above-average service", but some consider its fare "standard."

Frankie & Johnnie's/S | – | – | – | M |
(Hoboken) **F8**

163 14th St. (Garden St.), 659-6202

This attractive, commodious Italianate steakhouse attracts a stylish Hoboken crowd who wrote in about its friendly "family atmosphere" and high-quality NY-style steaks at NJ prices; the gorgeous bar (where the wedding scene from On The Waterfront *was filmed) is tops, with extras like piano music and valet parking.*

FRENCHTOWN INN, THE/S | 24 | 24 | 22 | $44 |
(Frenchtown) **A6**

7 Bridge St. (Front St.), 908-996-3300

U – "Top grades on all counts" are bestowed on this "sweet" Contemporary French "farmhouse" in western Hunterdon County, near the Delaware River; despite reports of "inconsistent" service and "uneven food", even critics say that "when it's good, it's very good."

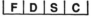
FRESH FIELDS CAFE | 24 | 16 | 22 | $33 |
(Chatham) **D8**
Hickory Square Mall, 641 Shunpike Rd. (Green Village
Rd.), 377-4072
U – Whether you find this shopping-center storefront
"cramped" or "cozy" is a moot point compared with
chef-owner Kevin Collins's "fresh and inventive"
Contemporary American cooking; though boosters feel
he "deserves more elegant surroundings", he and his
"friendly staff" offer "excellent food"; BYO.

FROG AND THE PEACH, THE/S | 24 | 21 | 22 | $42 |
(New Brunswick) **D6**
29 Dennis St. (Hiram St.), 908-846-3216
U – "California in New Jersey" is the claim to fame of
this "peach" of a Contemporary American in a
somewhat "disreputable" section of New Brunswick;
sleek decor provides a "pleasing" (some say "cold")
setting for "top-notch", "creative" food and "wonderful"
service; though "pricey", it's "in a pond by itself."

FROMAGERIE/S (Rumson) **F5** | 26 | 23 | 24 | $44 |
26 Ridge Rd. (Ave. of Two Rivers), 908-842-8088
U – Still "the best in the Shore area", this 20-year-old
"Classic French favorite" is holding its own despite
"high" tabs; diners "really feel like they're dining out" at
this "elegant" farmhouse that combines beautiful
atmosphere with "excellent food" and first class service;
coming with high expectations, a few feel it's "overrated."

Giovanna's/S (Plainfield) **C7** | 18 | 18 | 19 | $36 |
1462 South Ave. (Terrill Rd.), 908-753-6900
U – This "good, not excellent", older Italian has a quirky
location in a former bank building that, on the outside,
gives no indication of the "attractive" "art deco"
ambiance within; its fans commend the pasta dishes,
service and aura of "quiet" refinement.

Girafe (Basking Ridge) **C7** | 23 | 23 | 21 | $44 |
95 Morristown Rd., Rte. 202 (bet. N. Finley & Maple
Aves.), 908-221-0017
M – Those in the know say this tony, high-ticket New
American is "back on track" (a fact not fully reflected in
its ratings) under new management; "civilized" service,
a "fantastic wine list" and "elegant" ambiance mean you
"don't have to stick your neck out for a good meal here."

Golden Ko Shing/S | – | – | – | I |
(Parsippanny) **D8**
Arlington Plaza, 792 Rte. 46 W., 263-9000
This truly golden Chinese with modern decor serves
inexpensive Cantonese and Szechuan dishes; house
specialties include shrimp with garlic sauce and
pan-fried flounder; try the dim sum brunch on Sundays.

| F | D | S | C |

Good-Time Charley's/S

| – | – | – | M |

(Kingston) **C5**
40 Main St. (Ridge Rd.), 609-924-7400
*Located just north of Princeton, this mid-priced
Contemporary American features prime cuts of beef,
fresh seafood and daily specials at reasonable prices;
live rock bands play in the vintage bar–style setting.*

GRAND CAFE, THE (Morristown) **C8** | 23 | 22 | 23 | $44 |

42 Washington St. (bet. Court St. & Schuyler Place),
540-9444
*M – "Grand", indeed, this "elegant" formal French "rates
with the best in NYC", according to its many fans, who
cite "excellent food", "fantastic service" and "gracious"
ambiance; it's "expensive", and some call it "stuffy"
and "overrated", but for most, it's "always a treat";
remodeling has added a fireplace and convivial bar.*

GRENVILLE RESTAURANT/S | 22 | 25 | 22 | $37 |

(Bay Head) **G3**
Grenville Hotel, 345 Main Ave. (2 blocks north of Bridge
Ave.), 908-892-3100
*U – Despite high prices, this "romantic dining room" in
an elegant "old Victorian hotel" in seaside Bay Head
gets solid scores for its enjoyable New American food,
and raves for its "charming" atmosphere; brunch on the
ornate veranda is a "pleasure", and rooms right upstairs
are a plus; BYO.*

HAMILTON'S GRILL ROOM/S | 23 | 19 | 21 | $34 |

(Lambertville) **A5**
84½ Coryell St. (bet. Union St. & Lambert Lane),
609-397-4343
*U – The "best back-street find in NJ" is this "unique"
Mediterranean-style seafood grill located in a creatively
refurbished slaughterhouse in Lambertville's Porkyard;
an "eclectic setting" and an "inspired menu" offset
sometimes "uneven" service; BYO.*

Harry's Lobster House*/S | 18 | 11 | 18 | $31 |

(Sea Bright) **F5**
1124 Ocean Ave. (New St.), 908-842-0205
*M – This Shore standby serves a mainstream menu of
seafood and Continental standards in a casual setting
with an outdoor patio; Bruce Springsteen's rumored
allegiance notwithstanding, critics say "don't bother
unless you can't get in anywhere else."*

Haulout, The/S | 13 | 16 | 12 | $22 |
(Monmouth Beach) **E6**
Channel Club Marina, 33 West St. (Beach Rd.),
908-222-7592
*M – If you "go to watch the boats" on the Shrewsbury
River from this informal "waterfront spot", you may not
mind the "unpredictable" Italian and American food and
minimal service; if you go to eat, the early-bird menu is
your best bet.*

Hero'Chan*/S (Edgewater) **F9** | 19 | 28 | 16 | $29 |
(fka Chinzan-So)
Yaohan Plaza, 595 River Rd. (3 miles south of GW
Bridge), 945-9450
*M – Though the Japanese menu has changed since this
was Chinzan-So, the "fab" Hudson River-side view of
New York City and the "elegant" accommodations are
the same; while some rate the food a "few notches
down", the prices have dropped as well, making it "good
for first dates" and dinner with good friends.*

HIGHLAWN PAVILLION/S | 19 | 27 | 20 | $40 |
(West Orange) **E8**
Eagle Rock Reservation, Eagle Rock Ave. (near
Prospect St.), 731-3463
*M – Despite "major improvements" under chef Steve
Mellina (ex Manhattan Ocean Club), the food doesn't
equal the "breathtaking" view of Manhattan from this
architecturally "stunning" Contemporary American;
still, the food is good enough when combined with the
"magnificent setting" to produce noise, crowds and
"long waits."*

Hiro Japanese Restaurant/S | – | – | – | M |
(Teaneck) **F9**, 299 Queen Anne Rd. (Fort Lee Rd.),
692-1002
(Closter) **F10**, 97 Homan's Ave. (behind Closter Plaza),
768-7766
*Though we overlooked it on our questionnaire, this
mini-dynasty of Intown Japanese is popular among
locals for the "freshest sushi at reasonable prices" and
"unpretentious" surroundings; a third location, in Leonia,
handles only takeout, catering and delivery; BYO.*

Hong Nung Kalbi/S (Leonia) **E8** | – | – | – | I |
334 Broad Ave. (10th St.), 592-5959
*The delicious, authentic Korean food at this modest
Leonia spot has locals congregating for bulgogi and
other spicy, intriguing dishes; language barriers must be
hurdled, but prices are low if you're willing to experiment.*

Hudson Place (Montclair) **E9** | 21 | 15 | 20 | $33 |
98 Walnut St. (bet. Grove St. & Valley Rd.), 746-0789
*U – For good creative American food "with a Southern
accent", check out this "small find" with its "delicious but
limited menu"; "tight tables" and no liquor license are
nothing when you've got "pleasant service" and
chef-owner Michael Hudson's "sensational fried chicken."*

Hunt Club, The/S (Summit) **D7** | 20 | 22 | 21 | $36 |
Grand Summit Hotel, 570 Springfield Ave. (Morris Ave.),
908-273-3000
*M – The "basement atmosphere", however "English
clubby", produces mixed reactions to this Contemporary
American located in a 120-year-old hotel; though it's
"pricey", the place is not as "stuffy as the name suggests"
and generally gets good marks.*

Il Capo (Ridgewood) **F9** | 18 | 14 | 19 | $30 |
14 Oak St. (Ridgewood Ave.), 652-8080
*M – "Good effort", say those who frequent this "little BYO
storefront" Italian in Bergen County; fans praise the
pastas, in particular, and are "favorable" to the service by
tuxedoed waiters, but critics say there's "no place to wait
except in the street", and it "used to be better."*

Il Capriccio (Whippany) **D8** | 23 | 21 | 21 | $42 |
633 Rte. 10 E. (bet. Whippany & Jefferson Rds.), 884-9176
*M – For "sophisticated Italian food" at surprisingly
moderate prices try this longtime Morris County
favorite; recently remodeled, the "elegant" Palladian
setting is a "nice place to dine and people-watch", but
many find it "overblown."*

Il Giardino (Cedar Knolls) **E8** | 21 | 18 | 20 | $34 |
41 Ridgedale Ave. (Rte. 10), 984-9594
*M – "Another fancy" Italian restaurant sums up this
"classy" garden-style Essex County spot, with its plants
and fountain view; surveyors say the pricey food is
"good, not spectacular."*

IL MONDO VECCHIO (Madison) **D8** | 24 | 18 | 19 | $31 |
72 Main St. (Central Ave.), 301-0024
*U – Surveyors "have a love/hate relationship" with this
hyperpopular Morris County Italian: they love the
"delicious food", especially the "extended list of daily
specials", but hate the "deafening noise" and "frantic
scene"; when quiet, this double storefront is "romantic"
and "inviting", with "good" service and BYO that keeps
the tab in line.*

IL TULIPANO/S (Cedar Grove) **E8** | 25 | 23 | 23 | $43 |
1131 Pompton Ave. (bet. Stevens Ave. & Linsley Rd.),
256-9300
*M – A "classic NJ Italian", this "high-class", decade-old
Essex Countyite sports the "inevitable peach decor" and
"outstanding", if "expensive", Continental–Northern Italian
food; some "don't understand the great reviews", and note
that "familiar faces are treated with much more respect."*

Il Villagio (Carlstadt) **E8** | – | – | – | E |
651 Rte. 17 N. (Paterson Plank Rd.), 935-7733
*Long before the influx of trendy Italians, this "comfortable"
local landmark was serving traditional favorites to Bergen
County diners; its special-occasion prices are bolstered
by formal touches – an elegant dining room, valet parking
and a jackets-preferred dress code.*

Il Villino/S (Waldwick) **F9** | – | – | – | E |
53 Franklin Tpke. (E. Prospect St.), 652-8880
*Though we neglected to include this Bergen County
Northern Italian newcomer in our* Survey, *plenty of
people wrote-in this chic spot with its garden setting and
innovative food; prices are highish, but in line with local
standards, and having more than 20 wines by the glass
is a treat, especially with the four-course tasting menu
Sunday through Tuesday.*

INN AT MILLRACE POND/S | 22 | 24 | 21 | $38 |
(Hope) **A9**
Rte. 519 (near Rte. 521), 908-459-4884
*U – Worth the hike to "tranquil" Hope, this "beautiful"
antique gristmill turned inn has an "ideal country setting"
and fine, though pricey, "country squire" American
cuisine; "romantic dining" is enhanced by piano music;
Sunday brunch gets extra nods.*

Ironwood*/S (Basking Ridge) **C7** | 17 | 20 | 16 | $27 |
Basking Ridge Country Club, 185 Madisonville Rd.
(N. Maple Ave.), 908-766-8201
*M – The "pretty view of the golf course" and neaby
Watchung Hills get higher marks than the Continental–
Contemporary American food; regulars say it's "better
for lunch" or brunch, when you can enjoy the
"country-club surroundings."*

Italian Chalet, The/S (Denville) **C9** | 20 | 16 | 19 | $30 |
3150 Rte. 10 (Franklin Rd.), 366-0111
*M – This informal Morris County roadhouse gets "solid"
marks for big portions of "consistently good" Italian food
at family-style prices and "friendly", "attentive" service;
overall, it's "decent", but some mind the "long waits."*

Italianissimo (West Caldwell) **D8** | 19 | 13 | 16 | $29 |
Broadway Plaza, 40 Clinton Rd. (Passaic Ave.), 228-5158
M – "Huge portions" of "authentic Italian food" at "fair prices" are why no one minds the quirky, "cramped" quarters of this Essex County "trattoria" – some even say it's "like being in Italy"; friendly ambiance makes it a "neighborhood" favorite; BYO.

Jade Ho*/S (Denville) **C9** | 17 | 13 | 14 | $21 |
Denville Commons Mall, 3130 Rte. 10 W. (Franklin Rd.), 989-8558
M – "Modern Cantonese" food with an emphasis on Hong Kong–style seafood and dim sum is the attraction at this fair-priced but out-of-the-way BYO Chinese in northern Morris County.

Jamie's/S (Englewood Cliffs) **F9** | 23 | 23 | 23 | $41 |
574 Rte. 9W (¼ mile north of Palisade Ave.), 568-4244
M – "Perfect for that special occasion", this "elegant" and "comfortable" (if "a little glitzy") Contemporary American "attracts a country-club crowd" with its "beautifully prepared food" and "top-notch", white-glove service; critics call it "pretentious" and "nothing special for the price."

Jimmy's*/S (Asbury Park) **G4** | 21 | – | 18 | $29 |
1405 Asbury Ave. (Ridge Ave.), 908-774-5051
U – Extremely popular with locals, this Shore "family place" has a "busy bar", well-rated "homestyle" Italian food, and a comfortable bar-and-grill atmosphere, thanks to a redecoration near the time this Survey was conducted.

Joe & Maggie's Bistro/S | 23 | 19 | 21 | $35 |
(Long Branch) **G5**
591 Broadway (at Norwood & Bath Aves.), 908-571-8848
U – It's "so nice to have this restaurant" in a restaurant-shy Shore area; congoscenti laud the "creative food" on the seasonally changing "California cuisine" menu, and enjoy the "bistro" setting and staff that "tries to please."

Ken Marcotte/S (Westfield) **D6** | 23 | 20 | 21 | $38 |
115 Elm St. (E. Broad St.), 908-233-2309
U – For a "formal yet relaxed" evening, you can "bank on" this Nouvelle American in a former Essex County bank (check out the service bar in the old vault); chef-owner Ken Marcotte's "innovative" American-grill menu and a solid staff attract "fashionable" diners.

Khiva/S | 16 | 15 | 16 |$23|

(Morristown) **C8**, 11 South St. (De Hart St.), 267-4427
(Montclair) **E9**, 485 Bloomfield Ave. (Church St.),
529-0660

Khiva on the Barge/S

(Carlstadt) **E8**, Outwater Lane (Paterson Plank Rd.),
933-8270

*M – This trio of "gimmicky" "Mongolian BBQs" lets you
"create your own stir-fry" from a "great selection of fresh
veggies, beef, pork and chicken"; it's a "novel idea" that's
"ok once in a while" and "fun" for families; the Carlstadt
location on the Hackensack River is the prettiest.*

Koreana/S (Paramus) **F9** | – | – | – | M |

Mall at IV, Rte. 4 W. (Johnson Ave.), 487-8558
*Located in spiffy quarters in a roadside strip mall, this
comfortable newcomer attracts locals and adventurous
shoppers with authentic and exotic Korean specialties
and an unusually helpful staff.*

La Catena (Roselle Park) **E7** | 23 | 19 | 22 |$39|

386 E. Westfield Ave. (Sheridan St.), 908-298-0828
*M – Whether you find this jackets-only Northern Italian a
"gem" or an "expensive" "hole-in-the-wall" will largely
depend on your tolerance for "cramped quarters"; all
agree on "fine" food ("pasta and seafood to die for") and
"highly professional service"; the valet parking is a plus.*

La Cucina/S (Somerville) **C6** | 21 | 18 | 19 |$35|

Pathmark Shopping Ctr., 125 W. Main St. (N. Bridge St.),
908-526-4907
*U – Happy customers applaud the "always good" Italian
fare at this lavishly decorated, faux-Roman
shopping-center "trattoria"; though it's "noisy at times"
and the staff can be "overburdened", the "excellent
kitchen" and lively "outdoor cafe" win kudos.*

La Dolce Vita/S (Lambertville) **A5** | – | – | – | M |

11 Church St. (N. Main St.), 609-397-9111
*Though too new to rate, the charming brick-walled setting
and an interesting, high-quality menu at fair prices make
this creative Italian worth a try, especially in warm
weather, when you can sit at a table in the courtyard.*

Lady Jane's/S (Hoboken) **F8** | 21 | 16 | 18 |$28|

51 14th St. (Hudson St.), 659-9390
*U – "Very NY", this "fun bar" attracts local trendies with
its "warm atmosphere" and "quite good" up-to-the-
minute American food; the Sunday brunch is "terrific"
and validated parking is available; for more formal
dining, try the Victorian dining room on the left.*

Lafayette House*/S (Lafayette) **B10** | 18 | 15 | 16 | $22 |
Old Lafayette Village, Rte. 94 (Rte. 15), 579-3100
M – This little-known "family restaurant"/pub in an ersatz Early American shopping village in NW Sussex County is the only thing "for miles around"; surveyors call it "routine" but "dependable", especially if you "stick to burgers" and other simple fare in the informal downstairs tavern.

LA FONTANA (New Brunswick) **D6** | 25 | 25 | 24 | $43 |
120 Albany St. (Spring Alley), 908-249-7500
U – "The best in New Brunswick" (and one of NJ's top-rated Italians) rave fans of this "fabulous" aristocrat; yes, it's "expensive", but "romantic", "old-world atmosphere", "superb service", a winning wine list and "original food" make it well worth the tab.

Lahiere's (Princeton) **C4** | 21 | 20 | 21 | $41 |
11 Witherspoon St. (Nassau St.), 609-921-2798
M – "Go with an old Princetonian" to this clubby but "friendly" 74-year-old "landmark" where you can "see state politicians", sip wine from a "superior list" and enjoy a good Contemporary American menu in a "beautiful setting"; critics say it's "overbloated" and "overpriced."

Laico's/SX (Jersey City) **F8** | 20 | 9 | 13 | $23 |
67 Terhune Ave. (bet. Spring St. & Fowler Ave.), 434-4115
U – Fans say that big portions of "great" "down-home" Italian fare at "good prices" make the "lengthy waits" and "unassuming" ambiance "worthwhile" at this almost "impossible to find" "working-class neighborhood" joint; "forget the room", just mangia!

L'allegria (Madison) **D8** | 20 | 19 | 18 | $36 |
11 Prospect St. (Main St.), 377-6808
M – "Elegant decor" (newly renovated to resemble a Tuscan country courtyard), smooth service and "excellent, though pricey, food" make this Morris County Italian "nice for a romantic dinner for two"; if you found the food "standard", give it another try, given the arrival of a creative new chef.

Lantana/S (Secaucus) **F8** | 20 | 22 | 20 | $38 |
(fka Sonny D)
1148 Paterson Plank Rd. (Cedar Lane), 867-1065
M – A new personality, marked by lower prices, a more casual Italian style and a "huge" new mix-and-match menu, is a definite improvement, but may not be reflected in the above ratings; some claim the food is still "ordinary" at "extraordinary prices" and the glitzy decor is "Bensonhurst recidivist."

La Petite Auberge/S (Cresskill) **F9** | 21 | 20 | 21 | $39 |
44 E. Madison (bet. County & Piermont Rds.), 569-2270
M – Run by the sons of founder Jean Claude Brecq,
this "quaint", "romantic" Bergen County Classic French
with its "fabulous" wine list and "intimate", "country
setting" gets mixed reviews; but for most it's a "favorite."

Laughing Lion, The/S (Dover) **D9** | – | – | – | M |
40 N. Sussex St. (Rte. 46), 328-1800
Across from Dover's Town Hall, this westernmost Morris
County "plain-Jane" Italian is tasty, "congenial" and
reasonably priced; it's "crowded" on weekends, but with
so little competition, that's really no surprise.

LE CHATEAU (Tenafly) **F9** | 24 | 23 | 23 | $43 |
115 County Rd. (Central Ave.), 871-1500
U – "Sit by the fireplace" and "feel like you're in
Burgundy" at this north Bergen County French; diners
give it high marks for "dependable" "traditional French"
fare, "cheerful service" and a "fine country setting", saying
they've "never had a bad meal" at this "old reliable."

LE DELICE (Whippany) **D8** | 25 | 23 | 24 | $49 |
302 Whippany Rd. (Park Ave.), 884-2727
M – "Wonderful food and service" are hallmarks of this
"expensive", "formal but friendly" Morris County French
Contemporary with a "beautiful" setting in a flower-filled
pink house; though some find it "uneven", most "rate it
with top NY restaurants" as a "special-occasion" place.

Le Papillon/S (Morristown) **C8** | 20 | 19 | 19 | $37 |
142 South St. (bet. Pine & Elm Sts.), 539-8088
M – This airy, "pretty" Morris County Classic French
draws mixed comments: "fair" and "mediocre" vs.
"delicious" and "tasty"; while foes say it's "trying to be
too upscale", friends say it fills a void; good ratings
suggest you give it a try.

LE PETIT CHATEAU/S | 24 | 23 | 23 | $45 |
(Bernardsville) **C7**
121 Claremont Rd. (Main St.), 908-766-4544
M – A recent "redecoration has made a marked improve-
ment" at this "wonderful country inn" where the owner's
high standards ensure "consistently excellent" Classic
French fare and "friendly service"; though a few find it
"overrated", high ratings suggest it's worth a detour.

Le Plumet Royal*/S (Princeton) **C4** | 20 | 23 | 21 | $41 |
Peacock Inn, 20 Bayard Lane, Rte. 206 (Nassau St.),
609-921-0050
U – Little-known, this "beautiful" Classic French dining
room in an historic Queen Anne Colonial inn is said to
be the "best in Princeton", with "consistently" "delicious
food", polished service and a pretty garden.

Lighthouse (W. New York) **F8** | 15 | 13 | 16 | $28 |
60th St. & River Rd., 854-1004
M – An "excellent view of NY" is the main draw at this nautical old-time "riverfront" Southern Italian and not the "huge portions" of "very average food"; fans cite "Grandma's home cooking" and "friendly service", but others say it's "no longer worth going to."

Little Kraut, The/S (Red Bank) **F5** | 17 | 16 | 17 | $32 |
115 Oakland St. (Bridge Ave.), 908-842-4830
M – "If you like German food", this gemütlich Shore staple may be your barrel of bock, especially during Oktoberfest, when the Terrace cafe throngs with people, pitchers and wurst on the grill; Germanophiles call it an "enjoyable spot with ok food", but phobes think it's "overblown", "overpriced" and "overcooked."

Lu Nello's (Totowa) **F9** | – | – | – | E |
331 Union Blvd. (1 mile north of Rtes. 80 & 46), 790-1410
Write-ins tell us that this bustling, "sophisticated" Italian has robust food, straight-arrow service and comfortable quarters that make up for highish prices and an "unlikely" Passaic County storefront location.

Manon*/SX (Lambertville) **A5** | 23 | 13 | 20 | $31 |
19 N. Union St. (Bridge St.), 609-397-2596
U – Though few know this "tiny", "charming" Lambertville BYO "storefront", those who do laud the "food and surroundings of Provence", "inventive" cooking by chef Jean-Michel Dumas and "personal service" overseen by wife Susan; "if only the place were larger."

MANOR, THE/S (West Orange) **E8** | 22 | 23 | 22 | $42 |
111 Prospect Ave. (Eagle Rock Ave.), 731-2360
M – "The gold standard in New Jersey", this "special-event haven" is "big", "glitzy" and worth a visit "at least once", if only for the "lavish" decor and the "dazzling" nightly "lobster buffet" (there's also "surprisingly good" à la carte Contemporary Continental dining in the Terrace garden); for every critic who calls this "catering-mill" "garish" and "overblown", there's a fan who says it's "beautiful" and just "the place for a special occasion."

Marcello/S (Harrington Park) **G10** | 22 | 20 | 21 | $40 |
12 Tappan Rd. (Schraalenburgh Rd.), 767-4245
M – Our respondents are mixed about this Italian: while some praise the "lovely setting" on six acres (complete with babbling brooks and honking geese), "congenial host" Marcello Sili and his "fantastic" food, others find the mirrored dining room "flashy" and "uncomfortable", and call the service "condescending"; solid ratings indicate that those who can afford it, "like it."

Marique's French Cuisine/S | – | – | – | M |
(Mendham) **B8**
25 E. Main St. (center of town), 543-9571
This "tiny", romantic, family-owned Country French in an
early 1800s building inspired lots of surveyors to write in
to describe its food as "equal to any NY restaurant",
plus likable service and the opportunity to keep the tab
reasonable by brown-bagging your wine.

Markers* (Jersey City) **F8** | 15 | 18 | 17 |$26|
Harborside Financial Ctr., Christopher Columbus Dr.
(Exchange Pl.), 433-6275
M – "Plain food in a handsome setting" describes this
"chainlike" American bistro; surveyors call it a "good
value" and a "nice casual place" for lunch but "so-so" at
dinner; despite its IHudson River location, there's no view.

Marlboro Inn, The/S (Montclair) **E9** | 15 | 18 | 16 |$31|
334 Grove St. (Watchung Ave.), 783-5300
U – The "attractive old setting" of "Montclair's only hotel",
in operation since the late 1800s, is "better" than the
old-time Continental fare; still, it's beloved by the
"Mother's Day crowd" for its "lovely atmosphere" and
"nice brunch"; BYO "keeps prices down."

Marra's/S (Ridgewood) **F9** | 20 | 15 | 16 |$31|
16 S. Broad St. (Ridgewood Ave.), 444-1332
U – "More than satisfying", this BYO North Bergen
storefront serves "surprisingly good pasta" and other
Italian staples, with fresh seafood a specialty; it's small,
and the "waiting area is the sidewalk."

Max's/S (Raritan) **B6** | 22 | 13 | 19 |$28|
63 W. Somerset St. (Wall St.), 908-725-4553
M – Confusion with Max's hot dog place in Long Branch
makes this elegant Northern Italian hard to rate, but raves
for its "delicious food" and "masculine" atmosphere are
unmistakable; with "crowded" quarters you may have "other
diners in your lap", but in this area, it's "the place to go."

Memories/S (Fort Lee) **F8** | 15 | 15 | 17 |$29|
116 Main St. (Central Rd.), 947-2500
M – The shtick here is "lots of old pieces of Fort Lee"
memorabilia, but while some nostalgia-lovers call it a
"good local spot" run by "nice people", for most the
standard American-Continental food is "not memorable."

Memphis Pig Out/S | 19 | 12 | 15 |$22|
(Atlantic Highlands) **G5**
67 First Ave. (7 blocks north of Rte. 36), 908-291-5533
M – "For when you want messy", this Shore-town
Memphis-style BBQ is "lots of fun", full of kids, "cute pig
decor" and more kids; it's also a good buy on an
abundant salad bar and delicious homemade desserts.

Meson Madrid/S | 18 | 12 | 16 | $28 |

(Palisades Park) **F9**

343 Bergen Blvd. (Central Blvd.), 947-1038

M – "Hustling and bustling", this popular Bergen County Spaniard packs 'em in for "huge quantities" ("giant lobsters") of "typical Spanish food" in a comfortable but somewhat "tacky" "roadhouse" setting; expect "long waits" and lots of "noise."

Mexicali Rose/S (Montclair) **E9** | – | – | – | M |

10 Park St. (Bloomfield Ave.), 746-9005

In a hard-luck location, this likable SW-style BYO Mexican may endure, thanks to fresh, tasty food (check out the unique specials, two or three steps above Tex-Mex), friendly service and reasonable prices in an atrium filled with south-of-the-border artifacts.

Michael's Backstreet Cafe*/S | 20 | 14 | 18 | $27 |

(Irvington) **E8**

18 Union Ave. (bet. Nye & Springfield Aves.), 371-2355

U – "Like being in New Orleans", this low-atmosphere "neighborhood cafe", presided over by chef-owner Michael Brown, serves "the most authentic Cajun and Creole food in New Jersey", "worth a detour" to a "most unlikely location" just off the Garden State.

Mike Doolan's* | 18 | 15 | 20 | $24 |

(Spring Lake Heights) **G4**

Doolan's Hotel, 700 Hwy. 71 (bet. Essex & Sussex Aves.), 908-449-3666

U – "A real bargain", this "solid" "all-around Shore place" collects more praise for its "friendly service" ("Mike really works the patrons") than for its "plain" but "good" Americanized French-Continental food.

Milano* (Summit) **D8** | 18 | 13 | 18 | $30 |

34 Maple St. (Springfield Ave.), 908-522-1010

M – Some folks from the "neighborhood" like this "pleasant" little BYO Italian where you can order a "delicious meal" "without going to the bank" first; even those who like the "fresh, earthy food", however, say the wait "between courses" can be "deadeningly long"; with minimal ambiance this is "strictly a local" place.

Mr. Tong/S | 20 | 18 | 18 | $26 |

(E. Rutherford) **F8**, 900 Paterson Plank (Rte. 17), 933-7799

(Fairfield) **E8**, 160 Passaic Ave. (Rte. 46), 808-2708

U – These "better-than-average Chinese" with "excellent" food, "pleasant" service and "nice", if "stark", surroundings please nearly everyone; no one seems to mind "high prices" (for Chinese) for a meal that's "yummy, just like Manhattan."

Muirhead* (Ringoes) **B5** | 21 | 22 | 22 | $43 |
43 Rte. 202 (3½ miles south of Flemington Circle),
908-782-7803
*U – For a "different experience", this "delightful"
"family-run" Hunterdon County inn that's only open on
Fridays and Saturdays offers a different menu each
night; the fact that the Continental food is "back in the
'60s" (rack of lamb, beef Wellington) matters little in light
of the location in a "beautiful" "converted" farmhouse.*

MUMFORDS'/S (Long Branch) **G5** | 24 | 17 | 19 | $31 |
45 Atlantic Ave. (Rte. 36, at Ocean Ave.), 908-222-2657
*U – The "Shore's shining star" is this "imaginative" New
American, whose owners use vegetables and herbs
from their organic garden to create "delicious"
"innovative yuppie char cooking"; a "no-reservations"
policy on weekends means waiting, and the
second-floor setting is funky.*

Namaskaar/S (Paramus) **F9** | – | – | – | M |
Mall at IV, Rte. 4 W. (Johnson Ave.), 342-8868
*Though most NJ Indians are located in bare-bones
storefronts, this spiffy new contender has a casually
sophisticated ambiance and delicious versions of all the
subcontinent favorites; if service is lax, then fair prices,
including a lunch buffet at $8.95, compensate.*

NANINA'S IN THE PARK/S | 24 | 20 | 21 | $39 |
(Belleville) **E9**
540 Mill St. (Franklin Ave.), 751-1230
*U – For 38 years, this Essex County Italian "hasn't
changed and shouldn't"; "old-fashioned" "rich, generous"
Italian food, "dark elegant atmosphere", "white-glove
service" and "one of the best wine lists in NJ" make this
"local favorite" a "tradition"; for a truly "special occasion",
"reserve the wine cellar" for a nine-course, seven-wine
feast at $114 per person.*

Neelam/S | 19 | 14 | 18 | $24 |
(Berkeley Heights) **D7,** 295 Springfield Ave. (Snyder
Ave.), 908-665-2212
(South Orange) **E8,** 115 S. Orange Ave. (Valley St.), 762-1100
*M – Surveyors say this neighborhood BYO duo serves
"consistently good Indian food" – "tandoor dishes are the
specialty"; "friendly" service helps to offset "uninspiring"
decor, and the $7.95 buffet lunch is a "real bargain."*

Nero's/S (Livingston) **E8** | – | – | – | M |
618 S. Livingston Ave. (Northfield Rd.), 994-1410
*Fans wrote in about this "warm", "consistent" Italian, a
"hangout for the 'in' crowd" for more than 20 years; the
comfortable old-world ambiance and large portions of
familiar favorites at moderate prices sustain a following.*

F	D	S	C

Net Lane's Fisherman*/S | 17 | 11 | 15 | $23 |
(Asbury Park) **G4**

1605 Ocean Ave. (Seventh Ave.), 908-775-0282
M – Across from the Boardwalk, this old-line "standard Shore sort" of seafooder gets decent marks for "fresh fish, rather simply prepared", and friendly service; critics say the nautical "decor is lacking" and call this place "Red Lobster at the beach."

Newmain Taste Thai*/S | 22 | 15 | 14 | $34 |
(Chatham) **D8**

225 Main St. (N. Passaic St.), 635-7333
U – "Good-tasting Thai food" is the specialty of this "sooo serious" Morris County storefront; though even fans say it's "too expensive for ethnic food", it sure is "excellent"; "order quickly, it's slow" coming.

New Top O' The Mast*/S | 15 | 17 | 16 | $29 |
(South Seaside Park) **G2**

23rd Ave. on the Ocean (gateway to Beach State Park), 908-793-3355
M – Big and "brassy", with a "good view" through its bay windows, this revitalized Shoreside American has yet to establish itself; but it's right on the beach, with an outdoor clam bar in season, an elaborate Sunday brunch buffet and plenty of special deals.

North Sea Village/S (Livingston) **E8** | 18 | 13 | 15 | $23 |
28 N. Livingston Ave. (Rte. 10), 992-7056
U – Adventurous diners flock to this Essex County Chinese where "Hong Kong–style fresh" seafood is the specialty and the weekend dim sum is as good as Chinatown's; the place is "noisy", "crowded" and low on decor, but for an "authentic Chinese experience", ask for the "gourmet menu" or the daily specials.

Ocean Gate House*/S | 18 | 18 | 15 | $33 |
(Ocean Gate) **G2**

401 Monmouth Ave. (E. Bayview Ave.), 908-269-2888
M – "Considering there's nothing else around", this Continental near Toms River is surprisingly good, with an elegant Williamsburg mien, good-value early-bird specials and a pastry chef on premises; critics warn it's "getting less special all the time."

Old Bay Restaurant*/S | 17 | 18 | 18 | $31 |
(New Brunswick) **D6**

61-63 Church St. (Nielson St.), 908-246-3111
M – One of New Brunswick's prime "social" scenes, this "noisy" Cajun-Creole, with "decent food" and a setting that recalls 19th-century New Orleans (wooden floors, tin ceilings and all that jazz), may be no world-beater, but its live entertainment and freewheeling bar are fun.

Olde Mill Ford Oyster House/S | – | – | – | E |
(Milford) **A6**
17 Bridge St. (Rte. 519), 908-995-9411
*Little known but worth the trip, this Traditional American
and seafood restaurant set in an 1829 home along the
Delaware is like "eating at Grandmother's", sloping
plank floors, mismatched chairs and all; the "seafood is
tops", absolutely fresh and simply prepared; BYO, wait
on the porch (no reserving), then order the crab cakes –
possibly NJ's best.*

Old Mill Inn/S | 18 | 21 | 19 | $30 |
(Spring Lake Heights) **G4**
Old Mill Rd. (bet. Rtes. 71 & 35), 908-449-1800
*M – "As comfortable as an old shoe", this "scenic"
"Colonial inn" is a "Jersey Shore institution"; the
Traditional American food matches the "beautiful"
ambiance and "gracious" service, and is "always
dependable", attracting a loyal, "older" clientele.*

Olive Branch Cafe/S | 20 | 15 | 18 | $27 |
(Morristown) **C8**
106 Speedwell Ave. (Spring St.), 539-0944
*M – An "interesting", if "limited", menu of "creative"
Italian and Mediterranean specialties defines this "tiny",
easily affordable Morris County "storefront" with its
"cozy warm atmosphere" and "very good food"; it's
BYO, with wine delivery from a local store a nice touch.*

Owl Tree, The*/S | 18 | 19 | 20 | $27 |
(Harvey Cedars) **G1**
7908 Long Beach Blvd. (80th St.), 609-494-8191
*M – "Best on LBI" may not be saying much, but scores
indicate that this dual-personality Italian may be worth a
try; downstairs, the "light fare is great" in a pubby setting;
upstairs, the "Victorian" Top of the Tree, is "pretty" and
the more formal menu is "good", if a little overreaching.*

Palmer's*/S (Princeton) **C4** | 21 | 25 | 22 | $42 |
Nassau Inn, 10 Palmer Square (Hulfish & Nassau Sts.),
609-921-7500
*M – This ambitious New American hasn't caught on,
despite a luxurious formal setting in a refurbished 200-
year-old hotel;"good service" and a creative, seasonal
menu of local ingredients are pluses, but critics cite steep
prices, and prefer the Tap Room's pub setting instead.*

Pals Cabin/S (W. Orange) **E8** | 14 | 13 | 15 | $26 |
265 Prospect Ave. (Eagle Rock Ave.), 731-4000
*M – "Great for dinner with the kids or a fast meal after
work", this "extremely popular" American restaurant–
cum–coffee shop is a "local institution" despite "just ok"
food, "nothing-spectacular decor" and service; sensibly
priced steaks, burgers and beer are the main draws.*

Pamir/S (Morristown) **C8** | 20 | 14 | 17 | $26 |

85 Washington St. (Rte. 24), 605-1095
M – You don't have to be an "authority on Afghan" to appreciate the "unusual and interesting" cuisine served in this somewhat "dark and dingy" Morris County BYO storefront; though most surveyors think it's "not as good" as the NYC original, it's still a "true find – inexpensive and accommodating."

Panevino/S (Livingston) **E8** | 16 | 16 | 15 | $23 |

637 W. Mt. Pleasant Ave., Rte. 10 (Eisenhower Circle), 535-6160
M – A "nice place for a casual and quick bite", this "trendy" "trattoria" specializes in "pasta and pizza" from a "wood oven" and "noisy" ersatz Tuscan ambiance; it's "best for lunch", especially at a table on the "attractive" patio; critics nail it as "nothing special."

Panico's (New Brunswick) **D6** | 22 | 20 | 21 | $40 |

103 Church St. (George St.), 908-545-6100
M – Recent personnel and menu changes are lifting the ratings of this "excellent upscale Italian", with its "creative food", "good" service and wine list, and "plush" "supper-club" atmosphere; it's "expensive", but "outstanding food" and an aura of "quiet" elegance make it "great for business dinners."

Pappardelle (Cliffside Park) **F9** | 23 | 14 | 17 | $35 |

671 Palisade Ave. (Lawton Ave.), 945-2339
U – At this "intimate" North Bergen "storefront bistro", chef-owner Nicholas Davino's "excellent and innovative" Italian food and modest prices attract a significant following; though service can be "slow", this "hidden treasure" is "worth a detour"; BYO.

Park & Orchard/S | 23 | 15 | 19 | $28 |
(East Rutherford) **F8**

240 Hackensack St. (Union St.), 939-9292
M – A "gourmet vegetarian delight" with "big helpings" of "healthy, delicious Eclectic" food and a "top wine list" create "long waits" (no reserving) at this "cavernous" restaurant near the railroad tracks; some mind the "noise" and the "stark" "factory" setting, but this place is still "wildly popular."

PARK ONE ELEVEN | – | 17 | 21 | $37 |
(Ridgewood) **F9**

111 E. Ridgewood Ave. (Oak St.), 444-7111
M – Changes in management have outdated our surveyors' high food ratings, however, with "some true talent in the kitchen" (chef Peter Loria, ex-banquet chef at Highlawn Pavilion) this pricey BYO American can still be recommended for an "enjoyable and relaxing meal" though decor in the "unpretentious", brick-walled storefront is a "little bare."

Peking Duck House/S (Closter) **F10** | 19 | 14 | 17 | $24 |
411 Piermont Rd. (Homon Rd.), 767-8779
*M – Because it's "one of the only places in NJ to offer
Peking duck with no advance notice", duck-lovers pack
this Bergen County "standby"; "great dim sum",
"imaginative tableside preparation" and "always-
dependable" Chinese food make up for the "tacky"
decor in this former steakhouse.*

Peking Pavilion*/S | 22 | 20 | 20 | $25 |
(Red Bank) **F5**, 58 Oakland St. (bet. Shrewsbury &
Maple Aves.), 908-219-0888
(Manalapan) **D4**, 425 Rte. 33 W. (½ mile west of
Freehold Raceway), 908-308-9700
*M – "Creative" "Hong Kong"–style food and "elegant",
contemporary decor are available at "both locations" of
this little-known but well-rated dynasty, near the Shore
and Freehold Raceway; expect "fancy Chinese at fancy
prices"; Red Bank serves weekend dim sum.*

Per Forza!/S (Basking Ridge) **C7** | – | – | – | M |
60 S. Finley Ave. (Henry St.), 908-221-0203
*Loyalists remind us that this "surprising" BYO "hole-in-
the-wall" serves an ever-"improving menu" of Italian
classics at moderate prices; lots of specials and a
"cozy", if close, dining room make this a local "favorite."*

Periwinkles/S (Sea Bright) **G5** | 18 | 15 | 17 | $29 |
1070 Ocean Ave. (Peninsula Ave.), 908-741-0041
*M – Across from the beach, this petite spot serves a
weekly changing menu of "moderately priced"
Continental and French specials in an old-fashioned
storefront environment, to so-so ratings.*

Perryville Inn*/S (Perryville) **B9** | 21 | 19 | 18 | $40 |
Perryville Rd. (I-78, exit 12), 908-730-9500
*M – In rural Hunterdon County, this mostly Continental
"class country" inn in a romantic old red-brick building
presents a country-club atmosphere and an "updated"
(some say "uneven") menu that makes it a "cozy spot"
for a relaxing meal, especially at brunch.*

Pheasants' Landing*/S | 17 | 21 | 21 | $30 |
(Belle Mead) **C5**
301 Amwell Rd., Rte. 514, (Rte. 206), 908-359-4700
*U – A setting in a restored Victorian farmhouse is the
big plus of this otherwise just "pretty good" Continental,
popular for its Sunday champagne brunch buffet; the
more casual pub, The Nest, is hip for a burger and a
beer when there's live entertainment.*

Phoenix Garden Too/S | 21 | 8 | 14 | $23 |
(Ridgefield) **G8**
88 Rte. 46 W. (Grand Ave.), 313-0088
*U – Forget the "glorified diner" setting and the stone-faced
service: go for some of "the best" Cantonese food in NJ,
including "exquisite" "salt and pepper shrimp" and about
400 other "unusual" items that have diners wondering
"is this really suburbia?"; daily dim sum is a bonus.*

Pierre's* (Morristown) **C8** | 26 | 19 | 23 | $35 |
26 Washington St. (Schuyler Ave.), 539-7171
*M – If you can't get to Paris, get to this "small, new
and très bien" bistro shoehorned into a "cramped" but
atmospheric storefront; it's got an excellent, if limited,
menu that changes every two weeks; it's a "real comer",
owned by the founders of Hoboken's Brass Rail.*

P.J. Clarke's/S (Short Hills) **D8** | 13 | 13 | 13 | $24 |
The Mall at Short Hills, JFK Pkwy. & Rte. 24, 376-7800
*M – "Good for the middle of the week if you're tired of
cooking", this "fern bar" with an unfortunate mall
location strikes some as "upgraded fast food" and,
despite "tasty burgers" and "big salads", it doesn't
measure up to its Manhattan parents.*

Portobello/S (Oakland) **E10** | – | – | – | M |
155 Ramapo Valley Rd. (High Mountain Rd.), 337-8073
*This "comfortable", casual Bergen County Italian
continues to serve "consistently good" favorites at
"reasonable prices" in its brand-new location with chic
white-on-white decor.*

PRATOS (Carlstadt) **E8** | 19 | 24 | 20 | $40 |
335 Paterson Plank Rd. (Rte. 17), 460-1777
*M – The "beautiful" "castle atmosphere" is what "you
pay for" at this theatrical Northern Italian, the very
definition of NJ "posh"; the "extensive menu" is "pricey"
but well-executed, making it a "good choice near the
Meadowlands"; critics say "too big for its britches."*

Prima Donna/S (East Hanover) **E8** | 21 | 21 | 21 | $38 |
341 Rte. 10 E. (River Rd.), 887-4949
*M – This "old-fashioned formal Italian" with its swanky
(some say "stuffy") atmosphere, straight-backed service
and "pricey" "old-world cuisine" gets some criticism as a
"fading lady", but a "new chef" is scoring points.*

Priory, The/S (Newark) **E8** | 15 | 19 | 18 | $23 |
233 W. Market St. (Warren St.), 242-8012
*M – Surveyors "really like" the "interesting decor" in this
Downtown former church, but can't say the same for the
Southern Soul Food or a location that's "dangerous" at
night; it's a "good place when visiting the Museum" and
has an "excellent" Sunday jazz champagne brunch.*

Pronto Cena (Jersey City) **F8** | 22 | 22 | 17 | $35 |
87 Sussex St. (Washington St.), 435-0004
M – "A miracle" in restaurant-poor Jersey City is this "stylish"
Italian trattoria with its creative Tuscan menu and chic,
SoHo-style ambiance, full of original art; N.B. post-Survey
chef and menu changes throw ratings into doubt.

Raritan River Club | – | – | – | M |
(New Brunswick) **D6**
85 Church St. (New St.), 908-545-6110
"Live music" and a "beautiful", atrium-style setting provide
the backdrop for an easy-to-take American- Continental
menu that's heavy on steak and seafood standards.

Ray's Restaurant*/S (Keyport) **F5** | 23 | 14 | 19 | $22 |
Keyport Marina, 340 W. Front St. (Broadway), 908-739-4710
U – "Don't tell people, for God's sake", say those who
want to keep this comfortable, low-budget BYO Italian in
the Marina to themselves; friendly service, fresh,
creative food with an accent on seafood and an
appealing terrace explain why people "love this place."

Richard's Cafe Americain/S | – | – | – | E |
(Madison) **D8**
4 Cook Plaza (Main St.), 822-9697
This pretty Morris County storefront has won a loyal
following with its diverse Contemporary American menu;
chef-owner Jim Riley's new à la carte menu format (with
a $41.95 six-course prix fixe–only on Saturdays) offers
"plenty to eat and sample."

Rispoli's/S (Montclair) **E9** | 20 | 16 | 18 | $31 |
5 N. Fullerton Ave. (Bloomfield Ave.), 509-8544
M – "Good", "solid" Italian food and a "lively" (if "cramped")
setting make this "decent local place" "worth a visit",
though not a detour; BYO holds prices down and the
specials can be interesting.

Ristorante Bellavista*/S | 16 | 14 | 13 | $31 |
(Long Branch) **G5**
228 New Ocean Ave. (Joline Ave.), 908-229-4720
M – Diners divide over this "seaside" Italian-Continental
in a restored 100-year-old Victorian, with a knotty-pine
tap room in front and a more formal dining room in back
(plus a grapevine-shaded patio); ratings suggest it
needs to improve to justify its price.

Riverfront Cafe, The (Harrison) **E8** | 21 | 19 | 18 | $31 |
600 Cape May St. (Frank Rogers Blvd.), 485-3202
M – Ignore the run-down industrial area and focus on
the Contemporary French–Italian blend at this quirky
but likable Hudson County cafe; once inside, you'll find
the tile-walled bistro-style setting "small" but attractive,
with a decent wine list and good food.

RIVER PALM TERRACE, THE/S | 25 | 15 | 20 | $39 |
(Edgewater) **G9**
1416 River Rd. (Palisades Terrace), 224-2013
U – The local crowd doesn't mind being "jammed in" at this "noisy", "NYC-style steakhouse", where the "food's the thing": beautifully prepared steak, chops, veal, lobster, fish and great side dishes like cottage fries; it's pricey, but "you'll never have to cross the bridge again."

Rod's 1890's Restaurant/S | – | – | – | M |
(Convent Station) **E7**
Rte. 24 (Madison Ave.), 539-6666
Respondents suggested this popular write-in; though the steak-and-prime-rib-intensive menu is rather predictable, the memorabilia-filled setting provides "romantic dining" and lots of fun, especially for groups.

Rosemary and Sage | – | – | – | E |
(Riverdale) **E10**
28 Hamburg Tpke. (Newark-Pompton Tpke.), 616-0606
Don't let the inauspicious exterior of this new Morris County Contemporary American fool you: there's good food inside at the hands of owners Brooks Nicklas and Wendy Farber; expect attentive service and a simple but attractive setting.

Rudolfo/S (Gladstone) **C7** | 22 | 22 | 22 | $43 |
(fka Maria's)
12 Lackawanna Ave. (Main St.), 908-781-1888
M – New owner Rudolfo Hisena has created a "plush", "lovely" spot with "well-prepared" Classic Italian cuisine and "excellent" service; though "expensive", improved food and "elegant" ambiance make this out-of-the-way Somerset County spot worth it, "once you find it."

RUGA (Oakland) **E10** | 25 | 19 | 21 | $38 |
4 Barbara Lane (north end of Rte. 208), 337-0813
U – Respondents love the "innovative and interesting" New American food but "hate the noise level" at this otherwise "fine, classy", New Yorky spot in northern Bergen County; the food's as "creative" as the "lovely paintings" by artist Edward Ruga.

Ruth's Chris Steak House/S | 21 | 18 | 19 | $41 |
(Weehawken) **F8**
Lincoln Harbor, 1000 Harbor Blvd. (19th St.), 863-5100
M – "Very good but not excellent" steaks at stiff prices keep this sleek chain "out of the major leagues" for many, who think "it's never quite like the original New Orleans version" and wish the view was of the Hudson, not "ugly condos"; still, "if you love beef", expect a "good meal here."

RYLAND INN/S (Whitehouse) **B7** | 24 | 24 | 22 | $46 |
Old Rte. 22 W. (8 miles west of Bridgewater Commons),
908-534-4011
*U – "Born again and fantastic" – at last the Modern
American food is up to the setting of this "warm, rich,
country inn", now under the wing of Townsquare's Dennis
Foy, with chef Craig Shelton (ex NYC's Bouley) at the
helm; Shelton's fare is "not cheap" but it's "magnifique";
N.B. the 24 food rating albeit excellent is outdated and
underrates the extraordinary food quality now being served.*

Sabatini's/S (Caldwell) **D8** | 20 | 18 | 20 | $34 |
435 Bloomfield Ave. (Passaic Ave.), 403-0224
*M – This "pretty, local" Italian has "two parts" – a "nice
cafe" specializing in brick oven pizzas, and a "more
formal" dining room serving "typical Northern Italian"
favorites; most say it's "one of the best BYO places
around", though arguably "expensive for what you get."*

SADDLE RIVER INN | 27 | 25 | 25 | $46 |
(Saddle River) **F10**
2 Barnstable Court (corner of E. Allendale & W. Saddle
River Rds.), 825-4016
*U – "Numero Uno" in our New Jersey ratings, this
"elegant" inn set "in a converted old barn" "charms" our
respondents "again and again" with its "rustic
ambiance", "enthusiastic service" and the "delicious"
Continental–Classic French cuisine of chef-owner Hans
Egg; jackets and reservations are essential; BYOW.*

Saint's Cafe (Teaneck) **F9** | 17 | 17 | 17 | $30 |
827 Teaneck Rd. (Rte. 4), 833-1160
*M – "Funky wine bar–bistro atmosphere" plus "decent"
Continental and Italian favorites make this "corner bar
made good" a nifty "neighborhood place" for "pleasant"
meals; insiders say "the simpler, the safer."*

Sammy's Olde Cider Mill/S | 22 | 8 | 14 | $41 |
(Mendham) **B8**
353 Rte. 24 W. (Oak Knoll Rd.), 543-7675
*M – Legions "love this dive", an ex-speakeasy that's
now an "unattractive", "astronomical" "basement" of a
steakhouse where you "order when you enter and eat when
you're called"; what's the attraction? "big portions" of "great
steak and fries", and "the best lobster", but "prepare to wait."*

Sam's Grill/S (Raritan) **B6** | 20 | 19 | 18 | $32 |
(fka Sam's)
777 Rte. 202 (1 mile south of Somerville Circle),
908-707-1777
*M – Now that they've "downscaled the menu", fans say this
Somerset County roadhouse is "one of the best buys in the
state" for Californian grill food and an airy ambiance; "the
food has gone down a notch", but "so have the prices."*

Sandpiper*/S (Spring Lake) **G3** | 17 | 18 | 21 | $29 |
Sandpiper Hotel, 7 Atlantic Ave. (First Ave.),
908-449-4700
*M – "Warm and inviting in summer", this "middling" but
popular BYO American grill in a "pleasant" old Victorian
hotel near the ocean aims to please with "creative food"
and "piano player music"; its Thursday night $19.95
seafood buffet is a steal.*

Santoro's Restaurant/S | – | – | – | M |
(Teaneck) **F9**
439 Cedar Lane (Palisade Ave.), 836-9505
*"Kosher Italian cooking" and thin-crust pizzas are the
draws at this Bergen County "neighborhood" storefront
with its updated decor; doubters say it's "ok if kosher is
what you need, but otherwise why bother?"*

Sea Shack/S (Hackensack) **F9** | 20 | 14 | 19 | $31 |
293 Polifly Rd. (Rte. 17), 489-7232
*M – "Fresh", "basic seafood" in a "relaxed" atmosphere
has made this Bergen County roadhouse "something of
an 'in' place for local business lunches"; tables are too
close, however, and some claim the food is "not as
good as they say."*

SERGEANTSVILLE INN/S | 23 | 24 | 22 | $36 |
(Sergeantsville) **A5**
Rte. 523 (corner of Rte. 604), 609-397-3700
*U – Most consider this rambling stone country inn a
"winner all the way", with "creative" Continental food,
"lovely" service and a "warm, wonderful ambiance"
that's perfect for a "secret rendezvous" or "cold-winter
dining by the fire"; it's pricey but "worth it."*

Sergio's/S (Millburn) **E8** | 20 | 18 | 20 | $32 |
343 Millburn Ave. (Main St.), 379-7020
*U – "Attentive service" and "consistently good", "beautifully
presented" Ligurian specialties have given a "great
reputation" to this BYO Essex County Italian hidden
upstairs "in a faceless office building"; it's a "long-term
player" in a world of change, and worth a visit.*

SESTRI/S (Gillete) **D7** | 24 | 18 | 23 | $35 |
342 Valley Rd., Rte. 512 (Union County border),
908-647-0697
*U – "Wow!"; "New York meets Milan" at this chic
Regional Italian that's part old-world cafe with a
fireplace and mirrored-back bar, and part formal dining
room with a mauve-and-peach decor; either way, the
"lusty food" is "terrific", though a few say "poor acoustics
mar an otherwise pleasant experience."*

Settebello (Morristown) **C8** | – | – | – | M |
2 Cattano Ave. (Speedwell Ave.), 267-3355
*This bustling, popular Morris County Regional Italian
(younger sibling to Piccolo in Pine Brook), with its
attractive exposed-brick walls and delicious, reasonably
priced food is gaining attention; BYO.*

Shadowbrook/S (Shrewsbury) **F5** | 16 | 23 | 18 |$37 |
Rte. 35 (Newman Springs Rd.), 908-747-0200
*M – "Beautiful gardens" and a setting in a Georgian
mansion filled with art and antiques make this formal
restaurant–cum–catering hall ideal for "weddings", but
surveyors say the Continental food is "boring" and
"overpriced"; "take Grandma", but "not for the food."*

Shanghai Red's/S (Weehawken) **F8** | 14 | 22 | 15 |$31 |
Lincoln Harbor, Pier D-T (River Rd.), 348-6628
*U – "Look but don't eat" at this "chain restaurant" "right
on the water at Lincoln Harbor"; the theatrical SF Gold
Rush decor and the bar can be "fun if you're single", but
the "awesome view of the NY skyline" is better than the
"assembly-line" trendoid Continental-American food;
"stick with the simple stuff", drinks or Sunday brunch.*

Shinwa/S (Alpine) **F10** | 22 | 23 | 20 |$40 |
5-9 Rte. 9W (Palisades Pkwy.), 767-6322
*U – "For Japanese purists", this "over-opulent" Bergen
County spot serves up "inspirational, authentic food" at
high prices, including "first-rate sushi", "great
homemade" noodle dishes and "ultrasophisticated"
specialties; "elegant but chilly" decor and attentive
service make it "great for a festive Japanese meal";
N.B. at $25, the all-you-can-eat brunch is a bargain.*

Shore Casino*/S | 12 | 17 | 18 |$30 |
(Atlantic Highlands) **G5**
Municipal Yacht Harbor, Atlantic Highlands Marina (off
Rte. 36), 908-291-4300
*M – Outstanding views of the harbor and Sandy Hook
Bay keep this old-line Italian-American (veal, steaks,
prime rib, etc.) "always crowded"; service is ok, but the
food has "seen better days."*

Shrewsbury/S (Long Branch) **G5** | – | – | – | E |
Ocean Place Hilton, 1 Ocean Blvd. (B'way),
908-571-4000
*An "innovative menu" and "beautiful" formal decor
highlight this Contemporary American hotel dining room;
most surveyors say it's "great" but "overpriced" for the
Shore; for a more casual setting and lovely views, try
Pleasure Bay instead, the hotel's all-day American.*

Shubox Cafe/S (Cedar Grove) **E8** | – | – | – | M |
256 Pompton Ave., Rte. 23 (S. Mountain Ave.), 239-8880
*Cute as a button, this Essex County Eclectic has tasty
homemade food with a healthy slant, and "nice informal
atmosphere" that make it a good place "to take kids";
wine and beer only.*

Silver Pond/S | – | – | – | M |
(Fort Lee) **F9**, 230-234 Main St. (bet. Anderson &
Palisade Aves.), 392-8338
(East Hanover) **E8,** Pathmark Shopping Ctr., 240 Rte. 10
W., 887-1193
*Outposts of a popular Queens restaurant, these spiffy
Chinese have a clientele devoted to their authentic,
seafood-intensive Hong Kong–style Cantonese food
and comfortable art deco settings; friendly service and
weekend dim sum are additional reasons to visit.*

Silver Spring Farm/S (Flanders) **C8** | – | – | – | E |
Flanders-Drakestown Rd. (Flanders-Netcong Rd., off
Rte. 206), 584-6660
*For over three decades, this French charmer, with its
homey, country setting, has offered dependable, if
rather old-fashioned, special-occasion dining; it's a good
place for comfort food, Gallic-style.*

Sinclaire's/S (Westfield) **D6** | 20 | 17 | 18 | $36 |
240 North Ave. (Central Ave.), 908-789-0344
*M – This "pleasant" Union County bastion of elaborately
prepared and "imaginative seafood" has fans who tout it
for the "best fish in Jersey"; critics call it "overrated" and
say the premises "should be redecorated"; your call.*

Sing Ya/S (Englewood Cliffs) **F9** | – | – | – | M |
520 Sylvan Ave. (Rte. 9W), 568-9855
*This Bergen County newcomer offers Hong Kong–style
food and interesting dim sum in an attractive, airy
greenhouse setting, with amiable service (though a little
lacking in English-language skills).*

Sirin Thai*/S (Glen Ridge) **E9** | 15 | 12 | 18 | $26 |
13 Herman St. (Bloomfield Ave.), 429-2422
*U – "Friendly owners" are the strong point of this
comfortable, low-atmosphere Thai storefront; it may be "too
authentic even for adventurous diners", i.e. too "spicy", but
there are plenty of dishes you don't see everywhere.*

Sonoma Grill/S (East Rutherford) **F8** | – | – | – | M |
64 Hoboken Rd. (Paterson Plank Rd.), 507-8989
*Too new to rate, this promising American Contemporary is
owned by chef and wine maven Dennis Foy (ex Le Delice);
this much-awaited bistro is a casual, moderately priced
neighborhooder with an eclectic, grill-intensive menu and
lots of specials.*

Sorrento's*/S (East Rutherford) **F8** | 17 | 12 | 18 | $23 |
132 Park Ave. (3 blocks north of Rutherford train station), 507-0038
M – "Solid midweek Italian fare" characterizes this small BYO storefront "family place" that "everyone keeps a secret"; complimentary crostini and grilled vegetables and soppressata are favorites, but surveyors with tender backs say "dump the chrome-frame chairs."

Spain/S (Newark) **E8** | 20 | 12 | 16 | $26 |
419 Market St. (Raymond Blvd.), 344-0994
U – "Tons of great Spanish food" make diners "forget about the surroundings" at this "typical", "crowded" Downtown tavern-cum-restaurant; fans who "love this place" come to "overdose on green sauce" and "garlic", and take a lot of it home in doggie bags; attended parking at night is a plus in an iffy neighborhood.

Spanish Tavern/S | 20 | 15 | 19 | $28 |
(Newark) **E8**, 103 McWhorter St. (Green St.), 589-4959
(Mountainside) **E7**, 1239 Rte. 22 E. (New Providence Rd.), 908-232-2171
M – Suburbanites who don't like Newark hike to Mountainside, but either way, "bring your earplugs" and "be prepared to wait" for large portions of Spanish food, including "great" paella and mariscada; some say "mediocre", but scores suggest otherwise.

Squan Tavern*/S (Manasquan) **G3** | 19 | 11 | 16 | $22 |
15 Broad St. (Main St.), 908-223-3324
U – "Pizza, pasta and cheap red wine" keep locals coming back to this "standby"; it's not trendy, but reasonably priced Italian food, friendly family owners and a "comfortable" "tavern atmosphere" constantly fill this casual Shore-town spot.

Stage Left/LS (New Brunswick) **D6** | – | – | – | M |
5 Livingston Ave. (George St.), 908-828-4444
Promising but too new to rate, this chic little seasonal American has an enviable Theater District location plus comfortable art-hung ambiance, late-night supper, an interesting wine list and sensible prices.

Stefano's*/S (Fanwood) **E7** | 24 | 19 | 22 | $34 |
Mansion Hotel, 295 South Ave. (Maron Rd.), 908-889-7874
U – A "very imaginative" Northern Italian menu with noteworthy "specials" makes this intimate hotel dining room a "secret treasure" to its fans, who say you "cannot go wrong" here.

STONY HILL INN/S | 20 | 24 | 21 | $39 |
(Hackensack) **F9**
231 Polifly Rd. (Rte. 17), 342-4085
*M – "Accommodating service" and "good" food in a
"restored Colonial landmark" make this old-line
Continental-Italian a "place to celebrate", "impress your
date" or clinch a deal; though detractors insist it's "too
pricey" and the "food is no match" for the "beautiful
decor", solid numbers make it a good bet.*

Taj Palace*/S (Montclair) **E9** | 18 | 13 | 17 | $24 |
702 Bloomfield Ave. (Valley Rd.), 744-1909
*M – Expect "consistently tasty" Indian food and "close
tables" at this "wonderful hole-in-the-wall" where the
staff greets you like a long-lost friend; N.B. the
well-meaning staff may "urge you to order more than
you need or want"; BYO.*

Teresa's Pizzetta Caffe/S | – | – | – | M |
(Princeton) **C4**
21 Palmer Sq. E. (Chambers Walk), 609-921-1974
*An attractive European-style cafe that serves mid-priced
authentic Italian dishes, including a variety of small
pizzas (the eponymous pizzetta), and also specializes in
Italian coffees and desserts.*

Terrace Cafe/S (W. Caldwell) **D8** | – | – | – | E |
Regency Bldg., 555 Passaic Ave., 2nd fl. (Bloomfield
Ave.), 575-6334
*This likable Eclectic is struggling with an odd location on
the second floor of a shopping center; unique (if not
always successful) combinations of Chinese, SW and
Caribbean flavors and ingredients, friendly staff and
low-key ambiance make it worth a visit.*

Terra Cotta/S (Maplewood) **E7** | 21 | 19 | 20 | $32 |
168 Maplewood Ave. (Baker St.), 763-1176
*U – A funky, "very small and intimate" BYO Essex
County storefront that has a following for its "romantic"
antique-filled atmosphere and "interesting"
Contemporary American menu; the "changing menu
makes you want to return", but few tables mean it's hard
to get a reservation.*

Tewksbury Inn/S (Oldwick) **A7** | 18 | 18 | 18 | $31 |
Main St. (Rte. 571), 908-439-2641
*M – 200 years old but still "waiting to be discovered",
this "neat country inn" attracts a "rowdy crowd" to the
barroom singles scene downstairs, and more sedate
diners to the upstairs dining room, for "pleasant"
Traditional American–Continental food; "country
ambiance", an "eager" staff and a garden patio in
summer make it worth a stop.*

Tivoli Gardens/S (Princeton) **C4** | – | – | – | M |
Scanticon Princeton, 100 College Rd. E. (Rte. 1),
609-452-7800
This sylvan restaurant with a pretty garden view offers a
seafood-leaning Continental menu at decent prices; try
the "Tivoli at Twilight" $16.95 prix fixe, which combines
buffet and à la carte selections.

Tommy Gray's Steak House*/S | 20 | 19 | 16 | $39 |
(Summit) **D8**
38 Maple (bet. Springfield Ave. & Union Pl.), 908-277-1000
M – The consensus on this "meat-lover's dream" is
"good food" but "better when it was Toto"; the men's
club ambiance is comfortable, and the steakhouse
menu appealing, but uneven food quality and service
mean that this newcomer at times "just misses."

Tony da Caneca/S (Newark) **E8** | 19 | 13 | 18 | $26 |
72 Elm Rd. (bet. Garrison & Houston Sts.), 589-6882
M – Many are "addicted" to the lusty Spanish/
Portuguese food at this "comfortable", "authentic"
"neighborhood" spot, "without the noise and bustle" of
Newark's other Iberians; "affordable" prices and friendly
waiters make this "worth the search."

Trattoria Nicola*/S (Somerset) **C5** | 25 | 15 | 23 | $36 |
900 Easton Ave. (Foxwood Dr.), 908-745-4846
U – A "real find"; clever owners have turned an old root
beer stand into a "friendly", "casual" Northern Italian
cafe, and "inventive chef" Tommy Alicino spins out
"excellent cuisine" in a contemporary vein; BYOW and
reserve early.

Trumpets/S (Montclair) **E9** | 15 | 17 | 15 | $32 |
6 Depot Sq. (Walnut St.), 746-6100
M – The "attraction here is the jazz", but a few raters
call the Eclectic menu "surprisingly good"; more
demanding types say "go for the jazz, eat at home"; the
"best plan" may be "snack and jazz" or Sunday brunch.

Tuptim/S (Montclair) **E9** | 21 | 17 | 20 | $25 |
600 Bloomfield Ave. (Valley Rd.), 783-3800
M – "Lovely ambiance" and "generally very good food"
make this likable Thai a "pleasant experience"; tasty,
tongue-tingling food and friendly service make this "one
of the best Thais in the area."

Turkish Kitchen*/S | 26 | 14 | 21 | $27 |
(Weehawken) **F8**
3506 Park Ave. (35th St.), 863-1011
U – "Who knew Turkish food was so good?"; this
modestly priced "friendly" and "attractive" BYO
"storefront" serves sophisticated renditions of fragrant
Turkish specialties; parking may be a problem.

Tuzzio's*/S (Long Branch) **G5** | 16 | 12 | 14 | $22 |
224 Westwood Ave. (Morris Ave.), 908-222-9614
M – Hearty Italian food and pizzas make this
comfortable "family-type place" a "best value",
especially with the $7.95 four-course early-bird or the
Wednesday lobster dinner that costs a mere ten-spot.

Union Landing/S (Brielle) **G3** | – | – | – | M |
622 Green Ave. (Rte. 35), 908-528-6665
This nautical Shore seafooder on the Manasquan River
has its own dock and an outdoor dining patio; surveyors
say this "less expensive family-type place" is dependable,
with good value early-birds; BYO in winter.

UNION PLACE (Summit) **E8** | 26 | 19 | 24 | $41 |
7 Union Pl. (Summit Ave.), 908-277-3444
U – One of the top five for food in NJ, this "shockingly
good" BYO storefront has been wowing diners with its
wonderful Contemporary French and Italian food,
"friendly" service and "cozy" feel; still, some complain of
"minimal ambiance" and "cramped" quarters; reserve in
advance and leave those bulky crinolines at home.

Valentino's Ristorante/S | 18 | 18 | 17 | $35 |
(Morristown) **C8**
150 South St., Rte. 24 (Elm St.), 993-8066
M – "You can get a nice meal" at this "neighborhood
Italian" that was one of the first area spots to espouse
the new-wave trattoria trend (interesting pastas, olive oil
on the table, an antipasto cart); Valentino memorabilia
and a "decent wine list" are pluses.

Vic's Bar & Restaurant*/S | 21 | 8 | 13 | $16 |
(Bradley Beach) **G3**
60 Main St. (Evergreen Ave.), 908-774-8225
U – "Fabulous thin-crusted pizza" – "the best at the
Shore" or "anywhere" – is available at this knotty-pine-
encrusted old-timer that's "as good today as it was 30
years ago"; there's a "long wait on weekends", but who
cares when the "NY tomato pie is indescribable?"

Villa Amalfi/S (Cliffside Park) **F9** | 22 | 21 | 20 | $40 |
793 Palisade Ave. (bet. Marion & Columbia Aves.),
886-8626
M – Whether this is an "old-time first-class Italian" or
just a "glitzy" place for local "wiseguys" is for you to
decide, but solid ratings indicate that "excellent"
Traditional Italian-Continental food vies with "attentive
and professional" service and "great early-bird specials"
for a place in fans' hearts.

Villa Cesare/S (Hillsdale) **F9** | 18 | 18 | 20 | $39 |
322 Evergreen St. (bet. Kinderkamack Rd. & Broadway),
664-0773
*M – This 60-year-old "not inexpensive" Bergen County
bastion of Northern Italian cuisine inspires fierce debate:
"old-fashioned and good" vs. "a ghost of its past";
"old-world feel" and "old-line" "professional service" win
praise, but modernists say "tired, tired, tired."*

Wallington Exchange/S | 13 | 12 | 16 | $30 |
(Wallington) **F8**
365 Main Ave. (Midland Ave.), 472-5457
*M – "New Jersey's answer to Little Russia" is this often
boisterous place for plentiful ethnic food and corny
entertainment"; with gypsy violinists and polkas, it's
"always like a party", but the "hearty", "full-bodied fatty
foods" get mixed reviews: "pleasant" vs. "run-of-the-mill."*

WaterLot Cafe*/S (Red Bank) **F5** | 14 | 20 | 16 | $26 |
Oyster Point Hotel, 146 Bodman (Rte. 35), 908-530-8200
*U – The Contemporary American food is "irrelevant"
compared with the "incomparable view" of the Navesink
River from this attractive hotel restaurant; college-
student service and variable food quality make this
chancy at best, so opt for the $16.95 buffet brunch.*

Wyckoff's Steak House*/S | 13 | 15 | 15 | $26 |
(Westfield) **D6**
(fka Throckmorton's)
932 South Ave. (½ mile west of Westfield Circle),
908-654-9700
*M – A new, lower-priced, steak-seafood-burger menu
and more casual mien have yielded mixed results for
the owners of the old special-occasion Throckmorton's;
fans say the "new food is an improvement", but critics –
and sliding ratings – suggest it "went downhill."*

Yankee Clipper, The/S | 16 | 20 | 17 | $31 |
(Sea Girt) **G4**
1 Chicago Blvd. (Ocean Ave.), 908-449-7200
*U – "Good for the beach" is the best to be said about the
"average" seafood at this Monmouth County institution,
but a "beautiful view of the ocean" ensures its success;
the full-menu Surf Room upstairs has the best view,
downstairs is the noisy Sandbar Pub with its casual
menu; keep it simple or hit the Sunday brunch buffet.*

Yaohan Plaza (Edgewater) **F9** | – | – | – | I |
595 River Rd. (3 miles south of G.W. Bridge), 941-9113
*As close as the Metropolitan area gets to Japan, this
huge Japanese supermarket offers not just one or two,
but 12 fast food facilities built around a food court;
there's nothing else like it and it's a bargain all the way
from soup to sushi.*

Yea Jeon/L (Fort Lee) **F8**　　| – | – | – | M |

1616 Palisade Ave. (Main St.), 944-0505
*If you hanker for something exotic at 3 AM, this huge,
bustling Korean, conveniently located above a parking
garage, offers big portions of bulgogi, kimchi and other
spicy specialties 24 hours a day; English is not a strong
suit here – but you can point in any language.*

YVES (Montclair) **E9**　　| 25 | 23 | 23 | $41 |

30 S. Fullerton Ave. (Bloomfield Ave.), 744-8282
*U – More people should know about this "pretty
storefront bistro", where chef-owner Patrick Yves
Pierre-Jerome "pushes the envelope for creative food in
the 'burbs" with his "sublime" Contemporary French
cuisine (try the duck pastilla with port-wine sauce or the
crème brûlée); the "place is as tiny as its name is short",
but the staff is "charming" and the menu "changes with
the seasons."*

Zio Michel/S (Cliffside Park) **F9**　　| – | – | – | M |

496 Anderson Ave. (Edgewater Rd.), 201-945-3484
*Though tiny (just 13 tables), this three-year-old, family-
owned BYO Northern Italian Bergen County storefront
packs a lot of punch with an inventive menu that
includes homemade rice balls, stuffed lobster, fresh fish
and pasta dishes, all at moderate prices; its customers
wrote in to tell us that we'd missed a good thing.*

NORTHERN NEW JERSEY INDEXES

TYPES OF CUISINE

Afghan
Pamir

American (Contemporary)
Anton's
Arthur's Landing
Baumgart's Cafe
Bernard's Inn
Cafe Main
Carijon's
Chatfield's
Court Cafe
Court Street
Creations
Culinary Renaissance
Dennis Foy's
Dining Room
Dove Island Inn
Evergreen
Forsgate
40 Main Street
Fresh Fields Cafe
Frog and the Peach
Girafe
Good-Time Charley's
Grenville
Highlawn Pavillion
Hudson Place
Hunt Club
Inn at Millrace
Ironwood
Jamie's
Joe & Maggie's
Ken Marcotte
Lady Jane's
Lahiere's
Manor
Mumfords'
Palmer's
Park One Eleven
Richard's
Riverfront Cafe
Rosemary and Sage
Ruga
Ryland Inn
Sandpiper
Shrewsbury
Sonoma Grill
Stage Left
Terra Cotta
Terrace Cafe
WaterLot

American (Traditional)
Alchemist/Barrister
Arthur's St. Moritz
Arthur's Tavern
Black Horse Inn
Bluffs Hotel
Brass Rail
Breakers
Brielle Yacht Cl.
Cliff House Grill
Colligan's
Cypress Inn
Don's
East Hill Grill
Eggiman's
Evelyn's
Haulout
Italian Chalet
Lafayette
Markers
Mike Doolan's
Net Lane's Fisherman
New Top O' The Mast
Olde Mill Ford
Old Mill Inn
Pals Cabin
Raritan River Club
Rod's 1890's
Shadowbrook
Shanghai Red's
Shore Casino
Shrewsbury
Spanish Tavern
Tewksbury Inn
Vic's

Bar-B-Q
Memphis Pig Out

British
Alchemist/Barrister

Cajun/Creole
Michael's Backstreet

Northern New Jersey

Old Bay
Priory

Tivoli Gardens
Yankee Clipper

Californian
Sam's Grill

Chinese
Cathay 22
Chengdu 46
China 17
Four Seas
Golden Ko Shing
Jade Ho
Mr. Tong
North Sea Village
Peking Duck House
Peking Pavilion
Phoenix Garden Too
Silver Pond
Sing Ya

Continental
Armory
Auberge Swiss
Black Forest Inn
Black Horse Inn
Black Orchid
Bluffs Hotel
Brass Rail
Breakers
Casa Dante
Colligan's
Farm House
Fromagerie
Harry's
Il Tulipano
Ironwood
Jamie's
Lafayette
Little Kraut
Manor
Marlboro Inn
Memories
Mike Doolan's
Muirhead
Ocean Gate House
Periwinkles
Perryville Inn
Pheasants'
Priory
Richard's
Ristorante Bellavista
Riverfront Cafe
Saddle River Inn
Saint's Cafe
Sergeantsville Inn
Shadowbrook
Stony Hill Inn
Tewksbury Inn

Dim Sum
Four Seas
Golden Ko Shing
Jade Ho
North Sea Village
Peking Duck House
Peking Pavilion
Phoenix Garden Too
Silver Pond
Sing Ya

Eclectic
Cafe Louis
New Top O' The Mast
Park & Orchard
P.J. Clarke's
Ruga
Shubox Cafe
Terrace Cafe
Trumpets

French Bistro
Chez Andre
Court Street
Pierre's

French Classic
Black Swan
Chez Andre
Chez Catherine
Chez Madeleine
Claude's Ho-Ho-Kus
Fromagerie
Hamilton's Grill Room
La Petite Auberge
Le Chateau
Le Papillon
Le Petit Chateau
Le Plumet Royal
Manon
Marique's
Periwinkles
Silver Spring Farm

French Contemporary
Black Orchid
Cafe Panache
Frenchtown Inn
Grand Cafe
Le Delice
Riverfront Cafe
Union Place
Yves

Northern New Jersey

German
Black Forest Inn
Little Kraut

Hamburgers
Arthur's St. Moritz
Arthur's Tavern
Don's
Markers
P.J. Clarke's
Wyckoff's

Hungarian
Aranka's

Indian
Chand Palace
Namaskaar
Neelam
Taj Palace

International
Le Chateau
Perryville Inn

Italian (Northern)
Beaugard's
Bel'vedere
Cafe Panache
Capri Mia
Cucina di Roma
Eccola
Farmingdale House
Il Capo
Il Capriccio
Il Giardino
Il Tulipano
Il Villagio
Il Villino
Italian Chalet
La Catena
Lu Nello's
Max's
Milano
Olive Branch
Owl Tree
Pappardelle
Pratos
Prima Donna
Rudolfo
Sabatini's
Sergio's
Shore Casino
Stefano's
Stony Hill Inn
Trattoria Nicola
Valentino's
Villa Cesare
Zio Michel

Italian (North & South)
Abin's
Al Dente
Aldo & Gianni
Archer's
Assaggia
Baci
Black Orchid
Cafe Main
Cafe "Z"
Casa Dante
Cella Luna
De Angelo's
De Anna's
Ferraro's
Frankie & Johnnie's
Giovanna's
Haulout
Il Mondo Vecchio
Italianissimo
Jimmy's
La Cucina
La Dolce Vita
La Fontana
Laico's
L'allegria
Lantan
Laughing Lion
Lighthouse
Marcello
Marra's
Nanina's in the Park
Nero's
Panevino
Panico's
Per Forza!
Portobello
Pronto Cena
Ray's
Rispoli's
Ristorante Bellavista
Santoro's
Sestri
Settebello
Sorrento's
Squan Tavern
Teresa's
Tuzzio's
Vic's
Villa Amalfi

Japanese
East
Hero'Chan
Hiro
Shinwa

Northern New Jersey

Jewish
*Santoro's
(*Kosher)

Korean
Hong Nung Kalbi
Koreana
Yea Jeon

Mexican/Tex-Mex
Adelitas
Azteca
Casa Comida
Casa Maya
East L.A.
Mexicali Rose

Mongolian
Khiva
Khiva on the Barge

Pizza
Ferraro's
Santoro's
Squan Tavern
Tuzzio's
Vic's

Portuguese
Europa South
Tony da Caneca

Russian
Wallington Exchange

Seafood
Arthur's Landing
Bahrs
Bluffs Hotel
Charles' Sea Garden
Clam Broth House
Crab's Claw
Cypress Inn
Doris and Ed's
Eggiman's
Evelyn's
Hamilton's Grill Room
Harry's
Net Lane's Fisherman
New Top O' The Mast
North Sea Village
Olde Mill Ford
Old Mill Inn
Sammy's
ea Shack

Sinclaire's
Tivoli Gardens
Union Landing
Wyckoff's
Yankee Clipper

Southern
Hudson Place
Priory

Spanish
Casa Vasca
Don Manuel
Don Pepe
Europa South
Fornos of Spain
Meson Madrid
Spain
Spanish Tavern
Tony da Caneca

Steakhouses
Arthur's St. Moritz
Arthur's Tavern
Cliff House Grill
Cypress Inn
East Hill Grill
East L.A.
Frankie & Johnnie's
River Palm Terrace
Rod's 1890's
Ruth's Chris
Sammy's
Tommy Gray's
Wyckoff's

Swiss
Auberge Swiss

Thai
Bangkok City
Newmain Taste Thai
Sirin Thai
Tuptim

Turkish
Turkish Kitchen

Vegetarian
(Most Chinese, Indian
and Thai restaurants)
Chand Palace
Evergreen
Park & Orchard

LOCATION BY TOWN

Alpine
  Shinwa
Asbury Park
  Jimmy's
  Net Lane's Fisherman
Atlantic Highlands
  Memphis Pig Out
  Shore Casino
Bank
  Peking Pavilion
Basking Ridge
  Girafe
  Ironwood
  Per Forza!
Bay Head
  Bluffs Hotel
  Grenville
Beach Haven
  Charles' Seafood
Belle Mead
  Pheasants'
Belleville
  Nanina's in the Park
Belmar
  Evelyn's
Bergenfield
  Chez Madeleine
Berkeley Heights
  Auberge Swiss
  Azteca
  Neelam
Bernardsville
  Bernard's Inn
  Le Petit Chateau
Bradley Beach
  Vic's
Brielle
  Brielle Yacht Cl.
  Union Landing
Caldwell
  Sabatini's
Carlstadt
  Il Villagio
  Khiva on the Barge
  Pratos
Cedar Grove
  Il Tulipano
  Shubox Cafe
Cedar Knolls
  Il Giardino
Chatham
  Dennis Foy's
  Fresh Fields Cafe
  Newmain Taste Thai
Cliffside Park
  Cliff House Grill
  De Angelo's
  Pappardelle

Villa Amalfi
Zio Michel
Clifton
  Bel'vedere
  Chengdu 46
Closter
  Hiro
  Peking Duck House
Convent Station
  Rod's 1890's
Cresskill
  La Petite Auberge
Denville
  Italian Chalet
Dover
  Laughing Lion
Dumont
  Beaugard's
East Hanover
  Cafe "Z"
  Prima Donna
East Rutherford
  Mr. Tong
  Park & Orchard
  Sonoma Grill
  Sorrento's
Edgewater
  Hero'Chan
  River Palm Terrace
  Yaohan Plaza
Englewood
  Baci
  Baumgart's Cafe
  East Hill Grill
Englewood Cliffs
  Jamie's
  Sing Ya
Fairfield
  Mr. Tong
Fanwood
  Stefano's
Farmingdale
  Farmingdale House
Fort Lee
  Archer's
  Memories
  Silver Pond
  Yea Jeon
Franklin Park
  Aranka's
Frenchtown
  Frenchtown Inn
Gillete
  Sestri
Gladstone
  Chatfield's
  Rudolfo

Northern New Jersey

Glen Ridge
  Sirin Thai
Hackensack
  Sea Shack
  Stony Hill Inn
Harrington Park
  Marcello
Harrison
  Riverfront Cafe
Harvey Cedars
  Owl Tree
Highlands
  Bahrs
  Doris and Ed's
Hillsdale
  Villa Cesare
Hoboken
  Arthur's Tavern
  Bangkok City
  Brass Rail
  Cafe Louis
  Cella Luna
  Clam Broth House
  Court Street
  East L.A.
  Frankie & Johnnie's
  Lady Jane's
Ho-Ho-Kus
  Claude's Ho-Ho-Kus
Hope
  Inn at Millrace
Irvington
  Michael's Backstreet
Jamesburg
  Forsgate
Jersey City
  Casa Dante
  Laico's
  Markers
  Pronto Cena
Keyport
  Ray's
Kingston
  Good-Time Charley's
Lafayette
  Lafayette
Lake Mohawk
  Arthur's St. Moritz
Lambertville
  Anton's
  De Anna's
  Hamilton's Grill Room
  La Dolce Vita
  Manon
Lavallette
  Crab's Claw
Leonia
  Hong Nung Kalbi
ittle Silver
  Farm House

Livingston
  Don's
  Nero's
  North Sea Village
  Panevino
Long Branch
  Casa Comida
  Joe & Maggie's
  Mumfords'
  Ristorante Bellavista
  Shrewsbury
  Tuzzio's
Madison
  Creations
  Four Seas
  Il Mondo Vecchio
  L'allegria
  Richard's
Manalapan
  Peking Pavilion
Manasquan
  Squan Tavern
Maplewood
  Chez Andre
  Terra Cotta
Mendham
  Black Horse Inn
  Marique's
  Sammy's
Metuchen
  Culinary Renaissance
Meyersville
  Casa Maya
Middleville
  Carijon's
Milford
  Olde Mill Ford
Millburn
  Cafe Main
  40 Main Street
  Sergio's
Monmouth Beach
  Haulout
Montclair
  Adelitas
  Hudson Place
  Khiva
  Marlboro Inn
  Mexicali Rose
  Rispoli's
  Taj Palace
  Trumpets
  Tuptim
  Yves
Montvale
  Aldo & Gianni
Morris Plains
  Arthur's Tavern
Morristown
  Black Orchid

Northern New Jersey

Chand Palace
Grand Cafe
Khiva
Le Papillon
Olive Branch
Pamir
Pierre's
Settebello
Valentino's
Mountainside
Silver
Newark
Abin's
Casa Vasca
Don Manuel
Don Pepe
Fornos of Spain
Priory
Silver
Spain
Tony da Caneca
New Brunswick
Frog and the Peach
La Fontana
Old Bay
Panico's
Raritan River Club
Stage Left
North Brunswick
Arthur's Tavern
Oakland
Portobello
Ruga
Ocean Gate
Ocean Gate House
Oldwick
Tewksbury Inn
Palisades Park
Meson Madrid
Paramus
China 17
Koreana
Namaskaar
Parsippanny
Chand Palace
Golden Ko Shing
Perryville
Perryville Inn
Perth Amboy
Armory
Pine Brook
Don Pepe
Piscataway
Al Dente
Plainfield
Giovanna's
Point Pleasant Beach
Europa South

Princeton
Alchemist/Barrister
Black Swan
Lahiere's
Le Plumet Royal
Palmer's
Teresa's
Tivoli Gardens
Ramsey
Cafe Panache
Raritan
Max's
Sam's Grill
Red Bank
Cucina di Roma
Little Kraut
WaterLot
Ridgefield
Phoenix Garden Too
Ridgewood
Il Capo
Marra's
Park One Eleven
Ringoes
Muirhead
Riverdale
Rosemary and Sage
Roselle Park
La Catena
Rumson
Fromagerie
Saddle River
Saddle River Inn
Sea Bright
Harry's
Periwinkles
Sea Girt
Yankee Clipper
Secaucus
Lantan
Sergeantsville
Sergeantsville Inn
Short Hills
Dining Room
P.J. Clarke's
Shrewsbury
Shadowbrook
Somerset
Trattoria Nicola
Somerville
Court Cafe
La Cucina
South Hackensack
Capri Mia
South Orange
Neelam
South Seaside Park
New Top O' The Mast

Northern New Jersey

Sparta
  Arthur's St. Moritz
  Silver Spring Farm
Spring Lake
  Breakers
  Sandpiper
Spring Lake Heights
  Eggiman's
  Mike Doolan's
  Old Mill Inn
Springfield
  Cathay 22
Stanhope
  Black Forest Inn
Stillwater
  Dove Island Inn
Stockton
  Colligan's
Summit
  Hunt Club
  Milano
  Tommy Gray's
  Union Place
Teaneck
  East
  Hiro
  Saint's Cafe
  Santoro's
Tenafly
  Le Chateau
Totowa
  Lu Nello's
Union
  Cafe "Z"
Upper Montclair
  Evergreen

Waldwick
  Il Villino
Wallington
  Wallington Exchange
Wanamassa
  Cypress Inn
Weehawken
  Arthur's Landing
  Ruth's Chris
  Shanghai Red's
  Turkish Kitchen
West Caldwell
  Italianissimo
  Terrace Cafe
Westfield
  Chez Catherine
  Ferraro's
  Ken Marcotte
  Sinclaire's
  Wyckoff's
West New York
  Clam Broth House
  Lighthouse
West Orange
  Highlawn Pavillion
  Manor
  Pals Cabin
Whippany
  Il Capriccio
  Le Delice
Whitehouse
  Ryland Inn
Wood-Ridge
  Assaggia

SPECIAL FEATURES AND APPEALS

Bar/Singles Scenes
Alchemist/Barrister
Anton's
Arthur's Landing
Arthur's Tavern
Brass Rail
Cella Luna
Chatfield's
Court Street
East L.A.
Frankie & Johnnie's
Highlawn Pavillion
Lady Jane's
Lafayette
Lantan
Lighthouse
Markers
Memphis Pig Out
New Top O' The Mast
Old Mill Inn
Owl Tree
Panevino
P.J. Clarke's
Pronto Cena
Raritan River Club
Saint's Cafe
Shanghai Red's
Tewksbury Inn
Trumpets
Union Landing
Wyckoff's
Yankee Clipper

Breakfast
(All hotels and the
following standouts)
Baumgart's Cafe
East L.A.
Farm House
Haulout
Pals Cabin
Ray's

Brunch
(Best of the many)
Arthur's Landing
Black Horse Inn
Brielle Yacht Cl.
Cafe Louis
Carijon's
Cella Luna
Chatfield's
Claude's Ho-Ho-Kus
Court Street
East L.A.
Farm House
Forsgate

Frankie & Johnnie's
Frenchtown Inn
Grenville
Hunt Club
Inn at Millrace
Ironwood
Jade Ho
Lady Jane's
Lafayette
Le Plumet Royal
Manon
Manor
Marlboro Inn
North Sea Village
Old Bay
Old Mill Inn
Perryville Inn
Pheasants'
Phoenix Garden Too
Portobello
Priory
Rod's 1890's
Sandpiper
Sergeantsville Inn
Shanghai Red's
Shinwa
Shrewsbury
Sing Ya
Sonoma Grill
Terra Cotta
Trumpets
WaterLot
Yankee Clipper

Business Dining
Aldo & Gianni
Archer's
Arthur's Landing
Assaggia
Auberge Swiss
Bel'vedere
Bernard's Inn
Black Orchid
Black Swan
Brass Rail
Carijon's
Casa Dante
Chengdu 46
Chez Catherine
Claude's Ho-Ho-Kus
Cliff House Grill
Court Cafe
Cucina di Roma
Culinary Renaissance
Dennis Foy's
Dining Room
Doris and Ed's

Northern New Jersey

Dove Island Inn
East
East Hill Grill
Forsgate
40 Main Street
Frenchtown Inn
Frog and the Peach
Giovanna's
Girafe
Grand Cafe
Hero'Chan
Highlawn Pavillion
Hunt Club
Il Capriccio
Il Giardino
Il Tulipano
Il Villagio
Inn at Millrace
Ironwood
Jamie's
Ken Marcotte
La Cucina
La Fontana
Lahiere's
Lantan
La Petite Auberge
Le Chateau
Le Delice
Le Petit Chateau
Le Plumet Royal
Lu Nello's
Manor
Marcello
Marique's
Nanina's in the Park
Nero's
Ocean Gate House
Old Bay
Old Mill Inn
Palmer's
Panevino
Panico's
Perryville Inn
Pratos
Prima Donna
Ray's
Richard's
Riverfront Cafe
River Palm Terrace
Rod's 1890's
Rudolfo
Ruga
Ruth's Chris
Ryland Inn
Sabatini's
Saddle River Inn
Sea Shack
Shadowbrook
Shinwa

Sinclaire's
Sonoma Grill
Stage Left
Stony Hill Inn
Terrace Cafe
Tommy Gray's
Union Landing
Valentino's
Villa Amalfi
Villa Cesare
WaterLot
Wyckoff's

Dancing
(Nightclubs and the following; check times)
Archer's
Arthur's Landing
Crab's Claw
Marcello
Saint's Cafe
Shadowbrook
Shrewsbury
Squan Tavern
Stony Hill Inn
Tuzzio's
Union Landing
Vic's
Villa Amalfi
Wyckoff's
Yankee Clipper

Delivers
(Call to check range and charges, if any)
Abin's
Alchemist/Barrister
Aranka's
Baci
Baumgart's Cafe
East Hill Grill
Four Seas
Good-Time Charley's
Markers
Sing Ya

Entertainment
(Check days, times and performers)
Aranka's (gypsy music)
Archer's (bands)
Armory (guitar, piano)
Arthur's (bands)
Arthur's St. Moritz (bands)
Baci (jazz)
Bernard's (jazz, piano)
Black Forest Inn (piano)
Black Horse Inn (guitar)

Northern New Jersey

Black Orchid (piano)
Black Swan (piano)
Brass Rail (jazz)
Breakers (piano)
Brielle Yacht Cl. (bands)
Cafe Main (guitar)
Cafe "Z" (piano)
Carijon's (piano)
Chatfield's (bands, piano)
Clam Broth House (DJ)
Claude's (accordion)
Colligan's (piano)
Crab's Claw (bands)
Creations (piano)
Cypress Inn (piano)
Dennis Foy's (piano)
Dining Room (bands)
East Hill Grill (jazz)
Eggiman's (piano)
Europa South (vocalists)
Forsgate (piano)
40 Main Street (opera)
Frankie/Johnnie's (jazz)
Good-Time (bands)
Highlawn Pavillion (piano)
Hunt Club (piano)
Il Capriccio (piano)
Il Giardino (piano)
Il Tulipano (piano)
Inn at Millrace (piano)
Ironwood (guitar)
Jamie's (piano)
La Cucina (piano)
Lafayette (guitar)
Lahiere's (varies)
Lantan (piano, vocalists)
Laughing Lion (jazz)
Le Chateau (varies)
Le Delice (jazz, piano)
Lighthouse (accordion)
Manor (bands)
Markers (jazz)
Marlboro Inn (piano)
Mike Doolan's (piano)
New Top/Mast (varies)
Old Bay (blues, jazz)
Old Mill Inn (vocalists)
Olive Branch (guitar, jazz)
Owl Tree (bands)
Palmer's (piano)
Pals Cabin (piano)
Panico's (piano)
Pheasants' (bands)
Pratos (varies)
Prima Donna (piano)
Priory (jazz)
Raritan River Club (piano)
Ray's (vocalist)
Rod's 1890's (bands)
Saint's Cafe (DJ)

Sam's Grill (jazz, piano)
Sandpiper (piano)
Sestri (piano)
Shore Casino (bands)
Shrewsbury (band)
Stony Hill Inn (piano)
Terrace Cafe (jazz, guitar)
Tewksbury Inn (varies)
Tivoli Gardens (dancing)
Tommy Gr. (piano, vocalist)
Trumpets (jazz)
Union Landing (TK)
Villa Amalfi (band, piano)
Villa Cesare (piano)
Wallington Exch. (varies)
WaterLot (band, guitar)
Wyckoff's (bands)
Yankee Clipper (DJ, piano)

Fireplaces

Anton's
Arthur's St. Moritz
Arthur's Tavern
Auberge Swiss
Azteca
Bernard's Inn
Black Forest Inn
Black Horse Inn
Casa Comida
Chatfield's
Claude's Ho-Ho-Kus
Cliff House Grill
Crab's Claw
Cypress Inn
Dennis Foy's
Dove Island Inn
Eggiman's
Europa South
Farm House
Forsgate
Fromagerie
Grand Cafe
Grenville
Inn at Millrace
Ironwood
Lafayette
La Petite Auberge
Le Chateau
Le Plumet Royal
Marcello
Marique's
Mike Doolan's
New Top O' The Mast
Perryville Inn
Rod's 1890's
Ryland Inn
Sergeantsville Inn
Sestri
Settebello
Shanghai Red's

Northern New Jersey

Shinwa
Stony Hill Inn
Tivoli Gardens
Union Landing
Villa Cesare

Health/Spa Menus

(Most places cook
to order to meet
any dietary requests;
call in advance to
check; almost all
health food spots,
Chinese, Indian and
other ethnics have
health-conscious meals,
as do the following)

Arthur's Landing
Evergreen
Forsgate
Fresh Fields Cafe
Good-Time Charley's
Ironwood
La Dolce Vita
Le Chateau
Shrewsbury

Historic Interest

Alchemist/Barrister
Anton's
Bahrs
Baumgart's Cafe
Bernard's Inn
Black Horse Inn
Chatfield's
Clam Broth House
Claude's Ho-Ho-Kus
Colligan's
Eggiman's
Farm House
Frankie & Johnnie's
Frenchtown Inn
Grenville
Hamilton's Grill Room
Highlawn Pavillion
Il Mondo Vecchio
Inn at Millrace
Lady Jane's
Lahiere's
Le Plumet Royal
Marcello
Marique's
Marlboro Inn
Muirhead
Olde Mill Ford
Palmer's
Perryville Inn
Pheasants'
Priory

Ristorante Bellavista
Rod's 1890's
Ryland Inn
Saddle River Inn
Sandpiper
Sergeantsville Inn
Shadowbrook
Stony Hill Inn
Tewksbury Inn
Union Landing

Hotel Dining

Bernard's Inn
   Bernard's Inn
Bluffs Hotel
   Bluffs Hotel
Breakers Hotel
   Breakers
Doolan's Hotel
   Mike Doolan's
Grand Summit Hotel
   Hunt Club
Grenville Hotel
   Grenville
Headquarter Plaza Hotel
   Black Orchid
Hilton at Short Hills
   Dining Room
Inn at Millrace Pond
   Inn at Millrace
Mansion Hotel
   Stefano's
Marlboro Inn
   Marlboro Inn
Shrewsbury
   Pleasure Bay
   Shrewsbury
Oyster Point Hotel
   WaterLot
Peacock Inn
   Le Plumet Royal
Sandpiper Hotel
   Sandpiper
Scanticon Princeton
   Black Swan
   Tivoli Gardens
Westfield Manor
   Chez Catherine

"In" Places

Assaggia
Bernard's Inn
Cella Luna
Chez Catherine
Dennis Foy's
Highlawn Pavillion
Lu Nello's
Park & Orchard
Saddle River Inn
Sonoma Grill

Northern New Jersey

Stage Left
Union Place

Late Dining
(All hours are after 11 PM)

Alchemist/Barrister (12)
Cafe Main (12)
Crab's Claw (12)
Lighthouse (12)
Owl Tree (1)
Squan Tavern (12)
Stage Left (1)
Turkish Kitchen (12)
Vic's (12)

Noteworthy Newcomers (31)

Adelitas
Assaggia
Azteca
Cafe "Z"
Cella Luna
China 17
Cliff House Grill
Creations
Culinary Renaissance
East Hill Grill
Eccola
Evelyn's
Il Mondo Vecchio
Jade Ho
Joe & Maggie's
Koreana
La Dolce Vita
Mexicali Rose
Namaskaar
Neelam
New Top O' The Mast
Pierre's
P.J. Clarke's
Rosemary and Sage
Silver Pond (E. H'over)
Sing Ya
Sonoma Grill
Stage Left
Terrace Cafe
Tommy Gray's
Turkish Kitchen

Offbeat

Adelitas
Aranka's
Baumgart's Cafe
Cafe Louis
Evergreen
Fornos of Spain
Hudson Place
Khiva
Koreana
Lady Jane's

Laico's
Memphis Pig Out
Michael's Backstreet
Namaskaar
Pamir
Priory
Sammy's
Sirin Thai
Tony da Caneca
Turkish Kitchen
Wallington Exchange

Outdoor Dining
(G = Garden,
 S = Sidewalk,
 W = Waterside location)

Alchemist/Barrister (G)
Anton's (G)
Armory (G,W)
Arthur's Landing (W)
Bahr's (W)
Bangkok City (S)
Bluff's Hotel (W)
Brass Rail (S)
Breakers (W)
Brielle Yacht Cl. (G,W)
Cafe Louis (G,S)
Carijon's (G)
Cella Luna (S)
Chatfield's (G)
Chez Andre (G)
Clam Broth House (S)
Claude's Ho-Ho-Kus (G)
Colligan's (G)
Cypress Inn (G)
De Anna's (G)
Doris & Ed's (W)
Dove Island Inn (G)
East L.A. (S)
Evergreen (G)
Forsgate (G)
Frankie & Johnnie's (S)
Frog and the Peach (G)
Grenville (G)
Hamilton's Grill (G,W)
Harry's (S)
Haulout (W)
Highlawn Pavillion (G)
Ironwood (G)
Khiva on the Barge (W)
La Cucina (S)
La Dolce Vita (G)
Lady Jane's (S)
Le Plumet Royal (G)
Little Kraut (G)
Marlboro Inn (G)
Net Lane's (W)
New Top O' Mast (G,W)
Ocean Cate (W)
Old Mill Inn (W)

Northern New Jersey

Panevino (G)
Ray's (G,W)
Rispoli's (G)
Rist. Bellavista (G,W)
Ruth's Chris (G,W)
Ryland Inn (G)
Shanghai Red's (G,W)
Shrewsbury (G,W)
Terrace Cafe (G)
Tewksbury Inn (G)
Union Landing (G,W)
Waerlot Cafe (W)
Yankee Clipper (W)

Parties & Private Rooms

(All major hotels, plus
the following; best of
the many)
Alchemist/Barrister
Aldo & Gianni*
Anton's*
Aranka's*
Archer's*
Arthur's Landing*
Arthur's St. Moritz*
Baci
Beaugard's
Black Horse Inn*
Brielle Yacht Cl.*
Cafe Panache
Carijon's*
Casa Vasca*
Cella Luna
Chez Madeleine
Claude's Ho-Ho-Kus*
Colligan's*
Cucina di Roma*
Culinary Renaissance
Dennis Foy's*
Doris and Ed's
Dove Island Inn*
East Hill Grill*
Farm House*
Farmingdale House*
Forsgate*
40 Main Street
Frankie & Johnnie's*
Frenchtown Inn*
Fresh Fields Cafe
Frog and the Peach
Fromagerie*
Girafe*
Good-Time Charley's*
Grand Cafe*
Hamilton's Grill Room*
Hero'Chan*
Highlawn Pavillion*
Il Mondo Vecchio*

Il Tulipano*
Il Villino*
Ironwood*
Jamie's*
Joe & Maggie's*
Ken Marcotte*
Khiva*
Lady Jane's*
La Fontana*
L'allegria*
Lahiere's*
Lantan*
La Petite Auberge*
Le Chateau*
Le Delice*
Le Papillon*
Le Petit Chateau*
Manor*
Marcello*
Max's
Michael's Backstreet*
ike Doolan's*
Muirhead*
Mumfords'*
Nanina's in the Park*
New Top O' The Mast*
Old Bay*
Old Mill Inn*
Panico's*
Park One Eleven
Pheasants'*
Pratos*
Prima Donna*
Priory*
Pronto Cena*
Raritan River Club*
Ristorante Bellavista*
Riverfront Cafe
Rod's 1890's
Rudolfo*
Ruth's Chris
Ryland Inn*
Saddle River Inn*
Sergeantsville Inn*
Shadowbrook*
Shanghai Red's*
Silver Spring Farm*
Sonoma Grill*
Stony Hill Inn*
Teresa's*
Terra Cotta*
Tony da Caneca*
Trattoria Nicola
Trumpets
Union Landing
Villa Amalfi*
Wallington Exchange
Yves
(*Private Rooms)

Northern New Jersey

People-Watching
Alchemist/Barrister
Archer's
Arthur's Landing
Arthur's Tavern
Baci
Beaugard's
Black Horse Inn
Brass Rail
Cafe Main
Casa Dante
Cella Luna
Chatfield's
Chez Catherine
Clam Broth House
Court Street
Crab's Claw
Dennis Foy's
East Hill Grill
East L.A.
Frankie & Johnnie's
Fresh Fields Cafe
Frog and the Peach
Grand Cafe
Highlawn Pavillion
Il Capriccio
Il Tulipano
Jamie's
Ken Marcotte
La Fontana
Lahiere's
Le Delice
Manor
Marcello
Markers
Old Mill Inn
Owl Tree
Panevino
Panico's
Park & Orchard
Pronto Cena
River Palm Terrace
Rudolfo
Ruga
Ryland Inn
Saddle River Inn
Saint's Cafe
Sammy's
Shanghai Red's
Sonoma Grill
Stage Left
Tommy Gray's
Trumpets
Union Landing
Wyckoff's

Power Scenes
Archer's
Arthur's Landing
Bernard's Inn
Black Orchid
Black Swan
Cafe Panache
Casa Dante
Chez Catherine
Claude's Ho-Ho-Kus
Court Cafe
Dennis Foy's
Dining Room
Forsgate
40 Main St.
Frog and the Peach
Fromagerie
Girafe
Grand Cafe
Highlawn Pavillion
Il Tulipano
Jamie's
Ken Marcotte
La Fontana
Lahiere's
L'allegria
Le Delice
Le Plumet Royal
Manor
Marcello
Nanina's in the Park
Old Mill Inn
Palmer's
Panico's
Pratos
Prima Donna
River Palm Terrace
Ruga
Ruth's Chris
Ryland Inn
Saddle River Inn
Shinwa
Tommy Gray's
Villa Amalfi

Pre-Theater/
Early-Bird Menus
(Call to check
 prices and times)
Bel'vedere
Breakers
Charles' Sea Garden
Court Street
Crab's Claw
Cypress Inn
Evelyn's
Golden Ko Shing
Haulout
Joe & Maggie's
Mike Doolan's
Net Lane's Fisherman
New Top O' The Mast

Northern New Jersey

Ocean Gate House
Old Mill Inn
Periwinkles
Ruth's Chris
Shrewsbury
Stage Left
Terrace Cafe
Tuzzio's
Union Landing
Villa Amalfi
Yankee Clipper
Yves

Prix Fixe Menus

(Call to check
  prices and times)
Arthur's Landing
Bel'vedere
Black Horse Inn
Breakers
Brielle Yacht Cl.
Cafe Louis
Charles' Seafood
Chez Andre
Chez Catherine
Claude's Ho-Ho-Kus
Court Street
Crab's Claw
Cypress Inn
Dennis Foy's
Dining Room
Dove Island Inn
Evelyn's
Farm House
Forsgate
Fresh Fields Cafe
Grenville
Haulout
Hero'Chan
Hunt Club
Il Villino
Jamie's
Joe & Maggie's
Khiva
Khiva on the Barge
La Fontana
Lantan
Le Delice
Manon
Manor
Marlboro Inn
Memories
Mike Doolan's
Muirhead
Neelam
Net Lane's Fisherman
New Top O' The Mast
Ocean Gate House
Old Mill Inn

Pals Cabin
Park One Eleven
Peking Duck House
Periwinkles
Pheasants'
Pierre's
Portobello
Pratos
Priory
Pronto Cena
Rispoli's
Rod's 1890's
Rosemary and Sage
Ruth's Chris
Sammy's
Sandpiper
Santoro's
Sea Shack
Sestri
Shanghai Red's
Shinwa
Shore Casino
Shrewsbury
Taj Palace
Terrace Cafe
Tivoli Gardens
Trumpets
Tuzzio's
Union Landing
Villa Amalfi
Wallington Exchange
WaterLot
Yankee Clipper
Yves
Zio Michel

Pubs

Alchemist/Barrister
Arthur's Tavern
Brass Rail
Clam Broth House
Frankie & Johnnie's
Inn at Millrace
Lady Jane's
Lafayette
Markers
Memphis Pig Out
Owl Tree
P.J. Clarke's
Yankee Clipper

Quiet Conversation

Archer's
Bernard's Inn
Black Forest Inn
Black Horse Inn
Black Orchid
Brass Rail
Brielle Yacht Cl.

Northern New Jersey

Carijon's
Chez Andre
Chez Catherine
Cucina di Roma
Dennis Foy's
Dining Room
Dove Island Inn
Eggiman's
Farmingdale House
Forsgate
Frenchtown Inn
Fromagerie
Giovanna's
Girafe
Grand Cafe
Grenville
Hunt Club
Il Giardino
Inn at Millrace
Jamie's
Ken Marcotte
Lantan
La Petite Auberge
Le Chateau
Le Delice
Lighthouse
Marcello
Marique's
Marlboro Inn
Ocean Gate House
Old Mill Inn
Olive Branch
Palmer's
Perryville Inn
Prima Donna
Ruth's Chris
Ryland Inn
Silver Spring Farm
Stony Hill Inn
Terrace Cafe
Yves

Romantic Spots

Alchemist/Barrister
Anton's
Archer's
Armory
Arthur's Landing
Arthur's St. Moritz
Auberge Swiss
Bel'vedere
Bernard's Inn
Black Forest Inn
Black Horse Inn
Black Orchid
Bluffs Hotel
Brass Rail
Breakers
Brielle Yacht Cl.

Cafe Panache
Carijon's
Chez Andre
Chez Catherine
Chez Madeleine
Claude's Ho-Ho-Kus
Cucina di Roma
Dennis Foy's
Dining Room
Dove Island Inn
Europa South
Farmingdale House
40 Main Street
Frenchtown Inn
Frog and the Peach
Fromagerie
Giovanna's
Girafe
Grand Cafe
Grenville
Hamilton's Grill Room
Haulout
Hero'Chan
Highlawn Pavillion
Il Giardino
Inn at Millrace
Italianissimo
Jamie's
La Fontana
Lahiere's
La Petite Auberge
Le Chateau
Le Delice
Manon
Manor
Marcello
Marique's
Marlboro Inn
Muirhead
New Top O' The Mast
Ocean Gate House
Olde Mill Ford
Old Mill Inn
Palmer's
Panico's
Pappardelle
Perryville Inn
Pheasants'
Prima Donna
Pronto Cena
Rispoli's
Rudolfo
Ruth's Chris
Ryland Inn
Saddle River Inn
Sergeantsville Inn
Shadowbrook
Shanghai Red's
Shinwa

Silver Spring Farm
Stony Hill Inn
Terra Cotta
Tewksbury Inn
Trattoria Nicola
WaterLot
Yankee Clipper

Senior Appeal
Aranka's
Black Horse Inn
Bluffs Hotel
Brielle Yacht Cl.
Chez Catherine
Cypress Inn
Doris and Ed's
Dove Island Inn
Europa South
Farm House
Forsgate
Frenchtown Inn
Fromagerie
Grenville
Inn at Millrace
Joe & Maggie's
Lafayette
Lahiere's
La Petite Auberge
Le Chateau
Le Delice
Le Petit Chateau
Le Plumet Royal
Manor
Marique's
Marlboro Inn
Mike Doolan's
Muirhead
Nanina's in the Park
Net Lane's Fisherman
New Top O' The Mast
Ocean Gate House
Olde Mill Ford
Old Mill Inn
Palmer's
Pals Cabin
Perryville Inn
Pheasants'
Ristorante Bellavista
Rod's 1890's
Ruth's Chris
Ryland Inn
Saddle River Inn
Sandpiper
Shadowbrook
Silver Spring Farm
Tewksbury Inn
Tuzzio's
Union Landing
Wallington Exchange

WaterLot
Yankee Clipper

Smoking Prohibited
Baumgart's Cafe
Manon
Marlboro Inn
Pierre's
Santoro's
Shubox Cafe
Union Place

Teas
Marlboro Inn

Teenagers & Other Youthful Spirits
Alchemist/Barrister
Aldo & Gianni
Aranka's
Arthur's Tavern
Azteca
Bahrs
Baumgart's Cafe
Cafe Main
Cafe "Z"
Casa Comida
Casa Maya
Cathay 22
Cella Luna
Charles' Sea Garden
Chengdu 46
China 17
Culinary Renaissance
Cypress Inn
Don Manuel
Don's
East
Farm House
Four Seas
Khiva
Khiva on the Barge
Lady Jane's
Laughing Lion
Le Petit Chateau
Lighthouse
Markers
Marra's
Memphis Pig Out
Mexicali Rose
New Top O' The Mast
North Sea Village
Pals Cabin
Panevino
Park & Orchard
Peking Duck House
Phoenix Garden Too
P.J. Clarke's
Pronto Cena

Northern New Jersey

Ray's
Rod's 1890's
Sammy's
Sandpiper
Santoro's
Shanghai Red's
Shubox Cafe
Sonoma Grill
Squan Tavern
Tewksbury Inn
Tony da Caneca
Tuzzio's
Union Landing
Vic's
Wallington Exchange
WaterLot
Wyckoff's
Yankee Clipper

Wheelchair Access

(Check for bathroom
  access; almost all
  hotels plus the
  following)
Abin's
Adelitas
Alchemist/Barrister
Al Dente
Aldo & Gianni
Anton's
Aranka's
Armory
Arthur's Landing
Arthur's St. Moritz
Arthur's Tavern
Assaggia
Auberge Swiss
Azteca
Baci
Bahrs
Bangkok City
Black Forest Inn
Brass Rail
Cafe Louis
Cafe Main
Cafe Panache
Cafe "Z"
Capri Mia
Carijon's
Casa Comida
Casa Dante
Casa Maya
Casa Vasca
Cathay 22
Cella Luna
Chengdu 46
Chez Andre
Chez Madeleine
China 17

Clam Broth House
Claude's Ho-Ho-Kus
Colligan's
Court Cafe
Court Street
Crab's Claw
Creations
Cucina di Roma
Culinary Renaissance
Cypress Inn
De Angelo's
De Anna's
Dennis Foy's
Don's
Dove Island Inn
East
East L.A.
Eccola
Eggiman's
Europa South
Evelyn's
Farmingdale House
Ferraro's
Fornos of Spain
Forsgate
40 Main Street
Four Seas
Frankie & Johnnie's
Fresh Fields Cafe
Frog and the Peach
Giovanna's
Girafe
Golden Ko Shing
Good-Time Charley's
Grand Cafe
Hamilton's Grill Room
Harry's
Haulout
Hero'Chan
Highlawn Pavillion
Hiro
Hudson Place
Il Capo
Il Giardino
Il Mondo Vecchio
Il Villagio
Il Villino
Ironwood
Italianissimo
Italian Chalet
Jade Ho
Jamie's
Jimmy's
Joe & Maggie's
Ken Marcotte
Khiva
Khiva on the Barge
Koreana
La Cucina
La Dolce Vita

Northern New Jersey

Lafayette
La Fontana
L'allegria
Lantan
La Petite Auberge
Laughing Lion
Le Papillon
Le Petit Chateau
Lighthouse
Little Kraut
Lu Nello's
Manon
Manor
Markers
Marique's
Marra's
Memories
Meson Madrid
Milano
Mumfords'
Namaskaar
Nero's
Net Lane's Fisherman
New Top O' The Mast
North Sea Village
Ocean Gate House
Old Bay
Old Mill Inn
Olive Branch
Palmer's
Pals Cabin
Pamir
Panevino
Panico's
Pappardelle
Park & Orchard
Park One Eleven
Per Forza!
Periwinkles
Perryville Inn
Pheasants'
Phoenix Garden Too
Pierre's
P.J. Clarke's
Portobello
Pratos
Prima Donna
Priory
Pronto Cena
Raritan River Club
Ray's
Richard's
Rispoli's
Ristorante Bellavista
Riverfront Cafe
River Palm Terrace
Rod's 1890's
Rosemary and Sage
Rudolfo

Ruth's Chris
Ryland Inn
Sabatini's
Saddle River Inn
Sammy's
Sam's Grill
Sergio's
Sergeantsville Inn
Sestri
Settebello
Shadowbrook
Shanghai Red's
Shinwa
Shore Casino
Shubox Cafe
Silver Pond
Sinclaire's
Sing Ya
Sonoma Grill
Spain
Spanish Tavern
Squan Tavern
Stage Left
Stony Hill Inn
Teresa's
Terrace Cafe
Terra Cotta
Tewksbury Inn
Tommy Gray's
Tony da Caneca
Trattoria Nicola
Tuptim
Union Landing
Union Place
Valentino's
Villa Amalfi
Wyckoff's
Yankee Clipper
Zio Michel

Winning Wine Lists

Assaggia
Chez Catherine
Claude's Ho-Ho-Kus
Crab's Claw
Dennis Foy's
Dining Room
Doris and Ed's
Dove Island Inn
40 Main Street
Frog and the Peach
Grand Cafe
Il Capriccio
La Fontana
Lahiere's
La Petite Auberge
Le Delice
Manor
Nanina's in the Park

Northern New Jersey

Ocean Gate House
Park & Orchard
Sonoma Grill
WaterLot

Young Children
(Besides the normal
fast-food places)
Alchemist/Barrister*
Aldo & Gianni
Bahrs*
Baumgart's Cafe*
Bluffs Hotel*
Brielle Yacht Cl.*
Cafe Louis
Cafe Main*
Cafe "Z"
Casa Comida*
Cathay 22
Cella Luna*
Charles' Sea Garden*
Chatfield's*
Clam Broth House *
Crab's Claw*
Cypress Inn*
Don Manuel
Don's*
East *
Eggiman's*
Europa South*
Evelyn's*
Farm House*
Forsgate
Four Seas
Grenville*
Italian Chalet*

Jimmy's*
Khiva on the Barge*
Khiva*
Lafayette*
Lantan*
Laughing Lion
Little Kraut*
Markers*
Marra's
Memphis Pig Out*
Mexicali Rose*
Mike Doolan's*
Net Lane's Fisherman*
New Top O' The Mast*
North Sea Village
Ocean Gate House*
Old Mill Inn*
Owl Tree*
Pals Cabin*
Park & Orchard*
Peking Duck House
Pheasants'
Phoenix Garden Too
Ray's*
Ristorante Bellavista
Sammy's*
Santoro's
Shrewsbury*
Shubox Cafe*
Sorrento's
Squan Tavern
Tuzzio's
Union Landing
Vic's
(*Children's menu served)

WINE VINTAGE CHART 1981-1991

These ratings are designed to help you select wine to go with your meal. They are on the same 0–to–30 scale used throughout this *Survey*. The ratings reflect both the quality of the vintage and the wine's readiness to drink. Thus if a wine is not fully mature or is over the hill, its rating has been reduced. The ratings were prepared principally by our friend Howard Stravitz, a law professor at the University of South Carolina.

WHITES	81	82	83	84	85	86	87	88	89	90	91
French:											
Burgundy	15	20	15	11	28	29	13	23	27	20	14
Loire Valley	—	—	—	—	17	18	14	19	25	24	15
Champagne	23	29	23	—	25	24	—	—	26	25	—
Sauternes	25	—	28	—	21	26	—	27	26	23	—
California:											
Chardonnay	—	—	—	18	22	25	19	26	22	28	25

REDS	81	82	83	84	85	86	87	88	89	90	91
French:											
Bordeaux	23	29	25	14	28	24	22	24	26	24	19
Burgundy	—	18	25	—	28	13	22	24	24	26	23
Rhône	16	16	25	—	25	21	14	25	24	23	17
Beaujolais	—	—	—	—	18	17	18	22	25	23	24
California:											
Cabernet/ Merlot	22	23	16	27	26	25	25	17	20	24	23
Zinfandel	—	—	—	18	18	17	20	15	16	19	19
Italian:											
Chianti	14	16	13	—	25	15	—	23	—	24	—
Piedmont	13	25	—	—	25	12	17	20	25	22	11

Bargain sippers take note—some wines are reliable year in, year out, and are reasonably priced as well. These wines are best bought in the most recent vintages. They include: Alsatian Pinot Blancs, Côtes du Rhône, Muscadet, Bardolino, Valpolicella and inexpensive Spanish Rioja and California Zinfandel.

Shinwa
Il Viel

Pour Quoi
251 8008

Este St
307 1515

assagio
Citrus Grill
914 35 2 5533
~~212 595 0500~~

Merlo
Clos du Bois

Ivy Inn Hasbrouck
201 393 7699

Amandas Tobaken
201 798 0101
908 Washington St
5pm & 20 –

Cafe Matisse   935
Rutherford   2995

Chez Madeleine ⎫ 767
Petit Paris   ⎭ 0063

NORTHVALE
Nojane Grill (Westfield)

Soho on George (New Brunswick)
                  "   "

Stage Left Restaurant

        N. Bergen
Stephen's Cafe 854
                9666
7722 Bergenline Ave.

C'est La Vie

Cafe L'Amore

455 Ramapo Valley Rd
Oakland
   337 5628

Take 202 exit
turn R onto Ramapo
   Valley Rd

Grand Cafe Morrestown

Baselico - Millburn

Chengdu 46   973 777 8850
1105 RT 46 E   Clifton

Epernay
Montclair